The happier *Terence* all the choir inspir'd,
His soul replenish'd, and his bosom fir'd;
But say, ye *Muses*, why this partial grace,
To one alone of *Afric's* sable race;
From age to age transmitting thus his name
With the first glory in the rolls of fame?

("To Maecenas")

Books by William H. Robinson

Early Black American Poets

Early Black American Prose

Nommo: An Anthology of Modern Black African and Black American Literature

Phillis Wheatley: In The Black American Beginnings

The Free African Union Society & the Free African Benevolent Society 1780–1824

Black New England Letters

Phillis Wheatley: A Bio-Bibliography

Critical Essays on Phillis Wheatley

CONTENTS

PREFACE

Presented here are a sketch of Phillis Wheatley and her Boston; an examination of her poetry; a display of all of her extant poems and letters; a selection of her variant poems and letters in facsimile; and a facsimile of her complete, famous volume, *Poems on Various Subjects, Religious and Moral* (London, 1773). The facsimile volume includes all of the original prefatory matter and the original frontispiece engraving of Phillis's portrait. Because, corrected, it is still seminal for any Wheatley biographical rendering, the 1834 memoir of Phillis, written by a collateral descendant of Phillis's mistress, is included in the appendices. Also in the appendices are the Latin and Biblical originals of poems which Phillis translated or paraphrased; a letter by George Washington, discussing Phillis, and another Washington letter, to Phillis herself; and a biographically helpful excerpt from a letter to the Earl of Dartmouth. Annotations have been supplied wherever it was thought they might prove helpful. The original spellings and punctuation have been retained.

The accounts of Phillis Wheatley, her Boston, and her poetry have drawn heavily on corrected earlier biographical comments, but just as heavily on information derived from manuscript and printed letters written to and about Phillis by American and European personalities, from 18th-century newspapers, magazines, pamphlets, and broadsides, later books of various kinds, legal documents, literary anthologies, diaries, and, of course, her own writings. Because they might have easily become plentiful to the point of distraction, many footnotes have been avoided, but a selective bibliography has been offered.

Until or unless the still missing almost several dozen Wheatley poems are ever found and published, this book will likely remain the most complete collection of her writings. All told, there can be counted a total of almost 150 titles of Wheatley poems, but many of these are of variants of published pieces, and a great many others are of non-extant poems. This volume publishes a total of eighty odd poems and their variants, and thirty-five prose pieces made up of a Wheatley prayer, three selections she wrote from dictation, the four sets of her proposals (printed in 1772, 1773, 1779, and 1784) for two projected volumes of her work, newspaper notices including information dictated by Wheatley, and twenty-six of her notes and letters and their variants. There is an un-counted—because unknown—number of still more, non-extant poems, which are only referred to by Wheatley contemporaries.

Again, as with earlier books, it is my own pleasure to acknowl-edge here my indebtedness to the able, ready, and generous assist-ance of American and European archivists, college and university library and special collections personnel. I thank also authorities at my own institution, Rhode Island College, for both their administrative and their financial considerations for me as I researched and wrote the book. For his Spanish translation, I thank Dr. E. Steven Tegu, a colleague now retired. Other Wheat-ley scholars will recognize at once my indebtedness to them. Thanks are especially due, again, to Dr. Henry-Louis Gates, Jr., of Yale University for his extraordinary personal and professional exertions on behalf of scholars, students, and general readers of Afro-American letters. As usual, singular thanks are tendered to D.C.R. for singular reasons.

William H. Robinson
Providence, R.I., 1983

ACKNOWLEDGMENTS

Thanks are hereby tendered to the following authorities for their permissions to print and/or reprint the information indicated:

To the American Antiquarian Society, for permission to print "To the University of Cambridge, Wrote in 1767"; "On the Death of the Rev'd Dr. Sewall. 1769"; "An Elegy to Miss Mary Moorhead, on the Death of her Father, the Rev. Mr. John Moorhead."

To the Boston Athenaeum, for their permission to print "AN/ ELEGY,/ Sacred to the/ MEMORY/ of the REVEREND AND LEARNED/ DR. SAMUEL COOPER . . . / By PHILLIS PETERS."

To Bowdoin College Library, for its permission to print "The following thoughts on his Excellency Major General Lee being/ betray'd into the hands of the Enemy by the treachery of a pretended/ Friend; to the Honourable James Bowdoin Esqr. . . ."

To the Trustees of the Boston Public Library for their courtesy in permitting the printing of a Phillis Wheatley letter to "The Rev'd Mr. Saml Hopkins," dated May 6, 1774.

To Dr. S.H. Mayor, Director, the Cheshunt Foundation, Cambridge University, England, for permission to print, from the papers of the Countess of Huntingdon, four letters from Phillis Wheatley to the Countess of Huntingdon, dated Oct. 25, 1770, and a variant; June 27, 1773; July 17, 1773; and two versions of "On the Decease of the rev'd Dr. Sewell."

To the Right Honourable the Earl of Dartmouth for making his manuscripts available to me at the County Record Office, Strafford, England, and for granting permission to print a Phillis Wheatley letter to the Earl, dated Oct. 12, 1772; a biographical sketch of Phillis dictated by Nathaniel Wheatley and written by Phillis; and a poem to the Earl, submitted under cover of the aforementioned letter.

To the Henry Huntington Library of San Marino, California, for its permission to reprint the broadside, #41245, "An Ode of Verses on the much-lamented Death of the Rev. Mr. George Whitefield, ..."

To the Historical Society of Pennsylvania, for permission to print and reprint "To the King's most Excellent Majesty on his repealing the american Stamp Act"; "To Mrs. Leonard on the Death of her Husband"; "To the Hon'ble THOMAS HUBBARD, Esq; on the Death of Mrs. THANKFULL LEONARD"; and a Phillis Wheatley letter to "the Rev'd M͟r Sam͟l Hopkins," dated February 9th, 1774.

To Professor Mukhtar Ali Isani and *Early American Literature*, for permission to reprint "On the Death of J.C. An Infant."

To Houghton Library of Harvard University, for its permission to print "Poem on the death of Charles Eliot aged 12 m͞o To Mr. S. Eliot."

To the Massachusetts Historical Society, for permission to print "An Address to the Atheist . . ."; "Atheism"; "An Address to the Deist"; "Poem on the Death of Charles Eliot . . ."; "An Elegy, Sacred to the Memory of Revd/ Samuel Cooper, D.D. By Phillis Wheatley"; and six letters from Wheatley to Obour Tanner, dated July 19, 1772; Oct. 30, 1773; March 21, 1774; May 6, 1774; May 29, 1778; May 10, 1779" and a letter to the Earl of Dartmouth, dated Oct. 10, 1772.

To the Medford Historical Society, Dr. Valeriana, President, for permission to print from the Timothy Fitch papers a Timothy Fitch letter to Captain Peter Quinn, dated January 12, 1760, and another to Quinn from Fitch, dated September 4, 1761.

To the Moorland-Spingarn Research Center, Howard University, for permission to print "On Friendship."

To the William Perkins Library, Duke University, for its permission to print a letter dictated by Nathaniel Wheatley and written by Phillis Wheatley to William Channing, dated Nov. 12, 1770.

To the Quaker Collection at Haverford College Library, for permission to print a Phillis Wheatley to Obour Tanner letter, dated May 19, 1772.

To the Schomburg Center for Research in Black Culture, the New York Public Library, Astor, Lenox and Tilden Foundations, for permission to print Phillis's prayer of "Sabbath—June 13, 1779."

To Lord Levin and Melville, for permission to print four letters in the Scottish Record Office (GD26/13/663), Phillis Wheatley letters to John Thornton, dated April 21, 1772; December 1, 1773; March 29, 1774; October 30, 1774.

To the Manuscript Division of the Library of Congress, the Hugh Upham Clark papers, for permission to print a Phillis Wheatley letter to Colonel David "Worcester" [sic for Wooster]; a Phillis Wheatley letter to "Madam," (i.e., Mrs. Mary Wooster) dated July 15, 1778, embodying a poem, "On the Death of General Wooster."

The Library Company of Philadelphia, for permission to print "Atheism," "Deism," "America," "To the Honble Commodore Hood on his pardoning a deserter," "On the Death of Mr. Snider Murder'd by Richardson," "on Atheism."

To the National Urban League, for its permission to reproduce the drawing of Phillis Wheatley.

PHILLIS WHEATLEY AND
HER WRITINGS

ON PHILLIS WHEATLEY
AND HER BOSTON

In a letter dated "Boston 12th January 1760," to his employee, "Captain Peter Quinn" (i.e., Gwyn or Gwinn), Timothy Fitch (1725–1790), a one-time successful slave-trading merchant of Boston, gave his slaving orders:

Sir You haveing the Command of my Schooner Phillis your orders Are to Imbrace the First Favorable Opertunity of Wind & Weather & proceed Directly for the Coast of Affrica, Touching First at Sinagall if you fall in with it On your arrival then Cum to Anchor with your VeSsell & go up to the Facktory[1] in your Boat & see if you Can part with Any of your Cargo to Advantage . . . if you Could Sell the whole of your Cargo there to a Good Proffett & take Slaves & Cash Viz. Cum Directly Home. . . . You must Spend as little Time as poSsible at Sinagal & then proceed Down the Coast to Sere Leon & then make the best Trade you Can from place to place till you have disposed of all your Cargo & purchase your Compleat Cargo of Young Slaves which I Suppose will be about 70 or Eighty More or LeSs I would Reacommend to you gowing to the Isle Delos if you Cant Finish at Sereleon . . . be sure to bring as Fiew Women & Girls as possibl . . . hope you wont be Detaind Upon the Coast Longer than ye 1st of May by Any Means, the Consequence you know We have Experienced to be Bad, You & your people & Slaves will get Sick which will ruin the Voyage. Whatever you have left Upon hand after April, Sell it altogeather for what you Can Get if even at the First Cost Rather than Tarry Any Longer . . . be Constantly Upon your Gard Night & Day & Keep good Watch that you may Not be Cutt of by Your Own Slaves tho Neavour So Fiew on Board Or that you Are Not Taken by Sirprise

1. *Facktory*. There were a number of establishments strung along the African slave-trading coasts for the collection and exchange, by barter and cash, of various goods to various people, but mostly African slaves to white people. Factors were the European, American, and, occasionally, African merchant-managers of these places.

by Boats from the Shore which has often ben the Case[2] Let your Slaves be well Lookd after properly & Carefully Tended Kept in Action by Playing Upon Deck . . . if Sick well Tended in ye Half Deck & by All Means Keep up Thare Spirretts & when you Cum off the Coast bring off a Full Allowance of Rice & Water for a Ten Week PaSage Upon this your Voyage Depends in a Grate Measure . . . by all Means I Reacommend Industry, Frugality & dispatch which will Reacommend you to further BuSsiness. Your Wages is Three pounds Ten Sterling per Month Three Slaves, privildge[3] & Three % but of the Cargo of Slaves Delivered at Boston, This is all you are to have. . . .

With this cargo of slaves, Gwinn arrived in Boston on August 16, 1760, and left for Africa again in the fall. With another shipload of slaves numbering "about 70 or Eighty More or Less," Gwinn returned to Boston on July 11, 1761, but was noted "cleared outward for Africa" as soon as August 12 of that year. One reason for such a hasty departure might have been the undisguised disappointment of Fitch at the wretched condition of Gwinn's most recent, July 1761, cargo of slaves. Almost doubling his cargo of sale goods, in hopes of securing "140 to 150 Prime Slaves" to be sold at Charleston, South Carolina, Fitch again directed Gwinn to Senegal, West Africa. From "Boston September 4th 1761," Fitch's slaving orders directed Gwinn that

. . . as you'l be very Earley upon the Coast you are not to take any Children & Especilly Girls, if you can avoid it by any means & as fiew Woman as PoSsible, & them Likely but as many Prime Young Men Boys as you Can get from 14 to 20 Years of Age Take no Slave on Board that has the Least defect or Sickly . . . make no Doubt

2. Fitch's cautions to Gwinn were given seriously. The history of the American slave trade is characterized by the uncounted, untold numbers of African slave revolts and killings of slave ship captains and their crew members. Elizabeth Donnan edited a four-volume work, *Documents Illustrative of the History of the Slave Trade to America* (Carnegie Institute of Washington Publication No. 409, 1922; reprinted New York, Octagon Books, 1969). In volume III alone (*New England and the Middle Colonies*), Donnan mentions, in incidental footnotes, the African slave rebellions and murders of more than fifty captains and crew members of New England slaving ships between 1731 and 1805. More such revolts and murders are found in the other three of her volumes and in other accounts of the African slave trade to America. Even more such murders can be found in accounts of the traffic to other countries.

3. *Three Slaves, privildge.* Slave ship captains were often given, as bonuses, a predetermined number of slaves they kidnapped or purchased. Text of the Fitch letters is from a typescript of the Fitch manuscripts at the Medford Historical Society.

You'l be able to Pick Your Slaves. I had Rather you would be Two Months Longer on the Coast then to Bring off Such a Cargo as Your Last which were very small & the meanest Cargo I Ever had Come. . . .

This "meanest Cargo I Ever had Come," had tied up at a wharf on Beach Street, July 11, 1761, a block from the Newbury Street home of John Avery (1711–1790), a seasoned agent for Boston slave ship captains. After having the survivors of the black cargo cleaned and greased and made presentable for sale, Avery, as usual, advertised his human wares in the *Boston Evening Post* and the *Boston Gazette and Country Journal* for July 29 and for several weeks thereafter:

To Be Sold

A Parcel of likely Negroes, imported from Africa, cheap for cash, or short credit; Enquire of John Avery, at his House next Door to the White-Horse, or at a Store adjoining to said Avery's Distill-House, at the South End, near the South Market; Also, if any Persons have any Negro Men, strong and hearty, tho' not of the best moral character, which are proper Subjects for Transportation, may have an Exchange for small Negroes. . . .

Among these "small Negroes" was the female child who would shortly become the internationally famous Phillis Wheatley, black poet. Some years later, a descendant of Phillis's owners would describe her Boston arrival:

Aunt Wheatley was in want of a domestic. She went aboard to purchase. In looking through the ship's company of living freight, her attention was drawn to that of a slender, frail, female child, which at once enlisted her sympathies. Owing to the frailty of the child, she procured her for a trifle, as the captain had fears of her dropping off his hands, without emolument, by death. . . .

Phillis's first biographer, another descendant of Phillis's owners, would report that, concerned for the comfort of her own old age, Mrs. Susanna Wheatley wished to acquire a young, black, female personal domestic to replace the now aging domestic who, with other household domestics, had long tended Mrs. Wheatley. That lady therefore

visited the slave-market, that she might make a personal selection from the group of unfortunates offered for sale. There she found several robust, healthy females, exhibited at the same time with

Phillis, who was of a slender frame, and evidently suffering from change of climate. She was, however, the choice of the lady, who acknowledged herself influenced to this decision by the humble and modest demeanor and the interesting features of the little stranger.

The poor, naked child, (for she had no other covering than a quantity of dirty carpet about her like a fillibeg) was taken home in the chaise of her mistress, and comfortably attired. She is supposed to have been about seven years old, at this time, from the circumstance of shedding her front teeth. . . .

Whether Phillis was actually purchased from the White Horse Tavern, next door to John Avery's house on the corner of Newbury (today's Washington) Street and Avery Street, or, which is more probable, from aboard the schooner that brought her to Boston from Africa, is not known. Both before and after the time of Phillis's sale, black slaves were bought and sold in various parts of Boston—Ann Street, the northern edge of Boston Commons, in various taverns or warehouses, at auctions, or, often, from aboard slave ships tied up at any of the many wharves of the town. It is known that Phillis was sold to Mrs. Wheatley "for a trifle"—perhaps something less than £10 sterling, the going price for prime male slaves in 1761 in Newport, Rhode Island, then being £35 sterling—and that she was carried to the Wheatley mansion on the corner of King Street and Mackerel Lane (today's State and Kilby Streets).

Ever since she had been kidnapped from her parents and native childhood life, enslaved in the hold of a schooner, and forcibly transported with some seventy or eighty other hapless black Africans, Phillis had dealt as best a suddenly orphaned child could with the profound business of being a human chattel.

In a sense, purchased as she was, Phillis might be said to have been grimly lucky, if that is the word. Purchased with a total of fewer than 100 other slaves for stowage in a typical Yankee slaver, she was part of a cargo that was "loose-packed." If she had been part of the "140 to 150 Prime Slaves" whom Captain Gwinn would be directed to purchase on his voyage after delivering her to Boston in July of 1761, she would then have been part of a "tight packed" cargo in a sloop about 67 feet long, 20 feet wide, and 9 feet deep, having a captain and a crew of eight, and she might not have even survived the voyage across more than 4000 miles of Atlantic Ocean. Fancying that they were shrewdly saving money, which would otherwise be spent on crew members, Yankee slave ship captains typically preferred smaller schooners, sloops, sometimes brigs of no more than 30 to 100 tons burden. They also preferred to buy slaves selectively, in hand-picked lots, often sailing hundreds of miles of African coastline to do so, unlike captains of many large slave ships of Liverpool, France, and Spain, who liked to purchase as many as eight or nine hundred slaves at a single sale. On the Clipper ship, *Nightingale*, of 1020 tons burden, built in Portsmouth, New Hampshire, in 1851, Captain Francis Bowen, "The Prince of Slavers," was illegally carrying 961 slaves off the coast of Congo (Kinshasa) when it was captured by American naval, anti-slavery squadron forces in 1861; the American slave trade to and from the coast of Africa was "abolished" in 1807.

Captain Gwinn had been ordered to work the slave markets at Senegal, Sierra Leone, and the Isles de Los (off the coast of Guinea) in that order. If Phillis had been among the first slaves purchased, at Senegal, she would have remained captive as the schooner sailed to other ports in search of enough slaves to make up the complement of seventy or eighty. She would not have been free of this boat until some eight months later, in Boston, in July of 1761, when she was purchased by Mrs. Susanna Wheatley.

During these months, Phillis and the gradually swelling number of other slaves were made to understand that they lived under constant threat of being punished, whipped, or even killed if they did not obey often confusing orders from strange, white-skinned crew members, some of them no more than teenagers. She and the others learned that they had to do whatever these white strangers (and callous black crew members) indicated, whenever, wherever, and however these men gestured or growled. Aboard the *Phillis*, slaves were to awaken, eat meals of rice and water, dance twice a day for exercise, toilet, submit to chained and darkened and foul-smelling storage, and sleep whenever they were ordered. To avoid the fisted abuse of an annoyed crew member who might be obliged to clean up, slaves who became spontaneously seasick—most of them had never seen the sea before in their lives—would try vainly to regulate their vomiting. Defiantly, some slaves would try to starve themselves to death; others died of the bloody flux (severe dystentery) and were dropped overboard; others, if they saw the chance, would leap overboard with upraised, clenched fists. Now

7

Phillis found that she had, somehow, to absorb and assimilate the threats and the cultural shock of living daily among these people. How long she would survive, she did not know: in the hold, other blacks made it clear that these white-skinned people cannibalized black people.

To assure the thin black child and to divert her from these and other such fears, Mrs. Susanna Wheatley may have sympathetically encouraged her to look about her. Enroute from her place of purchase to the Wheatley residence—her home for the next fourteen years—Phillis could only glimpse aspects of the several worlds that would make up the Boston of her time. There was, Phillis must have noticed, such a bustling of so many peoples, white skinned, coppery skinned, swarthy, black skinned, including Prince, Mrs. Wheatley's own servant who neatly maneuvered the Wheatley chaise homeward through daytime traffic. There were burly merchant seamen, sailors in French and Spanish and British uniforms; important-looking gentlemen in white wigs, some sporting knobbed canes, waistcoats with deep pockets and flashing buttons, smoothened breeches buckled before the knee; other men wore plain work clothes; followed by a black or white servant, women in full dresses and piled wigs strolled from shop to shop; noisy vendors bawled their wares, sometimes to the accompaniment of hand-swung bells, as they walked from place to place; lumbering oxen pulled drays of lumber as drivers whipped them and cursed aloud to no one and everyone; stray hogs waddled wherever; chickens hysterically squawked down any nearby alley away from the grasp of wild-eyed boys in pursuit.

There were, Phillis would have noticed, all kinds of frame and brick buildings, one, two, and three stories high, residences, shops for tailors, bakers, butchers, grocers, candle-makers, cordwainers. In wooden stalls, some with waist-high shelves jutting from their fronts, stood or sat white hawkers, their white and black servants dissonantly singing out their goods; black chimney sweeps, boys and girls and men, shouldered or twirled their brooms and carried sootened blankets as they harmonized their desire for work— "Sweep 'em down, ladies; sweep 'em down to the ground"— hoping to earn the fixed rate of twopence a chimney, or a shilling for a three-story job. Here and there, Phillis may have noticed red flags draped from front windows, which, she would learn, signified a quarantine home infected with smallpox. Dominating the skyline were the steeples of the several meeting houses.

And there were the smells. From goods stacked outside of shops along the way came the smells of tarred rope, oakum, turpentine, logwood, redwood; and the musky, tarty smells of West Indian imported spices, oranges, bananas, mangoes, cherries; and the smells of varieties of teas and coffees, imported from England. From open windows and doors of ordinaries, or taverns, came smells of domestic and/or West Indian rums, and prepared meals, and pipe tobacco, and beers and spirits. Lacing all of these odors were those of all kinds of seafood: lobsters, crabs, eels, scup, whiting, mackerel, haddock, shark, and cod, always plentiful cod. Even in Phillis's day, it was known that two hundred kinds of fish crowded New England waters. Too, there were always the wet smells of the fitful breezes coming in from the surrounding Atlantic Ocean.

Turning, finally, from Cornhill into King Street itself, Phillis would surely have noticed, near the intersection, the pillories, sit-down and stand-up stocks, and, directly beneath the windows of the Writing School, the whipping post that was painted "Hellfire red," where, periodically, barebacked malefactors, male and female, were carted to have a legally determined number of stripes laid on as crowds taunted and jeered.

It all may have impressed young Phillis as a great, sprawling metropolis, crowded with all kinds of people, speaking Babels of tongues. Actually, the Boston of her day, as she would soon learn, was no more than a small peninsula, shaped roughly like a much hammered and crudely flattened spoon, jutting northeasterly into the large, crescent-shaped Boston harbor, and joined southwesterly to the mainland by its "handle," a half-mile stretch of narrow lowlands called Boston Neck. Altogether, Phillis's Boston was only some two miles long and a bit more than 700 yards at its widest points, made up of something more than 750 acres that featured three large hills—Beacon Hill in the west-central part of town; Fort Hill at the easternmost edge; and the smallest rising, the fifty-foot high Copp's Hill, in the north—and several smaller hills, all much levelled today. (In the adjacent colony of Rhode Island and the Providence plantations, over a half-dozen men, mostly gentried farmers, owned several dairy farms that, separately, were four, five, even ten times larger than all of Phillis's Boston.) Nor were there really as many people there as Phillis may have imagined. In 1765, for instance, Boston had a population of

15,520, of which about 1000 were blacks, by one count. In the Boston of 1762, Boston Selectmen counted only eighteen free blacks.

By the time Phillis arrived in Boston in the summer of 1761, most blacks throughout the colonies had long since been forcibly fixed into lowly positions of meniality, servitude, slavery. Indulging harbored repugnance at the disparities—real and imagined—between black and white racial, cultural, and intellectual differences, southern whites assumed—or vigorously pretended to assume—that blacks naturally belonged to a grossly inferior species of humankind, fit properly for chattel slavery. The presence of blacks was to be suffered for their own moral, intellectual, and spiritual improvement, some said. What they meant was that the presence of blacks was to be suffered for the economic advantage of whites. Monopolizing the religious, civil, judicial, and economic powers, southern whites could and did act—with impunity—against the hapless blacks. If need be, whites would even write laws that would justify, legally, their assumptions of black inferiority, and their consequent enslavement of these peoples. An early Virginia example will illustrate. White 17th-century Virginians surely thought of themselves as Englishmen and were proud to bring English law from the motherland to the colonies. English law had long held that the status of a child was determined by the status of its father. Virginia legislators of 1662, however, were fully aware that if they followed English legal precedence in this matter, in the colonies, the many hundreds of children born of white men and black women would be legally free. This would be an intolerable affront to white male supremacy and domination. Easily as important as such psychological buttressing, it was foreseen that an increasingly expanding population of free, mulatto children on hand would not serve the purpose—to exploit a controlled, unpaid work force—for which blacks were imported in the first place. The legislators simply changed the law. Henceforth "Children got by an Englishman upon a Negro woman shall be bond or free according to the status of the mother. . . ." Henceforth all Virginia children of white male masters and Negro women were to be regarded as legal slaves, and as such they were put to work to swell the plantation gangs of other slaves. Following the lead of Virginia, other southern colonies also devised laws that were designed to maximize the powers of white male masters, and to legally obliterate any semblance of common humanity among black slaves, except as chattel.

Because its rugged hilly lands of thin and rocky soils and its harsher weather were so unlike the broad fertile lands of the sunny and agricultural South, New Englanders had no need for such elaborate legal machinery for controlling slavery. Indeed, as has been noted, it is hard to understand why black slavery and its concomitant slave codes were ever even necessary in New England. A class of indentured servants—black or white or both—could have handled the labor needed for necessarily diversified ways of making a living in New England. The chief economy was based on maritime undertakings, and if blacks did not secure work as deck hands or cooks aboard merchant ships, there was not that much for them to do ashore. It has been reckoned that throughout the history of colonial New England, blacks made up no more than 2% of the area's population. They worked at diversified occupations, mostly as household domestics. Black New England slaves led lives of curiously ambiguous status. Sometimes they were regarded as legal chattel, suffering all of the attendant evils; at other times, they were regarded as quasi-persons, enjoying a limited number of the rights and privileges that all New England freemen enjoyed more fully. However ambiguous their status, most New England blacks, slave or free, were made by whites to function as much like discrete inferiors as possible. During Phillis's lifetime, no black children could be counted among the more than 800 young scholars distributed between the two grammar or Latin schools and the three vocational writing schools. In the various places of Christian worship in the Boston of 1768, all blacks, including Phillis Wheatley, were relegated to either the rear of first floor congregations, or, usually, the galleries of the second floors. Built in 1710, the oldest Meeting House in Chelsea, Massachusetts, across the bay, had one entrance for black men and another for black women, both entrances leading upstairs to the reserved galleries. Long before Phillis's time in Boston, most denominations of Christian churches had ruled that while black slaves might be baptized and receive religious freedom thereby, such baptism in no way changed their civil status as black slaves.

There were not many good, paved streets, the main thoroughfare then being the nearly one-mile long "Handle," the low-lying way of Boston Neck, leading northerly from the mainland along

Orange Street into Newbury and Marlboro and Cornhill Streets (all of which make up today's Washington Street), and continuing easterly into King Street, and out into the harbor by way of Long Wharf. Although dotted with thirty various-sized islands, the excellent harbor was capacious enough to accommodate some 500 vessels riding at anchor. Serrating the northeastern tip of the town and all of its eastern coastline were some 80 wharves, the most important of which was the well-made Long Wharf, running from the end of King Street easterly into the harbor for about half a mile, made even more useful by the T-shaped smaller wharf appended midway along its western edge, thereby allowing ships to unload or load easily, without the need for quays or lighters or other intermediary cargo craft.

On the northeastern corner of King Street and Mackerel Lane (today's Kilby Street), Phillis's new home was one of the finer residences on that bustling, fashionable, seaside street, called the busiest street in town. The home was owned by 59-year-old John Wheatley and occupied by him, his wife, Susanna, their 18-year-old twin children, Nathaniel and Mary, and several aging black household domestics of both sexes. Three other Wheatley children, Susanna, John, and Sarah, had all died young. John Wheatley (1703–1778) was a very successful merchant-tailor (one of his clients being the generously wealthy and noticeably stylish John Hancock) who owned the *London Packet*, a three-masted schooner merchantman of 200 tons burden, and several dockside warehouses, wharfage, and several pieces of residential real estate on nearby Union Street. He also owned a thriving wholesale store on King Street, selling such items as "Casks of good Lisbon wine, Bohea Tea, Rice, Turpentine, Spermacetti Candle, warranted pure table fish. . . ." A year before Phillis landed, after the most devastating of many Boston fires—this one had destroyed more than 300 buildings—John Wheatley filed a personal and real estate fire damage claim of more than £300; the Boston Selectmen quickly gave him permission to repair his home. Like many Bostonians of his day, he was a pious Congregationalist, as was his equally pious wife, whom he married in 1741 at the trim New South Church, located snugly on Seven Star Lane (today's Summer Street, near Otis). A long-time, no-nonsense businessman, he advertised his retirement in July of 1771, promising to pay all of his creditors immediately, and requiring all of his debtors to pay up at once. On September 11, he sued a tardy John Sale of Chelsea for £113 16s. "Lawful Money." Even before he retired, John Wheatley tolerated no business shortcomings, suing Stephen Welcome of Salem, Massachusetts, as early as 1749, for a default in repayment of a loan of "sixtyfive pounds."

Susanna (Wheeler) Wheatley (1709–1774) was a deeply religious woman of dedicated and sober Christian zeal. Aged 52 when she purchased Phillis as her personal servant, she professed a preoccupation with living the life and dying the death of a serious believer. "The earnest of the Spirit and foretaste of the Glory which shall be reveal'd, has long been the subject of my pursuit," she would write in 1771. She cultivated a longtime admiration of, and unabashed passion for, the spellbinding sermon, especially as preached by the enormously popular English evangelist, the eloquent Reverend George Whitefield (1714–1770), who often toured the colonies, visiting Boston six times before he died suddenly of an asthmatic attack in Newburyport, Massachusetts. (Susanna and John Wheatley may have been among the transfixed congregation at the New South Church in September of 1740, when, as a guest speaker, Whitefield preached so fiery a sermon that so galvanized the excited assembly that five members were reportedly trampled to death.)

She also cherished a fond admiration for the Reverend Samson Occom (1732–1792), a converted Mohegan Indian Christian minister from Connecticut, a friend and correspondent of Phillis. In December of 1765, Occom and a white fellow divine, the Reverend Nathaniel Whitaker, would sail from Boston for London and Scotland where they would lecture for two years, raising the record-breaking amount of nearly £12,000 for the promotion of Occom's alma mater, Moor's Charity Indian School of Lebanon, Connecticut, before it would be moved in 1770 to Hanover, New Hampshire, to become the Dartmouth College of today. For all of her Christian zeal, however, Mrs. Susanna Wheatley was also a wife and a practical woman. On the eve of Occom and Whitaker's departure for London, she wrote them a combined letter of warm wishes, noting that she "was much concerned for your families, in your absence & shall endeavor to raise up friends to assist them & hope God in his good Providence will not be unmindful of them. . . ." Dated "Norwich June 12!ʰ 1766," there is extant a receipt of a one dollar gift from Mrs. Wheatley to the ministers' wives, Mrs. Sarah Whitaker and Mrs. Mary Occom. In bold token of her fervent notions of Christian uplift for all Christians, Susanna Wheatley defended Occom from malicious charges that, an Indian after all, he drank excessively while he was abroad. Some years later, in January of 1773, she even housed Occom with her while he was a guest speaker in the pulpit of Reverend John Moorhead's nearby Presbyterian Church in Long Lane (today's Federal Street). "It is a duty incumbent on us to help each other in our Christian course," she would explain, especially proud that Occom's preaching had packed the church for both the morning and the evening services.

Even before his father announced his retirement from business, young Nathaniel Wheatley (1743-1783) was assuming increasing amounts of responsibilities for the family business, and he did so with impressive efficiency. Since the late 1760s he had been advertising that the Wheatley King Street wholesale store was selling casks of good Lisbon wine, Bohea tea, rice, turpentine, spermecetti candles, among other goods. When his father did retire in 1771, Nathaniel bought out his father's holdings, including wharves and real estate, and the King Street mansion. Also serving as financial exchange agent for such powerful merchants as John Hancock, Aaron Lopez (the Jewish slave-trader of Newport, Rhode Island), and Joseph Rotch, Sr., of New Bedford, Boston, and London, Nathaniel would soon develop the family concern to the point at which it simply outgrew Boston-based possibilities and needed international expansion. That would be one reason he would relocate to London in 1773, when he would marry into the thriving mercantile family of the Enderbys of Thames Street. Nathaniel, too, was fond of Samson Occom. Graciously accepting a financial loss that resulted from differing rates of exchange in one international transaction that would, nevertheless, benefit the Mohegan minister, Nathaniel dictated a letter for Phillis to write to Eleazor Wheelock, President of Dartmouth College in 1770, "This I have done out of pure regard for Mr. Occom for I think him a very just man. . . ." Nathaniel would encourage Phillis at other times by other dictations of letters for her to write.

Mary Wheatley was a simple, sickly girl who enjoyed being Phillis's childhood tutor and lifelong friend. Like others in her family, she was a member of the New South Congregational Church, marrying there, in January 1771, the popular and outspoken Reverend John Lathrop (1740-1816), "the Revolutionary

Preacher," pastor of the Old North Church. Similar to so many other colonial American wives, Mary would spend the seven years of her brief marriage producing almost as many children. In her case, she even birthed two children in one year. When young Miss Ann Green Winslow recorded in her diary for March 2, 1772, that she dined with the pious Mrs. Lathrop and a Mrs. Carpenter, Mary had already delivered her first son, John Lathrop, Jr., on January 13; she was pregnant again with Jane Tyler, who would be born on December 18 of that same year. There were four other children, but only two of the six survived into adulthood. After a siege of sickness that may have been complicated by an incompleted pregnancy, Mary would die in 1778, only 35 years old.

Phillis's new American home was situated in the very heart of colonial Boston's political, social, and commercial bustles. At the southern end of her street, a few short blocks from her home, was the Old Colony House (today's memorial Old State House), the administrative unit for the town, unhappy arena for a succession of besieged Royalist governors—Bernard, Hutchinson, Gage, Howe—all of whom would be ultimately and raucously driven to a more politically congenial London. The worst riots in the riotous history of pre-Revolutionary War Boston would explode on or quite near King Street. Although only eleven or twelve years old in 1765, Phillis could hardly forget that summer's mob-sprawling Stamp Act riots against the British-imposed act, which in fifty-five sections, demanded a Stamp duty from half a penny to twenty shillings "on any skin or vellum or parchment or sheet or piece of paper on which anything should be engrossed, written or printed." On August 16, led by several dozen Patriot tradesmen and town artisans, a mock funeral procession, bearing a bier on which was flung an effigy of Andrew Oliver, newly appointed Stamp Master for Boston, marched in angry protest against the despised Stamp Act. At first, most of the seething marchers walked solemnly, almost rhythmically, through the then open promenade of the street-level floor of the Old Colony House (unnerving the wide-eyed Governor Bernard upstairs trying to conduct official business). But, growing uglier by the stomping footstep, the crowd picked up speed, swarmed down King Street, yelling "Liberty! Property, and no stamps!" over and over again. They veered to their right into Mackerel Lane—just past the Wheatley household—spilled down to an office structure they believed to have been newly erected for the business of the Stamp Master. In a few noisy, cursing minutes, the mob barehandedly tore the office to pieces, some of them jubilantly carrying away souvenir planks down to the elegant Oliver residence near Fort hill, where they tore down the garden fence, smashed several windows, drank some of Oliver's wine, and stared from behind menacing bonfires outside, before finally drifting out of sight.

On August 26, this same mob and others, this time even more disorderly under the practised direction of the seasoned South End gang-leader, "Captain" Ebenezer Macintosh, frightened the entire town and much of the province with the imminent threat of violent mob rule. Milling about the Old Colony House, a crowd suddenly spurted across the street and with bare fists and staves attacked the home of William Story, registrar for the Court of the Admiralty, smashing his windows, flinging official papers to the alleys and streets. Another mob raced to the Hanover Street home of Benjamin Hallowell, a customs official, rampaged his place, and drank up most of the wines and liquors in the basement. Then, some of them almost falling down drunk, the mobs joined and stormed up Hanover Street until they reached Fleet Street, where they wheeled down one block to Garden Court, and the resplendent town mansion of the heartily detested, officious Lieutenant-Governor, Thomas Hutchinson. All night long, the howling, cursing, wild-eyed mobs almost completely tore to the ground, from its cupola down to its much-admired and well-tended lawns of lovely flowers and fruit trees, one of the most splendid mansions in all of New England. The next morning, thousands of gathered spectators, beholding the ruins, were stunned, revolted, and frightened.

Nor could Phillis easily forget the predictable British military retaliation for Boston's most recent display of civil disobedience. When variously uniformed detachments of His Majesty's troops landed in Boston in the fall of 1768, they would parade directly in front of Phillis Wheatley's King Street home. Paul Revere made an engraved panorama of the harbor full of identified British ships, and inscribed the landing: "On the arrival of the Ships of War, and landing of the Troops—on fryday, Sepr 30, 1768, the Ships of War, armed schooners, Transports &c came up to the Harbour and anchored around the Town; their cannons loaded, a spring on their cables, as for a regular siege. At noon on Saturday October 1st the fourteenth & twenty-ninth Regiments, a detachment from the 59th Regt. and a train of Artillery with the pieces of cannon, landed on Long Wharf; there formed and marched with insolent parade, Drums beating, Fifes playing, colours flying up KING STREET. . . ." Phillis would not have overlooked the eight or ten black drummer boys of the 29th Regiment, with their brown bearskin pointed hats, their yellow coats faced with red, their drums trimmed in the regimental yellow; about fifteen at this time, she was not much younger than most of the boys. It was all frightening and thrilling enough to move Phillis, later that year or early in 1769, to react poetically in a non-extant poem, "On the Arrival of the Ships of War, and Landing of the Troops."

She would write verses also on her reactions to subsequent revolutionary events that took place near her home. She would versify the slaying of "the first martyr for the cause," in her piece, "On the Death of Master Seider [sic] who was killed by Ebenezer Richardson. 1770," elsewhere titled "On the Death of Mr. Snider Murder'd by Richardson." In February of 1770, young Snider was accidentally shot to death in a fracas not far north of Phillis's home. The next month, the "Boston Massacre" of March 5 happened in front of the Old Colony House, down the street from where Phillis lived. The funeral for the four martyred victims of the "Massacre" was larger than any before held in the history of Boston, various sources reporting various thousands of persons at the gathering. "Such a concourse of people I never saw before," wrote John Rowe, believing the number of mourners to be, extravagantly, "Ten or Twelve Thousand." Escorting the corpses from their respective homes (the bodies of black Crispus Attucks and white James Caldwell, being "strangers," i.e., non-residents of Boston, were escorted from Fanueil Hall), groups of mourners converged at the head of King Street to form a common funeral procession of record-breaking thousands, who all trooped down to the Old Granary Burial Grounds on Treamont Street (today's Tremont Street). Shortly after witnessing the ceremony, Phillis hurriedly wrote out a metrical response in another non-extant poem, "On the Affray in King-Street, on the Evening of the 5th of March, 1770" (twelve anonymous lines which may be hers appeared in *The Boston Evening Post* for March 12, q.v., below).

In addition to the Old Colony House, other municipal buildings were within walking distance from Phillis Wheatley's King Street home. The scene of many noisy mass meetings of outraged and rebellious Patriots, Fanueil Hall was only one block north.

The graceful Province House, long the official residence for royal governors of the Province of Massachusetts, sat back, in three-storied architectural reserve, from the dusty, much-travelled Marlborough Street (part of today's Washington Street), almost opposite the Old South Meeting House. The site of the trial of Captain Preston and eight of his fellow British soldiers involved in the celebrated "Boston Massacre," the combined jail and courthouse, newly completed in 1767, stood on Queen Street (today's Court Street), practically an arching, northwesterly extension of Phillis's King Street. In the next block west of the courthouse-jail was the cluster of the three-storied Granary building (on the site of today's Park Street Church), storing and retailing grain for times of emergency need; the Work House; Bridewell ("for the distracted"), and the Almshouse, large enough to accommodate several hundred indigents—all of these buildings in a row on Park Street between Tremont and Beacon Streets.

Shortly after arriving in Boston, Phillis would become, predictably enough, a committed, lifelong Christian, and, as such, churches would come to mean much to her. Not so incidentally, several ministers, of various denominations, would come to mean very much to her career as a poet. Conveniently close to her residence were many churches, several of whose pastors would offer spiritual guidance and poetical instruction that would, in turn, inspire versified tributes of gratitude from Phillis. Especially cherished, and only a few blocks from her home, was her own Old South Congregational Church, which she would join on August 18, 1771, she then being about eighteen years old. However widely known a poet she might become, Phillis was black, and as such she with other blacks in this and other Boston churches would be baptized only after the regular services were concluded. (On November 1, 1772, for instance, two black females, Hannah Dunmore and a Cloe ". . . were rec^{d} into/ Reverend Samuel Stillman's Second Baptist Church/ . . . *after the divine Service.*" (Italics are mine.)

The congregation of the Old South Church, the nearly 200-foot-high steeple of which still stands on the corner of Washington and Milk Streets, was led for almost sixty years by the venerable Reverend Joseph Sewall, until his death in 1769 when he was ninety years old. Especially fond of Sewall, Phillis would write five (or six) versions of an elegy on his passing. Practically around the corner from her own church was the Long Lane (today's Federal Street) Church of the Scotch Presbyterian, Reverend John Moorhead, whose death in 1773 Phillis would acknowledge in an unusually dramatized broadside. A block west of the Old Colony House stood the Brattle Street Church of the handsome, eloquent, poetry-writing Patriot minister, the Reverend Samuel Cooper, whose death in 1783 would move Phillis to compose an elegy that was printed early the following year. As an addendum to the early 1771 London reprinting of his celebrated sermon on the death of the Reverend George Whitefield, the corpulent, much-married Reverend Ebenezer Pemberton of the North End's New Brick Church, only blocks from Phillis's home, would thoughtfully include her already popular, widely reprinted elegy on Whitefield. When Phillis needed a signed attestation certifying that she, a black slave girl, had actually written the poems of her volume, the Reverends Moorhead, Pemberton, and Cooper would be joined by four other Boston clergymen—Charles Chauncy, Mather Byles, Andrew Eliot, and Samuel Mather.

Around the corner from "Puffing Pem's" New Brick Church was the historic Old North Church, of Paul Revere fame, then pastored by John Lathrop, husband to Mary Wheatley, Phillis's childhood tutor and longtime friend. Phillis's relationship with the Lathrops was both religious and personal. Her first visit to the Lathrop home in the North End was memorable to the servants because, "it was the first time they ever carried tea to a colored woman." As Lathrop often preached emotion-laden sermons on several Tory or British military provocations, he may well have inspired Phillis's poetic pieces on the same events, such as the slaying of the young Snider boy, and the "Boston Massacre." When, in the fall of 1776, she was with Lathrop in Providence, Rhode Island, where he was temporarily filling an empty Congregational pulpit, Phillis composed and mailed her tributary poem to newly appointed Commander-in-Chief of the Continental Army, General George Washington. While she was in London in the summer of 1773, Lathrop would write to a friend of his admiration for the black poet:

> Yes Sir, the famous Negro Phillis is a servant of Mrs. Lathrop's mother. She is indeed a singular genius. Mrs. Lathrop taught her to read, and by seeing others use the pen, she learned to write. . . . She is now in London with Lady Huntingdon and . . . I hope her going to England may do her no hurt.

19

Phillis probably met the Reverend Timothy Pitkin (1727-1811) during his travels between his Congregational Church in Farmington, Connecticut, and Dartmouth College in Hanover, New Hampshire, where he was a trustee from 1769 to 1773. A son of the governor of Connecticut, and a wealthy graduate of Yale University, he worked with converted Indian ministers, including the Reverend Samson Occom. In 1752, Pitkin married Temperance Clap, daughter of the president of Yale, and a sister-in-law to Phillis's military friend, General David Wooster of New Haven. When Temperance died in 1772, giving birth to an eighth child, Phillis wrote two versions of a comforting and personalized eulogy to Pitkin; if she had not failed in having Bostonians subscribe for a second projected volume of her work she wanted to publish in 1779, she would have included a letter she wrote to Pitkin. See the 1779 proposals, below, for letter #2, "To the Rev. Mr. T.P. Farmington." Phillis also corresponded with the Reverend James Thomas (1699-1790) whom she would meet during her visit to London in the summer of 1773.

In addition to housing all kinds of business shops and second-story owner residences—an ambitious Mr. Lewis, a black hair stylist, lived and worked on the street—King Street also had its share of busy, noisy taverns, each of them public houses but often meeting places for members of fraternal organizations, and openly antagonistic political groups. It was at the Royal Exchange Tavern, across the way from the Old Colony House, that the vociferous James Otis was badly beaten in a political confrontation that left him with head wounds that surely accelerated his fitful bouts of madness. Directly across the street from the Wheatley home was the Tory-patronized Admiral Vernon's Head, once licensed by Thomas Hubbard, whose daughter, Thankfull, would be the object of three of Phillis's poems. Down Mackerel Lane from the Wheatley place was the noisy, Whiggish Bunch of Grapes Tavern. In good weather, Phillis might regularly have seen Colonel John Hancock and some of his dazzlingly bedecked militiamen, the ceremonial Independent Cadets, manfully striding into, and later otherwise staggering out from, this place after a Wednesday's drilling down on Boston Commons.

By 1771, Boston featured ten printers, eight booksellers, six printer-booksellers, several newspaper publishers, most of them clustered on, or in the immediate vicinity of, King Street. John Fleming and John Mein, two testy Scotsmen, were proud of their newspaper, *The Boston Chronicle*, and of their circulating library of more than 1000 volumes of Scottish and English works housed in their shop at the head of the street. Mein, however, would soon convert the newspaper into such a flagrantly Tory propaganda sheet that he would incite Patriot reaction sufficient to hasten his departure for London. An even larger stock of volumes was sold or rented from the bookstore of James Rivington, close to Fleming and Mein's place, until the manager, William Miller, died in 1765. John Green and Joseph Russell issued their *Weekly Advertiser* from their King Street shop, while neighboring merchants and booksellers, Cox and Berry, across the street from the Brattle Street Church, sold sundry items, and "a large collection of the most esteemed Books. . . ," one of the more memorable of these books being Phillis Wheatley's *Poems*. From his place on nearby Marlborough Street, John Boyles, printer and bookseller, would help bring out the *News Letter*. From the adjacent Court Street (then Queen Street) printing shop came the Whiggish *Boston Gazette and Country Journal* of Benjamin Edes and John Gill, while Thomas Fleet's *Evening Post* issued from his handsome residence-shop on Cornhill Street (today's Washington Street, a block before State Street). From his busy shop on Union Street, the determined Isaiah Thomas brought out first his *Massachusetts Spy*, thrice weekly, then his *Massachusetts Spy; Or, Thomas's Boston Journal*, twice weekly, until British hostility to his Whiggish views prompted him to flee to Worcester, where he would resume with *The Massachusetts Spy; Or American Oracle of Liberty* in 1775. From Union Street also, Ezekiel Russell would edit the short-lived *Censor*, propaganda organ for Tories. All of these and other newspaper publishers, and Boston printing houses and booksellers would be important to Phillis, because, for one occasion or another, at one time or another, her name and her poetry would apear in newspapers, broadsides, pamphlets, magazines, or volumes that would be either printed in or sold from one of these establishments.

Unless he were financially able, a writer in Phillis's time, as now, could not simply compose poems that were printed upon his or her simple demand. Whether in newspapers or magazines, whether broadsides, ballads, pamphlets, or books, the printing of poems cost money. A printer might absorb the costs for turning out a supply of broadsides that celebrated some outstanding current event, but he would certainly hope that he could thereby attract paying customers enough to have made the investment worth his while. A newspaper or a magazine publisher who featured a poetry section would similarly risk expenses for printing solicited pieces, gambling that readers would thereby become sufficiently interested in future issues of the publication as to become subscribers. Ordinarily, advertisements of poems, or proposals for subscribers to a projected volume would be paid for by someone other than the printer—a popular minister's congregation, a writer's friends, even, if possible, the writer him or herself. Printing being a business, there were monies involved, certainly more money than an unsalaried black female servant such as Phillis Wheatley could ever expend. And yet she published more than fifty poems in her lifetime.

From the start, it would be Mrs. Susanna Wheatley who would bear much of the financial burdens required to promote the career of her beloved black protégée. Mrs. Wheatley may have imagined that when she purchased Phillis she was thereby providing for the comfort of her own old age, but, as matters quickly turned out, she would spend the rest of her life assisting Phillis's fame in every way she could. Much taken by the shy black girl's gentle demeanor, and impressed by the child's early display of uncommon intellectual abilities and potential, Mrs. Wheatley would relieve the girl of routinized household duties; instead she had the able young girl tutored in Latin and English and the Bible by her daughter, Mary. Mrs. Wheatley herself, by precept and example, instructed Phillis in puritanical Christian piety and genteel decorum. Rewardingly precocious, Phillis proved to be a singularly gifted student. Her master, John Wheatley, would publicly attest as much:

> Without any Assistance from School Education, and by only what she was taught in the Family, she, in sixteen Months Time from her Arrival, attained the English Language, to which she was an utter Stranger before, to such a Degree, as to read any, the most difficult Part of the Sacred Writings, to the great Astonishment of all who heard her.
>
> As to her Writing, her own Curiosity led her to it; and this she learnt in so Short a Time, that in the Year 1765, she wrote a Letter to the Rev. Mr. Occom, the Indian Minister, while in England.
>
> She has a great Inclination to learn the Latin Tongue, and has made some Progress in it. . . .

To nurture the young prodigy's talents, Mrs. Wheatley saw to it that a special fire was kept in her upstairs apartment during bone-numbingly cold Boston winter nights, and she permitted a candle to burn all night in Phillis's room. On a stand beside the girl's bed were placed ink and quill and writing paper, the better for Phillis to write down at once any poetic thoughts that, she complained, did not always stay with her. A small-boned girl of delicate constitution, Phillis would suffer chronically poor health —asthma and a suspicion of tuberculosis—all of her life. Despite constant medical care, she often lapsed into recurring sieges of illnesses; most of her letters to her lifelong black friend and fellow domestic, Obour Tanner, in nearby Newport, Rhode Island, complain of her health. When she fell into especially serious sickness, she was sent by Mrs. Wheatley to the country for recuperation. "I have been in a very poor state of health all the past winter and Spring," she wrote Obour in the summer of 1772, "and now reside in the country for the benefit of its more wholesome air. I came to town this morning to spend the Sabbath with my master and mistress."

It was Mrs. Wheatley who eagerly circulated Phillis's growing reputation by arranging for the touted girl to visit and be visited by the most prominent ministers and merchants and politicians, Whigs and Tories, in town. In the fall of 1772, she would be visited by a Thomas Wooldridge, a minor English functionary who toured the American colonies on behalf of his superior, the Earl of Dartmouth. To see for himself the "very extraordinary female Slave," he visited the Wheatley household, and was amazed to behold a black person writing poetry. He found "by conversing with the African, that she was no Impostor. . . . I was astonish'd, and could hardly believe my own Eyes. I was present while she wrote. . . ." A story has come down that tells of Phillis's visit with Mrs. (Eunice Plaisted) Timothy Fitch, second wife of the wealthy merchant of Medford, Massachusetts, who owned the slave ship on which she was brought from Africa. The Fitch daughters were at first amused with Phillis's stories of her various experiences, but soon grew uneasy as teatime drew near, dreading the idea of sitting at the same table for tea with a black woman, however talented and celebrated. But Mrs. Fitch simply insisted that they all sit together, after which the daughters were so beguiled with Phillis's charming conversation that they "forgot her color." Several visitors to the Wheatley home would be obliged by a persuasive Mrs. Wheatley to listen to her little black genius recite an original poem, or two, or three. In such ways Phillis got to be known to Governor Thomas Hutchinson, Lieutenant-Governor Andrew Oliver, James Bowdoin, John Hancock, Harrison Gray, and many eminent divines. Visitors who courteously wished to convey the proper encouragement to the pious little poet often left her with books. The Reverend Charles Chauncy, for instance, inscribed a gift copy of Thomas Amory's *Daily Devotions Assisted and Recommended in Sermons* with "The gift of Dr. Charles Chauncy to Phl^s Wheatley, Boston Oct. 14, 1772." In turn, she would later make a gift of this same book to Thomas Wallcutt, one of the founders of the Massachusetts Historical Society.

Often thinking of Phillis as something of an actual daughter, Mrs. Wheatley would try, in vain, to keep her from familiarity with other blacks, even other Wheatley household servants. At one time while Phillis was visiting some distinguished Boston home, the weather changed for the worse, and ever fretful over Phillis's chronically poor health, Mrs. Wheatley ordered Prince, one of her servants,

> to take the chaise, and bring home her *protegee*. When the chaise returned, the good lady drew near the window, as it approached the house, and exclaimed—"Do but look at the saucy varlet—if he hasn't the impudence to sit upon the same seat with my Phillis!" And poor Prince received a severe reprimand for forgetting the dignity thus kindly, though perhaps to him unaccountably, attached to the sable person of "my Phillis."

Although not documented, as is the case with practically all accounts of the largely unrecorded early black colonial life, it is not at all unlikely that, later, when alone, both Prince and Phillis found Mrs. Wheatley's attempts at intraracial segregation amusing. Phillis had other black contacts, of course, her closest black friend being Obour Tanner, equally pious soul mate. When or how Phillis and Obour first met is unknown, but their friendship endured, as is testified to by seven letters from Phillis to Obour between 1772 and 1779. Sometimes they came by the post, but more usually these letters would be delivered through the kindness of a friend or a travelling black servant. On one known occasion, an especially noteworthy friend delivered a letter from Obour in Newport to Phillis in Boston. In her reply of October 30, 1773, Phillis, temperamentally reserved but also a nineteen- or twenty-year-old young lady, commented, twice, on the mailman. "The young man by whom this is handed you seems/ to me to be a very clever man, knows you very well, & is/ very complaisant and agreeable," she wrote in a postscript. So described, this young man may have been the handsome, ambitious John Peters, a free black whom Phillis would marry five years later. Despite the threat of penalties, colonial American privacy of the mail was hardly guaranteed; it would be even less so with letters written by blacks. Knowing this, literate blacks would often exchange personal matters orally. Writing to officers of the Free African Union Society of Newport, Rhode Island, Prince Hall would include little or nothing specific about plans which he and other black Bostonians were laying for the establishment of a quasi-secret relief society:

> . . . Your brother [Henry] Stewart will inform you by word of mouth of some proposals we made to him, which I do not care to write at this time. . . .
>
> Prince Hall, Boston, Sep. 16th, 1789.

Whatever casual black social contacts Phillis might have enjoyed would have to have been developed almost surreptitiously, for by enforced and approving design, she was made to spend most of her waking time either reading or writing her "poetic performances" before curious guests, or close beside her mistress reading and discussing the Bible, or visiting among ladies of Boston's first families, holding forth on "feminine topics." As much is clear from an explanatory note that introduced her poem "Recollection," (q.v.), which Phillis wrote toward the end of 1771 and which so impressed an unknown female acquaintance, "L," that she mailed the piece for publication in the March, 1772, issue of the *London Magazine*. "The following," explained "L" to the London editor, "was occasioned by being in company with some young ladies of family, when one of them said she did not remember, among all the poetic pieces she had seen, ever to have met with a poem upon RECOLLECTION. The African (so let me call her, for so in fact she is) took the hint, went home to her master's, and soon sent the following."

Along with others, this unknown "L" would be helpful to Phillis, but no one would ever do as much for the poet as would her mistress. It was likely Mrs. Wheatley who wrote the introductory and explanatory headnote to "On Messrs Hussey and Coffin," which was printed in the *Newport* (R.I.) *Mercury* for December 21, 1767, and is the first known poem published by fourteen-year-old Phillis. As it is probable that both Phillis and her mistress were in attendance at the Old South Church one or more of the four times that the Reverend George Whitefield preached there throughout the month of August, 1770, the month before he would die suddenly in Newburyport, Massachusetts, it is also likely that Mrs. Wheatley's known admiration for the English evangelist moved Phillis to write several versions of an elegy on the minister's death. It would be Mrs. Wheatley who would help to internationalize Phillis's poetic reputation by putting her in correspondence contact with such influential persons as the wealthy Selina Hastings, Countess of Huntingdon, (1702–1791) as early as 1770; and with the even wealthier English millionaire and Christian philanthropist John Thornton (1720-1790); and with William Legge, the Earl of Dartmouth (1731-1801), "His Majesty's Principal Secretary of State for North America," a financial supporter and religious follower of the Countess of Huntingdon. These and other English and American personages were part of an international Christian missionary circle whose American interests focused on support of Moor's Indian Charity School of Lebanon, Connecticut. When this school was moved to Hanover, New Hampshire, over the protests of Legge, and white students enrolled—to the everlasting resentment of the Indian, Reverend Samson Occom—it was renamed for the Earl of Dartmouth. Thornton Hall at the college was named in thanks for the financial support of John Thornton. A fervent Christian enthusiast who would expend over £500,00, almost her entire fortune, for the promotion of early English dissident Methodism, the countess, touched by Phillis's eulogy of the Reverend Whitefield, her onetime personal chaplain, would eventually serve as Phillis's English patron of sorts. It would be through her insistence that Phillis's portrait was engraved and made the frontispiece for the 1773 London edition of Phillis's *Poems on Various Subjects, Religious and Moral*. In her letters to Mrs. Wheatley, the countess sometimes spoke warmly of Phillis, writing on May 13, 1773, ". . . Your little poetess, remember me to her. May the Lord keep her heart alive with the fire of that other that never goes out. . . ." Several letters Phillis wrote to the countess are extant. With John Thornton, said to have spent two to three thousand pounds sterling annually on charitable causes, "perhaps £150,00" in his lifetime, Phillis would continue a pious correspondence from 1771 to 1774.

Delighted at seeing Phillis's poem, "On Messrs Hussey and Coffin," in the *Newport Mercury* of 1767, Mrs. Wheatley would have her poet select twenty-eight of her manuscript poems, whose titles would be advertised in the *Boston Censor* for February 29, March 14, and April 18, 1772, as part of proposals to subscribers for a projected volume that was to have been published in Boston in that year. But Phillis's proposals were rejected for both political and racist reasons. Much supported by Loyalist Governor Hutchinson and his equally Loyalist brother-in-law, Lieutenant-Governor Andrew Oliver, the *Boston Censor* was pointedly ignored by hostile Patriot Bostonians, and the paper ceased publication after only seven months of unheeded existence. Bostonians rejected the proposals for other reasons also. A friend and student of Phillis's earliest manuscript poems, merchant John Andrews, exchanged many letters between 1772 and 1776 about the increasingly politicized Boston scene with his brother-in-law and fellow merchant, William Barrell, in Philadelphia. In eight of the letters, running from early March, 1772, through February 18, 1774, he discusses Phillis and her poetry as no other person could. In his letter of May 29, 1772, from Boston, Andrews wrote,

> . . . It is about two months since I subscribed for Phillis's poems, which I expected to have sent you long ago, *but the want of spirit to carry on anything of the kind here has prevented it, as they are not yet published.* . . . (Italics are mine.)

He was more specific in a letter of February 24, 1773:

> . . . In regard to Phillis's poems they will originate from a London press, as she was [illegible; blam'd?] by her friends for printing them here & made to expect a large emolument, if she sent ye copy home [sic, i.e., London] which induc'd her to remand it of ye printers & also of *Capt Calef, who could not sell it by reason of their not crediting ye performances to be by a Negro, since which she has had had* [sic] *a paper drawn up & sign'd by the Gov. Council, ministers & most of the people of note in this place, certifying the authenticity of it*; which paper Capt Calef carried last fall, therefore we may expect it in print by the Spring ships, it is supposed the Coppy will sell for £100 Sterlg. . . . (Italics are mine.)

By the time her proposals appeared, Phillis had already published three poems in London and four poems in Boston; advertisements for her elegy on the death of Reverend George Whitefield had been printed in more than a dozen newspapers in Pennsylvania, New York, and Boston (at least ten times in Boston newspapers alone). The elegy itself had appeared in broadside and pamphlet form about a dozen times in Philadelphia, New York, Newport, and at least five times in Boston. Still, not enough Boston subscribers—printers usually required 300—could or would agree that the poems of the proposals were written by a Negro. Lacking sufficient subscribers, the volume was not then or there printed, as originally planned.

Mrs. Wheatley was undoubtedly shaken by the rejection of her beloved protégée's proposals, but she was not overwhelmed. Indeed, she may have resolved, as soon as it was clear that Phillis's proposals attracted little reader response, that Phillis's poems certainly would be published, and if not in bigoted Boston then in the more civilized, sophisticated London. She may thus have had Captain Robert Calef, who commanded the Wheatley-owned schooner, *London*, regularly between Boston and London, to engage one Archibald Bell, an obscure London printer of religious works. Once familiar with the peculiar history of the Phillis Wheatley publishing project, however, Bell would insist on some kind of written verification of the black girl's authorship. Accordingly, such a paper was prepared. Prefaced to all but one of the several original London editions and to successive American reprinted editions, the attestation began:

To the PUBLICK

As it has been repeatedly suggested to the publisher, by Persons, who have seen the manuscript, that Numbers would be ready to suspect they were not really the writings of PHILLIS, he has procured the following Attestation, from the most respectable Characters in *Boston*, that none might have the least Ground for disputing their *Original*.

We whose names are under-written, do assure the World, that the Poems specified in the following Page, were (as we verily believe) written by PHILLIS, a young Negro Girl, who was but a few years since, brought an uncultivated barbarian from Africa, and has ever since been, and now is, under the disadvantage of serving as a slave in a Family in this Town. . . .

The paper was signed by Hutchinson, Oliver, councilmen Thomas Hubbard, John Erving, James Pitts, Harrison Gray, James Bowdoin, and John Hancock, Joseph Green, Richard Carey, and the Reverends Charles Chauncy, Mather Byles, Ed. [sic for Eb(enezer)] Pemberton, Andrew Eliot, Samuel Cooper, Samuel Mather, John Moorhead, and her master, John Wheatley.

As printed preface to the volume, this attestation is undated, but the first London edition of the poems did not carry this particular preface piece at all. That was because the London publisher, Archibald Bell, had already printed it in several London newspapers as part of his extended promotional campaign to interest London subscribers. In the newspaper printings that used the attestation, e.g., the *Morning Post and Advertiser* for September 13, and 18, and the *London Chronicle* for September 9–11, the document is undated, but in *Lloyd's Evening Post and British Chronicle* for September 10–13, 13–15, it is dated "Boston. Octo. 8, 1772," although it was in Bell's possession even earlier, as noted in published proposals for the volume in the (London) *Morning Post and Advertiser* throughout August, 1773. To curious London readers, Bell's proposals noted, "N.B. The original attestation, signed by the above gentlemen, may be seen by applying to Archibald Bell," at No. 8 Aldgate Street.

It could not have been the simplest of matters for Mrs. Wheatley to secure the names of these men to the attestation, factioned by powerfully financial family cliques and political antagonism as they were. It is a tribute to her persuasiveness and sophistication that she was able to get a diametrically opposed lot of men to sign a common paper, even one as innocuous as one that simply testified to the authenticity of a slave poet's genuineness. It may well have taken Mrs. Wheatley until October 8 to have all of the politicians, merchants and ministers sign the attestation.

Having determined to publish Phillis's poems abroad, Mrs. Wheatley had Phillis diplomatically revise several of the pieces listed by titles in the 1772 proposals that had been rejected by Bostonians. From the original specificity of sometimes naming the Bostonians to whom the poems were dedicated, Phillis revised toward a generality that would make more sense to Londoners who were now to be her reading audience. Thus the original title of "To Mrs. *Leonard*, On the Death of her Husband" was changed to "To A Lady on the Death of her Husband," and "To Mrs. *Boylston* and Children, on the Death of her Son and their

Brother" was generalized to "To A Lady and her Children, on the Death of her Son and their Brother." The original title, "To the Rev. Mr. *Pitkin* on the Death of his Lady" may have feelingly personalized the poet's compassion for Pitkin and his Connecticut and Boston and Dartmouth College friends, but as he may not have been as well known in London, Phillis revised the title to "To A Clergyman on the Death of His Lady." For the same reasons, the 1772 American title, "To *James Sullivan*, Esq: and Lady on the Death of her Brother and Sister, and a Child, Avis, aged 12 Months" became "To A Gentleman and Lady on the Death of the Lady's Brother and Sister, and a Child of the Name Avis, aged One Year." As the extant manuscript shows, the poem, "On the Death of Master *Seider* [sic] who was killed by *Ebenezer Richardson*" is bluntly pro-American and just as bluntly anti-English, and would be better left out of a volume that was to be published in London. Likewise, pieces with titles like "On the arrival of the Ships of War, and landing of the Troops" (about the provocative British military occupation of Boston in 1768) and "On the Affray in King Street, on the Evening of the 5th of March" (referring to the inflammatory "Boston Massacre" of 1770) would best be left out of such a book. On the other hand, there are included in the book, "To the King's Most Excellent Majesty. 1768," which flatters King George for repealing the hated Stamp Act, and the poem, "To Captain H——D, of the 65th Regiment." In this short piece, Phillis may have meant to hail only the British captain's virtues, but she does so in lines of military praise, such as,

> Go, hero, brave, still grace the post of fame,
> And add new glories to thine honoured name,
> Still to the field, and still to virtue true:
> *Brittania* glories in no son like you.

Both Phillis and Mrs. Wheatley knew exactly what they were doing.

When Thomas Wooldridge had visited the Wheatley household in the fall of 1772, to see for himself the much discussed slave poet, Phillis had written, before his very eyes, a poem and covering letter to Dartmouth, and a brief biographical sketch of herself signed for Nathaniel Wheatley, whose name is undersigned with the date "Oct. 12th 1772." Mrs. Wheatley then had Phillis revise and slightly expand this sketch by adding a few flattering details and by having this version signed "John Wheatley./ *Boston, Nov.* 14, 1772." Phillis also prepared a traditional preface, singularized by her clever inclusion of a reminder to her readers that she was a slave:

> . . . As to the Disadvantages she has laboured under, with Regard to Learning, nothing needs to be offered, as her Master's Letter in the following Page will sufficiently shew the Difficulties in this Respect she has had to encounter. . . .

The London editions of the book would also include a dedication to "the Right Honourable the/ COUNTESS of HUNTINGDON," which Phillis mistakenly dated *"Boston, June* 12,/ 1773." As she would leave Boston on May 8 and arrive in London on June 17, the dedication must have been written while she was at sea enroute to London.

Finally, having gathered the preface, the revised biographical sketch, the attestation, and manuscripts for 39 poems, Mrs. Wheatley gave the entire package to Captain Calef for delivery to Archibald Bell in London. Calef would leave Boston on November 19, with instructions to urge Bell to seek the permission of the countess to allow Phillis to dedicate the volume to her ladyship.

In London, Calef handed over all of the manuscripts to Bell who, in turn, read them before the countess for her inspection and approval. She was impressed. These and other events were detailed by Calef in a letter he wrote from London on January 5, 1773, to Mrs. Wheatley. The countess, Calef wrote,

> was fond of having the Book Dedicated to her; but one thing she desir'd which she said she hardly thot would be denied her, that was to have Phillis' picture in the frontispiece. So that, if you could get it done it can be Engrav'd here. I do imagine it can be Easily done, and think would contribute greatly to the Sale of the Book. . . .

Accordingly, Phillis sat for her portrait. That Mrs. Wheatley engaged Scipio Moorhead, black artist and servant to the Reverend and Mrs. John Moorhead of Boston's Long Lane Presbyterian Church, to paint Phillis's picture is most probable but undocumented. Phillis certainly knew the Moorhead family. Her friend, the Indian minister, Samson Occom, was a Wheatley houseguest when he preached, in January of 1773, at Moorhead's church. At Moorhead's death in December, 1773, Phillis wrote an interesting broadside elegy for Mary, the daughter. It is known that Moorhead's wife, Sarah, had a reputation as an instructor of drawing, Japanning (lacquer work in the Japanese style), and painting on glass, and that she also instructed Scipio. The January 7, 1773, issue of the *Boston News Letter* noted that

> At Mr. McLean's, watch-maker, near the Town Hall, a Negro man whose extraordinary genius has been assisted by one of the best Masters in London; he takes faces at the lowest Rates. Specimens of his Performances may be seen at said Place.

As the Town Hall, another local name for the Old Colony House, was down the street from where Phillis lived, both she and her mistress may have visited McLean's place to observe the artistic "performances," which may indeed have been painted by Scipio Moorhead. Phillis did write a flattering poem, "To S[cipio] M[oorhead] A Young African Painter, on seeking his Works," which she included in her volume of poems. Phillis's likeness is said to have been faithful. Either an original portrait or an impression of the engraving struck off immediately and sent to Mrs. Wheatley, adorned the living room mantelpiece of the King Street mansion. Visiting with Mrs. Wheatley during Phillis's brief absence abroad, a grand-niece of that lady had her attention excitedly directed toward the likeness. "See, look at my Phillis, does she not seem as though she would speak to me!"

Concerned as she always was with the publicizing of Phillis's poems, Mrs. Wheatley may have had something to do with the promotionally timely reprinting in the *Boston Post Boy* for March 1, 1773, and in the *Essex Gazette* for March 16–23, of Phillis's Poem, "Recollection," complete with the original accompanying letters by "L" and the note by Phillis to the dedicatee, "Madam," all of which had been first printed in the *London Magazine* for March, 1772. April issues of the *News Letter* and the *Post Boy and Advertiser* ran ostensible advertisements of "Proposals/ for printing in London by Subscription,/ A volume of Poems,/ Dedicated by Permission to the Right Hon. the/ Countess of Huntingdon/ Written by Phillis,/ A Negro Servant of Mr. Wheatley, of Boston/ in New England. . . ." With little effort one can hear, in the language and timing of this notice, the muted voice of Susanna Wheatley who, in a pique of un-Christian retaliation, was saying that, despite earlier rejection by Bostonians of Phillis's 1772 proposals, the black poetess's volume would most assuredly be published, and in London, and dedicated to the Countess of Huntingdon, and with her ladyship's permission, and that Phillis's likeness would be part of the book as "an elegant Frontispiece"; Bostonians who wished to become a part of this historic publication might do so by subscribing immediately.

Pressing on in her determined effort to get Phillis's poems into print in London, Mrs. Wheatley made the most of her warm correspondence with the countess. In February, 1773, she had written to the countess, and noted that she would gladly welcome into her Boston home any of the countess's itinerant preachers whom she might send her way. "I shall think my self greatly honour'd in entertaining those who are devoted to the/ cause of Christ . . ./ P.S. When your Ladiship sends any/ of the Gentlemen this way, please/ to direct them to John Wheatley,/ Merch't in Kingstreet, Boston." Heartened by Captain Calef's report of the London progress of Phillis's volume, Mrs. Wheatley wrote to Lady Huntingdon on April 30, 1773, to announce Phillis's trip to London under the escort of her son, Nathaniel:

> . . . Phillis being in a poor state of/ Health, the Physicians advise to the sea air/ and as my son is coming to England upon/ some Business, and as so good an opportunity presented I thot it my duty to send her &/ as your Ladiship has Condescended to take/ so much notice of my Dear Phillis as to permit her/ Book to Dedicate to you, and desiring her/ Picture in the Frontispiece: I flatter my-/ self that your good advice and Counsel/ will not be wanting. I tell Phillis to/ act wholly under the direction of your/ Ladiship. I did not think it worth/ while nor did the time permit to fit her/ out with cloaths, but I have given her/ money to Buy what you think most pro-/ per for her. I like she should be dress'd/ plain. Must beg the favour of your/ Ladiship to advise my son to some Chris-/ tian House for Phillis to board at. . . .

For weeks thereafter news of Phillis's pending departure for London was printed in many newspapers in New England, New York, and Pennsylvania. Over a half-dozen of these notices also printed her poem, "Farewel to America," (q.v.), a sentimental piece, originally in fifteen self-indulging ballad stanzas lamenting Phillis's parting from her mistress. In the newspaper notices of Phillis's sailing to London, she was hailed as "the extraordinary negro poetess," or "the ingenious negro poet." Even after Phillis actually sailed on May 8, Mrs. Wheatley contrived to keep her name before the public. The *Boston Post Boy and Advertiser* for May 6 had reported "The Ship London, Capt Calef, sails on Saturday/ for London, in whom goes passengers Mr. Nathaniel Wheatley/ Merchant, also Phillis, Servant to Mr. Wheatly the extraordinary Negro poet, at the Invi-/ tation of the Countess of Huntingdon." In the name of accuracy and in the name of naming, Mrs. Wheatley had this same newspaper print "a correction" in its May 13 issue: "It was maintained in our last that Phillis the Negro poet, had taken her passage to England in consequence of an invitation from the Countess of Huntingdon, which was a mistake."

On what must have been the next London-bound ship after Phillis's departure from Boston, Mrs. Wheatley mailed a copy of Phillis's poem, "Farewel to America," along with a presumptuous covering letter dated "Boston, New England, May 10, [1773] to the editor of the *London Chronicle*:

> You have no doubt heard of Phillis the extraordinary negro girl here, who has by her own application, unassisted by others, culti-vated her natural talents for poetry in such a manner as to write several pieces which (all circumstances considered) have great merit. This girl, who is a servant to Mr. John Wheatley of this place, sailed last Saturday for London, under the protection of Mr. Na-thaniel Wheatley: since which the following little piece of her's has been published here: [The poem, "Farewell to America/ ad-dressed to Mrs. Susanna W——. By/ Phillis Wheatley" follows.]

Whether or not the *Chronicle* editor had ever heard of Phillis, he obligingly ran Mrs. Wheatley's headnote and the poem in the July 1–3 issue.

Mrs. Wheatley's promotion of Phillis did not cease even with this kind of thing. She urged Jonathan Williams, a Boston neigh-bor, to mention Phillis in his letters to his uncle-in-law, Ben-jamin Franklin, colonial agent for Pennsylvania, then in Lon-don. So prodded, Franklin would visit with Phillis, but not without incident.

Phillis's brief month and a half visit in London was one of the most exciting times of her short life. She was an acknowledged celebrity among fellow celebrities and English peers. She was caught up in a whirlwind of social and literary activities. When she was not correcting and/or revising the signatures of her manuscript, which had been in the printing process since before she left Boston, she was visiting and being visited by several of London's famous personalities. Phillis describes her activities best in a letter written to an American friend shortly after she returned to Boston. To Colonel David Wooster of New Haven, she would write on October 18, 1773:

> . . . I take the/ Freedom to transmit to you, a short sketch of my voyage and re-/ turn from London where I went for the recovery of my health as ad-/ vis'd by my Physician. I was receiv'd in England with such kindness/ Complaisance, and many marks of esteem and real Friendship/ as astonishes me on the reflection, for I was no more than 6/ weeks there—Was introduced to Lord Dartmouth and had/ near half an hour's conversation with his Lordship, with whom/ was Alderman Kirkman,—Then to Lord Lincoln, who visited/ me at my own Lodgings with the Famous Dr. Solander, who/ accompany'd Mr Banks in his late expedition round the World./ Then to Lady Cavendish, and Lady Carteret Webb,—Mrs Pal-/ mer a Poetess, an accomplish'd Lady.—Dr. Thos Gibbons, Rhe-/ toric Proffessor, To Israel Mauduit Esqr Benjamin Franklin/ Esqr F.R.S. Grenville Sharp Esqr who attended me to the Tower &/ show'd the Lions, Panthers, Tigers, &^{c} The Horse Armoury, small/ Armoury, the Crowns, Sceptres, Diadems, the Font for christening/ the Royal Family, Saw Westminister Abbey, British Museum/ Coxes Museum, Saddler's wells, Greenwich Hospital, Park/ and Chapel, the royal Observatory at Greenwich, &^{c} &^{c} too/ many things & places to trouble you with in a Letter.— The Earl of Dartmouth made me a Compliment of 5 Guineas, and desir'd me to/ get the whole of Mr Pope's Works, as the best he could recommend/ to my perusal, this I did, also got Hudibrass, Don Quixote & Gay's Fables/ —was presented with a Folio Edition of Milton's Paradise Lost, prin-/ ted on a Silver Type, so call'd from its elegance, (I suppose) By M^r/ Brook Watson, Merch^t whose Coat of Arms is prefix'd.—

There were others, not mentioned in this letter, with whom Phillis spent some time: John Thornton and his family of three sons and a daughter; the ailing Baron George Lyttelton, distinguished English statesman and man of letters, whom she visited at his Hill Street London home a month before he would die in late August. There was, too, a Reverend Dr. James Thomas of London. Captain Calef, who had family roots in nearby Homerton, may have also arranged for Phillis to meet some of his people there. Several of Phillis's London acquaintances are said to have begun preparations for her to be presented to the King and Queen of England as soon as the Court of St. James reopened. However, these plans were cut short. Back in Boston, Mrs. Wheatley was failing rapidly. Fearing that she might pass on before beholding her cherished poetess for a final time, she urged Phillis to return, in a letter she must have mailed quite soon after Phillis sailed from Boston. Beginning September 16, Boston newspapers noted the return of the "extraordinary Negro poet."

There had been some disappointments on her trip abroad. Phillis was pleased and flattered that Benjamin Franklin had visited with her in her London apartment, but she may have also noticed that, during his courtesy call, he seemed somewhat disconcerted. Phillis may never have learned that Franklin had been indeed perturbed during his interview, for as he wrote to his nephew-in-law, Jonathan Williams, in Boston:

> . . . Upon your recommendation I went to see the black poetess and offered her any service I could do for her. Before I left the house I understood her master was there, and had sent her to me, but did not come into the room himself, and I thought was not pleased with the visit. I should perhaps have inquired first for him; but I had heard nothing of him, and I have heard nothing since of her.

> London, 7 July, 1773.

Even after Phillis's return to Boston, Mr. and Mrs. Wheatley continued to press Jonathan Williams to mention their prized prodigy in his letters to Benjamin Franklin, still in London. But, remembering Nathaniel Wheatley's apparent pique at Franklin's visit with Phillis, Williams was duly hesitant: "The Black Poetess master and mistress prevaild on me to mention her in my letters but as it turned out I am sorry I did," he wrote to Franklin on October 17.

A greater disappointment of the trip was the fact that Phillis had been unable personally to greet her patron, the Countess of Huntingdon. Aging—her Ladyship was 71 years old that summer —and ill, the countess was confined, throughout Phillis's London stay, to Trevacca, the Methodist missionary school she supported on her Talgarth estate in South Wales, and the two of them never met. Phillis expressed genuine regret over this matter in two letters, the red sealing wax still showing to this day the "P W" imprint of her monogrammed ring. From London on "June 27th," shortly after she arrived there, she wrote,

Madam. It is with pleasure I acquaint your Ladiship of my safe arriv/ al in London after a fine passage of 5 weeks, in the Ship London, with my young Master: (advis'd by my Physicians for my Health) have/ Brought a letter from Rich'd Carey Esqr. but was disappointed by your/ absence of [word obscured by Phillis's red sealing wax] the honour of waiting upon your Ladiship with it. I wou^d have inclos'd it,/ but was doubtful of the safety of the conveyance.

I should think my self very happy in seeing your Ladyship,/ and if you was so desirous of the Image of the Author as to propose it/ for a Frontispiece I flatter myself that you would accept the Reality.

I conclude with thanking your Ladyship for permitting the/ Dedication of my Poems to you; and am not insensible, that under/ the Patronage of your Ladyship, not more eminent in the station/ of life than in your exemplary Piety and Virtue, my feeble/ efforts will be shielded from the severe trials of unpitying criticism/ and being encourag'd by your Ladyship's Indulgence, I the more freely/ resign to the world these Juvenile productions. . . .

The countess had invited both Phillis and Nathaniel to her estate in South Wales, but before Phillis could prepare for such a trip, the urgent message to return to Boston came from Mrs. Wheatley. On July 17, 1773, Phillis wrote:

Madam/ I rec'd with the mix'd sensations of pleasure & disappoin^t/ ment your Ladiships' message favored by Mr. Rien acquainting us with/ your pleasure that my Master & I should wait upon you in S^o. Wales, de/ lighted with your Ladiships Condescention to me so unworthy of it Am sorry/ to acquaint your Ladiship that the Ship is certainly to sail next Thurs [day? on? word or words obscured by her sealing wax] which I must return to America. I long to see my friends there,/ [I? am? word or words obscured by sealing wax] extremely reluctant to go without having first seen your Ladiship/ . . . My master is yet undetermind about going home and/ sends his dutiful regards to your Ladiship.

Dutifully Phillis left London on the next sailing of the *London* for Boston. Planning even then for his November wedding to Mary Enderby of the wealthy and successful mercantile London firm, Nathaniel did not return with Phillis.

Having left London with Captain Calef on July 26, Phillis could not have witnessed all of the promotion and publicity staged by Archibald Bell on behalf of London sales of her book of poems. Throughout August, Bell had run proposals for the book in the *London Morning Post and Advertiser* for the 6th, 9th, 11th, 12th, and 16th issues of that month; Phillis may have seen them herself:

Just published
PROPOSALS
For Printing By Subscription
A Volume of POEMS.
Written By
PHILLIS
A Negro Servant to Mr. Wheatley
of
Boston in New England.
The real Author of these Poems is properly attest/ ded by the Governor, Lieutenant-Governor, and great/ part of the council in Boston./ Proposals at large, with an account of this Sur-/ prising Girl, may be had, by applying to A. Bell,/ bookseller, No. 8, Aldgate-Street; by E. Johnson,/ Ave-Mary-lane; S. Leacroft, Charing-cross; C. Da-/ vis, Sackville-Street, Picadilly; Messrs. Richardson/ and Urquhart, Royal-Exchange; and at the Bar of the/ New England coffee-house./ N.B. The original attestation, signed by the above/ Gentlemen, may be seen, by applying to Archibald/ Bell, as above.

The actual London publication of Phillis's volume in early September was widely noted by area newspapers and magazines. Bell went so far as to prepare copy for two versions of this news. In *Lloyd's Evening Post and British Chronicle* for September 10–13, 13–15, and in the *Public Advertiser* for the 13th, he printed a lengthy notice of the book's appearance as "Dedicated, by Permission, to the Right Hon./ the Countess of Huntingdon./ *This Day is Published,/* Price 2s. sewed, or 2s. 6d. neatly bound, adorned with/ an elegant engraved Likeness of the Author." This notice of the publication is straightforward and includes a printing of the attestation which is here dated "Boston. Oct. 28, 1772." Bell also prepared a variant version of this publication news in which he reached almost show business spiel. In the *London Chronicle* for September 9–11, 11–14, and in the *London Morning Post and Daily Advertiser* for September 13, he announced the book as "This Day Sept. 11, will be published" and elsewhere in the piece indulged himself:

. . . The Book here proposed for publication displays per-/ haps one of the greatest instances of pure, unassisted/ genius, that the world ever produced. The Author is/ a native of Africa, and left not that dark part of the/ habitable system, till she was eight years old. She is/ now no more than nineteen, and many of the Poems/ were penned before she arrived at near that age.

They are wrote upon a variety of interesting subjects,/ and in a stile rather to have been expected from those/ who, to a native genius, have had the happiness of a/ liberal education, than from one born in the wilds of/ Africa.

The Writer, while in England a few weeks since,/ was conversed with by many of the principal Nobility/ and Gentry of this country, who have been signally/ distinguished for their learning and abilities, among whom was the Earl of Dartmouth, the late Lord Lyt-/ telton, and others, who unanimously expressed their/ approbation of her genius, and their amazement at the/ gifts with which Infinite Wisdom had furnished her.

But the Publisher means not, in this advertisement,/ to deliver any peculiar eulogiums on the present publi-/ cation; he rather desires to submit the striking beau-/ ties of its contents to the unbiased candour of the im-/ partial public. . . .

The attestation is also included in this information, but it is undated.

Because she was back in Boston when her volume of poems finally appeared in London, Phillis could not then have read the many English and Scottish notices and reviews of the collection. A dozen newspapers and magazines made note of the publication, many of them excerpting over a half-dozen poems from the book for display. At least two of the British reviewers scored the hypocrisy of those Bostonians, including Mr. and Mrs. Wheatley, who loudly touted the talented slave poet, but did nothing to free her from her slave status. Said one London reviewer:

. . . Youth, innocence, and piety, united with genius, have not yet been able to restore her to the condition and character with which she was invested by the Great Author of her being. So powerful is the custom in rendering the heart insensible to the rights of nature, and the claims of excellence!"

"We are much concerned," wrote another reviewer, "to find that this ingenious young woman is yet a slave. The people of Boston boast themselves chiefly on their principles of liberty. One such act as the purchase of her freedom, would, in our opinion, have done more honour than hanging a thousand trees with ribbons and emblems."

It would be hardly surprising then that, back in Boston, very shortly after her return, Phillis Wheatley, a slave for twelve years, was finally manumitted. In her October 18 letter to Colonel David Wooster in New Haven, she supplied details of her manumission. She also revealed, inadvertently, the conditions under which Mr. and Mrs. Wheatley probably subsidized the publication of the book:

> . . . Since my/ return to America my Master, has at the desire of my friends in/ England given me my freedom. The Instrument is drawn, so as/ to secure me and my property from the hands of the [Executive?] admin-/ istrators &^{C} of my Master, & secure whatsoever should be given me as/ my Own. A Copy is sent to Isra. Mauduit Esqr F.R.S.
>
> I expect my Books which are publish'd in London in Capt Hall, who will be here I believe in 8 or 10 days. I beg the favour/ that you would honour the enclos'd Proposals, & use your inte-/ rests; for the more subscribers there are, the more it will be for/ my advantage, as I am to have half the sale of the Books. Thus I/ am the more solicitous for, as I am now on my own footing/ and whatever I get by this is entirely mine, & it is the Chief I have to/ depend upon. I must also request you would desire the Printers/ in New Haven, not to reprint that Book, as it will be a great/ hurt to me, preventing any further Benefit that I might so/ receive from the sale of my Copies from England. The price is/ 2/6d Bound or 2/ Sterling sewed. If any should be so ungenerous/ as to reprint them the Genuine Copy may be known, for it/ is sign'd in my own handwriting. . . .

Phillis would not receive her books in Boston "in 8 or 10 days," as she had hoped; in fact it would be almost four months before a lot of 300 copies of her volume would become available to her and interested Bostonians. Archibald Bell had been busy with sales of his supply of the volume to London readers. Meanwhile Phillis would readjust to Boston and the Wheatley household, tending her mistress even more closely than ever; it was clear to all that Mrs. Wheatley was now dangerously ill. Whenever possible, there were more visits to area first families who would listen to Phillis tell of her recent trip. She continued with her writing, of course. In response to a letter of October 13 from her friend Obour Tanner, Phillis wrote on October 30 and mentioned her London trip, but not to the point of flaunting detail; instead she discussed the matter in terms of an object lesson in Christian humility.

> . . . I can't say but my voyage to England has conducted to/ the recovery (in a great measure) of my health. The Friends I found there among the nobility and gentry, their benevolent conduct towards me, the unexpected and unmerited/ civility and complaisance with which I was treated by all,/ fills me with astonishment . . ./ This I humbly hope has the happy Effect of lessening/ me in my own Esteem. . . . The God of the seas & dry land, has graciously Brought me home in safety. Join with me in thanks to him/ for so great a mercy, & that it may excite me to praise him/ with cheerfulness, ...

She went on to mention the waning condition of her mistress, and she did not fail to solicit Obour's help in securing buyers of the forthcoming book of poems. On the first of December she notified John Thornton in London of her safe arrival, but did not say a single word about her book. She did report on the languishing health of her dying mistress, but most of her letter is suffused with fervent supplications, which, she knew, would appeal to the stern, Christian preoccupations of the celebrated philanthropist. Given to pious pontifications, he would later write her a lengthy letter of Christian strictures against the folly of heeding popular acclaim of her poetic abilities:

> . . . Many a good man is often a snare, by too openly commending his good quali-/ ties, and not aware how undesignedly he spreads a net at the feet of his friend. Your/ present situation, and the kindness you meet with from many good people, and the respect/ that is paid to your uncommon genius, extorts this friendly hint from me. I have no reason/ to charge you with any indiscretions of this kind: I mean only to apprize you of the danger./ I feared for you when here, least the notice many took of you should prove a snare. . . .

In her letter of December 1, 1773, Phillis had also mentioned the recent death of the Reverend John Moorhead, but, deferentially, she did not mention that she would publish an elegy on his death on December 15.

In the *Boston Gazette and Country Journal* for January 17 and 24 and February 7, and in the *Gazette and Boston Weekly News Letter* for February 3, 10, and 17, 1774, notice of the availability in Boston of Phillis's long-awaited volume was finally printed. It was listed, somewhat misleadingly, as "This Day published, Adorned with an Elegant Engraving of the Author, Price 3s. 4d. L.M." (i.e., three shillings, four pence, Legal Money), and could be picked up at Cox and Berry's King Street store. In the *Boston Weekly News Letter* for February 24 and March 3 and 10, an enthusiastic Mr. Delile, itinerant instructor in French and Latin, wished to commemorate the publication by proposing that "Four Lines in Latin verse . . . be put under the/ Frontispiece of PHILLIS's Performances, by/ Benevolence for the Poet, and Regard for the/ Subscribers." No such inscription was added, but there was joy enough, especially in the Wheatley household, at the news of the appearance of Phillis Wheatley's POEMS/ On/ VARIOUS SUBJECTS,/ RELIGIOUS AND MORAL (London, Printed for A. Bell, Bookseller, Aldgate; and sold by/ Messrs. COX and BERRY, King-Street, BOSTON./ MDCCLXXIII.)

To William Barrell in Philadelphia, merchant John Andrews wrote from Boston on January 28, 1774, ". . . After so long a time have at last got Phillis's poems in print. . . . These don't seem to be near all her productions. She's an artful jade, I believe & intends to have the benefit of another volume. . . ." Although he may have put it bluntly, Andrews was exactly right about Phillis's artfulness. Indeed, throughout her American lifetime, it seems clear that, modest, shy, reverent, gentle, and unpretentious though she was, Phillis did not often lose sight of who and what and where she was; because she was that aware, she also never lost sight of the necessity of occasional artfulness to get on in her world. A free, responsible black woman, she realized, for instance, that it would be largely up to her to sell copies of her book for her support.

Two weeks after she solicited the assistance of Colonel David Wooster, she contacted her friend, Obour Tanner, on October 30, 1773, ". . . I enclose Proposals for my book, and beg you'd use your interest to get subscriptions, as it is for my benefit." Obour would dutifully sell at least a known half-dozen copies to her fellow Newporters, black and white, although there were surely more than six literate blacks in that town. In 1793 Obour Tanner was only one of seventeen free Newport blacks (and four free blacks of Providence) who would subscribe to *Systems of Doctrine*, an abstruse two-volume work written by Reverend Samuel Hopkins (1721–1803). Although Phillis's colonial contemporaries included a surprising number of literate blacks, several of whom read and wrote French, Latin, and Greek, most of them were at first otherwise too preoccupied to comment on the Boston slave poetess. It would not be until 1778 that Long Island-born versifier, Jupiter Hammon would acknowledge her fame in his "An Address to Miss Phillis Wheatly Ethiopian Poetess, in Boston, who came from Africa at eight years of age, and soon became acquainted with the gospel of Jesus Christ." If early American blacks did not mention Phillis often in their writings, they were certainly aware and proud of her. The 1801 American reprinted edition of her volume of *Poems* also carried a lengthy list of subscribers, among whom can be found the blacks, Reverends Absalom Jones and Richard Allen, James Forten, and others. Her Indian friend, the Reverend Samson Occom, could be depended on for help in selling her book. On May 6, 1774, she noted in a letter to Obour Tanner that "I have rec'd by some of the last ships/ 300 more of my Poems." In the June 17 issue of the *Connecticut Gazette* appeared the notice, "TO BE SOLD BY T. GREEN, POEMS ON VARIOUS SUBJECTS, RELIGIOUS AND MORAL, BY PHILLIS WHEATLEY, NEGRO SERVANT TO MR. JOHN WHEATLEY, OF BOSTON, IN NEW ENGLAND. *A few of the above are likewise to be sold by* SAMSON OCCOM." The good minister assumed the burden of trying to sell some of Wheatley's books even as he tried to sell copies of his own book. *A Choice Collection of Hymns*, which was published that same spring in New London. On September 9, a Deborah Cushing wrote from Boston to her husband in Philadelphia, and mentioned other ways by which Phillis herself sold copies of her poems:

> I rote you/ by M͏ͬ Gary and sent you one of Phillis Wheatley's books/ which you will wonder att/ but Mrs. Dickerson and Miss Clymer/ Mrs Bull with some other Ladys ware so pleas'd with Phillis and her performances that they bought her Books/ and got her to compose peices for them which put/ me in mind of Mrs Vanhorn to hume I thought it would/ be very agreabel. . . .

As soon as her books arrived in Boston from London, Phillis notified the Reverend Samuel Hopkins that she had "sealed up a package containing 17 for you, and 2 for Mr. Tanner, and one for M͏ͬ͏ˢ Mason. . . . I rec'd some time ago 20/ sterling, upon them by the hands of your Son in a Letter from Obour Tanner. . . ." It did not matter that Hopkins was privately on record as loathing all kinds of poetry. Even if she had known as much, Phillis would fully understand that Hopkins badly needed the prestige of her name and fame to help him in his attempts to raise funds for the education of two African-born slaves living in Newport—Bristol Yamma and John Quamine—at the College of New Jersey (Princeton University) for pioneering African missionary work. To Hopkins and his friends, Phillis sold at least twenty copies of her book. Hopkins would even pay "3s. 4d. L.M." rather than the later standard price of 2s. 6d. for the bound edition of the volume.

Feeling the headiness of almost six months of freedom, Phillis Wheatley then wrote a remarkable letter on February 11, 1774, to her friend, Samson Occom. Occom had written an indictment of professedly liberty-loving Christian slaveholders, especially such as were ministers:

> I will tell you who they are, they are the Preachers or ministers of the Gospel of Jesus Christ. It has been very fashionable for them to keep Negroe Slaves, which I think is inconsistent with their character and function. If I understand the Gospel aright, I think it is a Dispensation of Freedom and Liberty, both Temporal and Spiritual, and [if] the Preachers of the Holy Gospel of Jesus do preach it according to the mind of God, they preach True Liberty and how can such keep Negroes in slavery? And if ministers are True Liberty men, let them preach Liberty for the poor Negroes fervently and with great zeal, and those ministers who have Negroes set an example before their People by freeing their Negroes, let them show their faith by their Works. . . .

Phillis's letter is addressed to just such sentiments. It is arch, genteel, slicingly sarcastic but unmistakably condemnatory of all of those who regularly boasted of Christian charity but, incongruously, held slaves. Published first under a New London heading dated March 11 in the *Connecticut Gazette* of the same date, likely at the behest of Occom, then living at his birthplace of Mmoyoueeunnuck in New London, Phillis's letter would be reprinted in at least eleven New England newspapers throughout March and into April. It is her boldest anti-slavery protest in print, and reads, in part

> . . . in every human Breast, God has implanted a Principle, which we call Love of Freedom; it is impatient of oppression, and pants for Deliverance—and by the Leave of our Modern Egyptians I will assert that the same principle lives in us. God grant Deliverance in

44

his own Way and Time, and get him honour upon all those whose Avarice impels them to countenance and help forward the Calamities of their fellow Creatures. This I desire not for their Hurt, but to convince them of the strange Absurdity of their Conduct whose Words and Actions are so diametrically opposite. How well the Cry for Liberty and the reverse Disposition for the exercise of oppressive power over others agree I humbly think it does not require the penetration of a Philosopher to determine.

Mercifully, on March 3, a week before Phillis's protest letter appeared in print, Mrs. Susanna Wheatley, aged 65, died in the throes of religious ecstasy, crying out, "Come! come quickly! come, come! O pray for an easy and quick Passage!" Phillis was at the bedside during the death watch, and she was a part of the procession of mourners who wound down to the Old Granary Burial Place on Tremont Street, where her mistress and long-doting friend and benefactor was laid to rest with her three children who had died young. Mrs. Wheatley's Christian humility is said to have been such that she forbade Phillis from poetically memorializing any good deeds she proffered to her protégée; indeed, "on her death bed she requested that nothing might be written upon her decease." Phillis obeyed her mistress's wishes (indeed, this same kind of Christian humility in herself may explain why she did not write, or publish, anything of own family); nevertheless, she did share her grief with others in private letters. To Obour on March 21, she wrote

> . . . I have lately met with a great trial in the death of my/ mistress; let us imagine the loss of a Parent, Sister, or Brother, the tender-/ ness of all these were united in her. I was a poor little outcast &/ a stranger when she took me in, not only into her house, but I pre-/ sently became a sharer in her most tender affections. I was treated by her/ more like a child than her servant. . . .

She went on with other reflections of the death. She also noted her book-selling efforts.

Phillis also reported the death of her mistress, in some detail, to John Thornton on March 29. In his reply of August 1, Thornton commiserated and even suggested that he might replace Mrs. Wheatley as Phillis's spiritual guide. In her next letter, on October 30, 1774, Phillis said several things. She thanked him for his religious offer, but noted that the distance between them would make such an arrangement unlikely. She also flatly refused his hopes of having her join Bristol Yamma and John Quamine in Newport as missionaries to Africa. She told of how Nathaniel Wheatley, who had conveyed Thornton's letter of August 1, had returned to Boston "not before the 27th Ultimo after a tedious passage of near two months," but seemed, nevertheless, to approve of his father's allowing Phillis, now a free woman, to remain in the Wheatley mansion, now owned by Nathaniel. Phillis said something else in this same letter. She was genuinely grateful, she wrote, for

> . . . my old master's generous behaviour in granting me my free-dom, and still so/ kind to me. I delight to acknowledge my great obligations to him, this he did about/ 3 months before the death of my dear Mistress & at her desire, as well as his own/ humanity, of wch I hope ever to retain a grateful sense, and treat him with that respect/ which is ever due A paternal friendship—If this had not been the case, yet/ I hope I should willingly submit to servitude to be free in Christ—But since it/ is thus—Let me be a *Servant of Christ*, and that is the most perfect freedom.—

The extemporaneous expression of her sentiments here can be misleading. In her compulsion for Christian mortification, she had registered pious hyperboles earlier, both in her poetry and in her letters. In "Recollection," she had written

> . . . Now *eighteen years* their destin'd course have run,
> In due succession, round the central sun;
> How did each folly unregarded pass!
> But sure 'tis graven on eternal brass!
> To *recollect*, inglorious I return;
> 'Tis mine past follies and past crimes to mourn.
> The *virtue*, ah! unequal to the *vice*,
> Will scarce afford small reason to rejoice.

In writing on December 1, 1773, to John Thornton, of her safe return to Boston, she said, ". . . I presume you will join with . . . me/ in praise of God for so distinguishing a favour, it was amazing Mercy altogether/ unmerited by me; and if possible it is augmented by the consideration of the bitter re-/ verse, which is the deserved wages of my evil doings. . . ."

Phillis's piety was undeniably genuine and profound, as was her lasting gratitude and fond regard for the uncommonly privi-leged life and career which Mrs. and Mr. Wheatley had provided for her; at the same time, it is a matter of documentable fact that she was never really prepared to remain a slave or servant for the rest of her life, as her letter to Thornton suggests. It was with calculated casualness that she wrote her letter of October 30, 1774, to Thornton, and said that she had been freed "about 3 months before the death of my dear mistress." She knew very well that she had been a free woman longer than that. She had been manumitted between September 16, 1773, when Boston newspapers started reporting her arrival back from London, and October 18, of the same year, when she wrote to Colonel David Wooster, supplying some details of her manumission. This means that, Mrs. Susanna Wheatley dying in March of 1774, Phillis had been a free person for almost six months before the death of her mistress. Also, as she had noted in her letter to Wooster, she had not been freed merely by the belatedly spontaneous beneficence of her master and mistress. In her letter to Wooster, she had written "Since my return to America my Master, has at the desire of friends in England given me my freedom." Phillis seems, in her letter to Thornton, to be politely trying not to reveal her anxiety for her personal freedom, apprehensive that Thornton, a powerful and influential philanthropist of dogmatic piety, might misinterpret such concern as evidence of un-Christian vanity, evidence of a professedly un-Christian misfocusing on earthly social status.

But, as her writing points out, Phillis indeed did have an abiding interest in freedom, personal and general. The words "free" and "freedom" are used more than a dozen times throughout her poetry; in one poem, "Liberty and Peace," she uses "freedom" four times. In her eulogy on the death of her friend, General David Wooster, she is even more daringly specific about her feelings for freedom and against slavery. She records a dying Wooster's declamation to the skies:

> Permit, great power while yet my fleeting breath
> And Spirits wander to the verge of Death—
> Permit me yet to paint fair freedom's charms
> For her the Continent shines bright in arms
>
> . . .
>
> O still propitious be thy guardian care
> And lead *Columbia* thro' the toil of war.

          . . .
For ever grateful let them live to thee
And keep them ever Virtuous, brave, and free—
But how, presumptuous shall we hope to find
Divine acceptance with th'Almighty mind—
While yet, O deed ungenerous! they disgrace
And hold in bondage Afric's blameless race?
Let virtue reign—And thou accord our prayers
Be victory our's, and generous freedom theirs. . . .

In February of 1774, she wrote her anti-slavery letter to the Reverend Samson Occom, arguing against the hypocrisy of Christian slaveholders, who, as such, ran contrary to the principle of freedom, which, she wrote, God had implanted "in every human breast." In May of 1774, she received 300 more copies of her books from London. Interestingly, she advertised the volumes for sale in the *Boston Evening Post and Advertiser*, not, as subsequent advertisements would state, as the poems of a servant of Mr. John Wheatley of Boston; instead she advertised her books as the work of "Phillis Wheatley/ A Negro Girl/ Printed for the benefit of the Author." But to try and explain or justify such provisioning for herself as a free black woman might have been misunderstood by the single-minded John Thornton, a man who had been free and rich and white all of his accommodated life. In the business of human survival, one is often obliged to wear different faces in different places for the same reasons.

When Lieutenant-General Thomas Gage came from London to rebellious Boston in May of 1774, he did so as the newly appointed military governor of the Province of Massachusetts. With him he brought four regiments of soldiers, the first of a British military force which he would gradually augment with detachments of Royal troops from Quebec, from New York, from Newfoundland. By the beginning of 1775, Gage would be in command of over 4500 troops, eleven regiments and four companies of artillery, all of them crowded into and around the tiny Boston peninsula to punish the locals for their defiant and continued refusal to pay the British government for the estimated $90,000.00 damage loss incurred from the celebrated Boston Tea Party of December 1773.

As part of the punishment, traditional seats of administration were deliberately dislocated: the capital of the province was moved from Boston to Salem, and Plymouth was deemed the new seat of county customs. Boston Harbor was closed. The old Quartering Act of 1765 was newly extended and expanded to include now private homes to the list of possible abodes for Royal officers. When, on June 30, Vice Admiral Samuel Graves arrived in Boston with troops to relieve Admiral John Montagu as commander of the North American station and to enforce the blockading of the harbor, his command staff included a nephew, Lieutenant Thomas Graves, and, possibly, a Lieutenant Rochefort (or Rochford). These officers, young men both, may have been billeted in the Wheatley mansion; and, young men both, they may have tried to impress the popular black poetess of that address, with romantic stories of their past service in Africa. Graves, for instance, had served aboard the *Edgar* off the coast of Africa only recently. If it is true that these officers were so billeted, it might explain a grouping of three poems—two by Phillis and one by an anonymous hand—all three written within one month and published in the same magazine at the end of 1774 and the beginning of 1775.

Phillis wrote a poem, "To A Gentleman of the Navy," dated "Boston, October 30th, 1774," which was printed in Joseph Greenleaf's *Royal American Magazine* for December 1774. Appearing in this same issue, and in reaction to Phillis's poem, and dated "December 2, 1774," was an anonymous piece, "The Answer." "The Answer" flatters both Phillis as "the lovely daughter of the Affric shore," and her native country as "the guilded shore, the happy land,/ Where spring and autumn gently hand in hand; O'er shady forests that scarce know a bound,/ In vivid blaze alternately dance round." In reply to this piece, Phillis wrote a second poem, dated "December 5th, 1774." which the editor, Joseph Greenleaf, titled "PHILIS's Reply to the Answer in/ our last by the Gentleman in the/ Navy," which was published in the same magazine for January of 1775. In this second poem, Phillis develops the motif of flattering things African, and she may even have become autobiographical:

> . . . Charm'd with thy painting, how my bosom burns!
> And pleasing Gambia on my soul returns,
> With native grace in spring's luxuriant reign,
> Smiles the gay mead, and Eden blooms again,
> The various bower, the tuneful flowing stream,
> The soft retreats, the lovers golden dream,
> Her soil spontaneous, yields exhaustless stores:

For phoebus revels on her verdant shores.
Whose flowery births, a fragrant train appear,
And crown the youth throughout the smiling year, . . .
    There, as in Britain's favour'd isle, behold
The bending harvest ripen into gold!
Just are thy views of Afric's blissful plain,
On the warm limits of the land and main. . . .

Even if she is not referring to her remembered Gambian birth-place, she is certainly the first of black American poets to so praise things African.

The swarming masses of British troops may have immensely pleased resident Boston Loyalists, but they absolutely galled town Patriots. The troops even got on each other's nerves. Scuffles and fights, drunken brawls between soldiers and sailors and civilian inhabitants were almost daily occurrences. Soon, of the roughly 16,000 Bostonians, over 10,000 secured permission from General Gage to leave the town, after pledging and depositing with town Selectmen 538 guns, 406 bayonets, 647 cartridge belts, 1500 rounds of ammunition—a total of several thousand pieces. Reportedly, John Wheatley left town for Chelsea, across the bay. By May, 1775, the Reverend John Lathrop had fled Boston, which spared him the anguish at seeing his church, the famous Old North, of Paul Revere fame, pulled to the ground by the British for fire-wood in the first month of 1776. Intending to repair to his birthplace of Norwich, Connecticut, he stopped in Providence, Rhode Island, where he was invited to fill an empty pulpit of the First Congregational Church there, which he did from May, 1775, until March, 1776, after the British evacuated his adopted home-town of Boston, to which he returned.

Where Phillis was living during these years is uncertain. She spent some time with the Lathrops in Providence, for it was from there that she composed and mailed her poem and covering letter, dated "Providence, Oct. 26, 1775," to General George Washing-ton in Cambridge, Massachusetts. Phillis may have been visiting, especially, with her old friend and childhood tutor, Mary Wheat-ley Lathrop. Chronically ill, Mary Lathrop had lost three of four children by October 20, 1775, by which time she was again preg-nant with a fifth child, who would die on November 21, only eight days old. Phillis was not in the Wheatley place on King Street, just days before the occupying British troops would evacu-ate the town in March of 1776, when that mansion was struck by bombs accidentally lobbed across the bay by American soldiers on Charleston's Cobble Hill. The Boston Phillis would know after the evacuation was in the sprawling disarray of any small town recently garrisoned by bored soldiers. The high grounds of Copps's Hill, Fort Hill, Beacon Hill were gouged with gun entrenchments and strewn with broken, abandoned British artillery pieces. The population had shrunk to some 3000 souls, more than 1100 Boston Tories having fled with General Burgoyne's troops, leaving their stately residences to covetous designs of the Patriots. Many of the town's trees had been chopped down by British soldiers needing firewood to keep warm. The Liberty Tree, on the corner of Essex and Newbury (today's Washington) Streets was reduced to a stump. Not only had Reverend Lathrop's Old North Church of subsequent "One, if by land, and two, if by sea" fame been pulled to the ground by vindictive British troops in ostensible need for fuel, but Phillis's own church, the Old South, had also been badly gutted. The pulpit and seats and pews had been ripped away and used as fuel, making room for the exercising of the horses of the Queen's pride, the 17th Regiment of Light Dragoons. Deacon Thomas Hubbard's handsomely carved private pew, with its silken furnishings, was converted into a pig sty. Even the second-story galleries, where children and blacks were confined, were redone for the accommodation of refreshments (including liquors) and spectators, who cheered the cavortings of the cavalrymen below on the now gravel and dirt floors. The Old South would not be fully repaired and usable for another six years; meanwhile, the congregation secured permission to worship at the abandoned King's Chapel from 1777 to 1783. Members reopened with a purification service, for which they joined the choir in pointedly and lustily singing the anthem "He hath raised up the tabernacle of David that was fallen . . . he hath raised up the ruins; he hath built it as in the days of old, and caused his people to rejoice therein."

Phillis was back in Boston by December of 1776, perhaps in an apartment by herself, for on the 30th of that month she composed a spirited paean that lavishly (and misguidedly) praised Major General Charles Lee of the Continental Army. Unaware of Lee's deeper feelings of resentment toward his superior, General George Washington, Phillis poetically hailed a gallant loyalty that was questioned by others. She dedicated the poem to James Bowdoin who, more aware of Lee's genuine feelings than Phillis, kept the manuscript among his papers and out of public print, thereby sparing Phillis considerable embarrassment. This poem would not be published until 1863, by a Bowdoin descendant who found the manuscript among his ancestor's papers. Presumably, she was still in Boston when, from aboard the *Ranger* on an undated Friday, the renowned American naval hero, Captain John Paul Jones, wrote a note to his friend and fellow officer, Lieutenant Hector McNeil. "I am on the point of sailing," he said, and enclosed some of his non-extant writings, probably verses, which he wished to be put into the hands of "the celebrated Phillis the African favorite of the Nine and Apollo. . . ." As Jones was given official command of the newly built warship, *Ranger*, in June of 1777, and, delayed by poor winds, would leave America for France as late as November of that year, his letter would have to have been written sometime during the intervening five months.

It is most probable that by the time old John Wheatley drew up his will on February 14, 1778, he was not then himself living in his former King Street home. Then seventy-two years old, he may well have been taken in sometime earlier by his son-in-law, the Reverend John Lathrop, then living in his North End quarters. Having already sold and bequeathed the bulk of his estate to his son, Nathaniel, John Wheatley appointed his son-in-law as his executor and bequeathed the remainder of his estate to his daughter, Mary. Phillis's name is nowhere mentioned in John Wheatley's will. After the old man died on March 12, 1778, life for Phillis changed dramatically for the worse. Since 1774, Nathaniel had been living in London, happily married, where he would die in the spring of 1783, leaving a widow and three London-born daughters, all generously provided for in his will. Phillis was not among Nathaniel Wheatley's legatees. Her old Tory friends had deserted Boston with the British troops in March of 1776. Even Captain Robert Calef, skipper and by now a part owner of the schooner, *London* had returned in 1774 to his Homerton, England, family roots and would remain there until after the war. As were most Bostonians of the time, other Wheatley relatives were hard pressed to cope with the inflated prices of food and clothing and shelter. Also, many of her friends were now dead. Of the eighteen ministers, merchants, and politicians who signed the attestation for her volume of poems in 1773, almost half were dead by 1778; others were obliged to fend for themselves. That other kindly folk would be hard come by had been an arresting reality to Phillis since the death of her mistress in 1774. "The World is a severe schoolmaster," she had written to John Thornton in that year, "for its frowns are far less dang'rous/ than its smiles and flatteries. . . . I attended and find exactly true your thoughts on the behaviour/ of those who seem'd to respect me while under my mistresses patronage; you said/ right, for some of those have already put on a reserve. . . ." So situated, it was not surprising, a few days after the death of her ex-master, that Phillis accepted the marriage proposal of one John Peters. With both of them officially listed as "free Negroes," their mariage intentions were posted on April 1, 1778.

About John Peters, conflicting reports have come down, and the man remains something of an enigma. Phillis's first biographer describes him as a respectable colored man of Boston, who kept a grocery store in Court Street, very handsome, well mannered, wore a wig, carried a cane, and "quite acted out" the gentleman. He is said to have failed in business soon after marriage, too proud and indolent to work below his fancied dignity; one who beguiled Phillis to confide in his protection and betrayed her trust and his own. Having heard nothing of Phillis for some time after her marriage, several of Mrs. Wheatley's relatives sought the poetess out.

They found her in extreme poverty, two of three children dead, the third "sick unto death." Phillis was herself desperately ill and living in filth. "If a charitable individual, moved at the sight of so much distress, sent a load of wood, to render her more comfortable during the cold season, her husband was too much of a gentleman to prepare it for her use." Obour Tanner felt that "poor Phillis let herself down by marrying." Another source reports that Peters' was so shiftless and improvident that he was forced to relieve himself of debt by an imprisonment in 1784 in the county jail. This same source reports, contradictorily, that Peters worked as an apprentice baker when he was freed from jail. Another writer, who supposedly knew Peters personally, claimed that he was the intellectual superior of other Boston blacks of the day and was himself a kind of phenomenon; that it was no surprise to see him, a grocer, "become a lawyer under the name of Doctor Peters and plead before the tribunals the cause of blacks. The reputation he enjoyed procured him a fortune." Others remember John Peters as a lawyer also. Jane Tyler Lathrop, granddaughter to Mrs.

Susanna Wheatley, noted that he "was not only a very remarkable looking man, but a man of letters and information; and that he wrote with fluency and propriety, and at one time read law." Josiah Quincy (1772–1864) also recalled seeing Peters in Boston law courts.

Writers who see any fault at all with Phillis are few, one noting that the marriage failed because Phillis could never adjust to living as anything except the spoiled poetess she was raised to be. The grievous realities and uncompromising demands of coping with a less than genteel life as the wife of a failed, overly ambitious businessman were too much for her; she was overwhelmed and died of a broken heart. Through it all, however, Phillis is said to have never complained against her husband. When Peters was sent to debtor's jail in 1784, writes another, "Phillis was obliged to earn her own subsistence in a common negro boarding-house, at the west end of the town."

For all of its reported subsequent ups and downs, the marriage seems to have begun well enough. Indeed, John and Phillis Peters may at one time have had their own servants. By 1780, for instance, Peters could afford to live in a house on fashionable Queen Street (today's Court Street) on which he paid £150 in real estate taxes. This was not an inconsiderable sum and speaks of a more than modest dwelling, which, in Queen Street fashion, typically employed servants. At one time or another during Phillis's Boston lifetime, such prominent men as John Adams, General Howe, Harrison Gray, Josiah Quincy lived on that street, each with a retinue of servants. The amount of taxes which Peters paid in 1780 is all the more impressive when one recognizes that in that same year the handful of other free Boston blacks who owned property paid significantly less taxes. Prince Hall paid £16. 13. 4 (i.e., sixteen pounds, thirteen shillings, and four pence).

Letters written by Phillis during her first year of marriage—one to Obour Tanner on May 29 and another to the recently widowed Mrs. Mary Wooster in New Haven on July 25—betray no undue marital tensions. In the fall of that year, however, there was a distressing piece of news for Phillis to endure: her longtime friend and tutor for ten years, Mary Wheatley Lathrop, died, aged 35, resolutely pious to the end. "She viewed her dissolution coming on with a calmness" wrote her husband in his eulogy for her, "and often said she did not wish to recover health, and be exposed again to the temptations of this evil world, unless it were to honor her Lord and Redeemer more than ever before she had done." Notices of Mary's death were published in the *Boston Evening Post and General Advertiser* from February 13, almost consecutively, to May 1, 1779, as part of announcements for sales of a "Discourse,/ occasioned by the Death of Mrs. MARY/ LATHROP, who departed this Life September/ 24, 1778. Delivered the Lord's Day after/ Her Funeral, by her afflicted Consort, JOHN/ LATHROP. Published at the Desire of many who heard it,/ and the particular acquaintance of the Deceased." Very probably, Phillis Wheatley Peters was among the "particular acquaintance of the deceased."

Even before the news of Mary Lathrop's death was printed, Phillis Wheatley Peters was pregnant, and there are indications of strain. From Boston on May 10, 1779, Phillis wrote a short note to her friend, Obour Tanner, now in Worcester, Massachusetts, with her people who had fled the siege of Newport late in 1778. For a happy change, Phillis does not write of feeling sickly, but it is clear that all is otherwise not well:

> . . . tho' I have been silent, I have not been unmindful of you but a variety of/ hindrances was the cause of my not writing to you./ But in time to come I hope our correspondence will/ revive—and revive in better times—pray write me/ soon for I long to hear from you—you may depend on constant replies—.

Despite her expressed wish for a revival of their correspondence, this is the last extant letter from Phillis to Obour. Some years later, Obour, who would live on until 1835 when she died in Newport, gave seven manuscript letters from Phillis, dating from 1772 to 1779, to the wife of the Reverend William H. Beecher, when he was preaching in Brookfield, Massachusetts. Mrs. Beecher gave copies of these Wheatley letters to the Reverend Edward A. Hale, a member of the Massachusetts Historical Society, which society published the letters in 1864. Charles Deane, another member of that society, reprinted the letters in 1864. In 1877, the Reverend William Beecher, now a widower, released the original manuscript letters to the society, where six of them remain. The seventh manuscript is in the Quaker Collection at Haverford College.

Always delicate and sickly, Phillis composed a fervid prayer on the "Sabbath, June 13, 1779," on the eve of her first pregnancy.

She prays for the bodily strength needed to deliver successfully a healthy child, one worthy of dedication to Christian purpose. Her prayer also intimates something of a puritanical revulsion at the awareness of her obligatory personal involvement in conjugal realities:

> Oh my Gracious Preserver!/ hithertoo thou hast brot [me] be pleased when thou bringest/ to the birth to give [me] strength/ to bring forth living & perfect a/ being who shall be greatly instrumental in promoting thy [glory]/ Tho conceived in Sin & brot forth/ in iniquity yet thy infinite wisdom/ can bring a clean thing out of an/ unclean. . . .

Presumably, she delivered her first child before she prepared proposals for a second volume of her writings, which she published in the *Boston Evening Post and General Advertiser* for six weeks commencing October 30, 1779, and concluding on December 18. This volume was to be "Dedicated to the Right Honourable Benjamin Franklin Esq:/ One of the Ambassadors of the United States, at/ the court of France." Headed with her married name, "PHILLIS PETERS," the proposals list the titles of thirty-three poems and thirteen letters that were scheduled to be sold to subscribers for "*Twelve Pounds*, neatly Bound & Lettered, and *Nine Pounds* sew'd in blue paper. . . ." Such extraordinarily high sale prices for a book of poems and letters probably reflected something of John Peters's fanciful estimation of the worth of his wife's work; at the same time, prices for all goods in Boston were greatly magnified throughout the late 1770's. The inflation rate jumped 200 percent from 1775 to 1778. A Continental dollar was then worth no more than 2 2/3 of an English halfpence. Phillis's first biographer tells stories of the high prices in wartime Boston: a cow cost fifty dollars and a goose just as much. A loaf of bread cost two shillings; potatoes cost between nine and ten shillings a bushel; blacksmiths charged £6 10s. for shoeing a horse all around; tailors got £15 for making a suit for a man. Just over a year earlier, in her letter of July 15, 1778, to Mary Wooster in New Haven, Phillis had asked that widow to return any unsold copies of her 1773 volume of *Poems*, along with "the money for those that are sold—I can easily dispose of them here for 12/Lm?. . . ," (i.e., twelve shillings, legal money). Her assertion that she could easily sell her volume for twelve shillings a copy, when the original price, just five years earlier, was two shillings and sixpence is indicative of the worsening inflation picture in the colonies. Successive issues of Boston newspapers printed angry accounts of outraged citizens meeting to try and fix the frustratingly high prices being exacted even for "the necessaries of life."

Phillis could not now rely, in 1779 as in 1773, on the prestige of eighteen of "the most respectable Characters in *Boston*" to sign an attestation of her authorship. Indeed, by 1779, many of those who had signed the attestation for the 1773 volume of *Poems*—Andrew Oliver, James Pitts, Thomas Hubbard, the Reverends Andrew Eliot and John Moorhead, and her ex-master—were dead. Many of her old Tory friends either had fled Boston with the British troops in 1776 or were barely surviving in and around Boston at legally prescribed disadvantage. No doubt Phillis hoped that her dedication of her projected 1779 book to Benjamin Franklin would attract subscribers, but such was not to be the case. The costs of everyday survival at 1779's inflated rates being so extravagantly expensive, there would be little or no money in circulation for subscribing to a volume of poems costing twelve pounds. In any event, despite the six-week run of her proposals in 1779, the projected second volume of Phillis Wheatley's works was rejected by Bostonians, who were otherwise preoccupied. The book was never published completely, although five of the poems and perhaps three of the letters have been printed by various hands over the years. The other letters and poems whose titles are listed in the 1779 proposals may be lost.

At some time during her marriage, Phillis is reported as having left Boston with her child and husband for an obscure village, Wilmington, Massachusetts, just north of the town, where, again presumably, she gave birth to two more children. It is not known exactly when or why they moved to Wilmington. There is a gap in the Wheatley chronology of datings between 1780, when John Peters was listed as having paid taxes on his Queen Street residence, and 1784, when Phillis's eulogy on the death of the Reverend Samuel Cooper was printed. It was probably during these years that Phillis and her family moved to Wilmington. Phillis's biographer speculates that grim life in an inland village was simply too demanding for one of her previous life-style. She "suffered much from privation—from absolute want—and from painful exertions to which she was unaccustomed, and for which her frail constitution unfitted her." Her already fragile health began to deteriorate. Not surprisingly, Phillis returned to Boston with her three children to live for six weeks under the care of Mrs. Elizabeth Wallcutt (1721–1811), a niece of her mistress. At one time Mrs. Wallcutt and her daughter, Lucy, conducted a day school for "young Misses" on Purchase Street, where, one writer says, Phillis helped to earn her keep by assisting in the teaching of the charges. After six weeks, John Peters is said to have taken Phillis and their children from the Wallcutt home to an apartment he had prepared for them "in an obscure part of the metropolis."

Phillis's biographer, a proud Wheatley descendant, may have been more concerned with the good name of the Wheatleys than she was with the facts of the matter when she claimed that she never knew of Phillis's being referred to, after her marriage, as anything but Phillis Wheatley. Actually, every known piece of writing published by Phillis after her marriage uses her married name, as does a private letter of May, 1779, to Obour Tanner. Also, contrary to the low opinion of John Peters held by this biographer and other commentators, there is extant a 1784 petition written and signed by John Peters, in which he requests the officially necessary approbation from the Boston Selectmen for a license with which he could retail spirits from his North End, Prince Street shop near the Boston side of the Charlestown ferry. Neither the act of submitting such a petition, in a town in which not all merchants always did so, nor the stated intent of the document is that of an improvident man, especially when it is known that by 1784 the annual rent for a typical small Boston store was almost £30. Furthermore, the petition includes an official testimony on behalf of John Peters's character and financial ability and status:

> . . . your Petitioner has for the purpose of/ supporting himself & Family, opened a Shop near to Charlestown/ Ferry, lately occupied by Mr. Daladie, a Frenchman, who/ was indulged with a License from your Honors the last Year/ and as his Trade lays chiefly with the people from the/ Country, who choose to purchase their Articles at one place/ and Rum & other Liquors being required in smaller quantities/ than can be sold without a License to Retail
>
> Your Pet! [i.e., petitioner] humbly prays your/ Honors would grant him a License to Retail Spirits/ &c at his said Shop and thereby be upon a footing/ with other Shopkeepers in his way of Trade. And as in Duty Bound with pray? [i.e., prayers]
>
> John Peters (signed)

Boston   July 28, 1784.

On the third of this four-page petition is written a testimony:

The Selectmen of Boston hereby Certify that the/ within named
Petitioner as a Person of Sober life/ & Conversation suitably qualified & provided for the/ Exercise of the Employment of a Retailer
of Spiri-/ tous Liquors.

By order of the Selectmen
William Cooper, Town Clerk (signed)

On the last page are two notations of "approved" and one *"to lay*
Disallowed."

However, a later critic pointed out that, after a variety of
failures, Peters "finally imposed upon the credulous by pretend-
ing to be a physician," and that, falling on harder times after
Phillis's death, he was reduced to selling Phillis's gift books.
Inscribed on a flyleaf of one such book, the 1770 Foulis Glasgow
folio edition of John Milton's *Paradise Lost* is "Mr. Brook Watson
to Phillis Wheatley/ London July-1773." On another flyleaf is
written "This book was given by Brook Watson,/ former Lord
Mayor of London, to Phillis/ Wheatley—& after her death was
sold in/ payment of her husband's debts./ It is now presented to
the Library/ of Harvard University at Cambridge,/ by Dudley L.
Pickman of Salem./ March, 1824." (Sir Brook Watson [1735–
1807] was not Lord Mayor of London when Phillis visited that
city in the summer of 1773. A merchant and frequent visitor to
America and Halifax, he left the country in 1775, becoming, later,
a commissary general which position caused him to be passed
over for the Lord Mayorship in 1793, 1794, and 1795; he became
Lord Mayor of London in 1796.) This copy of *Paradise Lost* is
today housed in the Houghton Library of Harvard College.

In the Schomburg Center for Afro-American Research are two
other Wheatley giftbooks: volumes 2 and 3 of William Shenstone's
3-volume *Works in Verse and Prose*, 3rd ed. (London, 1773).
Bearing the book plate of William Gayton Pickman, the volumes
are subscribed "Mary Eveleigh to/ Phillis Wheatley Sepr 24/
1774," and also inscribed "Elizabeth Pickman." The other book is
volume 1 of the Tobias Smollett 4-volume translation of *Don
Quixote* (London, 1773), inscribed "To Phillis Wheatley" by "the
Earl of Dartmouth/ London, July 1773."

Phillis's complete set of Alexander Pope's *Works*, in thirteen volumes, the gift of Lord Dartmouth, are kept at the University of North Carolina at Charlotte. The whereabouts of other books owned by Phillis—John Gay's *Fables*; Samuel Butler's *Hudibras*; and her Bible, in which was supposedly found a manuscript prayer she wrote while she was pregnant in 1779—are unknown. Phillis's biographer does have corroboration for her account of Phillis's final days in sickness and wretched poverty, with two of her children dead, and the third "sick unto death," in a filthy apartment, "in a state of abject misery, surrounded by all the emblems of squalid poverty!" Touring revolutionary America in a search for techniques and legal, political, social, commercial, and military models he hoped he might use in revolutionarily severing his own native colony of Venezuela from its motherland of Spain, the financially prepared mulatto leader, Francisco de Miranda, entered into his diary for September 16, 1784, a brief sketch of Phillis's life that ended with

> Casose al fin un negro ladino llamado *Petters* con quien tuvo varios hijos, y en el dia está muriendose en la indigencia" (She finally married a clever Negro named Peters, by whom she had several children, and is today dying in indigence).

Others have subsequently also reported on Phillis's presumed poverty and difficult marriage. She died in utter destitution in her Court Street home, wrote an historian of colonial Boston. Wrote Henri Grégroire

> La sensible Phillis, qui avoit été gâte, élevée . . . en enfant n'entendoit rien â gouverner un ménage, et son mari vouloit qu'elle s'en occupât; il commença par des reproches auxquels succédèrent de mauvais traitements dont la continuité affligea tellement son épouse, qu'elle périt de chagrin. (The sensitive Phillis, who had been reared almost as a spoiled child, had little or no sense or need of how to manage a household, and her husband wanted her to do just that; he made his wishes known at first by reproaches and followed these with downright bad treatment, the continuation of which so afflicted his wife that she grieved herself to death).

Through all of her noted vexations, Phillis is said never to have complained.

While Phillis was far too self-respecting and intelligent and well-mannered to write of her personal situation publicly, there may have been other reasons that she did not complain of her dire need. It may be that reports of her abject misery and destitute death are mistaken exaggerations. Most of the writers who comment on Phillis's last years and death base their remarks on the biography of Phillis written by Margarette Matilda Odell in 1834, fifty years after the poet's death. But continuing scholarship has corrected several assertions in this biography. A proud, collateral descendant of Phillis's mistress, Mrs. Odell wrote that she had "never heard Phillis named, or alluded to, by any other appellation than that of 'Phillis Wheatley'—a name she sustained with dignity and honor. . . ." However, after Phillis's marriage to John Peters in April of 1778, she published proposals which solicited Boston subscribers to a proposed second volume of her writings, and she published three poems—all before she would die in 1784. In each of these four publications, Phillis used her married name. The proposals were printed in the *Boston Evening Post and General Advertiser* for October 30, November 6, and 27, and December 4, 11, and 18 of 1779. Each printing displayed her married name in capital letters, "PHILLIS PETERS." Printed in January of 1784, Phillis's eulogy on the death of the Reverend Samuel Cooper is billed as the work of PHILLIS PETERS. Another poem published in the same year, "Liberty and Peace" is advertised as "A Poem/ By Phillis Peters." A third poem of that year, "To Mr. and Mrs. —— On the Death of Their Infant Son by Phillis Wheatley" includes the publisher's note that this poem "was selected from a manuscript volume of Poems, written by PHILLIS PETERS, formerly PHILLIS WHEATLEY. . . ."

Mrs. Odell also complains that, when Phillis died, "Peters did not see fit to acquaint" Wheatley relatives "of the event, or to notify them of her interment." But there was notice of Phillis's funeral in the *Massachusetts Independent Chronicle and Universal Advertiser* for December 8, 1784. The obituary details, incidentally, do not seem to be those describing someone who died in destitution:

> Last Lord's Day, died Mrs. Phillis Peters formerly Phillis Wheatly aged 31, known to the literary world by her celebrated miscellaneous Poems. Her funeral is to be this afternoon, at 4 o'clock, from the house lately improved by Mr. Todd, nearly opposite Dr. Bulfinch's at West-Boston, where her friends and acquaintances are desired to attend.

One source believes that the house in which her funeral was held stood on or near the site of the Revere House in Bowdoin Square, formerly a portion of Cambridge Street, known also as the westerly end of Court Street. Located as it was, "nearly opposite Dr. [Thomas] Bulfinch's at West Boston," this newly renovated home was situated in one of the most prestigious of 18th-century Boston neighborhoods.

Nor does any of the three poems she published in 1784, the last year of her life, indicate a noticeably deprived poet. Printed as a six-page pamphlet in January of 1784, her elegy to the memory of the Reverend Samuel Cooper displays her obvious grief over the reality of the man's death, her personal loss of one she regarded as a longtime friend and mentor, but there is no word of her reportedly pathetic living conditions. Phillis may have made a subtle appeal for sales of her elegy as she included in the headnote to the piece: "To the CHURCH and CONGRE-GATION/ assembling in Brattle-Street, the following/ ELEGY,/ Sacred to the MEMORY of their late/ Reverend and Worthy PASTOR, Dr./ SAMuel cooper is, with/ the greatest Sympathy, most respectfully/ inscribed by their Obedient,/ Humble Servant,/ PHILLIS PETERS." When she wrote, in the elegy,

> . . . What deep-felt sorrow in each *Kindred* breast
> With keen sensation rends the heart distress'd!
> *Fraternal* love sustains a tenderer part,
> And mourns a BROTHER with a BROTHER's heart. . . .

she may well have been poetically remembering or thanking Samuel Cooper's brother, William, the town clerk who, just four months earlier, had signed John Peters's petition for a license to retail liquors from his Prince Street store. Her personalized sorrow is open at the loss of a man who, filling in the temporarily empty Old South Pulpit, had baptized her into that church, who had counselled since, and who, a poetaster himself, had been a friend to her writing efforts. In another personal vein, she suggests that the writing of this poem was the fulfillment of a long-standing request from Cooper:

> . . . The hapless Muse, her loss in COOPER mourns,
> And as she sits, she writes, and weeps, by turns;
> A Friend sincere, whose mild indulgent grace
> Encourag'd oft, and oft approv'd her lays. . . .
>
>   . . .
>
> —at Heaven's high call he flies;
> His task well finish'd, to his native skies.

Yet to his fate reluctant we resign,
Tho' ours to copy conduct such as thine:
Such was the wish, th'observant Muse survey'd
Thy latest breath, and this advice convey'd.

A four-page pamphlet, "Liberty and Peace,/ A Poem./ By Phillis Peters," rejoices in celebrating the official advent of peace. She may have been among the Boston spectators at the February, 1784, ceremony that hailed the signing of the Treaty of Peace with the ringing of bells and firing of cannons, and parading of town officials and dignitaries from the State House to the Old South for sermons and songs and, later after a 13-gun salute, to a massive dinner at Fanueil Hall. Again, the poem says nothing of her supposedly wretched domestic life. Instead she points with unabashed patriotism to a victorious America's new and acknowledged status as a major world power as though it were the unfolding of a preordained inevitability. Indeed, as though to underscore her having prophesied American victory, she quotes her own description of a personified freedom, italicized in the following lines, which she first wrote in her 1775 poem of praise for General George Washington:

Lo! Freedom comes. Th'prescient Muse foretold,
    All eyes th'accomplish'd Prophecy behold:
Her port describ'd, *"She moves divinely fair,*
Olive and Laurel bind her golden Hair."
She, the bright Progeny of Heaven, descends,
And every Grace her sovereign Step attends;
For now kind Heaven, indulgent to our Prayer,
In smiling *Peace* resolves the Din of *War.* . . .

In the September, 1784, issue of *The Boston Magazine* appeared the poem, "To Mr. and Mrs. *******, On the Death of Their Son." It is the last known published piece by Phillis, who died three months later. It is a typical Wheatley elegy such as she had been writing for almost fifteen years. (Indeed, it reads very much like a slightly revised version of "A Funeral Poem on the Death of C.E. an Infant of Twelve Months," that was published in her 1773 volume.) An editorial of the *Boston Magazine* pointed out,

The Poem, in page 488, of/ this Number, was selected/ from a manuscript volume of Poems,/ written by PHILLIS PETERS, formerly/ PHILLIS WHEATLEY—and is inserted/ as a Specimen of her Work; should this gain the Approbation of the Pub-/ lick and sufficient encouragement be/ given, a Volume will be shortly Pub-/ lished, by the Printers hereof, who/ receive subscriptions for said Work."

This would represent the thirteenth time she had printed solicitations for Boston subscribers for two of her volumes of writings. As in 1772 and 1773, so in 1779 and finally in 1784, her proposals were rejected. The projected second volume, of poems and letters, was never published completely.

Three months later it was finally over. On a cold Sunday, December 5, 1784, Phillis Wheatley Peters and the last of her three infant children died. Her biographer wrote "A Grandniece of Phillis's benefactress, passing up Court-Street, met the funeral of an adult and a child; a bystander informed her they were bearing Phillis Wheatley to that silent mansion. . . ." With no mention of the child's death, several area newspapers carried the obituary. The December issue of *The Boston Magazine* printed her obituary on page 630, "Mrs. Phillis Peters (formerly/ Phillis Wheatly). Known to the litera/ ry world by her celebrated miscella/ neous Poems. 31 (age)." On page 488 appeared the last published poem by Phillis, "To Mr. and Mrs. *******/ on the Death of their/ Infant," and on pages 619–620, an anonymous "Horatio" of "State Street" (formerly known as King Street, where Phillis had lived earlier) published a fifty-four line tribute, "Elegy on the Death of a Late/ Celebrated Poetess," which concludes:

> . . . Tho' now the business of her life/ is o'er,
> Tho' now she breathes and tunes her/ lyre no more;
> Tho' now the body mixes with the/ clay;
> The soul wings upward to immortal/ day;
> Free'd from a world of wo, and scene/ of cares,
> A lyre of gold she tunes, a crown of/ glory wears.
>   Seated with angels in that blissful/ place,
> Where she now joins in her Creator's/ praise,
> Where harmony with louder notes is/ swell'd,
> Where her soft numbers only are/ excell'd.

It is not known where, exactly, Phillis was buried. Throughout most of her American lifetime, Boston's blacks, of all classes, were interred in any of the five large town cemeteries, but, toward the end of the 18th century and on into the 19th, it became increasingly common for them to be buried along the northeastern edge of Copp's Hill in the North End, the adjacent area beginning to take on the conditions of a black ghetto. Prince Hall was buried there in 1807, and Phillis may have also been laid to rest there. But, as her funeral was reportedly viewed by "a grandniece of Phillis's benefactress" who was "passing up Court-Street" (Queen Street, in Phillis's day), and as it was a cold December, she was probably carried to the Old Granary Burial Grounds, on Tremont Street, for it was only a few blocks from Court Street (Queen Street) rather than to Copp's Hill, more than a dozen blocks away.

When, earlier, Phillis had left Boston with her husband and child for Wilmington, Massachusetts, she had left all of her manuscripts with Mrs. Elizabeth Wallcutt and her daughter, Lucy, in Boston, for safekeeping. Two months after Phillis's death, Peters placed a curt notice in the *Independent Chronicle and Universal Advertiser* for February 10, 1785:

> The person who borrowed a volume of manuscript poems & & of Phillis Peters, formerly Phillis Wheatley, deceased, would very much oblige her husband, John Peters, by returning it immediately, as the whole of her works are intended to be published.

Peters may have chosen to delay this request out of respect for Phillis's death, but, more probably, he may have been already incarcerated in debtor's jail—even, perhaps, at the time of Phillis's death—and released in early February, 1785. His long-standing resentment and pointed indifference to personal contact with the well-connected relatives of Phillis's former mistress are documented in the public newspaper manner he used to reclaim his deceased wife's private papers. No such volume of Phillis's complete works was ever published. At his importunity, Peters was given all of Phillis's manuscripts, and he said to have gone to the South some years later. It is not known what happened to all of the manuscripts. Something of a restless, brash black man, Peters would have to have left Boston some time after 1800. Unlisted in a 1789 Boston Directory, he was included in the 1790 first Federal census; a 1796 head count listed him as a laborer living at 224 Short Street in Boston's South End. Living with one other unidentified person, he was at his own modest, one-story house, valued at $200.00, on Prince Street in the North End; in this same year, official returns of that year's election race of "Persons voted as Senators for the County of Suffolk . . ." notes a John Peters receiving two votes. Listed, again as a laborer, in 1800, Peters was then living in Belknap's Lane in the West End. Thereafter his name disappears from Boston documentations.

However, as late as 1858, a writer declared that the Wheatley manuscripts were still extant, "owned by an accomplished citizen of Philadelphia, whose mother was one of the patrons of the author." The "accomplished citizen" was Dr. James Rush (1786–1869), son of the more distinguished Dr. Benjamin Rush (1746–1813) of Philadelphia; the mother who "was one of the patrons of the author" was Mrs. Julia Stockton Rush (1759–1848), wife of Benjamin.

Over the years several Wheatley manuscripts have surfaced from Philadelphia respositories. The Historical Society of Pennsylvania, in Philadelphia, houses two Wheatley manuscripts, one of a poem, "To the King's most Excellent Majesty on his repealing the american/ Stamp act," (a variant of the poem with a similar title published in the 1773 volume), and a letter from Wheatley to the Reverend Samuel Hopkins, dated "Boston Feb 9th 1774." The manuscripts of six early Wheatley poems are in the Library Company of Philadelphia (two in their Du Simitière papers, and four in their Rush collection of papers). All of the manuscript poems from both the Historical Society of Pennsylvania and the Library Company of Philadelphia are from Phillis's earliest pieces, 28 titles of which were listed in proposals she printed in Boston in 1772. None of these manuscript poems is from the 1779 proposals which listed the titles of 33 poems and 13 letters. Although all six poems are from two different groupings in the Library Company, they are all said to have been collected by Pierre Eugène Du Simitière (c. 1736–1784) and to have been the property of the Company since 1785. That would be the year that the Library Company purchased the 12-volume collection of the Swiss-born, naturalized American citizen Du Simitière, artist, draftsman, and passionate antiquarian of Americana. Always seeking out discarded art work, even in garrets of homes, the peripatetic collector may have first heard of or seen Phillis Wheatley when he was in Boston in 1767–1768, when he may have made a pencilled portrait that was offered for sale in 1949 to Mrs. Dorothy Porter, Curator Emerita of the Moorland-Spingarn Collection at Howard University.

The four early Wheatley manuscripts of "America," "Atheism," "On Atheism," and "To the Right Honorable Commodore Hood on His Pardoning a Deserter," grouped among the Rush papers at the Library Company of Philadelphia, may have been originally collected by Du Simitière and sold to the Rush family. On the other hand, these four manuscript poems may represent all that remains of what may have been many other Wheatley papers, which found their way into the Rush papers in quite another way. It is known that, since Phillis's death in 1784, John Peters had been in possession of "the whole of her works." When he left Boston for the South sometime after 1800, he may have taken Phillis's manuscripts with him and, knowing of Dr. Benjamin Rush's marked fondness for things African or Afro-American, he may have given, or more probably sold, the papers to the Rush family.

In 1931, T.T. Fletcher noted in the June 30 issue of the *Pittsburgh Courier* that, preparing a biography of Phillis and knowing that she had corresponded with Dr. Benjamin Rush of Philadelphia, he visited the Library Company of that city, where he found the manuscripts for the poems, "America," "Atheism," and "To the Right Honorable Commodore Hood on His Pardoning a Deserter." These poems, Fletcher wrote, "were given to that institution in 1869, by the will of Dr. James Rush, a son of Dr. Benjamin Rush." When Dr. James Rush died in 1869, he left his estate, including his distinguished father's enormous collection of books and all kinds of manuscripts, "amounting perhaps to 10,000 pieces," to be deposited in a building he erected as a memorial to his wealthy wife, Phoebe Ridgway. This building became the Ridgway branch of the Library Company. The Rush collection was later transferred to the main building of the Library Company, after some of the manuscripts descended to Benjamin Rush's granddaughter, Julia Biddle, which family in 1943 would sell the papers at several New York City auction sales.

Fletcher received permission to duplicate the manuscripts he found, but he did not publish them. In 1970, Robert Kuncio, a staff member, found and published these same three manuscripts and the manuscripts for several other poems, again in the Library Company of Philadelphia. In 1977, still another early manuscript poem by Wheatley, "Deism," was found by Phil Lapsansky, Chief of the Reference Division of the Library Company of Philadelphia. Other Wheatley manuscripts may yet turn up from these Philadelphia repositories or from archives or collections elsewhere. Biographically very important, a July 15, 1778, Wheatley manuscript letter and poem were released from a private collection as late as 1978. Still missing are five of the twenty-eight titles from her 1772 proposal list, and twenty-eight titles from the thirty-three titles listed in her 1779 proposals. Also missing are uncounted, because unknown, "performances" Phillis wrote at the requests of the likes of "Mrs Dickerson, Miss Clymer, Mrs. Bull with some other Ladys," mentioned in a letter by Deborah Cushing in 1774 to her husband in Philadelphia. Of the bulk of letters she received from American and English correspondents from 1766 to 1779, the manuscripts of only two remain—one from Thomas Wallcutt, written as a teenager to Phillis from Montreal, Canada, on November 17, 1774, and a copy of another written sometime in 1775 from the millionaire Christian philanthropist of London, John Thornton.

Phillis Wheatley is said to have died in an obscurity of sorts, but, as was true with her former mistress ten years earlier in 1774, her own Christian humility and abnegation may have prompted her also to discourage any great notice of her death, or engraved headstone, holding, perhaps, with the Quakers that the final resting place of a true believer should be known only to God. Of course, her relatively unnoticed death and her unknown resting place might have been attributable to the reported poverty of her last days. Whatever the reason her grave is unmarked, she made her own mark in other ways, on both her contemporaries and on successive generations of students, scholars, and general readers. A Jane Dunlap was moved enough by the popularity of Phillis's elegy on the death of the Reverend George Whitefield to write and print her own tribute to the man in her slim volume of verses in 1771:

> . . . Shall his due praises be so loudly sung
> By a young Afric damsels virgin tongue?
> And I be silent! and no mention make
> Of his blest name, who did so often speak. . . .

As frontispiece, a woodcut likeness of Phillis's engraved portrait in her 1773 volume was featured on *Isaac Bickerstaff's Boston ALMANACK for the Year of our Redemption 1782*. Printed first in the May 20, 1784, issue of the *Boston Independent Chronicle and Universal Advertiser*, and repeated in the November issue of *Gentleman and Lady's Town and Country Magazine*, Heman Harris's piece, "The Choice," cited flatteringly ". . . the Phillis of our age. . . ." By a pseudonymous "Horatio" of State Street (formerly Phillis's King Street), she was eulogized in his "Elegy on the Death of a Late/ Celebrated Poetess" in the December, 1784, *Boston Magazine*, which also printed her obituary. Beginning in 1786, Phillis's London-published volume of *Poems* was reprinted in America at least four more times by 1793. In London, a "second edition, corrected," was reprinted in 1787. Charles Crawford's *Observations Upon Negro Slavery* (Philadelphia, 1784) was one of the initiators of the tradition, which continues to this day, of books which cite Phillis.

Phillis has been long revered among black Americans. Under the dateline of "June 30, Chicago," the *Pittsburgh Courier* for 2 July 1930 reported that "The Industrial Branch of the Phillis Wheatley Association, 5128 S. Michigan, Chicago, resolved to request all Phillis Wheatley organizations or institutions at present in existence to set aside the third Sunday in each February as Phillis Wheatley Memorial Day." In the same year, *Phillis Wheatley*, A pamphlet for the National Phillis Wheatley Foundation, at 2170 East 47th Street, Cleveland, Ohio, Jane E. Hunter, President, urged May 7 as "Phillis Wheatley Day," May 7 being one of the dates in 1773 when Phillis published "Farewell to America." *Ten Years a Neighbor/ Phyllis* [sic] *Wheatley Settlement House* 1924–1934 (n.p., n.d./ 1934), unpaginated, is self-explanatory. Calling Phillis "the Mother of Black Literature in North America," a modern black woman writer has noted that, historically throughout black America, more YMCAs, schools, dormitories and libraries have been named for Phillis Wheatley than for any other black woman. In commemoration of the 1773 publication of her volume of *Poems on Various Subjects, Religious and Moral*, a Bicentennial Phillis Wheatley Poetry Festival was hosted in 1973 at Jackson State College, Jackson, Mississippi, featuring the tributary work of almost two dozen black American women poets and artists. Especially for this festival, a new color portrait of Phillis was offered, and the distinguished black sculptor, Señora Elizabeth Catlett Mora, of the National University of Mexico, presented a handsome bronze bust of Phillis.

Phillis Wheatley Peters may have died in a kind of obscurity, but she was by no means obscure.

ILLUSTRATIONS

Map of Phillis Wheatley's Boston—1796, shortly after her death. (A) Beech Street wharf, where Phillis and "about 70 to Eighty" other slaves landed in July, 1761. (B) John Wheatley's mansion, corner of King Street and Mackerel Lane (today's State and Kilby Streets), where Phillis lived from 1761 to about 1775; (C) The Old South Congregational Church, on Marlborough Street (today's Washington Street) between Milk Street and Spring Lane, which Phillis joined on August 18, 1771. (D) Queen Street (today's Court Street) shop (and residence) of John and Phillis (Wheatley) Peters, after their April, 1778 marriage. (E) Prince Street retail shop of John Peters in the summer of 1784. (F) Old Granary Burial Grounds, on the corner of today's Tremont and Park Streets, where Phillis was probably buried on December 8, 1784, in an unmarked grave.

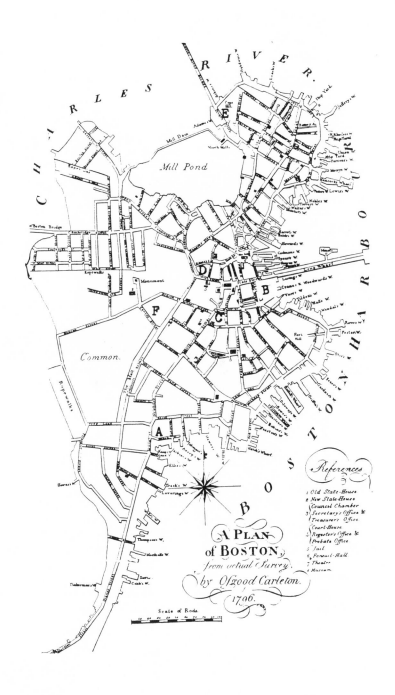

A PLAN
of BOSTON
from actual Survey
by Osgood Carleton.
1796.

Scale of Rods.

References

1 Old State-House
2 New State-House
  Council Chamber
3 Secretary's Office &
  Treasurer's Office
  Court-House
4 Register's Office &
  Probate Office
5 Jail
6 Fanueil-Hall
7 Theatre
8 Museum

A

A. The internationally popular English revivalist, the Reverend George Whitefield (1714–1770) was a frequent visitor to the American colonies, especially Boston. Phillis Wheatley's widely reprinted elegy on his death, published in America and London, established her international reputation.

B

J. Huntingdon

B. Selina Hastings, the Countess of Huntingdon (1702–1791), zealous supporter of dissident English Methodism, correspondent with
Phillis Wheatley, allowed the poet's volume of *Poems* to be
dedicated to her Ladyship. She also insisted that Phillis's portrait be
engraved as a frontispiece for the celebrated 1773 volume, thereby
making Phillis's book the first published volume by an American
female to include her own portrait as frontispiece.

THE OLD SOUTH.

A mid-19th century depiction of Boston's famous Old South Congregational Meeting House, with an insert of the interior. Phillis Wheatley became a member of this church on August 18, 1771, when, by the reckoning of her mistress, she was "of age," about eighteen years old. Originally built in 1669 and rebuilt in 1729, the structure stands today as an Historical Memorial site on Washington Street between Milk Street and Spring Lane. Since 1874, the congregation has worshipped at the New Old South in Copley Square.

The Life and Humble Confession of Richardson, the Informer

A depiction of the February 23, 1770, murder of eleven-year-old Christopher Snider (on the ground, right) by the despised Tory, Ebenezer Richardson, who fires from the second story window of his home, which is under siege by swarming mobs of Patriot Bostonians angry at both Richardson and his fellow Tory neighbor and importer, Theophilus Lillie, for refusing to sign a Bostonian non-importation ban. See the poem, "On the death of Mr Snider Murder'd by Richardson" in "Phillis Wheatley's Early Poems," below. The original of this depiction is at the Historical Society of Pennsylvania.

A

Like the text of her book of poems, Phillis's likeness has been changed over the years into variant renditions. Described as "A pen drawing from a rare print of Phillis Wheatley,/ By W.E. Braxton," (A) appeared in *Ebony and Topaz* (New York, 1927), p. 78. This is a most unusual depiction of Phillis, whose puritanical mistress insisted that Phillis "should be dress'd plain." (B) is a freely drawn version of the original engraving in Wheatley's volume, and was printed in E. and G. Duyckinck's *Cyclopedia of American Literature,* 2 volumes (New York, 1856), I, 367. Note changes from the original, especially the absence of the original chair and book, and the transformation of the original pewter inkstand into a glass ink bottle. (C) is an 1859 rendition found in Benson J. Lossing's *Eminent Americans.* Note that the original oval table has now become oblong and that Phillis's woolly hair is now waved; Phillis's last name is also misspelled. (D) is a copy of the newly prepared lithographic likeness of Phillis which pref-

B

Phillis Wheatley

aced the editions reprinted in Boston in 1834,
1835, and 1838. A silhouette of an unlikely,
bulky Phillis Wheatley is located at the American Antiquarian Society. Sculpted by Señora
Elizabeth Catlett Mora especially for the bicentennial commemoration of the publication
of Wheatley's *Poems on Various Subjects,
Religious and Moral* (London, 1773), held at
Jackson State College in Jackson, Mississippi
from November 4–7, 1973, a handsome, mod-
ernistic bronze bust of Phillis is housed at that
college.

C

Phillis Wheatley

D

Phillis Wheatley.

Negro Servant to Mr John Wheatley
of Boston

Pendleton's Litho. Boston

A

To the PUBLICK.

AS it has been repeatedly fuggefted to the Publifher, by Perfons, who have feen the Manufcript, that Numbers would be ready to fufpect they were not really the Writings of PHILLIS, he has procured the following Atteftation, from the moft refpectable Characters in *Bofton*, that none might have the leaft Ground for difputing their *original*.

WE whofe Names are under-written, do affure the World, that the POEMS fpecified in the following Page, * were (as we verily believe) written by PHILLIS, a young Negro Girl, who was but a few Years fince, brought an uncultivated Barbarian from *Africa*, and has ever fince been, and now is, under the Difadvantage of ferving as a Slave in a Family in this Town. She has been examined by fome of the beft Judges, and is thought qualified to write them.

His Excellency THOMAS HUTCHINSON, *Governor,*

The Hon. ANDREW OLIVER, *Lieutenant-Governor.*

The Hon. Thomas Hubbard,	*The Rev.* Charles Chauncey, D. D.
The Hon. John Erving,	*The Rev.* Mather Byles, D. D.
The Hon. James Pitts,	*The Rev* Ed. Pemberton, D.D.
The Hon. Harrifon Gray,	*The Rev.* Andrew Elliot, D.D.
The Hon. James Bowdoin,	*The Rev.* Samuel Cooper, D.D.
John Hancock, *Efq;*	*The Rev. Mr.* Samuel Mather,
Jofeph Green, *Efq;*	*The Rev. Mr.* John Moorhead,
Richard Carey, *Efq;*	*Mr.* John Wheatley, *her Mafter.*

N. B. The original Atteftation, figned by the above Gentlemen, may be feen by applying to *Archibald Bell*, Bookfeller, No. 8, *Aldgate-Street.*

---

* The Words " *following Page,* " allude to the Contents of the Manufcript Copy, which are wrote at the Back of the above Atteftation.

A and B are facsimiles of variant attestation pages from two of the four editions of Wheatley's book of poems published in the fall of 1773 in London. The first printing carried no dedication, no preface, no biographical sketch of Phillis, and no "To the PUBLICK" page (i.e., the attestation page), all of this information having already been used by Archibald Bell,

To the PUBLICK.

AS it has been repeatedly suggested to the Publisher, by Persons, who have seen the Manuscript, that Numbers would be ready to suspect they were not really the Writings of PHILLIS, he has procured the following Attestation, from the most respectable Characters in Boston, that none might have the least Ground for disputing their Original.

WE whose Names are under-written, do assure the World, that the Poems specified in the following Page, * were (as we verily believe) written by PHILLIS, a young Negro Girl, who was but a few Years since, brought an uncultivated Barbarian from Africa, and has ever since been, and now is, under the Disadvantage of serving as a Slave in a Family in this Town. She has been examined by some of the best Judges, and is thought qualified to write them.

His Excellency THOMAS HUTCHINSON, *Governor*,

The Hon. ANDREW OLIVER, *Lieutenant-Governor.*

The Hon. Thomas Hubbard,	*The Rev.* Charles Chauncy, D.D.
The Hon. John Erving,	*The Rev.* Mather Byles, D. D.
The Hon. James Pitts,	*The Rev.* Ed. Pemberton, D.D.
The Hon. Harrison Gray,	*The Rev.* Andrew Elliot, D.D.
The Hon. James Bowdoin,	*The Rev.* Samuel Cooper, D.D.
John Hancock, *Esq;*	*The Rev. Mr.* Samuel Mather,
Joseph Green, *Esq;*	*The Rev. Mr.* John Moorhead,
Richard Carey, *Esq;*	*Mr.* John Wheatley, *her Master.*

N. B. The original Attestation, signed by the above Gentlemen, may be seen by applying to *Archibald Bell*, Bookseller, No. 8, *Aldgate-Street.*

---

* The Words "*following Page,*" allude to the Contents of the Manuscript Copy, which are wrote at the Back of the above Attestation.

the London bookseller-printer in London newspapers promoting sales of the book for London readers. A second, 1773, London printing of the book did include these four prefatory pieces, but misspelled the last names of Governor Hutchinson (1) and Reverend Charles Chauncy (2) and the first name of the Reverend John Moorhead (3). A third, 1773, London printing also included these prefatory pieces and spelled

Hutchinson's, Chauncy's, and Moorhead's names correctly (B). ("*The Rev* Ed. Pemberton" should be "*The Rev. Eb[enezer] Pemberton*," and "*The Rev.* Andrew Elliot" should be "*The Rev.* Andrew Eliot.") The Providence, Rhode Island, Public library has another 1773 edition of Wheatley's *Poems*, whose flyleaf reads anonymously and in pencil, "The type in this edit. is/ entirely reset & press errors/ corrected— as/ p. 24—catchword 'Not' at foot of p. 9 has comma/ after it not in 1st ed./ p. 37. 8th line from top word/ "Goliath" is in italics/ in 1st ed. it is in roman/ . . . ." There were thus at least four printings or editions of *Poems* run in the fall of 1773 in London, in lots of 300 copies a printing. A fifth lot of these books arrived in Boston from London by the end of January, 1774. On May 6, 1774, Phillis wrote to her black friend, Obour Tanner, in Newport, "I have rec'd by some of the last ships/ 300 more of my Poems." In less than a year from its fall, 1773, first printing in London, some 1800 copies of *Poems on Various Subjects, Religious and Moral* (London, 1773) had been printed.

ON PHILLIS WHEATLEY'S POETRY

ON PHILLIS WHEATLEY'S POETRY

It is mixed praise to note that Phillis Wheatley's slim volume, *Poems on Various Subjects, Religious and Moral*, has been reprinted more than two dozen times since it was first published in London in 1773. Although many of these reprintings claim to reproduce the original London edition, most of them are in fact variantly or even carelessly done. For one thing, the poems follow different orders in different editions. There is one ordering of the poems in the 1786, 1787, 1793, 1804, and 1816 editions, but other reprintings reveal other orders. The ordering of one 1773 original is explained by the fact that there is misplaced pagination. The 1834, 1835, and 1838 reprintings show still another ordering of poems. As examples, in all of the eighteenth century and in the 1804 reprintings, the poem "On Being Brought from Africa to America," is fifth in order; in the 1802, 1834, 1835, and 1838 versions, this poem is third; in the 1801 edition, the poem is placed fourth. The 1802 edition prints "Farewel to America" with the date of "Boston, May 1775," when it should have been dated, as elsewhere, "Boston, May, 1773." The 1802 edition omits line 15 from "To the University at Cambridge in New-England," while the 1834, 1835 and 1838 editions omit line 3 of "On the Death of J.C. An Infant"; line 17 is left out of "To the University of Cambridge in New-England." The 1801 reprint omits an entire poem, "To the King's Most Excellent Majesty. 1768."

One reprinting, the 1793 edition, does include with other editions, line 10 of "To the King's Most Excellent Majesty. 1768," which reads "Live with heaven's choicest, constant blessings crown'd!" A 1916 edition omits the word "constant" from this same line. In earlier reprintings, line 25 of "On Imagination" reads "The frozen deeps may break their iron bands," but, in a 1797 excerpt from the poem, and in the 1834, 1835, and 1838 editions, the line reads "The frozen deeps may burst their iron bands." Line 24 of "Niobe in Distress" reads, in the 1834, 1835, and 1838 reprintings, "Seven Daughters beauteous as the rising morn," but elsewhere the line reads "Seven daughters beauteous as the op'ning morn." Line 105 of this same piece on Niobe in the 1834, 1835, and 1838 editions reads "To punish, and to scourge the rebel mind," while, in original editions of the volume, the line reads "To punish pride, and scourge the rebel mind." Line 10 of "On the Death of A Young Lady Five Years of Age" in a 1773 text reads "No more distress'd in our dark vale below," but in the 1834, 1835, and 1838 reprints, it reads "Nor suffer distress in this dark vale below." In a version of this same poem printed by William Wells Brown in 1865, line 13 reads "But hear, in heaven's best bowers, your child so fair," whereas other editions have the line reading "But hear in heaven's blest bowers your Nancy fair." Lines 21–22 of this poem in a 1773 edition read "Perfect in bliss, she, from her heavenly home,/ Looks down, and, smiling beckons you to come." In William Wells Brown's version, these lines read "Perfect in bliss, now from her heavenly home/ She looks, and, smiling, beckons you to come." In most editions, line 36 of this poem reads "Shall join your happy babe to part no more," but Brown's version substitutes "child" for "babe." In the 1773 original edition, line 31 of this poem reads "Eye him in all, his holy name revere," but in the 1834, 1835, and 1838 reprints and in Brown, the line reads "See him in all, his holy name revere." A Boston review of the 1834 reprinted edition quotes Phillis's "On Being Brought from Africa to America," but, unlike other printings of this poem, this review somehow misprints "Gave" for the original "Taught":

> 'Twas mercy brought me from my pagan land,
> Gave my benighted soul to understand. . . .

An 1884 reviewer of this volume quotes 22 lines from "On the Death of the Rev. Dr. Sewell, 1769," but omits a word in one line and substitutes a word in another line:

> By these made happy from his early youth.
> In blooming years that grace he felt . . .
> And henceforth seek, like him, the living bread. . . .

The original lines read:

By these made happy from his early youth.
In blooming years that grace divine he felt . . .
And henceforth seek, like him, for living bread. . . .

This kind of editorial "correction" of Wheatley's text is extensive, and reached extremes in Wilson Armistead's *A Tribute For The Negro* (Manchester, England, 1848), pp. 332-348. Here Armistead reprints one complete poem from Wheatley's volume, and excerpts from eight others. Many but not all of these reprintings include words and lines that are variant from their volume originals. In his *Tribute For The Negro*, Armistead's critical and biographical Wheatley commentary is no more than an expanded version of the selfsame remarks that were published, as part of an anonymous essay, "Intelligent Negroes," in *Chambers Miscellany of Useful and Entertaining Tracts* (Edinburgh, 1845), pp. 1-12. The expanded version of these remarks, as in *Tribute*, was reprinted verbatim in S.R.B. Attoh Ahoma's *Memoirs of West African Celebrities* . . . (Liverpool, 1905), pp. 199-217, under the by-line of Wilson Armistead. "Intelligent Negroes" reprints from four of Wheatley's 1773 volume poems. Each of these four excerpts includes punctuation, spelling, and word "differences" that are repeated in the same poems in his *Tribute For The Negro*. One of the four excerpts in "Intelligent Negroes" is a twenty-four line excerpt from Wheatley's "Thoughts on the Works of Providence," which carries a line with a word asterisked by Armistead:

What secret hand returns* the mental train. . . .

Armistead explains the asterisk: "*Returns, a common colloquial error for restores." When, a few years later, he came to reprint again the excerpt from "Thoughts on the Works of Providence" in his *Tribute* (1848), he printed this line "corrected" with no asterisked explanation:

What secret hand restores the mental train. . . .

Other "variants" found in Armistead's reprintings would seem to be similarly "corrections," and the text of his Wheatley offerings is, accordingly, unreliable.

Nevertheless, it seems that Armistead's Wheatley text has been cited, and in a once popular textbook of American literature. First published in 1858, and reaching a third edition by 1866, Charles Cleveland's *Compendium of American Literature, Chronologi-*

cally Arranged (New York, Boston, Chicago, and San Francisco) reprinted the eighteen-line excerpt from "On the Death of the Rev. Dr. Sewell, 1769," that is found in Armistead's *Tribute For The Negro*. Also, under the title of "On the Death of an Infant," (the same title Armistead had used for this piece) Cleveland reprinted a thirty-six line excerpt from "On the Death of C.E. an Infant of Twelve Months." In both of these Cleveland reprints are found each of the "variants" that are found in Armistead. If he was indebted to Armistead for these two pieces, Cleveland was not indebted for his reprinting of "A Farewell to America/ To Mrs. Susannah [sic] Wright," in thirteen quatrains. Armistead had printed "A Farewell to America/ Addressed to Mrs. Wheatley," in nine quatrains. (Phillis had originally printed the poem as "Farewell to America./ To Mrs. S.W." in fifteen quatrains, in a half-dozen New England newspapers, and in the 1–3 July 1773 edition of *The London Chronicle*. For her 1773 volume of *Poems*, she shortened and revised the piece to thirteen quatrains as "A Farewel to America./ To Mrs. S.W.") Cleveland may have found both the name of "*Mrs. Susannah* [sic] *Wright*," as the supposed dedicatee of the poem, and the thirteen-stanza version in E. and A. Duyckinck's *Cyclopedia of American Literature* (1856), which seems to be the first printing of the title as "Farewell to America./ To Mrs. *Susanna Wright*."

Not all of these and other such variants are due only to careless and/or indifferent printers and editors. Many well-meaning editors and printers inserted changes into Wheatley's texts hoping thereby to present her printed work as correctly as they could. In 1770, Henry Pelham wrote to his brother, Charles, in London, enclosing a copy of Wheatley's elegy on the death of the Reverend George Whitefield. The poem had been "examined by a Mr. Green . . . before it went to Press," he explained, and but one word of the manuscript had been changed "and that was the word Stars instead of star. . . ." In printing Wheatley's manuscript poem of 1772 to Lord Dartmouth in *The New York Journal* for June 3, 1773, the editor changed several words and omitted an embarrassingly poor two-line simile. Phillis's manuscript poem to Major General Charles Lee was dedicated to "The Honorable James Bowdoin Esqr." at the end of 1776, and she likely trusted that the piece would be printed by Bowdoin. But, perhaps because he knew more of the real facts about Lee's behavior than Phillis could, Bowdoin never released the manuscript for publication. It would not be until 1863 that a Bowdoin descendant found the manuscript and published it, with slight variants, in the *Proceedings of the Massachusetts Historical Society.*

It is true, then, that Phillis did not always have final control over whatever "improvements" or "corrections" were made to her manuscripts. It is also true that Phillis herself was forever rewriting her manuscripts, so that there is today a sizeable array of her own manuscript variants. There are extant at least four slightly variant manuscript versions of her poem on atheism; two variant manuscript versions of her poem on Deism; at least three manuscript versions of her elegy on the death of the Reverend Joseph Sewall, which differ from the printed version in her 1773 volume; two manuscript treatments of the death of Charles Eliot, which are variant from the version printed in the volume. Several of her pieces in print are also in variant versions.

In addition to having been made to serve as wrenched documentations for some later commentators' notions of racial inferiority or parity or superiority, Phillis's writings have been criticized for being extremely limited in topical range, excessively imitative in poetic technique, and self-deludingly aloof from the black realities of her times. Such comments can arise only from a partial reading of all of Wheatley's writings.

It is true that practically all of her writings are informed by a lifelong preoccupation with orthodox Christian piety. But that fundamental fact will not form the basis for deducing that her range was limited to Christian or Biblical or even pious concerns. Phillis composed over one hundred poems and published more than fifty pieces in her lifetime, certainly enough to display a wider range of topics than that for which she has been credited. In the thirty-eight pieces in her 1773 volume alone can be seen pieces on such matters as reconciliation, "the works of Providence," delightful companion lyrics of the Morning and the Evening, two Biblical renderings, a Latin translation, a tribute to a fellow black Bostonian who was also a poet and an artist, the human imagination. Most of these pieces are, however, variously structured elegies, versified comfortings for recent widows, widowers, parents grieving the death of their children or relatives.

In poems published before and after the 1773 volume, her range of poetic concerns includes topics of American patriotism, simple friendship, pioneering tributes to black Africa. Indications of still other topics may be reckoned from some of the titles of the thirty-three poems listed in her proposals for a 1779 volume, a volume that was never published: "Thoughts on the Times," "Farewell to England," "Epithalamium to Mrs. H——," "A Complaint." Likewise, her letters reveal a lively interest in several issues: antislavery, her chronic sickness, her ordeals as a bookseller and distributor of her own book, her manumission, the onset of Christian redemption of "heathen" Africans. The charge that she versified nothing but piety cannot be documented.

She may have written heartfelt condolences for personal Tory friends, but Phillis was plainly a Whig or American Patriot in her deepest political sympathies. This much is clear in a half-dozen poems she wrote. One of her very first efforts, "America," is a versified, allegorical chiding of Mother England for the imposition of unduly inhibiting taxation on her vigorous, growing son, New England, or America. Hailing King George III for his repeal of the Stamp Act, so despised in the colonies and especially in Boston where it had triggered mob riots, Phillis wrote two versions of a poem of American thanks to his majesty. The Earl of Dartmouth was appreciated in some of the colonies as a sometimes sympathetic recourse for American grievances. Congratulating him on his royal appointment as Secretary of State for North America, she greets his "blissful sway," because

> No more, *America*, in mournful strain
> Of wrongs, and grievance unredress'd complain;
> Which wanton *Tyranny* with lawless hand
> Had made, and with it meant t'enslave the land.

She also took occasion in this piece to testify of her own experiences as a kidnapped African slave to underscore the great hope with which, she was sure, her fellow colonists must greet Dartmouth's tenure. As she was herself a slave or unpaid servant, however indulged, when she wrote this poem, the piece can easily be read as her disdain for all kinds of slavery.

Eleven-year-old Christopher Snider's accidental killing by a goaded Tory, one Ebenzer Richardson, on February 23, 1770, in the North End, galvanized Patriot Americans into a swarming, outraged mob that almost lynched Richardson on the spot. Staged by the likes of wily Sam Adams, young Snider's funeral was worked up into the largest in Boston's history to that time, with ranks of Snider's school fellows leading thousands on foot and others in chaisses from the Liberty Tree to the Old Granary Burial Grounds. Newspapers and broadsides made much of the "slaughter." In her own poem, "On the Death of Mr. Snider killed by Richardson," Phillis speaks from the dead center of the seething, partisan crowd. She strains to couch the slaying and funeral of Snider, "the first martyr for the cause," in epic language. American Whigs here are seen as "the generous Sires," and Snider is "their young champion gasping on the ground." Richardson is made out to be "The Wretch appal'd," a "Tory chief," a "vaunted Heir" of the English, whom Phillis actually calls "the grand Usurpers."

In her paean to the newly appointed commander-in-chief of the Continental Army, George Washington, Phillis's political allegiances are again asserted as clearly American. She warns the oppressive British that they will ruefully learn, even as France had learned in the recent French and Indian Wars, that America, or Columbia, is heaven-destined to rise inexorably to become a shining exemplar of human freedom for all the world to see and emulate:

> One century scarce performed its destined round
> When Gallic powers Columbia's fury found:
> And so may you, whoever dare disgrace
> The land of freedom's heaven-defended race!
> Fix'd are the eyes of nations on the scales,
> For in their hopes of Columbia's arms prevails.
> Anon Britannia droops the pensive head,
> While round increase the rising hills of dead.
> Ah! cruel blindness to Columbia's state!
> Lament thy thirst for boundless power too late.

Resorting again to the rhetoric of the heroic epic, she poetically salutes Major General Charles Lee, "betray'd into the hands of the Enemy by the treachery of a pretended Friend." When she makes Lee extravagantly praise General Washington, she is grossly unaware of Lee's militarily disruptive resentment of Washington; but, in her partisan American advocacy, as orated by Lee in a defiant retort to his British captors, she is not at all confused:

> ". . . oh arrogance of tongue!
> "And wild ambition, ever prone to wrong!
> "Believ'st thou chief that armies such as thine
> "Can stretch in dust that heaven-defended line?

". . . What various causes to the field invite!
"For plunder *you*, and we for freedom fight.
"Her cause divine with generous ardor fires,
"And every bosom glows as she inspires!
". . . Yet those brave troops innum'rous as the sands
"One soul inspires, one General Chief commands.
"Find in your train of boasted heroes, one
"To match the praise of Godlike Washington. . . ."

"Liberty and Peace" celebrates the formal ending of the Revolutionary War, upbraids wrong-headed England, and counsels reconciliation but only on terms of competitive national parity:

Perish that Thirst of boundless Power, that drew
On *Albion's* Head the Curse to Tyrants due.
But thou appeas'd submit to Heaven's decree
That bids this Realm of Freedom rival thee!

Among her more successful poems are such pieces as "On the Works of Providence," "On Imagination," "Hymn to the Morning," "Hymn to the Evening," verses which allow her to give full rein to her innermost positive feelings about such matters. In her funeral elegies, human existence is viewed, typically and conventionally, as a dreary affair, a place of "dark abodes," of "sin and snares," where "the iron hand of pain" crushes everyone sooner or later. In her reflective pieces, on the other hand, human life is seen more favorably, especially as one is reminded that the earth is the Lord's and the fullness thereof; and that there is always available to ungrateful mankind the palliative of His Love. In "Thoughts on the Works of Providence," a world of unappreciated plenitude is hailed:

. . . Creation smiles in various beauty gay
While day to night, and night succeeds to day:
That *Wisdom*, which attends *Jehovah's* ways,
Shines most conspicuous in the solar rays:
Without them, destitute of heat and light,
This world would be the reign of endless night:
In their excess how would our race complain,
Abhorring life! how hate its length'ned chain!
. . . Hail, smiling morn, that from the orient main
Ascending dost adorn the heav'nly plain!
So rich, so various are thy beauteous dies,
That spread through all the circuit of the skies,

94

That, full of thee, my soul in rapture soars,
And thy great God, the cause of all adores.
O'er beings infinite his love extends,
His Wisdom rules them, and his Pow'r defends.
When tasks diurnal tire the human frame,
The spirits faint, and dim the vital flame,
Then too that ever active bounty shines,
Which not infinity of space confines.
. . . Infinite *Love* wher'er we turn our eyes
Appears: this ev'ry creature's wants supplies;
This most is heard in *Nature's* constant voice,
This makes the morn, and this the eve rejoice;
This bids the fost'ring rains and dews descend
To nourish all, to serve one gen'ral end,
The good of man; yet man ungrateful pays
But little homage, and but little praise. . . .

Widely anthologized as a display of sustained competence, "On Imagination" is especially interesting. Rejoicing at the marvelously potent faculty of human imagination, it illustrates how that attribute can, among other things, convert the severest winter into an idyllic if illusory summer:

Though Winter frowns, to Fancy's raptur'd eyes
The fields may flourish, and gay scenes arise;
The frozen deeps may break their iron bands,
And bid their waters murmur o'er the sand.

For all of the efficacy of the imagination, however, the poem closes with an awareness of its limitations. The winter of reality, Phillis concedes, will eventually force its being into human consciousness:

But I reluctant leave the pleasing views,
Which *Fancy* dresses to the delight the *Muse*:
Winter austere forbids me to aspire,
And northern tempests damp the rising fire;
They chill the tide of *Fancy's* flowing sea,
Cease then, my song, cease the unequal lay.

A soberly pious young lady who took her poetry writing quite seriously, Phillis never gave public vent to an impulse for ribaldry or uninhibited laughter. She seems to have been constitutionally disposed to a no-nonsense earnestness that would have been expressed even if she had remained in her native Africa. The nearest she got to anything like rapt lyricism was in passages of "Thoughts on the Works of Providence," and the companion pieces, "Hymn to the Morning" and "Hymn to the Evening." She invokes the muses for assistance in praising the morning, and, for a change, not concerned with the dead, she can sing:

> . . . *Aurora* hail, and all the thousand dies,
> Which deck thy progress through the vaulted skies:
> The morn awakes, and wide extends her rays,
> On ev'ry leaf the gentle zephyr plays;
> Harmonious lays the feather'd race resume,
> Dart the bright eye, and shake the painted plume.
>
> Ye shady groves, your verdant gloom display
> To shield your poet from the burning day:
> *Calliope* awake the sacred lyre,
> While thy fair sisters fan the pleasing fire:
> The bow'rs, the gales, the variegated skies
> In all their pleasure in my bosom rise.

In "To S[cipio] M[oorhead], A Young African Painter, On Seeing His Work," Phillis can confess frankly to her great pleasures at watching her fellow black artist and poet at work (Moorhead may have painted her portrait from which was engraved the frontispiece for her volume of poems):

> To show the lab'ring bosom's deep intent,
> And thought in living characters to paint,
> When first thy pencil did those beauties give,
> And breathing figures learnt from thee to live,
> How did those prospects give my soul delight,
> A new creation rushing on my sight?
> Still, wond'rous youth! each noble path pursue,
> On deathless glories fix thine ardent view:
> Still may the painter's and the poet's fire
> To aid thy pencil, and thy verse conspire! . . .

She is said to "have written with singular fluency, and she excelled in acrostics and other equally difficult tricks of literary dexterity." Answering a rebus posed by "I.B." (James Bowdoin?) in her volume, Phillis responded with her own rebus, which is the only extant example of this kind of manipulative play, although there is more than ample evidence of her literary dexterity throughout her poems.

Phillis's rebus concludes with four tetrameter couplets, and this is unusual for her, almost all of her pieces being written in iambic pentameters couplets. Because she did use this meter and rime scheme so very often—only three of her volume pieces partially use tetrameters—some of her critics have charged her with excessive indebtedness to the master of the heroic couplet, Alexander Pope. One critic[1] has gone so far as to complain,

> . . . The style of the poems is evidently formed, in a great degree, after that of Pope, a writer now in the golden age of his fame; and, indeed, we not infrequently meet with passages which remind us of the model so closely that we cannot but think the original editor or printer failed to do the writer the common justice of attaching the usual marks of quotation to matter, here and there, that had very much the air of an extract. . . .

Scrutiny of her work will reveal, however, that she was not as derivative of Pope as has been long asserted. In fact, recent scholarship is beginning to detail the extent to which she was not the extensive imitator of anyone.

Wheatley's originality is active enough in her special uses of the traditional elegiac form, as she manipulated elements of that form in several different ways. One traditional element of that elegy is the standard account of the heavenly happiness of the deceased. Usually, this account is in the form of testimony from the deceased, but with Phillis, the account is variously presented. Sometimes the deceased will speak of his or her satisfying heavenly bliss; at other times, Phillis will herself narrate such rapture. In "To Mr. and Mrs.******* On the Death of Their Infant Son," both the angels and infant's ghost tell of such unearthly joy. In her elegies on ministers, on the other hand—pieces on the deaths of the Reverends Sewall, Whitefield, Moorhead, and Cooper— there is no account of the pleasures of being in heaven. Instead, with these pieces, Phillis describes the earthly good deeds and ministrations of these divines. In some elegies, Phillis permits the grief of the surviving bereaved to be quoted; elsewhere she narrates their sorrow herself. Whenever appropriate, she thrusts into the texts her personal gratitude for religious instruction and/or poetic guidance she received from some of Boston's ministers who wrote verses. In her verses on the death of her own pastor, the Reverend Joseph Sewall, she writes:

1. "African Anecdotes. Memoir and Poems of Phillis Wheatley. Geo. W. Light: Boston," *The Knickerbocker or New York Monthly Magazine* IV (1834), 91.

> Listen, ye happy from your seats above,
> I speak sincerely, while I speak and love.
> . . . I, too, have cause this mighty loss to mourn,
> For he my monitor will not return.

Similarly, in her eulogy of Reverend Samuel Cooper, she expressed her thanks for his past poetic guidance:

> . . . The hapless Muse, her loss in COOPER mourns,
> And as she sits, she writes, and weeps, by turns;
> A Friend sincere, whose mild indulgent rays
> Encourag'd oft, and oft approv'd her lays. . . .

Because she wrote so many funeral pieces, Phillis might easily have fallen into clichéd expressions of death. Instead, she repeatedly found creatively different ways of describing the same phenomenon:

> Grim monarch! see, depriv'd of vital breath
> A young physician in the dust of death:
> Dost thou go on incessant to destroy,
> Our griefs to double, and lay waste our joys?
> *Enough* thou never yet wast known to say,—
> Though millions die, the vassals of thy sway:
> Nor youth, nor science, nor the ties of love,
> Nor ought on earth thy flinty heart can move
> The friend, the Spouse from his dire dart to save,
> In vain we ask the sovreign of the grave. . . .
> ("To A Lady on the Death of Her Husband.")

> We trace the pow'r of Death from tomb to tomb,
> And his are all the ages yet to come.
> 'Tis his to call the planets from on high,
> To blacken *Phoebus*, and dissolve the sky;
> His too, when all in his dark realm are hurl'd,
> From its firm base to shake the solid world;
> His fatal sceptre rules the spacious whole,
> And trembling nature rocks from pole to pole.
>   Awful he moves, and wide his wings are spread. . . .
> ("To A Lady on the Death of Three Relations.")

> On *Death's* domain intent I fix my eyes,
> Where human nature in vast ruin lies;
> With pensive mind I search the drear abode,
> Where the great conqu'ror has his spoils bestow'd;
> There the offspring of six thousand years

In endless numbers to my view appears;
Whole kingdoms in his gloomy den are thrust,
And nations mix with their primeval dust:
Insatiate still he gluts the ample tomb. . . .
>   ("To A Gentleman and Lady on the Death of the
>   Lady's Brother and Sister and a Child of
>   the Name Avis, Aged One Year.")

. . . Thy dread attendants, all-destroying *Pow'r*,
Hurried the infant to his mortal hour.
Could'st thou unpitying close those radiant eyes?
Or fail'd his artless beauties to surprise?
Could not his innocence thy stroke controul,
Thy purpose shake, and soften all thy soul?
>   ("On the Death of J.C. An Infant.")

In her translation of Ovid's Latin story of Niobe, Phillis is also quite original, a fact not unnoticed by E.A. Duyckinck as early as 1856:

> The longest piece of classicality in the volume is a paraphrase of the story of Niobe and her Children from Ovid, in which there is one line, at least, which would do honour to any pen. Apollo is preparing the slaughter of the sons in the race-course, the moment before that arrowy devastation:—

> With clouds incompass'd glorious Phoebus stands:
> *The feather'd vengeance quiv'ring in his hands.*

> This is not a translation of anything in Ovid, for that writer has neglected so striking a position for his Deity. Apollo, in the Metamorphoses, goes to work at once in the most business-like manner, and covers the field with the slain in the shortest possible time. Another touch of the poetic flight of the arrow is added to the original text in the death of Sipylus:—

> Then didst thou, Sipylus, the language hear
> *Of fate portentous whistling in the air.*

> Certainly, even with the assistance of a master, it was a most generous acquisition for a female slave to appreciate that fine classic story in this way.

More recently, another writer has noted that, in her translation Phillis "has not followed Ovid's interpretation of Niobe," and details the extent to which Phillis is clearly original.[2]

2. Emily S. Watts, *The Poetry of American Women from 1632 to 1945.* (Austin and London: University of Texas Press, 1977), p. 38.

Phillis asserts her creativity also in her versified paraphrase of two Biblical stories, "Goliath of Gath. 1 Sam. Chap. XVII" and "Isaiah LXIII. 1–8." In her rendering of the Goliath story, she even adds a character of her own creation, the angel who vainly chides the giant, and she inserts a dialogue between these two, which was not in the original. Verse 51 of 1 Samuel reads, "Therefore David ran, and stood upon the Philistine, and took his sword, and drew it out of the sheath thereof, and slew him, and cut off his head therewith." Phillis chose to vivify these details:

> The soul still ling'red in its lov'd abode,
> Till conq'ring *David* o'er the giant strode:
> *Goliath's* sword then laid its master dead,
> And from the body hew'd the ghastly head;
> The blood in gushing torrents drench'd the plains,
> The soul found passage through the spouting veins. . . .

For all of her display of her originality in elegies, translations, paraphrases, she is noticeably more limited in her use of rimes. As was often true even of the most able practitioners of the heroic couplet—Alexander Pope, John Dryden, Samuel Johnson—there is much repetition of the same rime words and even the same pairs of rime words. In the thirty-eight pieces in her volume, she repeats the word "God" as a rime in more than two dozen poems; "Love" rimes in more than a dozen verses; "Divine" is a rime in more than twenty poems. Perhaps her most overused rime word is "skies." In more than twenty poems, she employs "skies" almost thirty times. In one poem alone, "Thoughts on the Works of Providence," she uses "skies" to rime five times. As one might expect from the elegist that she was, there is much use of "death" or "dead" as rime words. She also repeats the same rime combinations: thus scattered throughout her works are repetitions of "spread/dead," "skies/arise," "sky/eye." The combination of "return/mourn" is found in at least a dozen pieces. These rimes and rime pairs are used also in poems published both before and after her 1773 volume.

Some of these and other kinds of repetitions are due to Phillis's being an occasional poet. The occasion for which she was most frequently called upon to versify was the same—death, which she deemed fitting to poeticize soon afterwards. She thus often wrote too hastily. The Reverend George Whitefield died on September 30, 1770, in Newburyport, Massachusetts; by the first week in

October, Boston newspapers were advertising, as "This Day Published," Phillis's elegy on that death. On the 3rd of September, 1772, Boston's John Andrews notified his brother-in-law, William Barrell, in Philadelphia, of the death of little Charles Eliot, Barrell's and Andrews's nephew. But by the first of that same month, Phillis had already composed two versions of an elegy for the deceased. The Reverend John Moorhead died on December 3, 1773 and was buried on December 6; by December 15 Phillis had published his eulogy. Just seven days after Mary Sanford Oliver died on March 17, 1773, Phillis's elegy was completed. Reverend Samuel Cooper died on December 29, 1783, and Phillis's tribute was dated "BOSTON, Jan. 1784." It is a poetic virtue of Phillis that, composing as quickly as she did for a standard poetic format, she was able to vary her elegies as well as she did. However, her hasty writings were not always free of repeated phrases, as in her references to "glowing breasts" or "glowing bosoms": "And ev'ry bosom with devotion glow'd" ("On the Death of the Rev. Mr. George Whitefield"); "And the dear Saviour glows in ev'ry breast" (On the Death of the Rev. Dr. Sewell); ". . . and all the bosom glows" ("To Maecenas"); "So may our breasts with ev'ry virtue glow" ("An Hymn to the Evening"); ". . . how my bosom burns" ("Philis's Reply to the Answer . . ."); "And every bosom glows as she inspires" ("On the Capture of General Lee").

Phillis is most comfortable with the "light" images conjured by such "burning" and "glowing" references. She is said to have remembered only a single detail for her native African childhood; she recalled that her mother poured out water before the sun at its daily rising. For all of her subsequent, potent indoctrination into suffusing Christianity, she never really forgot those primal African images of the sun, and light, and water. Indeed her references to the sun and light are so very frequent and broadcast throughout her poetry that they seem like ritualized supplications of a true believer in a "religion of light." She viewed the sun, or "mighty Sol," as generatively benign to mankind and nature, ordained by God "to reign/ the peerless monarch of th'ethereial train:/ . . . from him th'extended earth/ Vigour derives, and ev'ry flow'ry birth." Nurturing as it is, the sun is not the ultimate or even the first of lights. There was primordial light:

> . . . All-wise Almighty providence we trace
> In trees, and plants, and all the flow'ry race;

As clear as in the nobler frame of man,
All lovely copies of the Maker's plan.
The pow'r the same that forms a ray of light,
That call'd creation from eternal night.
"Let there be light," he said; from his profound
Old *Chaos* heard, and trembled at the sound:
Swift as the word, inspir'd by pow'r divine,
Behold the light around its maker shine,
The first fair product of th'omnific God,
And now through all his works diffus'd abroad. . . .

("Thoughts on the Works of Providence")

As she wrote, again in terms of light, in praise of a book of sermonizing written by an English minister:

Artists may paint the sun's effulgent rays,
But Amory's pen the brighter God displays.

("To the Rev. Dr. Thomas Amory . . .")

Typically, her invocations also feature similar imagery, although in such uses she refers to the "light" or "fire" of poetic inspiration:

For one bright moment, heavenly goddess! shine,
Inspire my song and form the lays divine . . .
While I each golden sentiment admire
In thee, the muse's bright celestial fire. . . .

("PHILIS's Reply to the Answer . . .")

At times, her use of "light" imagery can be both religious and military:

Celestial choir! enthron'd in realms of light,
Columbia's scenes of glorious toils I write.
While freedom's cause her anxious breast alarms
She flashes dreadful in refulgent arms . . .
See the bright beams of heaven's revolving light
Involved in sorrows and the veil of night! . . .
Wherever shines this native of the skies,
Unnumber'd charms and recent graces rise. . . .

("To His Excellency General Washington")

Repeatedly, her elegies describe heaven in terms of revered light, dazzling brightness. Heaven, for Phillis, is a place of "shining portals," "hills of light," "shining guards," and "refulgent domes," where the worthy deceased are seated "amidst the radiant throng." The young wife of a couple, recently deceased but reconciled in heaven with her husband who had died earlier, is made to offer comfort to her grieving parents:

> "Could ye, fond parents, see our present bliss,
> "How soon would you each sigh, each fear dismiss?
> "Amidst unutter'd pleasures whilst I play
> "In the fair sunshine of celestial day. . . ."
>
> ("To the Honourable T.H. Esq. . . .")

In her zeal to poetically paint the scenes of heaven, Phillis could sometimes become uncommonly ambitious. In one place, she wished she could employ her imagination or fancy:

> To rise from earth, and sweep th'expanse on high;
> . . . The monarch of the day I might behold,
> And all the mountains tipt with radiant gold,
> But I reluctant leave the pleasing views,
> Which *Fancy* dresses to delight the *Muse*;
> *Winter* austere forbids me to aspire,
> And northern tempests damp the rising fire;
> They chill the tide of *Fancy's* flowing sea,
> Cease then, my song, cease the unequal lay.
>
> ("On Imagination")

Realizing how easily some of her poetic aspirations might be construed as impious audacity or even downright egotistical blasphemy—the work of a mere mortal poet daring to poetically embellish the already perfected lights of heaven—she chided herself in print:

> . . . But of celestial joys I sing in vain:
> Attempt not, muse, the too advent'rous strain. . . .
>
> ("To A Lady and Her Children . . .")

In her piece on the death of the Reverend Samuel Cooper, she let it be known that she was familiar with the devices of grammatical rhetoric, which Cooper used so dramatically:

> . . . The Sons of Learning on thy lessons hung,
> While soft persuasion mov'd th'Illiterate throng,
> Who, drawn by rhetoric's commanding laws,
> Comply'd obedient, nor conceiv'd the cause.
> Thy every sentence was with grace inspir'd,
> And every period with devotion fir'd.

103

> Bright Truth thy guide without a dark disguise,
> And penetration's all-discerning eyes. . . .

Her own employment of various figures of speech, however, is uneven. Although she improved somewhat in its use over the years, Phillis did not often resort to the simile. In some early pieces, her similes simply do not work, as when she strains for pathos in likening the death of an infant to a violently uprooted plant:

> . . . As a young plant by hurricanes up torn,
> So near its parent lies the newly born—
> But 'midst the bright ethereal train behold
> It shines superior on a throne of gold:
> > ("To a Lady on the Death of Three Relations")

Or when she would compare the appointment of Lord Dartmouth as His Majesty's Secretary of State for North America to the advent of a personified Freedom, whose very appearance prompts the reactionary demise of a personified New England faction, which would be, in turn, likened to a disappearing owl:

> . . . While in thine hand with pleasure we behold
> The silken reins, and *Freedom's* charms unfold.
> Long lost to realms beneath the northern skies
> She shines supreme, while hated *faction* dies:
> Soon as appear'd the *Goddess* long desir'd,
> Sick at the view, she languish'd and expir'd;
> Thus from the splendors of the morning light
> The owl in sadness seeks the caves of night.
> > ("To the Right Honourable . . . Earl of Dartmouth . . .")

That she learned to use a more effective simile is clear from an example from her 1775 poem to General Washington, in which she sees the coming on of Freedom as a powerful hurricane, leading a train of military forces as plentiful and as driven as windblown leaves in autumn.

> . . . Muse! bow propitious while my pen relates
> How pour her armies through a thousand gates,
> As when Eolus heaven's fair face deforms,
> Enwrapp'd in tempest and a night of storms;
> Astonish'd ocean feels the wild uproar,
> The refluent surges beat the sounding shore;
> Or thick as leaves in Autumn's golden reign,
> Such, and so many, moves the warrior's train. . . .

With other tropes she did not improve. Excessive personifications remained a favored device to her last poems. In her use of alliteration, she was also often excessive, and too often gratuitous; alliteration seems to be used for its own sake and not to augment the sentiment of the line in which it appears. This kind of thing can end with being little more than a display of self-conscious cleverness and dexterity.

At times she alliterates the beginning of a line:

And *b*easts shall *b*e your animated tomb,

("Goliath of Gath")

His *r*ising *r*adiance drives the shades away—

("An Hymn to the Morning")

Or *w*ith new *w*orlds amaze th'unbounded soul.

("On Imagination")

At other times she alliterates the end of a line:

To Heavenly airs he tunes the *s*ounding *s*trings
("To Mr. and Mrs.******* On the Death of Their Infant Son")

Still live thy merits, where thy *n*ame is *kn*own
As the sweet Rose, its *b*looming *b*eauty gone. . . .
(". . . Elegy . . . to . . . Samuel Cooper . . .")

Swift as they move, hear each *r*ecess *r*ebound
But here I sit, and *m*ourn a grov'ling *m*ind

("To Maecenas")

Sometimes she will alliterate three times:

There *Wh*itefield *w*ings with rapid course his *w*ay
("On the Death of the Rev. Mr. George Whitefield. 1770")

"Inquire whose *s*on is he," the *s*ov'reign *s*aid,

("Goliath of Gath")

*S*ay what is *s*leep? and dreams how passing *s*trange!
("Thoughts on the Works of Providence")

She has alliterated almost entire lines:

The *l*ength'ning *l*ine moves *l*anguishing a*l*ong

("To Maecenas")

*S*till more, ye *s*ons of *s*cience, ye re*c*eive
("To the University of Cambridge in New England")

105

> The greatest gift than even a God can give
> ("On the Death of the Rev. Mr. George Whitefield")

And she can be intricately clever with her arrangements of double alliteration:

> In *s*ocial *b*anquet, and the *s*prightly *b*owl
> ("On the Capture of General Lee")

> Thus *h*aving *s*aid, he *h*eav'd a boding *s*igh
> ("On the Capture of General Lee")

And in still other arrangements:

> *F*air *F*lora may resume her *f*ragrant *r*eign
> ("On Imagination")

> Read o'er what *p*oets *s*ung, and *s*heperds *p*lay
> ("To Maecenas")

> *B*e your *c*omplaints on his *k*ind *b*osom laid
> ("On the Death of . . . Whitefield")

As late as 1784, three months before she would die, in her last known published poem, Phillis was still as manipulative with alliteration as earlier:

> These *s*aw *h*is entrance; *h*is *s*oft *h*and they press'd,
> "*H*ail: *th*ou! thrice welcome to *th*is *h*appy shore
> Sorrow and *s*in, those foes to human rest,
> *F*orever *b*anish'd *f*rom thy happy *b*reast."
> Gazing they spoke, and *r*aptur'd thus *r*eplies,
> The beauteous *s*tranger in th'etherial *s*kies,
> Thus safe conducted to your *b*less'd *a*bodes,
> With *s*weet *s*urprize I *m*ix a*m*ong the Gods;
> . . . Beyond your search, immortal *p*owers I *p*raise;
> Great Sire, I *s*ing, thy boundless love divine
> . . . Fain *w*ould we clasp *h*im, but *h*e *w*ings *h*is *f*light. . . .
> ("To Mr. and Mrs. ******* On the Death of Their Infant Son")

She can sometimes compound her uses of parison (the matching of words, or parts of speech in adjacent clauses or sentences):

> While Phoebus reigns above the starry train
> While bright Aurora purples o'er the main,
> So long, great Sir, the muse thy praise shall sing,
> So long thy praise shall make *Parnassus* ring. . . .
> ("To Maecenas")

106

. . . O could my muse thy seat on high behold,
How deckt with laurel, how enrich'd with gold!
O could she hear what praise thine harp employs,
How sweet thine anthems, how divine thy joys!

("On the Death of a Young Gentleman")

Ordinarily modest and restrained in her occasional uses of anaphora (repetition of the same word at the beginning of a sequence of clauses or sentences), she can let it get out of hand:

Sweeter than music to the ravish'd ear,
Sweeter than Maro's entertaining strains
Resounding through the groves, and hills, and plains.

("On Recollection")

This most is heard in *Nature's* constant voice,
This makes the morn, and this the eve rejoice;
This bids the fost'ring rains and dews descend
To nourish all, to serve one gen'ral end, ...

("Thoughts on the Works of Providence")

Where contemplation finds her sacred spring,
Where heav'nly music makes the arches ring,
Where virtue reigns unsully'd and divine,
Where wisdom thron'd, and all the graces shine,
There sits thy spouse amidst the radiant throng, ...

("To A Clergyman on the Death Of His Lady")

"E'er vice triumphant had possess'd my heart,
"E'er yet the tempter had beguil'd my heart,
"E'er yet on sin's base actions I was bent,
"E'er yet I knew temptation's dire intent;
"E'er yet the lash for horrid crimes I felt,
"E'er vanity had led my way to guilt,
"But soon arriv'd at my celestial goal,
"Full glories rush on my expanding soul."

(". . . On the Death of C.E. An Infant of Twelve Months")

She uses other tropes also, but only in an occasional metaphor is she notably effective, as when young David boasts of Goliath's impending doom and consumption by scavenging vultures and other animals:

. . . "The fate you threaten shall your own become,
And beasts shall be your animated tomb, ..."

In a compound of personification and apt synecdoche, she can relate the whole process in which England's trees are felled, processed, and used in the construction of sailing ships for its far-flung royal navy. Such action takes place, she writes, "in . . . Albion" (i.e., England)

> Where willing forests leave their native plain,
> Descend, and instant, plough the wat'ry main.
> Strange to relate! with canvas wings they speed
> To distant worlds; . . . .
>
> ("To a Gentleman of the Navy")

Perhaps the most persistent criticism of Phillis Wheatley has been that based on the usually unaesthetic grounds of her chosen subject matter. She did not write enough about blackness, some charge. She is said by others to have been callously indifferent to her contemporary black life generally, and archly above black slave life in particular. So contending, some see her as the progenitor of a posited black American literary tradition of black self-abnegation, black self-loathing. One writer would have it that so powerfully shaping were the unchallenged New England cultural pressures on a haplessly malleable young Phillis that she was compelled to develop into nothing else but a kind of psychologically malformed grotesquery—a black-white, colonial woman poet. There is perhaps some truth in some of these charges, but a greater truth is that Phillis was very much aware of being a black person, however celebrated a personality, in a world dominated numerically and culturally by white persons, and that she wrote of such matters in her volume of poems, in her miscellaneous poems, and in her letters.

It can be easily shown that almost every identifiable white person in Phillis's writings—politicians, ministers, merchants, Tories, Whigs—owned one or more black slaves or servants. Her famous, much-reprinted elegy on the death of the English evangelist, the Reverend George Whitefield, also saluted Selina Hastings, dowager Countess of Huntingdon, to whom Whitefield had served as private chaplain since 1749. But, his purportedly pious "Letter to the Inhabitants of Maryland, Virginia, North and South Carolina" (January, 1740) notwithstanding, Whitefield had been for some years the owner of 50-odd black slaves. These he purchased from monies of a special grant in 1764 for the purpose of clearing some 2000 acres of land twelve miles outside of Savannah, Georgia, for the building of Bethesda, his orphanage house.

By so erecting this building, Whitefield had helped cause the repeal of an anti-slavery provision which had been once a part of the Georgia charter. In a letter to the *Massachusetts Gazette and Boston Weekly News Letter* for February 8, 1770, an alarmed Bostonian professed great surprise and dismay and disgust at hearing of Whitefield's peculiarly hypocritical slave-holding acts. This reader

> was greatly surprised and grieved, not long since, to find *Mr. Whitefield's* Memorial to the Governor and Council of *Georgia*; that his plan is to buy a Number of Negroe Slaves, whose Labors are to support the President, Professors, and Tutors of his College, as well as Overseers. . . .

Whitefield's will of March 27, 1770, probated by February 6, 1771, bequeathed the "buildings, lands, negroes, furniture . . ." [of Bethesda] "to that elect lady, that mother in Israel, that mirror of true and undefiled religion, Right Honorable Selina, Countess Dowager of Huntingdon. . . ." Phillis may herself have read a printing of Whitefield's will in the supplement to the *Boston News Letter* of April 19, 1771. As soon as she could, after learning of her inheritance of Bethesda with its 50-odd black slaves, the countess dispatched a group of her own missionaries from London to Savannah to administer the estate. She also ordered that monies arising from the first sales from the trust, an amount that happened to total £26.05.65, be used to buy a black female slave for her. "I must request that a woman slave be purchased with it," she wrote, "and that she might be called Selina, after me." It is said that the countess was shown the error of her slave-buying overture in a letter from the American Quaker abolitionist, Anthony Benezet. Compensatorily, perhaps, by the first of 1773, the countess would agree that Phillis could dedicate her book of poems to her Ladyship, and she offered herself as a patron for Phillis's volume, and she even insisted that Phillis's engraved portrait be a frontispiece for the book.

Most of the eighteen Boston personages who signed the attestation to authenticate Phillis's genuine authorship of her volume of *Poems* owned black servants, including the Governor; the Lieutenant-Governor, Harrison Gray; and the Reverends Charles Chauncy, John Moorhead, Ebenezer Pemberton, Mather Byles. The only minister who signed this attestation and who was not a slave-owner was Andrew Eliot, who, an abolitionist in sentiment, vehemently refused his New North Church congregation's proffered gift of a black slave assistant. Another of the signers, Thomas Hubbard, had been a slave-dealer as early as 1740 when he advertised in the *Boston Weekly News Letter* of July 24: "Just imported and to be sold by Thomas Hubbard, Boston, a parcel of fine young Negro Boys and Girls; also Cotton Wool and Old West Indian Rum." James Bowdoin, another attestor, bought and sold several black male slaves in the 1760's. Scholar, poet, wit, satirist, and wealthy distiller merchant, Joseph Green, at his death in 1780, stipulated a £100 gift to his slave, Plato. Phillis was herself only one of several black servants to Mr. and Mrs. John Wheatley.

Phillis poetically hailed American Revolutionary War military leaders—George Washington, Charles Lee, David Wooster—all of whom commanded liberty-seeking units into which blacks were routinely not allowed to enroll except as fifers and drummers and valets—until times of emergencies. Although hard-pressed for new troops, General Washington wrote Congress that he would deny entrance to black recruits if so ordered. Major General Charles Lee left several of his blacks to friends in his will. Phillis also praised "The University of Cambridge, in New-England" at a time when blacks were not allowed to matriculate there, the first black man to graduate from Harvard College being Richard T. Greener, in 1870.

Phillis grew up in a Boston where almost everyone who could afford them, and there were not a great many, owned servants and/or slaves, black and/or white. It was *de rigueur*, fashionably required of those financially able, or pretentious enough to wish to display their real or imagined status, to have black-liveried postillions ornamenting carriages and chaisses, or black and white butlers, valets and domestics, and other menials. Not at all like the physically exhausting, exploitative plantation black world of the South, New England slavery amounted to institutionally sanctioned bound servitude; so argued Governor Hutchinson as he several times rejected anti-slavery legislation before him. Indeed, even a few blacks had slaves and servants of their own.

The great question, then, facing Phillis and the handful of other free blacks was what to do about finding one's black self living in a racially prejudiced and segregated society. To some, the answer may have seemed deceptively simple: able or determined blacks could leave the country, or they could remain and cope as best they could with the known racial climate. However, if such blacks decided to leave the country, they were not at all certain as to where they might migrate satisfactorily. Even in Africa there would be more than the usual problem of language; there would be the more serious matter of contending with a culture, however black, that would likely prove difficult if not intolerable to most black Americans, now even more deeply imbued than ever with the efficacious promises of Christianity and much impressed with the widely touted western notions of political provisions for the guarantees of accommodating the irrepressible human compulsion to be free individuals. It was such a compulsion that had driven blacks back in Africa to resist both African and white slavers in as many ways as were possible, including self-mutilations, escapes, slave ship mutinies, or watery suicides.

It is noteworthy that precious few blacks in Phillis's time actually returned from Europe or America or South America to an Africa of widespread native slavery. It had been in such a world that many of them had been kidnapped and sold into slavery, African and western, in the first place, and often by fellow black Africans. African-born contemporaries of Phillis who wrote or dictated their life stories recalled similar enslavements. Venture Smith remembered that he had been sold by black Africans to a white steward of a Rhode Island slave ship for "four gallons of rum and a piece of calico. . . ." Ottobah Cuguoano recalled that, as a thirteen-year-old boy, he had been sold by Africans to a white slaver for "a gun, a piece of cloth and some lead. . . ." Gustavus Vassa wrote that as a child he was frightened of Igbo slave dealers, and with good reason. At age eleven he, and his sister, were kidnapped by some Igbo slavers and sold into white slavery "for seventy two cowries" (white sea shells the size of fingernails, used as currency among some African tribes). Job Ben Solomon was inadvertently captured and sold into slavery by black Africans while he was himself on a slave-selling mission for his father.

Some blacks expressed the hope for ultimately returning to Africa, but relatively few actually sailed from Europe or America for the motherland. In the 1787 edition of his autobiography, Ottobah Cuguoana wrote of his strong desire to return, but there is evidence of his being in London as late as 1800. In that year, one John Jea published his life story in England, telling of his

111

being kidnapped as a boy with his entire family and sold into New York slavery. As a religiously inspired boy, he dared to speak out against the cruelties of his Dutch master, even at the risk of death, "thinking that after I was dead I should be at rest, and that I should go back again to my native Africa" (an idea generally cherished by slaves). Jea may have trusted that his spirit would return to Africa, but he directed his corporeal body along a greatly extended trek that led him to almost everywhere except Africa. "Not to please myself, but for the glory of God, and the good of souls," when he became a free man he travelled, as a ship's cook, from upstate New York to Boston; to New York; to Boston; to Salisbury, Massachusetts; to London; to Liverpool; to Manchester; to Yorkshire; to Sunderland; to New York; to Boston; to Amsterdam, where he preached in Dutch and English; to Rotterdam; to "Heilder, near Hamburg"; to Boston; to New Orleans; to Liverpool; to Newburyport, Massachusetts; to "Vennelia, [?] in the East Indies"; to Buones Ayres"; to Boston; to the West Indies; to Virginia; to Baltimore, where he was almost re-enslaved; to Limerick, Ireland, where he married his third wife, an Irish colleen; to Holland; to St. John's, Halifax. He was waylaid to France. The book ends with him and his wife living in Portsmouth, England.

It must be remembered that Phillis was herself kidnapped into slavery, as she revealed ruefully in her poem to Lord Dartmouth:

> . . . I, young in life, by seeming cruel fate
> Was snatch'd from *Afric's* fancy'd happy seat;
> What pangs excrutiating must molest,
> What sorrows labour in my parent's breast?
> Steel'd was that soul and by no misery mov'd
> That from a father seiz'd his babe belov'd. . . .

There should be little wonder then, that after enjoying an uncommonly fostered life of protection, privilege, patronage and international fame but especially after having serendipitously landed in a Christian realm, that she refused the blandishments of several of her closest friends and associates—Mrs. Susanna Wheatley, the Reverend Samson Occom—to return to Africa as a Christian missionary to the natives. As he would spend most of his life preaching among his fellow Indians throughout New England, Occom wrote a letter to Mrs. Susanna Wheatley on February 16, 1771, whose postscript added:

Please to remember me to Phillis and the rest of your Servants/ Pray madam, what harm would it be to send Phillis to her/ Native Country as a Female Preacher to her kindred,/ you know Quaker women are alow'd to preach, and why/ not others in an Extraordinary Case—

As she wrote the philanthropist, John Thornton, in London in 1774, who had also pressed her to join two blacks who were being prepared for African missionary work by the Reverend Samuel Hopkins of Newport:

. . . but/ why do you hon'd Sir, wish those poor men so much trouble as to carry/ me so long a voyage? Upon my arrival, how like a Barbarian shou'd/ I look to the Natives; I can promise that my tongue shall be quiet for a strong reason indeed, being/ an utter stranger to the Language of Anamaboe. Now to be Serious, This/ undertaking appears too hazardous and not sufficiently Eligible to go—/ And leave my British & American Friends. . . .

Although this letter was written before she could have clearly foreseen the eruption of war between her "British and American Friends," and although she had been personally friendly with several Boston Tory families, Phillis seemed resolved even then to live out the rest of her life as a black American. In so deciding, she chose one of the few options available to liberty-seeking colonial blacks. Blacks who would not emigrate could choose to side with the British or with the Americans and/or their French allies. Swearing a pox on all white houses, some blacks escaped to assimilation with neighboring or distant Indian tribes. Long frustrated by the hypocrisy of ostensibly Christian slave traffickers and Patriot American slave owners in the colonies, many thousands of blacks responded to the promises—actual and so construed—of Lord Dunmore in Virginia, Sir William Howe in Boston, and Sir Henry Clinton in New York that all black slaves who fought for his Majesty's military forces would be rewarded with their freedom. Uncounted hundreds of other blacks, slave and free, joined the French forces, which already included blacks among its naval personnel, and, in the 1779 Battle of Savannah, employed the nearly 600-man strong "Volunteer Chasseurs," blacks from Santo Domingo. In various engagements of the war between American and French forces against British and Hessian troops, there were thus the spectacles of blacks of America fighting blacks of America. By the end of the Revolutionary War, almost 15,000 blacks, many of them veterans, were among the British troops and Loyalist Americans who were evacuated from New York, Savannah, and Charleston, South Carolina. Of course, none of these blacks were really fighting for the British or the French cause so much as they were siding with those forces which they variously reckoned would soonest bring about their own freedom, their own liberty.

Similarly, of the 5000 blacks who fought on the American side, most were concerned with their personal freedom. Slaves agreed to hazard their lives in exchange for written and verbal promises of freedom. Some few free blacks joined the American forces out of a sense of adventure, financial need. It is not known how many blacks fought alongside Patriot American troops in a trust and belief that the vaunted political, economic, and social benefits would be shared by them or their black descendants. Phillis's belief in the American promise would seem to be confident; it certainly was idealistic. Her patriotic poems—to General Washington, General Lee, General Wooster and on the end of the war itself—are not, therefore, merely heroically inspired rhetorical exercises in pentameter couplets. She seems to have wanted to believe that it was divinely ordained for a free and especially Christian America to rise and loom on the world's horizon, a mighty example of the unfolding of God's will that all mankind be free. She repeats as much in each of her poems to American military leaders. America, she wrote, is

> . . . The land of freedom's heaven-defended race!
> Fix'd are the eyes of nations on the scales,
> For in their hopes Columbia's arm prevails. . . .
> ("To His Excellency General Washington")

Mortally wounded, her General Wooster is made to apostrophize to the heavens before he dies:

> . . . Permit me yet to paint fair freedom's charms
> For her the Continent shines bright in arms
> By thy high will, celestial prize she came—
> For her we combat on the field of fame . . .
> For ever grateful let them live to thee
> And keep them ever virtuous, brave, and free—
> ("On the Death of General Wooster")

Her Major General Charles Lee defies his British captors with a ringing reference to America's inevitable, righteous victory:

> . . . "Believ'st thou Chief, that armies such as thine
> "Can stretch in dust that heaven-defended line?
> "In vain allies may swarm from distant lands,
> "And demons aid in formidable bands. . . .
> "For plunder you, and we for freedom fight.
> "Her cause divine with generous ardor fires,
> "And every bosom glows as she inspires! . . .
> "So wills the Power who with convulsive storms
> "Shakes impious realms, and nature's face deforms; . . . ."
> ("On the Capture of Major General Lee, to I.B.")

That the Americans emerged triumphantly from the Revolutionary War was not at all startling to Phillis, who saw it as the manifestation of inexorable divine will. American freedom could never be denied:

> Lo! Freedom comes. Th'prescient muse foretold,
> All eyes th'accomplish'd Prophecy behold . . .
> She, the bright Progeny of Heaven, descends,
> And every Grace her sovereign Step attends;
> For now kind Heaven, indulgent to our Prayer,
> In smiling *Peace* resolves the Din of *War* . . .
> ("Liberty and Peace")

Phillis's explanation of the world as manifestation of God's will was shared by other literate blacks of her day. She seems convinced, for instance, that the state of universal black wretchedness was deservingly visited upon blacks by a just and demanding God. If only blacks would become earnest and devout Christians and seek God's forgiveness for their sins, then His mercy might deliver them from their worldwide misery. Jupiter Hammon (1711–1787), of Long Island, New York, carried the matter of Christian resignation to the point of seeming to counsel utter passivity, which was intolerable to many of his black audiences in Hartford, Connecticut, especially maimed veterans and widows of the recent Revolutionary War. In his known seven pieces of prose and verse, he repeats the same thing. His "An/ Evening's Improvement./ Shewing,/ the Necessity of beholding/ the Lamb of God. . . ." (undated but written "during the Revolution") says:

> . . . My dear brethren we are many of us seeking for a temporal freedom, and I pray God would grant your desire; if we are slaves it is by permission of the most high God; be not discouraged, but cheerfully perform the duties of the day, sensible that the same

power that created the heavens and the earth and causeth the greater light to rule the day and the lesser to rule the night, can cause a universal freedom. . . .

Inspired and counselled by Phillis's acquaintance, the missionary-minded Reverend Samuel Hopkins, the officers of the Free African Union Society of Newport, Rhode Island, also felt that the woes of the blacks were attributable to sinful blacks themselves. Urging, vainly, fellow Newport blacks to return to Africa, they would write in 1789:

> We, taking into consideration the calamitous state into which we are brought by the righteous hand of GOD, being strangers & outcasts in a strange land, attended with many disadvantages and evils, with respect to living, which are like to continue on us and on our children, while we and they live in this country, and the yet more wretched state of many hundreds of thousands of our brethren, who are in the most abject slavery, in the West Indies, and in the American States, many of whom are treated in the most inhumane and cruel manner, and are sunk down in ignorance, stupidity and vice, and considering the unhappy state and circumstances of our brethren, the nations in Africa, from whom we sprang, being in heathenish darkness & barbarity, and are, and have been for many years, many of them, so foolish and wicked as to sell one another into Slavery, by which means many Millions have either lost their lives, or been transported to a Land of Slavery; and whereas GOD has been pleased of late to raise up many to compassionate and befriend the African, not only in promoting their freedom, and using Means for their instruction, but by proposing and endeavoring to effect their return to their own country and their settlement there, where they may be more happy than they can be here. . . . We taking all this into view, think there is a special and loud call to us, and all the Blacks in America, to seek GOD by extraordinary fasting and prayer . . . humbly to confess the sins of our fathers, and our own sins; and to acknowledge the righteousness of GOD in bringing all these evils on us and our children & brethren And earnestly to cry to GOD for the pardon of our sins, and that he would, of his great mercy, deliver us and our brethren and the nations in Africa from the sins and miseries in which we and they are now involved; and pour down his holy spirit upon us and cause us and them to become a wise, virtuous and Christian People; And that he would, in his wise and good providence, open a safe and prosperous way for our returning to Africa. . . .

While they could reject these black Rhode Islanders' invitation to join in plans for an 18th-century black "Back-to-Africa" movement, the officials of a black Philadelphia self-help society could also indicate their similar reliance on God:

> . . . With regard to the emigration you mention to Africa, we have at present but little to communicate on that head, apprehending every pious man is a good citizen of the whole world; therefore let us, as with the heart of one man, continue daily in fasting from sin and iniquity . . . that the Lord thereby may be pleased to break every yoke and let the oppressed go free. . . .

For some time, Phillis had been lamenting the supposed direful absence of Christianity among her native Africans and rejoicing that she and her fellow black Americans had been brought, even as slaves, into the presence of God Almighty. She spoke of these matters in a letter to her friend, Obour Tanner, on May 19, 1772:

> . . . let us rejoice in and adore the wonders of God's infinite Love in bringing us from a land semblant of darkness itself, and where the divine light of revelation (being obscur'd) is as darkness. Here the knowledge of the true God and eternal life are made manifest; but there, profound ignorance overshadows the land. Your observation is true, namely, that there was nothing in us to recommend us to God. Many of our fellow creatures are pass'd by, when the bowels of divine love expanded toward us. May this goodness and long suffering of God lead us to unfeign'd repentance.
>
> It gives me very great pleasure to hear of so many of my nation, seeking with eagerness the way of true felicity. O may we all meet at length in that happy mansion. . . .

Delighted to learn of Reverend Samuel Hopkins's plans to educate two Newport, Rhode Island, blacks for Christian missionary work in Africa, she wrote him in 1774:

> . . . Methinks, Rev. Sir, this is the beginning of that happy period foretold by the Prophets, when all shall know the Lord from the least to the greatest. . . . My heart expands with sympathetic joy to see at distant time the thick clouds of ignorance dispersing from the face of my benighted country. Europe and America have long been fed with heavenly provision, and I fear they loath it, while Africa is perishing with a spiritual Famine. O that they could partake of the crumbs, the precious crumbs, which fall from the table of these distinguished children of the kingdom.
>
> Their minds are unprejudiced against the truth, therefore 'tis to

be hoped they would receive it with their whole heart. I hope that
which the divine royal Psalmist says by inspiration is now on the
point of being accomplished, namely, Ethiopia shall soon stretch
forth her hands unto God. . . .

So believing, Phillis would use her poetry to document further
that blacks were indeed rising from the depths of the barbarity
and heathenism and intellectual backwardness of which they
were accused by so many whites. She would do this by letting her
readers know, sometimes obtrusively, that a black could and did
write acceptable verses, all religiously informed, on a range of
conventional topics. Indeed many of her self-conscious revela-
tions of her black or African or Ethiopian identity are purely
gratuitous, having little or nothing to do with the poems in
which they appear. A measure of her racial consciousness in her
volume of poems has already been taken, but she is just as self-
conscious in her other poems and variants, and letters.

She begins two manuscript poems on Deism with a racial
identification that is hardly germane to the topic at hand:

> Must Ethiopians be employ'd for you?
> Much I rejoice if any good I do . . .

and

> Must Ethiopians be imploy'd for you
> Greatly rejoice if any good I do. . . .

In "America," which allegorically rebukes Mother England's
heavy taxation of her son, New England, Phillis insinuates her
own racial identity:

> New England first a wilderness was found
> Till for a continent 'twas destin'd round
> From feild to feild the savage monsters run
> E'er yet Brittania had her work begun
> Thy Power, O Liberty, makes strong the weak
> And (wond'rous instinct) Ethiopians speak. . . .

She may have signed an early manuscript poem, "on Atheism,"
with the self-conscious name of "Africania," and in a late 1774
poem, she established herself as the very first of black American
poets who would sing, even rhapsodize, about Africans and things
African, with such lines as

. . . Charm'd with thy painting, how my bosom burns!
And pleasing Gambia on my soul returns,
With native grace in spring's luxuriant reign,
Smiles the gay mead, and Eden blooms again,
The various bower, the tuneful flowing stream,
The soft retreats, the lovers golden dream,
Her soil spontaneous, yields exhaustless stores;
For phoebus revels on her verdant shores.
Whose flowery births, a fragrant train appear,
And crown the youth throughout the smiling year. . . .

("PHILIS's Reply to the Answer in/ our last
by the Gentleman in the/ Navy")

In other pieces too can be found self-conscious references to herself as a black poet. In different pieces, she is "an AEthiop" ("To the University of Cambridge . . ."); "the languid Muse in low degree" and "Afric's muse" ("Hymn to Humanity"); "Your vent'rous Afric" ("On Recollection"); ". . . last and meanest of the rhyming train!" ("Niobe in Distress . . .").

In several of her letters she also registered her racial awareness and concern, as in her letters to Obour Tanner, below, or to Lord Dartmouth on October 10, 1772, or to the Countess of Huntingdon on October 25, 1770, and on June 27 and July 17, 1773. In her letters she could even become defensively self-conscious about her race, as in a message to John Thornton in December of 1773:

. . . O pray that I may/ be one also, who shall join with you in songs of praise at the Throne of him, who/ is no respecter of Persons, being equally the great maker of all—Therefore disdain/ not to be called the Father of Humble Africans and Indians: though despis'd/ on earth on account of our colour, we have this Consolation if he enables us to/ deserve it, "That God dwells in the humble contrite heart."

It is grievously ironic that Phillis Wheatley should be charged with racial indifference, especially when it can be shown that a letter she wrote on February 11, 1774, and saw printed in ten New England newspapers from March through April of that year, was the first so widely distributed black-written, anti-slavery letter in Afro-American literature. She was by no means the first colonial black American to make her anti-slavery feelings known in print. Since the 17th century, New England blacks had petitioned, usually successfully, for their individual freedoms, while other blacks in other colonies had made their grievances against black slavery known in the forms of uncounted petitions. But, addressed to various colony and state governors and legislatures, these petitions (routinely denied in Massachusetts by the likes of Governor Hutchinson and John Adams) became official papers, and, as such, were very rarely printed for public consumption; instead they usually remained among other state papers in dusty archives for hundreds of years. It would not be until 1951 that historian Herbert Aptheker would locate and print a selection of twenty-two of them, which date from 1661 to 1797. On behalf of Boston blacks protesting the kidnapping of three free Boston blacks into slavery, Prince Hall wrote a petition to "The Honorable the Senit and House of Riprisentetives of the commonWelth of Massachusetts bay in general court assembled February 27 1788 . . ." that was selected by Isaiah Thomas for printing in his *Massachusetts Spy; or Worcester Gazette* of April 24, 1788. An earlier version of his *Gazette, Thomas's Massachusetts Spy; or the American Oracle of Liberty*, of June, 1775, selected for printing a petition for freedom by Worcester blacks. The first version of Thomas's newspaper, *Massachusetts Spy*, printed a black-written grievance as early as June, 1773. Having successfully petitioned for his personal freedom by September of 1773 from his Newburyport, Massachusetts, master, Richard Greenleaf, and pleading for other blacks still enslaved, including his own "no less than eleven relatives suffering in bondage," Caesar Sarter published a signed anti-slavery piece that covered almost the entire front page of the *Essex Journal and Merrimac Packet* of August 17, 1774. Unlike other early black-written anti-slavery notices that reached print and were addressed to Governors and colonial and state legislatures, Sarter's piece was addressed "To those who are Advocates for holding the Africans in Slavery. . . ." But, dated August 12, 1774, and printed five days later, it appeared several months after Phillis's protest letter appeared in the March 11, 1774, issue of the *Connecticut Gazette* (and reprinted again in Connecticut, twice in Rhode Island, twice in Salem, and four times in Boston). A freed woman for several months by the time she composed it, Phillis Wheatley's letter is a restrained, genteel, but unequivocal indictment of the colonial Christian hypocrisy that justified human slavery. It is all the more biting for its assumed stance of humility, its deft use of Biblical analogy, its politely sarcastic scoring of the patently absurd Christian racists. As reported in *The Massachusetts Spy* for March 24, 1774, the letter reads

Wednesday, March 23, Boston. The Following is an extract of a letter from Boston from Phillis, a Negro Girl of Mr. Wheatley's of this town, to the Reverend Samson Occom, which we are desired to insert as a specimen of her ingenuity. It is dated the 11th of February, 1774.

"Reverend and honoured Sir,"

"I have this Day received your obliging, kind Epistle, and am greatly satisfied with your Reasons respecting the negroes, and think highly reasonable what you offer in Vindication of their natural Rights: Those that invade them cannot be insensible that the divine Light is insensibly chasing away the thick Darkness which broods over the Land of Africa; and the Chaos which has reigned so long is converting into beautiful Order, and reveals more and more clearly the glorious Dispensation of civil and religious Liberty, which are so inseparably united, that there is little or no Enjoyment of one without the other: Otherwise, perhaps the Israelites had been less solicitous for their Freedom from Egyptian slavery; I do not say they would have been contented without it, by no means, for in every human Breast, God has implanted a Principle, which we call Love of Freedom; it is impatient of oppression, and pants for Deliverance—and by the Leave of our modern Egyptians I will assert that the same principle lives in us. God grant Deliverance in his own Way and Time, and get him honour upon all those whose Avarice impels them to countenance and help forward the Calamities of their fellow Creatures. This I desire not for their Hurt, but to convince them of the strange Absurdity of their Conduct whose Words and Actions are so diametrically opposite, How well the Cry for Liberty, and the reverse Disposition for the exercise of oppressive power over others agree I humbly think it does not require the penetration of a Philosopher to determine."

From the publication of this letter alone, the matter of Phillis Wheatley's racial consciousness would seem to be clear.

The fully detailed and shaded poetic portrait of Phillis has not yet been drawn because, for one thing, all of her known writings have not yet been seen. More than thirty of her known poems may be lost, as are the untold because unknown number of other pieces referred to by other writers. Similarly, not all of the letters written to her or all of the letters she wrote to others have been

121

preserved. Obour Tanner, for instance, wrote Phillis as many if not more letters than Phillis wrote to her, but not a single one of Obour's letters is known to exist. However, some of these missing letters and poems may yet be unearthed and made public. More than two dozen long unknown notes and letters and their variants written by Wheatley have been found or lately released from private collections, and published by various hands between 1834 and 1981, and since 1797 the finding and printing of Wheatley manuscript poems and variants has been going on.

Despite missing manuscript pieces and missing biographical details, more than enough is known to pronounce Phillis Wheatley Peters a surprisingly formidable, early black, female American survivor, and an impressively competent, if occasionally uneven, colonial poet, whose merits endure. It was no mean feat for a fragile, chronically sick African child of 7 or 8 years to survive the disorienting traumas of being kidnapped into American slavery; the life-threatening privations of a trans-Atlantic sea voyage in the suffocating hold of a crowded slave ship for two and a half months headed towards an unknown destination; bone cold numbing Boston winters, sometimes so cold that the harbor froze over, locking ships to their moorings, and freezing some people to death while sleeping in their beds; epidemics of diseases, especially smallpox, which wreaked a toll of Boston blacks in 1764, and which killed seventy-nine other Boston blacks in the siege of 1769-1770; an unfortunate marriage; the rigors of birthing three children, who all died in infancy; an American lifetime of trying to cope with pandemic racism.

The preface to Phillis's volume mentions that the poems were the products of her leisure time, written for the amusement of the author, not intended to be published, and printed only at the importunity of her best and most generous friends. The poems are presumed to have too much merit to be cast aside with contempt, as worthless and trifling effusions. All of this is, of course, a traditional "protest" stance, much used by poets. In reality, however, Phillis was far less casual about her poems and their publication than this preface asserts. She took her poetry writing and publication quite seriously, especially after she was manumitted in 1773 and needed her own income for her daily support. She was just as anxious to display a talented black poet's wares to a doubting white public. Towards these ends, she preserved her manuscripts for years, waiting for the opportunity to publish them.

When, in October of 1772, the Englishman, Thomas Wool-dridge, anxious to see the celebrated black poetess for himself, visited the Wheatley mansion, he reported to his superior, the Earl of Dartmouth that Phillis "showed me her letter to Lady Huntingdon, which I daresay your Lordship has seen." This letter to the countess would be the one Phillis had written on October 25, 1770; Phillis had kept a manuscript copy ever since. On January 28, 1774, John Andrews, a successful Boston merchant and student of Phillis's poems, wrote to his brother-in-law, William Barrell in Philadelphia, about the availability in Boston of the Wheatley volume that had been published in London the year before: "After so long a time have at last got Phillis's poems in print. . . . These don't seem to be near all her productions— She's an artful jade, I believe, & intends to have the benefit of another volume. . . ." It might have been a mistake to regard Phillis, at age 19 or 20, "an artful jade," but it would be no mistake to understand that the poems in the 1773 volume were not "near all her performances," and that she certainly did intend "to have the benefit of another volume," with or without the "importunity of her best and most generous friends."

The 1779 proposals for a second proposed volume of her writings included the titles for thirty-three poems and thirteen letters. Of these thirty-three titles, many are for poems known to have been written years earlier. In fact, one of these titles is dated, "Farewell to England 1773," written when she left London for a return to Boston in the summer of 1773. Two other titles are of poems which Phillis wrote in 1774. "To His Excellency General Washington" is the title for a poem she composed in Providence, Rhode Island, on "Oct. 26, 1775," and "On the Capture of General Lee, to J.B. Esq" is for a poem she wrote in "Boston, Decr. 30, 1776."

Most of the titles of the 13 letters listed in the 1779 proposals also go back many years earlier. "To the Right Hon. Countess H——" probably refers to the letter Phillis showed Wooldridge in the Fall of 1772, a copy of a letter Phillis wrote in 1770. Two other letter titles may refer to letters Phillis wrote to the countess from London in the summer of 1773. Six other letter titles refer to English friends she made while in London in the summer of 1773. Phillis had saved the manuscripts for some of these poems and letters for almost seven years. Such husbanding of one's written works is not usually done by one who would publish only at the importunity of her best and most generous friends. In any event, there were not enough such friends on hand in Boston when Phillis advertised her proposals for a second volume of her works on October 30, November 6 and 27, and December 4, 11, and 18 in the *Evening Post and General Advertiser*. Nor were such friends available later when, in the September, 1784, issue of *The Boston Magazine*, Phillis advertised for subscribers a final time. Her solicitations for Boston subscribers were rejected all seven times, and the volume ". . . of Poems,/ And/ Letters/ on Various Subjects,/ Dedicated to the Right Honourable,/ Benjamin Franklin Esq:/ One of the Ambassadors of the United States, at/ the Court of France," was never published in toto.

Nevertheless, she was able to write more than 100 poems and variants, to publish a collection of verses abroad, almost two dozen pieces as broadsides, pamphlets, and in magazines and newspapers throughout New England, in New York, Philadelphia, Williamsburg, London, Scotland, and Ireland—all within her brief lifetime. Drawing heavily on the vocabularies of the Bible, Latin epics, the patriotic cant of her day, and from a worn stock of neo-classical poetical expressions, her poetry can repeat themes, rimes, tropes excessively. Her punctuation and spelling, betraying her often hasty method of composition and her educational weaknesses, can be annoyingly erratic, so much so that to this day not all of her pieces are as clear as they might otherwise have been. Her persistent and sometimes strident piety can induce tedium. Considering the contemporary politics, the racist policy of the Continental Army and Navy, her steadfast American patriotism might strike all but "idealistically compatible" readers as downright incredulous, embarrassingly naive. But, over the years, Phillis had learned, perforce, how to maneuver in her various worlds of various and shifting allegiances: witness her diplomatic changes in her poems that were originally designed for American audiences, but were reshaped and eventually printed in London; witness her subtle and adroit handling of the pontifications of the millionaire Christian philanthropist, John Thornton of London, who addressed her in his one extant letter as "PH."

From the beginning of her poetic career in 1765, when she was about 11 years old, Phillis seems to have been aware that she was on constant display as a talented rara avis, a black oddity who read English and Latin and wrote acceptable poetry on acceptable topics. She may have wished to write more poems about things that struck her as poetic—piety, realms of nature, the eternal verities, the complexities of humanity—which need not have mentioned her color. But, a literary curiosity—to those unaware that blacks in 18th-century America and Europe had written and read and spoke in a variety of languages, including several American Indian dialects, Greek, Latin, Arabic Dutch, French, Spanish, and German—Phillis was made to be acutely aware of her blackness. As has been said, she injected her racial identity into a poem, often gratuitously, that was not even remotely concerned with her racial identity. But there are many of her pieces that are without racial identity, and in the last poem in her 1773 volume she identifies herself simply as ". . . The Author of These Poems." She was not always allowed to be so raceless. When she was not referring to herself as "Ethiop" or "Afric's muse," others—Mrs. Susanna Wheatley, white female ladies of quality, white printers of her pieces in newspapers and pamphlets and broadsides—inserted her race, just as extraneously as Phillis did. In both the many newspaper advertisements of her elegy on the death of the Reverend George Whitefield, and the elegy itself, as broadside or pamphlet, the various printers included copy that advised readers that the poem was the work of "Phillis, a Servant Girl of 17 Years of age, belonging to Mr. J. Wheatley, of Boston;—And has been but 9 Years in this/ country from Africa." A variant version of this elegy was printed in London with a headnote that pointed out that the poem was "Compos'd in America by a Negro/ Girl. . . ." Phillis's "Recollection" (in 58 lines) was printed in *The London Magazine, Or, Gentleman's Monthly Intelligencer* for March of 1772 with an introductory note by an anonymous American friend, "L," who informed the editor that the author of "Recollection" was ". . . a young *Negro woman*, who/ left her country at ten years of age, and has been in *this* eight years. . . ." A 1772 broadside elegy to Connecticut's Reverend Timothy Pitkin on the death of his wife includes, at the bottom of the page, a line, "The above Phillis Wheatley is a *Negro Girl*, about 18 Years/ Old, who has been in this country 11 Years." Joseph Greenleaf, editor of *The Royal American Magazine* ran a poem by Phillis in the December, 1774, issue, which prompted his observation, *"By particular request we insert the following Poem addressed, by/ Philis, (a young* Affrican, *of surprising genius) to a gentleman* of/ the navy, with his reply./ By this single instance may be seen the importance of education.—/ Uncultivated nature is much the same in every part of the globe./ It is probable Europe and Affrica would be alike savage or polite in the same circumstances; . . . ." Similarly in her 1772, 1773, 1779, and 1784 proposals was her race mentioned. Many times Phillis was so identified in a calculated if not subtle appeal to the sympathies or curiosities of potential buyers of her work; other times her race was mentioned as so much information. If literate Bostonians did not know that Phillis Wheatley was a black person, it could not be said to have been the fault of either Phillis or the promoters and printers of her poems.

Weaknesses, limitations, faults and all, Phillis could and did versify on a range of topics beyond Christian piety, and, to a limited extent, she worked beyond her favored heroic couplet, in blank verse, and other stanzaic patterns and meters. It is clear enough that she is much more subtle, more intellectually substantive than has been appreciated. It is also clear that she is much more the original poet than has been recognized. Her elegies, Latin translations, Biblical paraphrases are personally stylized and almost completely her own creations. That portion that makes up the best of her work stands as achieved poetry. Some of her pieces will be read as long as poetry is enjoyed.

Most important to many as an historical documentation of an atypically talented and privileged colonial, black Boston poet and woman, her life and work nevertheless deserve all of the continued attention that Phillis Wheatley has drawn.

Knowing, necessarily, all the while pretty much who and what and where she was—a black female poet in white America—she used her gifts for verse-making as a means of psychological survival, and as a repository for her deepest spiritual, Christian, patriotic, and racial interests. For her, the writing of poetry was a very real way of asserting her being, of documenting her Christian testimony, of declaring her aesthetic and human and racial worth in a world that could often seem like a menacing, impenetrable forest. Although she was fragile and sickly, gentle, kindly, and uncomplaining, she proved herself a worthy black American poet-pioneer. She led the way. As such, she lived, she lives, a very special life.

PHILLIS WHEATLEY'S EARLY POEMS
1765–1773

To the PRINTER.[1]

Please to insert the following Lines, composed by a Negro Girl (belonging to one Mr. Wheatley of Boston) on the following Occasion, viz. Messrs Hussey and Coffin, as undermentioned, belonging to Nantucket, being bound from thence to Boston, narrowly escaped being cast away on Cape Cod, in one of the late Storms; upon their Arrival, being at Mr. Wheatley's, and while at Dinner, told of their narrow Escape, this Negro Girl at the same Time 'tending Table, heard the Relation, from which she composed the following Verses.

On Messrs HUSSEY and COFFIN.

Did Fear and Danger so perplex your Mind,
As made you fearful of the Whistling Wind?
Was it not Boreas[2] knit his angry Brow
Against you? or did Consideration bow?
To lend you Aid, did not his Winds combine?
To stop your passage with a churlish Line,
Did haughty Eolus[3] with Contempt look down
With Aspect windy, and a study'd Frown?
Regard them not:—the Great Supreme, the Wise,
Intends for something hidden from our Eyes.
Suppose the groundless Gulph[4] had snatch'd away
Hussey and Coffin to the raging Sea;
Where would they go? where wou'd be their Abode?
With the supreme and independent God,
Or made their Beds down in the Shades below,
Where neither Pleasure nor Content can stow.
To Heaven their Souls with eager Raptures soar,
Enjoy the Bliss of him they wou'd adore.

1. Although she had been composing poems and writing letters since 1765, this is the first known published poem by Phillis Wheatley. It appeared in the *Newport* (R.I.) *Mercury* for December 21, 1767. The headnote was probably written by her mistress, Mrs. Susanna Wheatley. In her Proposals for 1772, see below, Phillis dated (and misdated) sixteen of her early poems; there she says that this poem was composed in 1766, but see the *Providence Gazette and Country Journal* (10 October 1767), p. 3: "Boston, October 5. Capt. Coffin, in a schooner, loaded with oil, was cast ashore in the storm mentioned in our last on the back of Cape Cod, but the vessell has since been got off and arrived here yesterday. . . . The oldest Seamen say they never experienced a more terrible gale."
2. *Boreas.* The North wind.
3. *Eolus (or Aeolus).* King of the four winds in Greek mythology.
4. *Gulph* (i.e., Gulf). Cape Cod Bay.

Had the soft gliding Streams of Grace been near,
Some favourite Hope their fainting hearts to cheer,
Doubtless the Fear of Danger far had fled:
No more repeated Victory crown their Heads.

Had I the Tongue of a Seraphim, how would I exalt thy
Praise; thy Name as Incense to the Heavens should fly, and the
Remembrance of thy Goodness to the shoreless Ocean of Beati/
tude! Then should the Earth glow with seraphick Ardour.

Blest Soul, which sees the Day while Light doth shine,
To guide his Steps to trace the Mark divine,

Phillis Wheatley.

An Address to the Atheist,/
By P. Wheatley at the age of
14 Years—1767[1]

Muse! where shall I begin the spacious feild
To tell what curses unbeleif doth yield?
Thou who dost daily feel his hand, and rod
Darest thou deny the Essence of a God?
If there's no heav'n, ah! whither wilt thou go,
Make thy Ilysium in the shades below?
If there's no God from whom did all things Spring
He made the *greatest* and *minutest* Thing
Angelic ranks no less his Power display
Than the least mite scarce visible to Day
With vast astonishment my soul is struck
Have Reason's powers thy darken'd breast forsook?
The Laws deep Graven by the hand of God,
Seal'd with Immanuel's all-redeeming blood:
This second point thy folly dares deny
On thy devoted head for vengeance cry
Turn then I pray thee from the dangerous road
Rise from the dust and seek the mighty God
His is bright truth without a dark disguise
And his are wisdom's all beholding Eyes:
With labour'd snares our Adversary great
Witholds from us the Kingdom and the seat
Bliss weeping waits thee, in her arms to fly
To her own regions of felicity
Perhaps thy ignorance will ask us where?
Go to the *Corner stone* he will declare.
Thy heart in unbeleif will harden'd grow
Tho' much indulg'd in vicious pleasure now—
Thou tak'st unusual means; the path forbear
Unkind to others to thyself severe
Methinks I see the consequence thou'rt blind
Thy unbeleif disturbs the peaceful Mind.
The endless scene too far for me to tread
Too great to utter from so weak a head.
That man his maker's love divine might know
In heavens high firmament he placed his Bow

1. The manuscript is in the Massachusetts Historical Society.

To shew his covenant for ever sure
To endless Age unchanging to endure
He made the Heavens and earth, that lasting Spring
Of admiration! To whom dost thou bring
Thy grateful tribute? Adoration pay
To heathen Gods? Can wise *Apollo* say
Tis I that saves thee from the deepest hell;
Minerva teach thee all thy days to tell?
Doth *Pluto* tell thee thou shalt see the shade
Of fell perdition for transgression made?
Doth *Cupid* in thy breast that warmth inspire
To love thy Brother, which is God's desire?
Atheist! behold the wide extended skys
And wisdom infinite shall strike thine eyes.
Mark rising Sol when far he spreads his Ray
And his commission read—"To rule the Day"
At night behold ~~the~~ its[2] silver Regent bright
And her command to lead the train of night
Lo! how the stars all vocal in his praise
Witness his Essence in celestial lays!

2. Phillis had first written "the" but wrote "its" over that word. See "Phillis
Wheatley's Variant Poems and Letters," below, for other versions of this verse.
Most of Wheatley's manuscript verses, and their revisions, included very little
punctuation.

An address to the Deist 1767[1]

Must Ethiopians be employ'd for you?
Much I rejoice if any good I do.
I ask O unbeliever, Satan's child
Hath not thy Saviour been too much revil'd
Th'auspicious rays that round his temples shine
Do still declare him to be Christ divine.
Doth not the great *Eternal* call him Son
Is he not pleas'd with his beloved One—?
How canst thou thus divide the Trinity
The blest the Holy the eternal three
Tis Satan's snares are fluttering in the wind
Whereby he doth ensnare thy foolish mind
God, the Eternal Orders this to be
Sees thy vain arg'ments to divide the three
Cans't thou not see the Consequence in store?
Begin th'Almighty monarch to adore?
Attend to Reason whispering in thine ear
Seek the Eternal while he is so near.
Full in thy view I point each path I know
Lest to the vale of black dispair I go
At the last day where wilt thou hide thy face
That Day approaching is no time for Grace
Too late percieve thyself undone and lost
To [sic] late own Father, Son, and Holy Ghost.
Who trod the wine-press of Jehovah's wrath?
Who taught us prayer, and promis'd grace and faith?
Who but the Son, who reigns supremely blest
Ever, and ever, in immortal rest?
The vilest prodigal who comes to God
Is not cast out but bro't by Jesus's blood
When to the faithless Jews he oft did cry
Some own'd their teacher some made him a lye[2]
He came to you in mean apparel clad
He came to save us from our sins, and had
Compassion more than language can express.
Pains his companions, and his friends distress
Immanuel on the cross those pains did bear

1. The manuscript is in the Massachusetts Historical Society. See "Phillis Wheatley's Variant Poems and Letters," below, for another version of this piece.
2. *Lye.* I.e., lie.

Will the eternal our petitions hear?
Ah! wond'rous Destiny his life he laid
"Father forgive them," thus the Saviour pray'd
Nail'd was king Jesus on the cross for us
For our transgressions he sustain'd the Curse.

America[1]

New England first a wilderness was found
Till for a continent 'twas destin'd round
From feild to feild the savage monsters run
E'r yet Brittania had her work begun
Thy Power, O Liberty, makes strong the weak
And (wond'rous instinct) Ethiopians speak
Sometimes by Simile, a victory's won
A certain lady had an only son
He grew up daily virtuous as he grew
Fearing his Strength which she undoubted knew
She laid some taxes on her darling son
And would have laid another act there on
Amend your manners I'll the task remove
Was said with seeming Sympathy and Love
By many Scourges she his goodness try'd
Untill at length the Best of Infants cry'd
He wept, Brittania turn'd a senseless ear
At last awaken'd by maternal fear
Why weeps americus why weeps my Child
Thus spake Brittania, thus benign and mild
My dear mama said he, shall I repeat—
Then Prostrate fell, at her maternal feet
What ails the rebel, Great Brittania Cry'd
Indeed said he, you have no cause to Chide
You see each day my fluent tears my food.
Without regard, what no more English blood?
Has length of time drove from our English veins.
The kindred he to Great Brittania deigns?
Tis thus with thee O Brittain keeping down
New English force, thou fear'st his Tyranny and thou didst frown
He weeps afresh to feel this Iron chain
Turn, O Brittania claim thy child again
Riech[2] o Love drive by thy powerful charms
Indolence Slumbering in forgetful arms
See Agenoria[3] deligent imploy's
Her sons, and thus with rapture she replys

1. Phillis's 1772 proposals list this poem as having been composed in 1768. The manuscript is in the Library Company of Philadelphia.
2. Reach? Phillis's spelling and punctuation were sometimes peculiar.
3. *Agenoria*. England.

Arise my sons with one consent arise
Lest distant continents with vult'ring eyes
Should charge America with Negligence
They praise Industry but no pride commence
To raise their own Profusion, O Brittain See
By this New England will increase like thee

On Friendship[1]

Let Amicitia[2] in her ample reign
Extend her notes to a celestial strain
Benevolent far more divinely bright
Amor like me doth triumph at the sight
When to my thoughts in gratitude imploy
Mental imaginations give me joy
Now let my thoughts in contemplation steer
The footsteps of the superlative fair

Phillis Wheatley

Boston
July 15, 1769

1. A photocopy of this manuscript is in the Moorland-Spingarn Research Center at Howard University. In her 1772 proposals, Phillis noted that this poem was composed in 1768. The above dated piece may be a revision of a non-extant 1768 version, or Phillis may have misremembered the date of composition.
2. *Amicitia.* Latin for "Friendship."

137

To the Honble Commodore Hood[1] on his pardoning a deserter[2]

It was thy noble soul and high desert
That caus'd these breathings of my grateful heart
You sav'd a soul from Pluto's dreary shore
You sav'd his body and he asks no more
This generous act Immortal wreaths shall bring
To thee for meritorious was the spring
From whence from whence, this candid ardor flow'd
To grace thy name, and Glorify thy God
The Eatherial spirits in the realms above
Rejoice to see thee exercise thy love
Hail Commodore may heaven delighted pour
Its blessings plenteous in a silent shower
The voice of pardon did resound on high
While heaven consented, and he must not die
On thee fair victor be The Blessings shed
And rest for ever on thy matchless Head

                                                Phillis

---

1. The manuscript is in the Library Company of Philadelphia. Commodore Samuel Hood (1724–1816) commanded the North American station, based at Boston, from 1767 through 1770.

2. From the *London Gentleman's Magazine, and Historical Chronicle* 39 (February, 1769), 105: "Boston, New England, Dec. 2. At a court martial aboard the Mermaid two sailors were sentenced to be flogged and one to be hanged; but just as sentence was to be executed upon the latter a reprieve arrived for him from Commodore Hood."

On the death of Mr Snider Murder'd by Richardson[1]

In heavens eternal court it was decreed
How the first martyr for the cause should bleed
To clear the country of the hated brood
He whet his courage for the common good
Long hid before, a vile infernal here
Prevents Achilles[2] in his mid career
Where'er this fury darts his Pois'nous breath
All are endanger'd to the shafts of death

1. In her 1772 proposals, Phillis reports this poem as having been composed in 1770. On February 23, 1770, Christopher Snider (also spelled Snyder, Seider, Sneider), an eleven-year-old Boston boy, was caught up in the fury of a crowd of local Patriots who were besieging the North End importing shop of a Tory, Theophilus Lily, who had defiantly refused to sign the locally popular Non-Importation Agreement that was designed to resist British tax ambitions on the colonies. A boisterous Tory and neighbor, Ebenezer Richardson, tried to help his fellow Tory friend, but was instead driven into his own home by the mob's mounting pressures; they smashed down his front door, and a hurled rock struck his wife. From a second-story window, in goaded desparation, Richardson shot into the jeering crowds below. With eleven slugs of swanshot (pea-sized pellets) in his chest and stomach, young Snider fell, and, despite emergency medical attention, "the young champion" died at nine o'clock that night, becoming thereby "the first martyr for the cause." Town church bells tolled mournfully, broadsides and newspapers lamented the death in heroic and propagandistic terms; fiery sermons against the British were preached on the following Sunday. Zealous Patriots, under the exploitive genius of the likes of Samuel Adams, made the most of the death and the funeral. Led by six of Snider's schoolmates, who bore the casket featuring patriotic Latin inscriptions on each of its sides, and followed by the family and friends of the deceased, 400 or 500 other schoolchildren, and thousands of mourners, the funeral procession was almost one mile long from its symbolic starting place at the Liberty Tree. It was the largest such procession in Boston's history. Snider was interred at the Old Granary Burial Grounds, on today's Tremont Street. Richardson was almost lynched on the spot, but was dragged from the scene of the killing to Fanueil Hall for trial, where an even greater crowd of over one thousand spectators heard him declared guilty of murder. However, claiming that Richardson acted in self-defense, the Tory Governor Hutchinson refused to sign the death warrant, and after a two-year imprisonment, Richardson was pardoned and freed by the King. Equating local Patriots with "generous Sires," and likening local Tories to "the hated brood" and "grand Usurpers" and "fair freedoms foes," this piece is the strongest of several pro-American and anti-British statements by Wheatley. The manuscript is in the Historical Society of Pennsylvania.
2. *Achilles.* The Greek hero of the classical poem, *The Illiad*, a work much admired by Wheatley. Phillis hopes that her readers will be reminded that, like young Snider, Achilles was cut off "in his mid career."

The generous Sires beheld the fatal wound
Saw their young champion gasping on the ground
They rais'd him up but to each present ear
What martial glories did his tongue declare
The wretch appal'd no longer can despise
But from the Striking victim[3] turns his eyes—
When this young martial genius did appear
The Tory chiefs no longer could forbear.
Ripe for destruction, see the wretches doom
He waits the curses of the age to come
In vain he flies, by Justice Swifty chaced
With unexpected infamy disgraced
Be Richardson for ever banish'd here
The grand Usurpers bravely vaunted Heir.
We bring the body from the wat'ry bower[4]
To lodge it where it shall remove no more
Snider behold with what Majestic Love
The Illustrious retinue begins to move
With Secret rage fair freedoms foes beneath
See in thy corse ev'n Majesty in Death

Phillis

---

3. *Striking victim.* Phillis may have meant to write "Stricken victim."
4. *We bring the body from the wat'ry bower.* Phillis seems to imagine that a group of sympathetic bystanders lifts Snider's mortally wounded body from the street that was becoming slushy from snow that was falling at the time.

POEMS
ON
VARIOUS OCCASIONS,
RELIGIOUS And MORAL
By
Phillis Wheatley
A Facsimile

PHILLIS WHEATLEY, NEGRO SERVANT to Mr JOHN WHEATLEY, of BOSTON.

Published according to Act of Parliament, Sept.ᵗ 1, 1773 by Arch.ᵈ Bell.

Bookseller Nᵒ 8 near the Saracens Head Aldgate.

Phillis Wheatley

P O E M S [1]

O N

VARIOUS SUBJECTS,

RELIGIOUS and MORAL.

BY

PHILLIS WHEATLEY,

NEGRO SERVANT to Mr. JOHN WHEATLEY,
of BOSTON, in NEW ENGLAND.

L O N D O N:

Printed for A. BELL, Bookseller, Aldgate; and sold by
Messrs. COX and BERRY, King-Street, *BOSTON*.
M DCC LXXIII.

Entered at Stationer's Hall.

DEDICATION.

To the Right Honourable the

COUNTESS of HUNTINGDON,

THE FOLLOWING

P O E M S

Are moſt reſpectfully

Inſcribed,

By her much obliged,

Very humble,

And devoted Servant,

Phillis Wheatley.

Boſton, June 12, [1]
1773.

PREFACE.

THE following POEMS were written originally for the Amusement of the Author, as they were the Products of her leisure Moments. She had no Intention ever to have published them; nor would they now have made their Appearance, but at the Importunity of many of her best, and most generous Friends; to whom she considers herself, as under the greatest Obligations.

As her Attempts in Poetry are now sent into the World, it is hoped the Critic will not severely censure their Defects; and we presume they have too much Merit to to be caſt aſide with Contempt, as worthleſs and trifling Effuſions.

As to the Diſadvantages ſhe has laboured under, with Regard to Learning, nothing needs to be of-fered, as her Maſter's Letter in the following Page will ſufficiently ſhew the Difficulties in this Reſpect ſhe had to encounter.

With all their Imperfections, the Poems are now humbly ſubmitted to the Peruſal of the Public.

The

The following is a Copy of a LETTER sent by the Author's Master to the Publisher.[1]

PHILLIS was brought from *Africa* to *America*, in the Year 1761, between Seven and Eight Years of Age. Without any Affittance from School Education, and by only what she was taught in the Family, she, in sixteen Months Time from her Arrival, attained the English Language, to which she was an utter Stranger before, to such a Degree, as to read any, the moft difficult Parts of the Sacred Writings, to the great Aftonishment of all who heard her.

As to her WRITING, her own Curiofity led her to it; and this she learnt in fo fhort a Time, that in the Year 1765, she wrote a Letter to the Rev. Mr. Occom, the *Indian* Minifter, while in *England*.[2]

She has a great Inclination to learn the Latin Tongue, and has made fome Progrefs in it.[3] This Relation is given by her Mafter who bought her, and with whom she now lives.

JOHN WHEATLEY.

Bofton, Nov. 14, 1772.

149

To the PUBLICK.[1]

AS it has been repeatedly suggested to the Publisher, by Persons, who have seen the Manuscript, that Numbers would be ready to suspect they were not really the Writings of PHILLIS, he has procured the following Attestation, from the most respectable Characters in Boston, that none might have the least Ground for disputing their original. [2]

WE whose Names are under-written, do assure the World, that the POEMS specified in the following Page, * were (as we verily believe) written by PHILLIS, a young Negro Girl, who was but a few Years since, brought an uncultivated Barbarian from Africa, and has ever since been, and now is, under the Disadvantage of serving as a Slave in a Family in this Town. She has been examined by some of the best Judges, and is thought qualified to write them.

His Excellency THOMAS HUTCINSON,[3] *Governor,*

The Hon. ANDREW OLIVER, *Lieutenant-Governor.* [4]

The Hon. Thomas Hubbard,	*The Rev.* Charles Chauncy, *D.D.*
The Hon. John Erving,	*The Rev.* Mather Byles, *D. D.* [5]
The Hon. James Pitts,	*The Rev* Ed. Pemberton, *D.D.*
The Hon. Harrison Gray,	*The Rev.* Andrew Elliot, *D.D.*
The Hon. James Bowdoin,	*The Rev.* Samuel Cooper, *D.D.*
John Hancock, *Esq;*	*The Rev. Mr.* Samuel Mather,
Joseph Green, *Esq;*	*The Rev. Mr.* John Moorhead,
Richard Carey, *Esq;*	*Mr.* John Wheatley, *her Master.*

N. B. The original Attestation, signed by the above Gentlemen, may be seen by applying to *Archibald Bell*, Bookseller, No. 8, *Aldgate-Street.* [6]

---

* The Words "*following Page,*" allude to the Contents of the Manuscript Copy, which are wrote at the Back of the above Attestation.

P O E M S

O N

VARIOUS SUBJECTS.

To M Æ C E N A S.[1]

M Æ C E N A S, you, beneath the myrtle
    shade,
Read o'er what poets sung, and shepherds play'd.
What felt those poets but you feel the same?
Does not your soul possess the sacred flame?
Their noble strains your equal genius shares   5
In softer language, and diviner airs.

   While *Homer* paints lo! circumfus'd in air,
Celestial Gods in mortal forms appear;

Swift as they move hear each recefs rebound,
Heav'n quakes, earth trembles, and the fhores re-
 found.   10
Great Sire of verfe, before my mortal eyes,
The lightnings blaze acrofs the vaulted fkies,
And, as the thunder fhakes the heav'nly plains,
A deep-felt horror thrills through all my veins. ³
When gentler ftrains demand thy graceful fong, 15
The length'ning line moves languifhing along.
When great *Patroclus* courts *Achilles*' aid,
The grateful tribute of my tears is paid;
Prone on the fhore he feels the pangs of love,
And ftern *Pelides* ⁴tend'reft paffions move.   20

Great *Maro*'s⁵ ftrain in heav'nly numbers flows,
The *Nine*⁶ infpire, and all the bofom glows.
O could I rival thine and *Virgil*'s page,
Or claim the *Mufes* with the *Mantuan* Sage;
Soon the fame beauties fhould my mind adorn, 25
And the fame ardors in my foul fhould burn:
Then fhould my fong in bolder notes arife,
And all my numbers pleafingly furprize;
            But

But here I sit, and mourn a grov'ling mind,
That fain would mount, and ride upon the wind.

Not you, my friend, these plaintive strains be-
come,
Not you, whose bosom is the *Muses* home;
When they from tow'ring *Helicon* retire,
They fan in you the bright immortal fire,
But I less happy, cannot raise the song,   35
The fault'ring music dies upon my tongue.

The happier *Terence* * all the choir inspir'd,
His soul replenish'd, and his bosom fir'd;
But say, ye *Muses*, why this partial grace,
To one alone of *Afric*'s sable race;   40
From age to age transmitting thus his name
With the first glory in the rolls of fame? [8]

Thy virtues, great *Mæcenas!* shall be sung
In praise of him, from whom those virtues sprung:

* He was an *African* by birth.

B 2   While

While blooming wreaths around thy temples
    spread,   45
I'll ſnatch a laurel from thine honour'd head,
While you indulgent ſmile upon the deed.

As long as *Thames* in ſtreams majeſtic flows,
Or *Naiads* in their oozy beds repoſe,
While *Phœbus* reigns above the ſtarry train,   50
While bright *Aurora* purples o'er the main,
So long, great Sir, the muſe thy praiſe ſhall ſing,
So long thy praiſe ſhall make *Parnaſſus* ring :
Then grant, *Mœcenas*, thy paternal rays,
Hear me propitious, and defend my lays.   55

On

On VIRTUE.

O Thou bright jewel in my aim I ftrive
 To comprehend thee. Thine own words
  declare
Wifdom is higher than a fool can reach.
I ceafe to wonder, and no more attempt
Thine height t' explore, or fathom thy profound. 5
But, O my foul, fink not into defpair,
Virtue is near thee, and with gentle hand
Would now embrace thee, hovers o'er thine head.
Fain would the heav'n-born foul with her converfe,
Then feek, then court her for her promis'd blifs.

Aufpicious queen, thine heav'nly pinions fpread,
And lead celeftial *Chaftity* along ;
Lo ! now her facred retinue defcends,
Array'd in glory from the orbs above.
Attend me, *Virtue*, thro' my youthful years ! 15
O leave me not to the falfe joys of time !
But guide my fteps to endlefs life and blifs.

Greatnefs,

155

Greatneſs, or *Goodneſs*, ſay what I ſhall call thee,
To give an higher appellation ſtill,
Teach me a better ſtrain, a nobler lay,   20
O thou, enthron'd with Cherubs in the realms of
    day !

To

To the University of CAMBRIDGE, in NEW-ENGLAND.[1]

WHILE an intrinfic ardor prompts to write,
 The mufes promife to affift my pen ;
'Twas not long fince I left my native fhore
The land of errors, and *Egyptian* gloom :
Father of mercy, 'twas thy gracious hand 5
Brought me in fafety from thofe dark abodes.

Students, to you 'tis giv'n to fcan the heights
Above, to traverfe the ethereal fpace,
And mark the fyftems of revolving worlds.
Still more, ye fons of fcience ye receive 10
The blifsful news by meffengers from heav'n,
How *Jefus'* blood for your redemption flows.
See him with hands out-ftretcht upon the crofs ;
Immenfe compaffion in his bofom glows ;
He hears revilers, nor refents their fcorn : 15
What matchlefs mercy in the Son of God !
When the whole human race by fin had fall'n, 2

           He

He deign'd to die that they might rife again,
And fhare with him in the fublimeft fkies,
Life without death, and glory without end.   20

 Improve your privileges while they ftay,
Ye pupils, and each hour redeem, that bears
Or good or bad report of you to heav'n.
Let fin, that baneful evil to the foul,
By you be fhunn'd, nor once remit your guard;   25
Supprefs the deadly ferpent in its egg.
Ye blooming plants of human race divine,
An *Ethiop* tells you 'tis your greateft foe;
Its tranfient fweetnefs turns to endlefs pain,
And in immenfe perdition finks the foul.   30

To

To the K I N G's Moſt Excellent Majeſty.
1768. [1]

YOUR ſubjeƈts hope, dread Sire—
The crown upon your brows may flouriſh
long,
And that your arm may in your God be ſtrong!
O may your ſceptre num'rous nations ſway,
And all with love and readineſs obey!

But how ſhall we the *Britiſh* king reward!   5
Rule thou in peace, our father, and our lord!
Midſt the remembrance of thy favours paſt,
The meaneſt peaſants moſt admire the laſt. *
May *George*, belov'd by all the nations round,
Live with heav'ns choiceſt conſtant bleſſings
crown'd! [2]   10
Great God, direƈt, and guard him from on high,
And from his head let ev'ry evil fly!
And may each clime with equal gladneſs ſee
A monarch's ſmile can ſet his ſubjeƈts free!

* The Repeal of the Stamp Aƈt.

C   Oı

On being brought from A F R I C A to A M E R I C A.[1]

'TWAS mercy brought me from my *Pagan*
      land,
Taught my benighted foul to underftand
That there's a God, that there's a *Saviour* too:
Once I redemption neither fought nor knew.
Some view our fable race with fcornful eye,   5
" Their colour is a diabolic die."
Remember, *Chriftians*, *Negros*, black as *Cain*,
May be refin'd, and join th' angelic train.

On

On the Death of the Rev. Dr. SEWELL. 1769.[1]

ERE yet the morn its lovely blushes spread,
See *Sewell* number'd with the happy dead.
Hail, holy man, arriv'd th' immortal shore,
Though we shall hear thy warning voice no more.
Come, let us all behold with wishful eyes   5
The saint ascending to his native skies;
From hence the prophet wing'd his rapt'rous way
To the blest mansions in eternal day.
Then begging for the Spirit of our God,
And panting eager for the same abode,   10
Come, let us all with the same vigour rise,
And take a prospect of the blisful skies;
While on our minds *Christ's* image is imprest,
And the dear Saviour glows in ev'ry breast.
Thrice happy saint! to find thy heav'n at last,   15
What compensation for the evils past!

C 2   Great

Great God, incomprehensible, unknown
By sense, we bow at thine exalted throne.
O, while we beg thine excellence to feel,
Thy sacred Spirit to our hearts reveal,   20
And give us of that mercy to partake,
Which thou hast promis'd for the *Saviour's* fake!

" *Sewell* is dead."   Swift-pinion'd *Fame* thus
    cry'd.
" Is *Sewell* dead," my trembling tongue reply'd,
O what a blessing in his flight deny'd !   25
How oft for us the holy prophet pray'd !
How oft to us the Word of Life convey'd !
By duty urg'd my mournful verse to close,
I for his tomb this epitaph compose.

" Lo, here a man, redeem'd by *Jesus'* blood, 30
" A finner once, but now a faint with God ;
" Behold ye rich, ye poor, ye fools, ye wife,
" Nor let his monument your heart surprize ;
" 'Twill tell you what this holy man has done,
" Which gives him brighter luftre than the fun.
                         " Liften,

" Liften, ye happy, from your feats above.

" I fpeak fincerely, while I fpeak and love,

" He fought the paths of piety and truth,

" By thefe made happy from his early youth!

" In blooming years that grace divine he felt,   40

" Which refcues finners from the chains of guilt.

" Mourn him, ye indigent, whom he has fed,

" And henceforth feek, like him, for living bread ;

" Ev'n *Chrift*, the bread defcending from above,

" And afk an int'reft in his faving-love.   45

" Mourn him, ye youth, to whom he oft has told

" God's gracious wonders from the times of old.

" I, too have caufe this mighty lofs to mourn,

" For he my monitor will not return.

" O when fhall we to his bleft ftate arrive?   50

" When the fame graces in our bofoms thrive."

On

On the Death of the Rev. Mr. G E O R G E
WHITEFIELD. 1770.[1]

HAIL, happy faint, on thine immortal throne,
Poffeft of glory, life, and blifs unknown;
We hear no more the mufic of thy tongue,
Thy wonted auditories ceafe to throng.
Thy fermons in unequall'd accents flow'd,   5
And ev'ry bofom with devotion glow'd;
Thou didft in ftrains of eloquence refin'd
Inflame the heart, and captivate the mind.
Unhappy we the fetting fun deplore,
So glorious once, but ah! it fhines no more.   10

Behold the prophet in his tow'ring flight!
He leaves the earth for heav'n's unmeafur'd
    height,
And worlds unknown receive him from our fight.
There *Whitefield* wings with rapid courfe his way,
And fails to *Zion* through vaft feas of day.   15
Thy pray'rs, great faint, and thine inceffant cries
Have pierc'd the bofom of thy native fkies.

Thou

Thou moon haſt ſeen, and all the ſtars of light,
How he has wreſtled with his God by night.
He pray'd that grace in ev'ry heart might dwell, 20
He long'd to ſee *America* excel;
He charg'd its youth that ev'ry grace divine
Should with full luſtre in their conduct ſhine;
That Saviour, which his ſoul did firſt receive,
The greateſt gift that ev'n a God can give, 25
He freely offer'd to the num'rous throng,
That on his lips with liſt'ning pleaſure hung.

" Take him, ye wretched, for your only good,
" Take him ye ſtarving ſinners, for your food;
" Ye thirſty, come to this life-giving ſtream, 30
" Ye preachers, take him for your joyful theme;
" Take him my dear *Americans,* he ſaid,
" Be your complaints on his kind boſom laid:
" Take him, ye *Africans,* he longs for you,
" *Impartial Saviour* is his title due: 35
" Waſh'd in the fountain of redeeming blood,
" You ſhall be ſons, and kings, and prieſts to God."

Great

Great *Countefs*, * we *Americans* revere
Thy name, and mingle in thy grief fincere;
New England deeply feels, the *Orphans* mourn, 40
Their more than father will no more return.

But, though arrefted by the hand of death,
Whitefield no more exerts his lab'ring breath,
Yet let us view him in th' eternal fkies,
Let ev'ry heart to this bright vifion rife;   45
While the tomb fafe retains its facred truft,
Till life divine re-animates his duft.

* The Countefs of *Huntingdon*, to whom Mr. *Whitefield*
was Chaplain.

On

On the Death of a young Lady of Five Years of Age. [1]

FROM dark abodes to fair etherial light
   Th' enraptur'd innocent has wing'd her flight;
On the kind bofom of eternal love
She finds unknown beatitude above.
This know, ye parents, nor her lofs deplore,   5
She feels the iron hand of pain no more;
The difpenfations of unerring grace,
Should turn your forrows into grateful praife;
Let then no tears for her henceforward flow,
No more diftrefs'd in our dark vale below.   10

Her morning fun, which rofe divinely bright,
Was quickly mantled with the gloom of night;
But hear in heav'n's bleft bow'rs your *Nancy* fair;
And learn to imitate her language there.
" Thou, Lord, whom I behold with glory crown'd,
" By what fweet name, and in what tuneful found

D   " Wilt

" Wilt thou be prais'd ? Seraphic pow'rs are faint
" Infinite love and majesty to paint.
" To thee let all their grateful voices raise,
" And saints and angels join their songs of
    " praise."   20

Perfect in bliss she from her heav'nly home
Looks down, and smiling beckons you to come;
Why then, fond parents, why these fruitless groans ?
Restrain your tears, and cease your plaintive moans.
Freed from a world of sin, and snares, and pain, 25
Why would you wish your daughter back again ?
No – bow resign'd.   Let hope your grief control,
And check the rising tumult of the soul.
Calm in the prosperous, and adverse day,
Adore the God who gives and takes away ;   30
Eye him in all, his holy name revere,
Upright your actions, and your hearts sincere,
Till having sail'd through life's tempestuous sea,
And from its rocks, and boist'rous billows free,
Yourselves, safe landed on the blisful shore, 35
Shall join your happy babe to part no more.

                                    OR

On the Death of a young Gentleman.

WHO taught thee conflict with the pow'rs
    of night,
To vanquish Satan in the fields of fight?
Who strung thy feeble arms with might unknown,
How great thy conquest, and how bright thy
    crown!
War with each princedom, throne, and pow'r
    is o'er,   5
The scene is ended to return no more.
O could my muse thy seat on high behold,
How deckt with laurel, how enrich'd with gold!
O could she hear what praise thine harp em-
    ploys,
How sweet thine anthems, how divine thy joys! 10
What heav'nly grandeur should exalt her strain!
What holy raptures in her numbers reign!
To sooth the troubles of the mind to peace,
To still the tumult of life's tossing seas,

D 2   To

To eafe the anguifh of the parents heart,   15
What fhall my fympathizing verfe impart ?
Where is the balm to heal fo deep a wound ?
Where fhall a fov'reign remedy be found ?
Look, gracious Spirit, from thine heav'nly bow'r,
And thy full joys into their bofoms pour ;   20
The raging tempeft of their grief control,
And fpread the dawn of glory through the foul,
To eye the path the faint departed trod,
And trace him to the bofom of his God.

To

To a Lady on the Death of her Hufband.[1]

GRIM monarch ! fee, depriv'd of vital breath,
A young phyfician in the duft of death :
Doft thou go on inceffant to deftroy,
Our griefs to double, and lay wafte our joy ?
Enough thou never yet waft known to fay, 5
Though millions die, the vaffals of thy fway :
Nor youth, nor fcience, nor the ties of love,
Nor aught on earth thy flinty heart can move.
The friend, the fpoufe from his dire dart to fave,
In vain we afk the fovereign of the grave. 10
Fair mourner, there fee thy lov'd *Leonard* laid,
And o'er him fpread the deep impervious fhade ;
Clos'd are his eyes, and heavy fetters keep
His fenfes bound in never-waking fleep,
Till time fhall ceafe, till many a ftarry world 15
Shall fall from heav'n, in dire confufion hurl'd,
Till nature in her final wreck fhall lie,
And her laft groan fhall rend the azure fky : [2]

Not

Not, not till then his active soul shall claim
His body, a divine immortal frame.   20

    But see the softly-stealing tears apace
Pursue each other down the mourner's face;
But cease thy tears, bid ev'ry sigh depart,
And cast the load of anguish from thine heart:
From the cold shell of his great soul arise,   25
And look beyond, thou native of the skies;
There fix thy view, where fleeter than the wind
Thy *Leonard* mounts, and leaves the earth behind.
Thyself prepare to pass the vale of night
To join for ever on the hills of light: 30
To thine embrace his joyful spirit moves
To thee, the partner of his earthly loves;
He welcomes thee to pleasures more refin'd,
And better suited to th' immortal mind.

G O L I.

G O L I A T H of G A T H.
1 SAM. Chap. xvii. [1]

YE martial pow'rs, and all ye tuneful nine,
Infpire my fong, and aid my high defign.
The dreadful fcenes and toils of war I write,
The ardent warriors, and the fields of fight :
You beft remember, and you befl can fing   5
The acts of heroes to the vocal ftring :
Refume the lays with which your facred lyre,
Did then the poet and the fage infpire.

Now front to front the armies were difplay'd,
Here *Ifrael* rang'd, and there the foes array'd ;   10
The hofts on two oppofing mountains ftood,
Thick as the foliage of the waving wood ;
Between them an extenfive valley lay,
O'er which the gleaming armour pour'd the day,
When from the camp of the *Philiftine* foes,   15
Dreadful to view, a mighty warrior rofe ;
In the dire deeds of bleeding battle fkill'd,
The monfter ftalks the terror of the field.

From

From *Gath* he fprung, *Goliath* was his name,
Of fierce deportment, and gigantic frame :   20
A brazen helmet on his head was plac'd,
A coat of mail his form terrific grac'd,
The greaves his legs, the targe his fhoulders preft :
Dreadful in arms high-tow'ring o'er the reft
A fpear he proudly wav'd, whofe iron head,   25
Strange to relate, fix hundred fhekels weigh'd ;
He ftrode along, and fhook the ample field,
While *Phœbus* blaz'd refulgent on his fhield :
Through *Jacob's* race a chilling horror ran,
When thus the huge, enormous chief began :   30

" Say, what the caufe that in this proud array
" You fet your battle in the face of day ?
" One hero find in all your vaunting train,
" Then fee who lofes, and who wins the plain ;
" For he who wins, in triumph may demand   35
" Perpetual fervice from the vanquifh'd land :
" Your armies I defy, your force defpife,
" By far inferior in *Philiftia's* eyes :

" Produce

" Produce a man, and let us try the fight,
" Decide the conteſt, and the victor's right." 40

Thus challeng'd he: all *Iſrael* ſtood amaz'd,
And ev'ry chief in conſternation gaz'd;
But *Jeſſe's* ſon in youthful bloom appears,
And warlike courage far beyond his years:
He left the folds, he left the flow'ry meads, 45
And ſoft receſſes of the ſylvan ſhades.
Now *Iſrael's* monarch, and his troops ariſe,
With peals of ſhouts aſcending to the ſkies;
In *Elah's* vale the ſcene of combat lies.

When the fair morning bluſh'd with orient
red, 50
What *David's* ſire enjoin'd the ſon obey'd,
And ſwift of foot towards the trench he came,
Where glow'd each boſom with the martial flame.
He leaves his carriage to another's care,
And runs to greet his brethren of the war. 55
While yet they ſpake the giant-chief aroſe,
Repeats the challenge, and inſults his foes:

E   Struck

Struck with the found, and trembling at the view,
Affrighted *Ifrael* from its poft withdrew.
" Obferve ye this tremendous foe, they cry'd, 60
" Who in proud vaunts our armies hath defy'd :
" Whoever lays him proftrate on the plain,
" Freedom in *Ifrael* for his houfe fhall gain ;
" And on him wealth unknown the king will pour,
" And give his royal daughter for his dow'r." 65

      Then *Jeffe's* youngeft hope : " My brethren
         " fay,
" What fhall be done for him who takes away
" Reproach from *Jacob*, who deftroys the chief,
" And puts a period to his country's grief.
" He vaunts the honours of his arms abroad, 70
" And fcorns the armies of the living God."

Thus fpoke the youth, th' attentive people ey'd
The wond'rous hero, and again reply'd :
" Such the rewards our monarch will beftow,
" On him who conquers, and deftroys his foe." 75

                              Eliab

Eliab heard, and kindled into ire
To hear his shepherd-brother thus inquire,
And thus begun? " What errand brought thee?
   " say
" Who keeps thy flock? or does it go astray?
" I know the base ambition of thine heart,   80
" But back in safety from the field depart."

Eliab thus to *Jesse's* youngest heir,
Expres'd his wrath in accents most severe.
When to his brother mildly he reply'd,
" What have I done? or what the cause to
   " chide?"   85

The words were told before the king, who sent
For the young hero to his royal tent :
Before the monarch dauntless he began;
" For this *Philistine* fail no heart of man :
" I'll take the vale, and with the giant fight: 90
" I dread not all his boasts, nor all his might."

E 2   When

When thus the king : " Dar'ft thou a ftripling go.

" And venture combat with fo great a foe ?

" Who all his days has been inur'd to fight,

" And made its deeds his ftudy and delight :   95

" Battles and bloodfhed brought the monfter forth,

" And clouds and whirlwinds ufher'd in his birth."

When *David* thus : " I kept the fleecy care,

" And out there rufh'd a lion and a bear ;

" A tender lamb the hungry lion took,   100

" And with no other weapon than my crook

" Bold I purfu'd, and chas'd him o'er the field,

" The prey deliver'd, and the felon kill'd : 2

" As thus the lion and the bear I flew,

" So fhall *Goliath* fall, and all his crew :   105

" The God, who fav'd me from thefe beafts of

    " prey,

" By me this monfter in the duft fhall lay."

So *David* fpoke.   The wond'ring king reply'd ;

" Go thou with heav'n and victory on thy fide :

" This coat of mail, this fword gird on," he

    faid,   110

And plac'd a mighty helmet on his head :

The

The coat, the fword, the helm he laid afide,

Nor chofe to venture with thofe arms untry'd,

Then took his ftaff, and to the neighb'ring brook

Inftant he ran, and thence five pebbles took. 115

Mean time defcended to *Philiftia's* fon

A radiant cherub, and he thus begun :

" Goliath, well thou know'ft thou haft defy'd

" Yon Hebrew armies, and their God deny'd :

" Rebellious wretch ! audacious worm ! for-
" bear, 120

" Nor tempt the vengeance of their God too far :

" Them, who with his omnipotence contend,

" No eye fhall pity, and no arm defend :

" Proud as thou art, in fhort liv'd glory great,

" I come to tell thee thine approaching fate. 125

" Regard my words. The judge of all the gods,

" Beneath whofe fteps the tow'ring mountain nods,

" Will give thine armies to the favage brood,

" That cut the liquid air, or range the wood.

" Thee too a well-aim'd pebble fhall deftroy, 130

" And thou fhalt perifh by a beardlefs boy :

" Such

179

" Such is the mandate from the realms above,

" And fhould I try the vengeance to remove,

" Myfelf a rebel to my king would prove.

" *Goliath* fay, fhall grace to him be fhown,   135

" Who dares heav'ns monarch, and infults his
   " throne ?"

" Your words are loft on me," the giant
   cries,

While fear and wrath contended in his eyes,

When thus the meffenger from heav'n replies :

" Provoke no more *Jehovah's* awful hand   140

" To hurl its vengeance on thy guilty land :

" He grafps the thunder, and, he wings the
   " ftorm,

" Servants their fov'reign's orders to perform."

The angel fpoke, and turn'd his eyes away,

Adding new radiance to the rifing day.   145

Now *David* comes : the fatal ftones demand

His left, the ftaff engag'd his better hand :

                                             The

The giant mov'd, and from his tow'ring height
Survey'd the ſtripling, and diſdain'd the ſight,
And thus began : " Am I a dog with thee ? 150
" Bring'ſt thou no armour, but a ſtaff to me ?
" The gods on thee their vollied curſes pour,
" And beaſts and birds of prey thy fleſh de-
    " vour."

David undaunted thus, " Thy ſpear and ſhield
" Shall no protection to thy body yield : 155
" *Jehovah's* name ——no other arms I bear,
" I aſk no other in this glorious war.
" To-day the Lord of Hoſts to me will give
" Vict'ry, to-day thy doom thou ſhalt receive ;
" The fate you threaten ſhall your own be-
    " come, 160
" And beaſts ſhall be your animated tomb,
" That all the earth's inhabitants may know
" That there's a God, who governs all below :
" This great aſſembly too ſhall witneſs ſtand,
" That needs nor ſword, nor ſpear, th' Almighty's
    hand ; 165
        " The

" The battle his, the conqueſt he beſtows,
" And to our pow'r conſigns our hated foes."

Thus *David* ſpoke ; *Goliath* heard and came
To meet the hero in the field of fame.
Ah ! fatal meeting to thy troops and thee,　170
But thou waſt deaf to the divine decree ;
Young *David* meets thee,　meets thee not in vain;
'Tis thine to periſh on th' enſanguin'd plain.

And now the youth the forceful pebble flung,
Philiſtia trembled as it whizz'd along :　175
In his dread forehead, where the helmet ends,
Juſt o'er the brows the well-aim'd ſtone deſcends,
It pierc'd the ſkull, and ſhatter'd all the brain,
Prone on his face he tumbled to the plain :
Goliath's fall no ſmaller terror yields　180
Than riving thunders in aerial fields :
The ſoul ſtill ling'red in its lov'd abode,
Till conq'ring *David* o'er the giant ſtrode :
Goliath's ſword then laid its maſter dead,
And from the body hew'd the ghaſtly head ;　185

　　　　　　　　　　The

The blood in gushing torrents drench'd the plains,
The soul found passage through the spouting
 veins.

And now aloud th' illustrious victor said,
" Where are your boastings now your cham-
 " pion's dead ?"
Scarce had he spoke, when the *Philistines* fled :
But fled in vain ; the conqu'ror swift pursu'd :
What scenes of slaughter ! and what seas of blood !
There *Saul* thy thousands grasp'd th' impurpled
 sand
In pangs of death the conquest of thine hand ;
And *David* there were thy ten thousands laid : 195
Thus *Israel's* damsels musically play'd,

Near *Gath* and *Ekron* many an hero lay,
Breath'd out their souls, and curs'd the light of
 day :
Their fury, quench'd by death, no longer burns,
And *David* with *Goliath's* head returns,   200
To *Salem* brought, but in his tent he plac'd
The load of armour which the giant grac'd.

       F   His

His monarch faw him coming from the war,
And thus demanded of the fon of *Ner.*

" Say, who is this amazing youth ?" he cry'd, 205
When thus the leader of the hoft reply'd ;
" As lives thy foul I know not whence he fprung,
" So great in prowefs though in years fo young :"
" Inquire whofe fon is he," the fov'reign faid,
" Before whofe conq'ring arm *Philiflia* fled." 210
Before the king behold the ftripling ftand,
Goliath's head depending from his hand :
To him the king : " Say of what martial line
" Art thou, young hero, and what fire was thine ?"
He humbly thus ; " the fon of *Jeffe* I : 215
" I came the glories of the field to try.
" Small is my tribe, but valiant in the fight ;
" Small is my city, but thy royal right."
" Then take the promis'd gifts," the monarch
        cry'd,
Conferring riches and the royal bride : 220
" Knit to my foul for ever thou remain
" With me, nor quit my regal roof again."

Thoughts

Thoughts on the WORKS of PROVIDENCE.

ARISE, my foul, on wings enraptur'd, rife
    To praife the monarch of the earth and
      fkies,
Whofe goodnefs and beneficence appear
As round its centre moves the rolling year,
Or when the morning glows with rofy charms,   5
Or the fun flumbers in the ocean's arms :
Of light divine be a rich portion lent
To guide my foul, and favour my intent.
Celeftial mufe, my arduous flight fuftain,
And raife my mind to a feraphic ftrain !   10

   Ador'd for ever be the God unfeen,
Which round the fun revolves this vaft machine,
Though to his eye its mafs a point appears :
Ador'd the God that whirls furrounding fpheres,
Which firft ordain'd that mighty *Sol* fhould
    reign   15
The peerlefs monarch of th' ethereal train :

            F 2   Of

Of miles twice forty millions is his height,
And yet his radiance dazzles mortal fight
So far beneath—from him th' extended earth
Vigour derives, and ev'ry flow'ry birth :   20
Vaft through her orb fhe moves with eafy grace
Around her *Phœbus* in unbounded fpace ;
True to her courfe th' impetuous ftorm derides,
Triumphant o'er the winds, and furging tides.

Almighty, in thefe wond'rous works of thine, 25
What *Pow'r*, what *Wifdom*, and what *Goodnefs*
    fhine ?
And are thy wonders, Lord, by men explor'd,
And yet creating glory unador'd !

Creation fmiles in various beauty gay,
While day to night, and night fucceeds to day : 30
That *Wifdom*, which attends *Jehovah's* ways,
Shines moft confpicuous in the folar rays :
Without them, deftitute of heat and light,
This world would be the reign of endlefs
    night :

                                                In

In their excefs how would our race complain, 35
Abhorring life! how hate its length'ned chain!
From air adult what num'rous ills would rife?
What dire contagion taint the burning fkies?
What peftilential vapours, fraught with death,
Would rife, and overfpread the lands beneath? 40

Hail, fmiling morn, that from the orient main
Afcending doft adorn the heav'nly plain!
So rich, fo various are thy beauteous dies,
That fpread through all the circuit of the fkies,
That, full of thee, my foul in rapture foars, 45
And thy great God, the caufe of all adores.

O'er beings infinite his love extends,
His *Wifdom* rules them, and his *Pow'r* defends.
When tafks diurnal tire the human frame,
The fpirits faint, and dim the vital flame, 50
Then too that ever active bounty fhines,
Which not infinity of fpace confines.
The fable veil, that *Night* in filence draws,
Conceals effects, but fhews th' *Almighty Caufe*;

Night

Night feals in fleep the wide creation fair,   55
And all is peaceful but the brow of care.
Again, gay *Phœbus*, as the day before,
Wakes ev'ry eye, but what fhall wake no more;
Again the face of nature is renew'd,
Which ftill appears harmonious, fair, and good. 60
May grateful ftrains falute the fmiling morn,
Before its beams the eaftern hills adorn!

Shall day to day and night to night confpire
To fhow the goodnefs of the Almighty Sire?
This mental voice fhall man regardlefs hear,   65
And never, never raife the filial pray'r?
To-day, O hearken, nor your folly mourn
For time mifpent, that never will return.

But fee the fons of vegetation rife,
And fpread their leafy banners to the fkies.   70
All-wife Almighty Providence we trace
In trees, and plants, and all the flow'ry race;
As clear as in the nobler frame of man,
All lovely copies of the Maker's plan.

The

The pow'r the fame that forms a ray of light, 75
That call'd creation from eternal night.
" Let there be light," he faid : from his profound
Old *Chaos* heard, and trembled at the found :
Swift as the word, infpir'd by pow'r divine,
Behold the light around its maker fhine, 80
The firft fair product of th' omnific God,
And now through all his works diffus'd abroad.

As reafon's pow'rs by day our God difclofe,
So we may trace him in the night's repofe :
Say what is fleep? and dreams how paffing
    ftrange ! 85
When action ceafes, and ideas range
Licentious and unbounded o'er the plains,
Where *Fancy's* queen in giddy triumph reigns.
Hear in foft ftrains the dreaming lover figh
To a kind fair, or rave in jealoufy ; 90
On pleafure now, and now on vengeance bent,
The lab'ring paffions ftruggle for a vent.
What pow'r, O man ! thy *reafon* then reftores,
So long fufpended in nocturnal hours ?

                                    What

What fecret hand returns the mental train,   95
And gives improv'd thine active pow'rs again ?
From thee, O man, what gratitude fhould rife !
And, when from balmy fleep thou op'tt thine
    eyes,
Let thy firft thoughts be praifes to the fkies.
How merciful our God who thus imparts   100
O'erflowing tides of joy to human hearts,
When wants and woes might be our righteous lot,
Our God forgetting, by our God forgot !

Among the mental pow'rs a queftion rofe,
" What moft the image of th' Eternal fhows ?"
When thus to *Reafon* (fo let *Fancy* rove)
Her great companion fpoke immortal *Love*.

" Say, mighty pow'r, how long fhall ftrife pre-
    vail,
" And with its murmurs load the whifp'ring
    " gale ?
" Refer the caufe to *Recollection's* fhrine,   110
" Who loud proclaims my origin divine,

                        " The

" The cause whence heav'n and earth began to be,

" And is not man immortaliz'd by me ?

" *Reason* let this moſt cauſeleſs ſtrife ſubſide."

Thus *Love* pronounc'd, and *Reaſon* thus re-
ply'd.   115

" Thy birth, celeſtial queen ! 'tis mine to own,

" In thee reſplendent is the Godhead ſhown ;

" Thy words perſuade, my ſoul enraptur'd feels

" Reſiſtleſs beauty which thy ſmile reveals."

Ardent ſhe ſpoke, and, kindling at her
charms,   120

She claſp'd the blooming goddeſs in her arms.

Infinite *Love* where'er we turn our eyes

Appears: this ev'ry creature's wants ſupplies ;

This moſt is heard in *Nature's* conſtant voice,

This makes the morn, and this the eve re-
joice ;   125

This bids the foſt'ring rains and dews deſcend

To nouriſh all, to ſerve one gen'ral end,

G   The

191

The good of man: yet man ungrateful pays
But little homage, and but little praife.
To him, whofe works array'd with mercy
 fhine,   130
What fongs fhould rife, how conftant, how di-
 vine!

To

To a Lady on the Death of Three Relations.

WE trace the pow'r of Death from tomb to
    tomb,
And his are all the ages yet to come.
'Tis his to call the planets from on high,
To blacken *Phœbus*, and diffolve the fky ;[1]
His too, when all in his dark realms are hurl'd, 5
From its firm bafe to fhake the folid world ;
His fatal fceptre rules the fpacious whole,
And trembling nature rocks from pole to pole.

Awful he moves, and wide his wings are fpread:
Behold thy brother number'd with the dead ! 10
From bondage freed, the exulting fpirit flies
Beyond *Olympus*, and thefe ftarry fkies.
Loft in our woe for thee, bleft fhade, we mourn
In vain ; to earth thou never muft return.
Thy fifters too, fair mourner, feel the dart 15
Of Death, and with frefh torture rend thine heart.

Weep not for them, who wiſh thine happy mind
To riſe with them, and leave the world behind.

   As a young plant by hurricanes up torn,   20
So near its parent lies the newly born —
But 'midſt the bright ethereal train behold
It ſhines ſuperior on a throne of gold :
Then, mourner, ceaſe; let hope thy tears reſtrain,
Smile on the tomb, and ſooth the raging pain. 25
On yon bleſt regions fix thy longing view,
Mindleſs of ſublunary ſcenes below;
Aſcend the ſacred mount, in thought ariſe,
And ſeek ſubſtantial, and immortal joys;
Where hope receives, where faith to viſion
    ſprings,   30
And raptur'd ſeraphs tune th' immortal ſtrings
To ſtrains extatic. Thou the chorus join,
And to thy father tune the praiſe divine.

To

To a Clergyman on the Death of his Lady. [1]

WHERE contemplation finds her sacred spring,
Where heav'nly music makes the arches ring,
Where virtue reigns unfully'd and divine,
Where wisdom thron'd, and all the graces shine,
There sits thy spouse amidst the radiant throng, 5
While praise eternal warbles from her tongue;
There choirs angelic shout her welcome round,
With perfect bliss, and peerless glory crown'd.

While thy dear mate, to flesh no more confin'd,
Exults a blest, an heav'n-ascended mind, 10
Say in thy breast shall floods of sorrow rise?
Say shall its torrents overwhelm thine eyes?
Amid the seats of heav'n a place is free,
And angels ope their bright ranks for thee;
For thee they wait, and with expectant eye 16
Thy spouse leans downward from th' empyreal
    sky:
                                    " O come

" O come away, her longing fpirit cries,

" And fhare with me the raptures of the fkies.

" Our blifs divine to mortals is unknown;

" Immortal life and glory are our own.   20

" There too may the dear pledges of our love

" Arrive, and tafte with us the joys above ;

" Attune the harp to more than mortal lays,

" And join with us the tribute of their praife

" To him, who dy'd ftern juftice to atone,   25

" And make eternal glory all our own.

" He in his death flew ours, and, as he rofe,

" He crufh'd the dire dominion of our foes ;

" Vain were their hopes to put the God to flight,

" Chain us to hell, and bar the gates of light." 30

She fpoke, and turn'd from mortal fcenes her eyes,

Which beam'd celeftial radiance o'er the fkies.

Then thou, dear man, no more with grief re-
　　tire,

Let grief no longer damp devotion's fire,

But rife fublime, to equal blifs afpire.   35

Thy

Thy sighs no more be wafted by the wind,
No more complain, but be to heav'n resign'd.
'Twas thine t' unfold the oracles divine,
To sooth our woes the task was also thine;
Now sorrow is incumbent on thy heart,   40
Permit the muse a cordial to impart;
Who can to thee their tend'rest aid refuse?
To dry thy tears how longs the heav'nly muse!

An

An HYMN to the Morning.

ATTEND my lays, ye ever honour'd nine,
   Assist my labours, and my strains refine;
In smoothest numbers pour the notes along,
For bright *Aurora* now demands my song.

Aurora hail, and all the thousands dies,   5
Which deck thy progress through the vaulted
    skies:
The morn awakes, and wide extends her rays,
On ev'ry leaf the gentle zephyr plays;
Harmonious lays the feather'd race resume,
Dart the bright eye, and shake the painted
    plume.   10

Ye shady groves, your verdant gloom display
To shield your poet from the burning day:
Calliope[2] awake the sacred lyre,
While thy fair sisters fan the pleasing fire:

            The

The bow'rs, the gales, the variegated ſkies   15
In all their pleaſures in my boſom riſe.

See in the eaſt th' illuſtrious king of day
His riſing radiance drives the ſhades away —
But Oh! I feel his fervid beams too ſtrong,
And ſcarce begun, concludes th' abortive ſong. 20

H   An

An H Y M N to the Evening.

SOON as the fun forfook the eaftern main
 The pealing thunder fhook the heav'nly
  plain;
Majeftic grandeur! From the zephyr's wing,
Exhales the incenfe of the blooming fpring.
Soft purl the ftreams, the birds renew their
 notes,   5
And through the air their mingled mufic floats.

 Through all the heav'ns what beauteous dies are
  fpread!
But the weft glories in the deepeft red:
So may our breafts with ev'ry virtue glow,
The living temples of our God below!   10

 Fill'd with the praife of him who gives the
  light,
And draws the fable curtains of the night,

           Let

Let placid flumbers footh each weary mind,
At morn to wake more heav'nly, more refin'd ;
So fhall the labours of the day begin   15
More pure, more guarded from the fnares of fin.

Night's leaden fceptre feals my drowfy eyes,
Then ceafe, my fong, till fair *Aurora* rife.

Isaiah lxiii. 1—8. [1]

S A Y, heav'nly mufe, what king, or mighty
  God,
That moves fublime from *Idumea's* road?
In *Bozrab's* dies, with martial glories join'd,
His purple vefture waves upon the wind.
Why thus enrob'd delights he to appear   5
In the dread image of the *Pow'r* of war?

 Comprefs'd in wrath the fwelling wine-prefs
   groan'd,
It bled, and pour'd the gufhing purple round.

 " Mine was the act," th' Almighty Saviour
   faid,
And fhook the dazzling glories of his head, 10
" When all forfook I trod the prefs alone,
" And conquer'd by omnipotence my own;
" For man's releafe fuftain'd the pond'rous load,
" For man the wrath of an immortal God:
          " To

" To execute th' Eternal's dread command   15
" My foul I facrific'd with willing hand ;
" Sinlefs I ftood before the avenging frown,
" Atoning thus for vices not my own."

His eye the ample field of battle round
Survey'd, but no created fuccours found ;   20
His own omnipotence fuftain'd the fight,
His vengeance funk the haughty foes in night ;
Beneath his feet the proftrate troops were fpread,
And round him lay the dying, and the dead.

Great God, what light'ning flafhes from thine
     eyes ?   25
What pow'r withftands if thou indignant rife ?

Againft thy *Zion* though her foes may rage,
And all their cunning, all their ftrength engage,
Yet fhe ferenely on thy bofom lies,
Smiles at their arts, and all their force defies.   30

On

On Recollection. [1]

MNEME [2] begin. Infpire, ye facred nine,
    Your vent'rous *Afric* in her great defign.
Mneme, immortal pow'r, I trace thy fpring :
Affift my ftrains, while I thy glories fing :
The acts of long departed years, by thee   5
Recover'd, in due order rang'd we fee :
Thy pow'r the long-forgotten calls from night,
That fweetly plays before the *fancy's* fight.

    Mneme in our nocturnal vifions pours
The ample treafure of her fecret ftores ;   10
Swift from above fhe wings her filent flight
Through *Phæbe's* realms, fair regent of the
    night ;
And, in her pomp of images difplay'd,
To the high-raptur'd poet gives her aid,
Through the unbounded regions of the mind, 15
Diffufing light celeftial and refin'd.

                      The

The heav'nly *phantom* paints the actions done
By ev'ry tribe beneath the rolling fun.

Mneme, enthron'd within the human breaft,
Has vice condemn'd, and ev'ry virtue bleft.   20
How fweet the found when we her plaudit hear?
Sweeter than mufic to the ravifh'd ear,
Sweeter than *Maro's* entertaining ftrains
Refounding through the groves, and hills, and
     plains.
But how is *Mneme* dreaded by the race,   25
Who fcorn her warnings, and defpife her grace?
By her unveil'd each horrid crime appears,
Her awful hand a cup of wormwood bears.
Days, years mifpent, O what a hell of woe!
Hers the worft tortures that our fouls can know.   30

Now eighteen years their deftin'd courfe have
     run,³
In faft fucceffion round the central fun.
How did the follies of that period pafs
Unnotic'd, but behold them writ in brafs!

                                        In

In Recollection fee them frefh return,   35
And fure 'tis mine to be afham'd, and mourn. ⁴

O *Virtue*, fmiling in immortal green,
Do thou exert thy pow'r, and change the fcene;
Be thine employ to guide my future days,
And mine to pay the tribute of my praife.   40

Of *Recollection* fuch the pow'r enthron'd
In ev'ry breaft, and thus her pow'r is own'd.
The wretch, who dar'd the vengeance of the fkies,
At laft awakes in horror and furprize,
By her alarm'd, he fees impending fate,   45
He howls in anguifh, and repents too late.
But O! what peace, what joys are hers t' impart
To ev'ry holy, ev'ry upright heart!
Thrice bleft the man, who, in her facred fhrine,
Feels himfelf fhelter'd from the wrath divine! 50

On

On Imagination.

THY various works, imperial queen, we fee,
    How bright their forms! how deck'd with
      pomp by thee!
Thy wond'rous acts in beauteous order ftand,
And all atteft how potent is thine hand.

From *Helicon's* refulgent heights attend,   6
Ye facred choir, and my attempts befriend:
To tell her glories with a faithful tongue,
Ye blooming graces, triumph in my fong.

Now here, now there, the roving *Fancy* flies,
Till fome lov'd object ftrikes her wand'ring
   eyes,   10
Whofe filken fetters all the fenfes bind,
And foft captivity involves the mind. [1]

I   *Imagi-*

Imagination! who can fing thy force?
Or who defcribe the fwiftnefs of thy courfe?
Soaring through air to find the bright abode,   15
Th' empyreal palace of the thund'ring God,
We on thy pinions can furpafs the wind,
And leave the rolling univerfe behind :
From ftar to ftar the mental optics rove,
Meafure the fkies, and range the realms
    above.   20
There in one view we grafp the mighty whole,
Or with new worlds amaze th' unbounded foul.

Though *Winter* frowns to *Fancy's* raptur'd
    eyes
The fields may flourifh, and gay fcenes arife ;
The frozen deeps may break their iron bands,   25
And bid their waters murmur o'er the fands.
Fair *Flora* may refume her fragrant reign,
And with her flow'ry riches deck the plain ;
Sylvanus may diffufe his honours round,
And all the foreft may with leaves be crown'd :   30
                Show'rs

Show'rs may descend, and dews their gems dis-
    close,
And nectar sparkle on the blooming rose.

Such is thy pow'r, nor are thine orders vain,
O thou the leader of the mental train:
In full perfection all thy works are wrought, 35
And thine the sceptre o'er the realms of thought.
Before thy throne the subject-passions bow,
Of subject-passions sov'reign ruler Thou;
At thy command joy rushes on the heart,
And through the glowing veins the spirits dart. 40

Fancy might now her silken pinions try
To rise from earth, and sweep th' expanse on
    high;
From *Tithon's* bed now might *Aurora* rise,
Her cheeks all glowing with celestial dies,
While a pure stream of light o'erflows the
    skies.   45
The monarch of the day I might behold,
And all the mountains tipt with radiant gold,

I 2

But

But I reluctant leave the pleasing views,
Which *Fancy* dresses to delight the *Muse*;
Winter austere forbids me to aspire,   50
And northern tempests damp the rising fire;
They chill the tides of *Fancy's* flowing sea,
Cease then, my song, cease the unequal lay,[3]

A Fu-

A Funeral POEM on the Death of C. E.
an Infant of Twelve Months.[1]

THROUGH airy roads he wings his inflant
    flight
To purer regions of celeftial light;
Enlarg'd he fees unnumber'd fyftems roll,
Beneath him fees the univerfal whole,
Planets on planets run their deftin'd round,   **5**
And circling wonders fill the vaft profound.
Th' ethereal now, and now th' empyreal fkies
With growing fplendors ftrike his wond'ring eyes:
The angels view him with delight unknown,
Prefs his foft hand, and feat him on his throne;
Then fmiling thus.   " To this divine abode,
" The feat of faints, of feraphs, and of God,
" Thrice welcome thou."   The raptur'd babe
    replies,
" Thanks to my God, who fnatch'd me to the
    " fkies,
                              " E'er

" E'er vice triumphant had poffefs'd my heart,   15
" E'er yet the tempter had beguil'd my heart,
" E'er yet on fin's bafe actions I was bent,
" E'er yet I knew temptation's dire intent ;
" E'er yet the lafh for horrid crimes I felt,
" E'er vanity had led my way to guilt,   20
" But, foon arriv'd at my celeftial goal,
" Full glories rufh on my expanding foul."
Joyful he fpoke : exulting cherubs round
Clapt their glad wings, the heav'nly vaults refound.

Say, parents, why this unavailing moan ?   25
Why heave your penfive bofoms with the groan ?
To *Charles*, the happy fubject of my fong,
A brighter world, and nobler ftrains belong.
Say would you tear him from the realms above
By thoughtlefs wifhes, and prepof'rous love ? 30
Doth his felicity increafe your pain ?
Or could you welcome to this world again
The heir of blifs ? with a fuperior air
Methinks he anfwers with a fmile fevere,
" Thrones and dominions cannot tempt me
       " there."   35

But

But ſtill you cry, " Can we the ſigh forbear,
" And ſtill and ſtill muſt we not pour the tear ?
" Our only hope, more dear than vital breath,
" Twelve moons revolv'd, becomes the prey of
    " death ;
" Delightful infant, nightly viſions give   40
" Thee to our arms, and we with joy receive,
" We fain would claſp the *Phantom* to our breaſt,
" The *Phantom* flies, and leaves the ſoul unbleſt."

To yon bright regions let your faith aſcend,
Prepare to join your deareſt infant friend
In pleaſures without meaſure, without end.

To

To Captain H——ᴅ, of the 65th Regiment.[1]

S A Y, mufe divine, can hoftile fcenes delight
  The warrior's bofom in the fields of fight ?
Lo ! here the chriftian, and the hero join
With mutual grace to form the man divine.
In H——ᴅ fee with pleafure and furprize,   5
Where *valour* kindles, and where *virtue* lies :
Go, hero brave, ftill grace the poft of fame,
And add new glories to thine honour'd name,
Still to the field, and ftill to virtue true :
Britannia glories in no fon like you.   10

To

To the Right Honourable WILLIAM, Earl
of DARTMOUTH, His Majefty's Principal Secretary of State for North-America, &c. [1]

HAIL, happy day, when, fmiling like the
morn,
Fair *Freedom* rofe *New-England* to adorn:
The northern clime beneath her genial ray,
Dartmouth, congratulates thy blifsful fway:
Elate with hope her race no longer mourns,   5
Each foul expands, each grateful bofom burns,
While in thine hand with pleafure we behold
The filken reins, and *Freedom's* charms unfold.
Long loft to realms beneath the northern fkies
She fhines fupreme, while hated *faction* dies: 10
Soon as appear'd the *Goddefs* long defir'd,
Sick at the view, fhe languifh'd and expir'd;
Thus from the fplendors of the morning light
The owl in fadnefs feeks the caves of night.

K   No

No more, *America*, in mournful ftrain   15
Of wrongs, and grievance unredrefs'd complain,
No longer fhall thou dread the iron chain,
Which wanton *Tyranny* with lawlefs hand
Had made, and with it meant t' enflave the land.

Should you, my lord, while you perufe my
    fong,   20
Wonder from whence my love of *Freedom* fprung,
Whence flow thefe wifhes for the common good,
By feeling hearts alone beft underftood,
I, young in life, by feeming cruel fate
Was fnatch'd from *Afric's* fancy'd happy feat: 25
What pangs excruciating muft moleft,
What forrows labour in my parent's breaft?
Steel'd was that foul and by no mifery mov'd
That from a father feiz'd his babe belov'd:
Such, fuch my cafe. And can I then but
    pray   30
Others may never feel tyrannic fway?

                          For

For favours paſt, great Sir, our thanks are due,
And thee we aſk thy favours to renew,
Since in thy pow'r, as in thy will before,
To footh the griefs, which thou did'ſt once de-
    plore.   35
May heav'nly grace the facred ſanction give
To all thy works, and thou for ever live
Not only on the wings of fleeting *Fame*,
Though praiſe immortal crowns the patriot's
    name,
But to conduct to heav'ns refulgent fane,   40
May fiery courſers ſweep th' ethereal plain,
And bear thee upwards to that bleſt abode,
Where, like the prophet, thou ſhalt find thy God.

K 2   ODE

O D E to N E P T U N E.

On Mrs. W—'s Voyage to England.

I.

WHILE raging tempefts fhake the fhore,
   While Æ'lus' thunders round us roar,
And fweep impetuous o'er the plain
Be ftill, O tyrant of the main;
Nor let thy brow contracted frowns betray,   5
While my *Sufannah* fkims the wat'ry way.

II.

The *Pow'r* propitious hears the lay,
The blue-ey'd daughters of the fea
With fweeter cadence glide along,
And *Thames* refponfive joins the fong.   10
Pleas'd with their notes *Sol* fheds benign his ray,
And double radiance decks the face of day.

III. To

III.

To court thee to *Britannia's* arms
   Serene the climes and mild the sky,
Her region boasts unnumber'd charms,   15
   Thy welcome smiles in ev'ry eye.
Thy promise, *Neptune* keep, record my pray'r,
Nor give my wishes to the empty air.

            Boston, October 10, 1772.

To

To a LADY on her coming to North-America
with her Son, for the Recovery of her Health.

INdulgent mufe! my grov'ling mind infpire,
  And fill my bofom with celeltial fire.

See from *Jamaica's* fervid fhore fhe moves,
Like the fair mother of the blooming loves,
When from above the *Goddefs* with her hand   5
Fans the foft breeze, and lights upon the land;
Thus fhe on *Neptune's* wat'ry realm reclin'd
Appear'd, and thus invites the ling'ring wind.

  " Arife, ye winds, *America* explore,
" Waft me, ye gales, from this malignant
  " fhore;   10
" The *Northern* milder climes I long to greet,
" There hope that health will my arrival meet."
Soon as fhe fpoke in my ideal view
The winds affented, and the veffel flew.

               Madam,

Madam, your spouse bereft of wife and son,   15
In the grove's dark recesses pours his moan ;
Each branch, wide-spreading to the ambient sky,
Forgets its verdure, and submits to die.

From thence I turn, and leave the sultry plain,
And swift pursue thy passage o'er the main :   20
The ship arrives before the fav'ring wind,
And makes the *Philadelphian* port assign'd,
Thence I attend you to *Bostonia's* arms,
Where gen'rous friendship ev'ry bosom warms :
Thrice welcome here ! may health revive again,   25
Bloom on thy cheek, and bound in ev'ry vein !
Then back return to gladden ev'ry heart,
And give your spouse his soul's far dearer part,
Receiv'd again with what a sweet surprize,
The tear in transport starting from his eyes !   30
While his attendant son with blooming grace
Springs to his father's ever dear embrace.
With shouts of joy *Jamaica's* rocks resound,
With shouts of joy the country rings around.

To

To a Lady on her remarkable Preservation
in an Hurricane in *North-Carolina*.

THOUGH thou did'st hear the tempest from
       afar,
And felt'st the horrors of the wat'ry war,
To me unknown, yet on this peaceful shore
Methinks I hear the storm tumultuous roar,
And how stern *Boreas* with impetuous hand   5
Compell'd the *Nereids* to usurp the land.
Reluctant rose the daughters of the main,
And slow ascending glided o'er the plain,
Till *Æolus* in his rapid chariot drove
In gloomy grandeur from the vault above :   10
Furious he comes.   His winged sons obey
Their frantic sire, and madden all the sea.
The billows rave, the wind's fierce tyrant roars,
And with his thund'ring terrors shakes the shores :
Broken by waves the vessel's frame is rent,   15
And strows with planks the wat'ry element.

                                       But

But thee, *Maria*, a kind *Nereid's* fhield
Preferv'd from finking, and thy form upheld :
And fure fome heav'nly oracle defign'd
At that dread crifis to inftruct thy mind   20
Things of eternal confequence to weigh,
And to thine heart juft feelings to convey
Of things above, and of the future doom,
And what the births of the dread world to come.

From toffing feas I welcome thee to land.   25
" Refign her, *Nereid*," 'twas thy God's command.
Thy fpoufe late buried, as thy fears conceiv'd,
Again returns, thy fears are all reliev'd :
Thy daughter blooming with fuperior grace
Again thou fee'ft, again thine arms embrace ;   30
O come, and joyful fhow thy fpoufe his heir,
And what the bleffings of maternal care !

L   To

To a LADY and her Children, on the Death
of her Son and their Brother. [1]

O'Erwhelming forrow now demands my fong:
　　From death the overwhelming forrow fprung.
What flowing tears? What hearts with grief op-
　　preft?
What fighs on fighs heave the fond parent's
　　breaft?
The brother weeps, the haplefs fifters join　　5
Th' increafing woe, and fwell the cryftal brine;
The poor, who once his gen'rous bounty fed,
Droop, and bewail their benefactor dead.
In death the friend, the kind companion lies,
And in one death what various comfort dies!　10

Th' unhappy mother fees the fanguine rill
Forget to flow, and nature's wheels ftand ftill,
But fee from earth his fpirit far remov'd,
And know no grief recals your beft-belov'd:

　　　　　　　　　　　　　　　He,

He, upon pinions fwifter than the wind, 15
Has left mortality's fad fcenes behind
For joys to this terreftrial ftate unknown,
And glories richer than the monarch's crown.
Of virtue's fteady courfe the prize behold!
What blifsful wonders to his mind unfold! 20
But of celeftial joys I fing in vain:
Attempt not, mufe, the too advent'rous ftrain.

No more in briny fhow'rs, ye friends around,
Or bathe his clay, or wafte them on the ground:
Still do you weep, ftill wifh for his return? 25
How cruel thus to wifh, and thus to mourn?
No more for him the ftreams of forrow pour,
But hafte to join him on the heav'nly fhore,
On harps of gold to tune immortal lays,
And to your God immortal anthems raife. 30

L 2   To

To a GENTLEMAN and LADY on the Death of
the Lady's Brother and Sifter, and a Child
of the Name *Avis*, aged one Year. [1]

ON *Death's* domain intent I fix my eyes,
　　Where human nature in vaft ruin lies :
With penfive mind I fearch the drear abode,
Where the great conqu'ror has his fpoils beftow'd ;
There there the offspring of fix thoufand years　5
In endlefs numbers to my view appears :
Whole kingdoms in his gloomy den are thruft,
And nations mix with their primeval duft :
Infatiate ftill he gluts the ample tomb ;
His is the prefent, his the age to come.　　　10
See here a brother, here a fifter fpread,
And a fweet daughter mingled with the dead.

But, *Madam*, let your grief be laid afide,
And let the fountain of your tears be dry'd,
In vain they flow to wet the dufty plain,　　15
Your fighs are wafted to the fkies in vain,

　　　　　　　　　　　　　　Your

Your pains they witnefs, but they can no more,
While *Death* reigns tyrant o'er this mortal fhore.

The glowing ftars and filver queen of light
At laft muft perifh in the gloom of night :   20
Refign thy friends to that Almighty hand,
Which gave them life, and bow to his command ;
Thine *Avis* give without a murm'ring heart,
Though half thy foul be fated to depart.
To fhining guards confign thine infant care   25
To waft triumphant through the feas of air :
Her foul enlarg'd to heav'nly pleafure fprings,
She feeds on truth and uncreated things.
Methinks I hear her in the realms above,
And leaning forward with a filial love,   30
Invite you there to fhare immortal blifs
Unknown, untafted in a ftate like this.
With tow'ring hopes, and growing grace arife,
And feek beatitude beyond the fkies.

On

On the Death of Dr. SAMUEL MARSHALL. 1771. ¹

THROUGH thickeft glooms look back, immortal fhade,
On that confufion which thy death has made ;
Or from *Olympus'* height look down, and fce
A *Town* involv'd in grief bereft of thee.
Thy *Lucy* fees thee mingle with the dead,   5
And rends the graceful treffes from her head,
Wild in her woe, with grief unknown oppreft
Sigh follows figh deep heaving from her breaft.

Too quickly fled, ah ! whither art thou gone ?
Ah ! loft for ever to thy wife and fon !   10
The haplefs child, thine only hope and heir,
Clings round his mother's neck, and weeps his
forrows there.
The lofs of thee on *Tyler's* foul returns,
And *Bofton* for her dear phyfician mourns.

When

When ſickneſs call'd for *Marſhall's* healing
    hand,   15
With what compaſſion did his ſoul expand?
In him we found the father and the friend:
In life how lov'd! how honour'd in his end!

And muſt not then our *Æſculapius* ſtay
To bring his ling'ring infant into day?   20
The babe unborn in the dark womb is toſt,
And ſeems in anguiſh for its father loſt.

Gone is *Apollo* from his houſe of earth,
But leaves the ſweet memorials of his worth:
The common parent, whom we all deplore,   25
From yonder world unſeen muſt come no more,
Yet 'midſt our woes immortal hopes attend
The ſpouſe, the ſire, the univerſal friend.

To

229

To a Gentleman on his Voyage to *Great-Britain*
for the Recovery of his Health. ¹

WHILE others chant of gay *Elyſian* ſcenes,
    Of balmy zephyrs, and of flow'ry plains,
My ſong more happy ſpeaks a greater name,
Feels higher motives and a nobler flame.
For thee, O R—, the muſe attunes her ſtrings, 5
And mounts ſublime above inferior things.

  I ſing not now of green embow'ring woods,
I ſing not now the daughters of the floods,
I ſing not of the ſtorms o'er ocean driv'n,
And how they howl'd along the waſte of heav'n, 10
But I to R— would paint the *Britiſh* ſhore,
And vaſt *Atlantic*, not untry'd before :
Thy life impair'd commands thee to ariſe,
Leave theſe bleak regions, and inclement ſkies,
Where chilling winds return the winter paſt,   15
And nature ſhudders at the furious blaſt.

                        O thou

O thou ftupendous, earth-enclofing man
Exert thy wonders to the world again !
If ere thy pow'r prolong'd the fleeting breath,
Turn'd back the fhafts, and mock'd the gates of
    death,   20
If ere thine air difpens'd an healing pow'r,
Or fnatch'd the victim from the fatal hour,
This equal cafe demands thine equal care,
And equal wonders may this patient fhare.
But unavailing, frantic is the dream   25
To hope thine aid without the aid of him
Who gave thee birth, and taught thee where to
    flow,
And in thy waves his various bleffings fhow.

May R— return to view his native fhore
Replete with vigour not his own before,   30
Then fhall we fee with pleafure and furprize,
And own thy work, great Ruler of the fkies !

M   To

To the Rev. Dr. THOMAS AMORY
on reading his Sermons on DAILY DEVOTION, [1]
in which that Duty is recommended and affifted.

TO cultivate in ev'ry noble mind
  Habitual grace, and fentiments refin'd,
Thus while you ftrive to mend the human heart,
Thus while the heav'nly precepts you impart,
O may each bofom catch the facred fire,   5
And youthful minds to *Virtue's* throne afpire!

When God's eternal ways you fet in fight,
And *Virtue* fhines in all her native light,
In vain would *Vice* her works in night conceal, [2]
For *Wifdom's* eye pervades the fable veil.   10

Artifts may paint the fun's effulgent rays,
But *Amory's* pen the brighter God difplays:
While his great works in *Amory's* pages fhine,
And while he proves his effence all divine,

         The

The Atheist sure no more can boast aloud   15
Of chance, or nature, and exclude the God;
As if the clay without the potter's aid
Should rise in various forms, and shapes self-made,
Or worlds above with orb o'er orb profound
Self-mov'd could run the everlasting round.   20
It cannot be   unerring *Wisdom* guides
With eye propitious, and o'er all presides.

Still prosper, *Amory !* still may'st thou receive
The warmest blessings which a muse can give,
And when this transitory state is o'er,   25
When kingdoms fall, and fleeting *Fame's* no more,
May *Amory* triumph in immortal fame,
A nobler title, and superior name !

On the Death of J. C. an Infant.

NO more the flow'ry scenes of pleasure rise,
 Nor charming prospects greet the mental
  eyes,
No more with joy we view that lovely face [1]
Smiling, disportive, flush'd with ev'ry grace.

 The tear of sorrow flows from ev'ry eye,   5
Groans answer groans, and sighs to sighs reply ;
What sudden pangs shot thro' each aching heart,
When, *Death*, thy messenger dispatch'd his dart ?
Thy dread attendants, all-destroying *Pow'r*,
Hurried the infant to his mortal hour.   10
Could'ft thou unpitying close those radiant
  eyes ?
Or fail'd his artless beauties to surprize ?
Could not his innocence thy stroke controul,
Thy purpose shake, and soften all thy soul ?

         The

The blooming babe, with shades of *Death* o'er-
　　spread,　　　　　　　　　　　　　　15
No more shall smile, no more shall raise its
　　head, 2
But, like a branch that from the tree is torn,
Falls prostrate, wither'd, languid, and forlorn.
" Where flies my *James?*" 'tis thus I seem to
　　hear 3
The parent ask, " Some angel tell me where 20
" He wings his passage thro' the yielding air ?"
Methinks a cherub bending from the skies
Observes the question, and serene replies,
" In heav'ns high palaces your babe appears :
" Prepare to meet him, and dismiss your tears." 25
Shall not th' intelligence your grief restrain,
And turn the mournful to the chearful strain ?
Cease your complaints, suspend each rising sigh,
Cease to accuse the Ruler of the sky.
Parents, no more indulge the falling tear :　　30
Let *Faith* to heav'n's refulgent domes repair,
There see your infant, like a seraph glow :
What charms celestial in his numbers flow
　　　　　　　　　　　　　　Melodious,

Melodious, while the foul-enchanting ſtrain
Dwells on his tongue, and fills th' ethereal plain?   35
Enough – for ever ceaſe your murm'ring breath ;
Not as a foe, but friend converſe with *Death*,
Since to the port of happineſs unknown
He brought that treaſure which you call your own.
The gift of heav'n intruſted to your hand   40
Chearful reſign at the divine command :
Not at your bar muſt ſov'reign *Wiſdom* ſtand.

An

An H Y M N to HUMANITY.
To S. P. G. Efq;

I.

LO! for this dark terreftrial ball
Forfakes his azure-paved hall
   A prince of heav'nly birth!
Divine *Humanity* behold.
What wonders rife, what charms unfold   5
   At his defcent to earth!

II.

The bofoms of the great and good
With wonder and delight he view'd,
   And fix'd his empire there:
Him, clofe comprefling to his breaft,   10
The fire of gods and men addrefs'd,
   " My fon, my heav'nly fair!

III. " Defcend

III.

" Defcend to earth, there place thy throne;
" To fuccour man's afflicted fon
  " Each human heart infpire: 15
" To act in bounties unconfin'd
" Enlarge the clofe contracted mind,
  " And fill it with thy fire."

IV.

Quick as the word, with fwift career
He wings his courfe from ftar to ftar, 20
  And leaves the bright abode.
The *Virtue* did his charms impart;
Their G——y! then thy raptur'd heart
  Perceiv'd the rufhing God:

V.

For when thy pitying eye did fee   25
The languid mufe in low degree,
  Then, then at thy defire
Defcended the celeftial nine;
O'er me methought they deign'd to fhine,
  And deign'd to ftring my lyre. 30

        VI. Can

VI.

Can *Afric's* mufe forgetful prove ?
Or can fuch friendſhip fail to move
    A tender human heart ?
Immortal *Friendſhip* laurel-crown'd
The fmiling *Graces* all furround   35
    With ev'ry heav'nly *Art.*

N   To

To the Honourable T. H. Efq; on the Death of his Daughter. [1]

WHILE deep you mourn beneath the
    cyprefs-fhade
The hand of Death, and your dear daughter laid
In duft, whofe abfence gives your tears to flow,
And racks your bofom with inceffant woe,
Let *Recollection* take a tender part,   5
Affuage the raging tortures of your heart,
Still the wild tempeft of tumultuous grief,
And pour the heav'nly nectar of relief:
Sufpend the figh, dear Sir, and check the groan,
Divinely bright your daughter's *Virtues* fhone: 10
How free from fcornful pride her gentle mind,
Which ne'er its aid to indigence declin'd!
Expanding free, it fought the means to prove
Unfailing charity, unbounded love!

She unreluctant flies to fee no more   15
Her dear-lov'd parents on earth's dufky fhore:
                      Impatient

Impatient heav'n's refplendent goal to gain,
She with fwift progrefs cuts the azure plain,
Where grief fubfides, where changes are no more,
And life's tumultuous billows ceafe to roar;　20
She leaves her earthly manfion for the fkies,
Where new creations feaft her wond'ring eyes.

To heav'n's high mandate chearfully refign'd
She mounts, and leaves the rolling globe behind;
She, who late wifh'd that *Leonard* might return,　25
Has ceas'd to languifh, and forgot to mourn;
To the fame high empyreal manfions come,
She joins her fpoufe, and fmiles upon the tomb:
And thus I hear her from the realms above:
" Lo! this the kingdom of celeftial love!　30
" Could ye, fond parents, fee our prefent blifs,
" How foon would you each figh, each fear dif-
　" mifs?
" Amidft unutter'd pleafures whilft I play
" In the fair funfhine of celeftial day,
" As far as grief affects an happy foul　35
" So far doth grief my better mind controul,

N 2

" To

" To fee on earth my aged parents mourn,

" And fecret wifh for T——l to return :

" Let brighter fcenes your ev'ning-hours em-
    " ploy :

" Converfe with heav'n, and tafte the promis'd
    " joy." 40

NIOBE

NIOBE in Diſtreſs for her Children ſlain by
APOLLO, from *Ovid's* Metamorphoſes, Book VI.
and from a view of the Painting of Mr. *Richard
Wilſon.* [1]

APOLLO's wrath to man the dreadful
      ſpring
Of ills innum'rous, tuneful goddeſs, ſing!
Thou who did'ſt firſt th' ideal pencil give,
And taught'ſt the painter in his works to live,
Inſpire with glowing energy of thought,   5
What *Wilſon* painted, and what *Ovid* wrote.
Muſe! lend thy aid, nor let me ſue in vain,
Tho' laſt and meaneſt of the rhyming train!
O guide my pen in lofty ſtrains to ſhow
The *Phrygian* queen, all beautiful in woe.   10

'Twas where *Meonia* ſpreads her wide domain
Niobe dwelt, and held her potent reign:
See in her hand the regal ſceptre ſhine,
The wealthy heir of *Tantalus* divine,

                         He

He moſt diſtinguiſh'd by *Dodonean Jove*,[2]   15
To approach the tables of the gods above :
Her grandſire *Atlas*, who with mighty pains
Th' ethereal axis on his neck ſuſtains :
Her other grand ſire on the throne on high
Rolls the loud-pealing thunder thro' the ſky.   20

Her ſpouſe, *Amphion*, who from *Jove* too ſprings,
Divinely taught to ſweep the ſounding ſtrings.

Seven ſprightly ſons the royal bed adorn,
Seven daughters beauteous as the op'ning morn,[3]
As when *Aurora* fills the raviſh'd ſight,   25
And decks the orient realms with roſy light
From their bright eyes the living ſplendors play,
Nor can beholders bear the flaſhing ray.

Wherever, *Niobe*, thou turn'ſt thine eyes,
New beauties kindle, and new joys ariſe !   30
But thou had'ſt far the happier mother prov'd,
{ If this fair offspring had been leſs belov'd :

What

244

What if their charms exceed *Aurora's* teint,
No words could tell them, and no pencil paint,
Thy love too vehement haftens to deftroy   35
Each blooming maid, and each celeftial boy.

Now *Manto* comes, endu'd with mighty fkill,
The paft to explore, the future to reveal.
Thro' *Thebes'* wide ftreets *Tirefia's* daughter came,
Divine *Latona's* mandate to proclaim: 40
The Theban maids to hear the orders ran,
When thus *Mæonia's* prophetefs began:

" Go, *Thebans!* great *Latona's* will obey,
" And pious tribute at her altars pay:
" With rights divine, the goddefs be implor'd,   45
" Nor be her facred offspring unador'd."
Thus *Manto* fpoke. The *Theban* maids obey,
And pious tribute to the goddefs pay.
The rich perfumes afcend in waving fpires,
And altars blaze with confecrated fires;   50
The fair affembly moves with graceful air,
And leaves of laurel bind the flowing hair.

Niobe

Niobe comes with all her royal race,
With charms unnumber'd, and superior grace:
Her *Phrygian* garments of delightful hue,   55
Inwove with gold, refulgent to the view,
Beyond description beautiful she moves
Like heav'nly *Venus*, 'midst her smiles and loves:
She views around the supplicating train,
And shakes her graceful head with stern dif-
          dain,   60
Proudly she turns around her lofty eyes,
And thus reviles celestial deities:
" What madness drives the *Theban* ladies fair
" To give their incense to surrounding air?
" Say why this new sprung deity preferr'd?   65
" Why vainly fancy your petitions heard?
" Or say why *Cæus'* offspring is obey'd,
" While to my goddeship no tribute's paid?
" For me no altars blaze with living fires,
" No bullock bleeds, no frankincense transpires, 70
" Tho' *Cadmus'* palace, not unknown to fame,
" And *Phrygian* nations all revere my name.
                              " Where'er

" Where'er I turn my eyes vaſt wealth I find.

" Lo! here an empreſs with a goddeſs join'd.

" What, ſhall a *Titaneſs* be deify'd,   75

" To whom the ſpacious earth a couch deny'd?

" Nor heav'n, nor earth, nor ſea receiv'd your

    " queen,

" 'Till pitying *Delos*⁶ took the wand'rer in.

" Round me what a large progeny is ſpread!

" No frowns of fortune has my ſoul to dread. 80

" What if indignant ſhe decreaſe my train

" More than *Latona's* number will remain?

"'Then hence, ye *Theban* dames, hence haſte

    " away,

" Nor longer off'rings to *Latona* pay?

" Regard the orders of *Amphion's* ſpouſe,   85

" And take the leaves of laurel from your brows."

Niobe ſpoke. The *Theban* maids obey'd,

Their brows unbound, and left the rights un-

    paid.

The angry goddeſs heard, then ſilence broke

On *Cynthus'* ſummit, and indignant ſpoke;   90

       O   " *Phœbus!*

" *Phœbus!* behold, thy mother in difgrace,

" Who to no goddefs yields the prior place

" Except to *Juno's* felf, who reigns above,

" The fpoufe and fifter of the thund'ring *Jove.*

" *Niobe* fprung from *Tantalus* infpires   95

" Each *Theban* bofom with rebellious fires ;

" No reafon her imperious temper quells,

" But all her father in her tongue rebels ;

" Wrap her own fons for her blafpheming breath,

" *Apollo !* wrap them in the fhades of death." 100

Latona ceas'd, and ardent thus replies,

The God, whofe glory decks th' expanded fkies.

" Ceafe thy complaints, mine be the tafk af-
    " fign'd

" To punifh pride, and fcourge the rebel mind." 7

This *Phœbe* join'd.—They wing their inftant
    flight ;   105

Thebes trembled as th' immortal pow'rs alight.

With   clouds   incompafs'd   glorious *Phœbus*
    ftands ;   4

The feather'd vengeance quiv'ring in his hands.

                                    Near

Near *Cadmus'* walls a plain extended lay,
Where *Thebes'* young princes pafs'd in fport the
    day :   110
There the bold courfers bounded o'er the plains,
While their great mafters held the golden reins.
Ijmenus firft the racing paftime led,
And rul'd the fury of his flying fteed.
" Ah me," he fudden cries, with fhrieking
    breath,   115
While in his breaft he feels the fhaft of death ;
He drops the bridle on his courfer's mane,
Before his eyes in fhadows fwims the plain,
He, the firft-born of great *Amphion's* bed,
Was ftruck the firft, firft mingled with the
    dead.   120

Then didft thou, *Sipylus,* the language hear
Of fate portentous whiftling in the air :
As when th' impending ftorm the failor fees
He fpreads his canvas to the fav'ring breeze,

O 2

So

So to thine horſe thou gav'ſt the golden reins,   125
Gav'ſt him to ruſh impetuous o'er the plains :
But ah ! a fatal ſhaft from *Phæbus'* hand
Smites through thy neck, and ſinks thee on the
 ſand.

Two other brothers were at *wreſtling* found,
And in their paſtime claſpt each other round :   130
A ſhaft that inſtant from *Apollo's* hand
Transfixt them both, and ſtretcht them on the
 ſand :
Together they their cruel fate bemoan'd,
Together languiſh'd, and together groan'd :
Together too th' unbodied ſpirits fled,   135
And ſought the gloomy manſions of the dead.

Alphenor ſaw, and trembling at the view,
Beat his torn breaſt, that chang'd its ſnowy hue.
He flies to raiſe them in a kind embrace ;
A brother's fondneſs triumphs in his face :   140
Alphenor fails in this fraternal deed,
A dart diſpatch'd him (ſo the fates decreed :)
         Soon

Soon as the arrow left the deadly wound,
His iſſuing entrails ſmoak'd upon the ground.

What woes on blooming *Damaſichon* wait !   145
His ſighs portend his near impending fate.
Juſt where the well-made leg begins to be,
And the ſoft ſinews form the ſupple knee,
The youth ſore wounded by the *Delian* god
Attempts t' extract the crime-avenging rod,   150
But, whilſt he ſtrives the will of fate t' avert,
Divine *Apollo* ſends a ſecond dart ;
Swift thro' his throat the feather'd miſchief flies,
Bereft of ſenſe, he drops his head, and dies.

Young *Ilioneus*, the laſt, directs his pray'r,   155
And cries, " My life, ye gods celeſtial ! ſpare."
Apollo heard, and pity touch'd his heart,
But ah ! too late, for he had ſent the dart :
Thou too, O *Ilioneus*, are doom'd to fall,
The fates refuſe that arrow to recal.   160

On

On the fwift wings of ever-flying *Fame*
To *Cadmus'* palace foon the tidings came :
Niobe heard, and with indignant eyes
She thus exprefs'd her anger and furprize :
" Why is fuch privilege to them allow'd ?   165
" Why thus infulted by the *Delian* god ?
" Dwells there fuch mifchief in the pow'rs above ?
" Why fleeps the vengeance of immortal *Jove ?*"
For now *Amphion* too, with grief opprefs'd,
Had plung'd the deadly dagger in his breaft. 170
Niobe now, lefs haughty than before,
With lofty head directs her fteps no more.
She, who late told her pedigree divine,
And drove the *Thebans* from *Latona's* fhrine,
How ftrangely chang'd !——yet beautiful in
      woe,   175
She weeps, nor weeps unpity'd by the foe.
On each pale corfe the wretched mother fpread
Lay overwhelm'd with grief, and kifs'd her dead,
Then rais'd her arms, and thus, in accents flow,
" Be fated cruel *Goddefs !* with my woe;   180
                                               " If

" If I've offended, let thefe ftreaming eyes,

" And let this fev'nfold funeral fuffice :

" Ah ! take this wretched life you deign'd to fave,

" With them I too am carried to the grave.

" Rejoice triumphant, my victorious foe,   185

" But fhow the caufe from whence your triumphs

    " flow ?

" Tho' I unhappy mourn thefe children flain,

" Yet greater numbers to my lot remain."

She ceas'd, the bow-ftring twang'd with awful

    found,

Which ftruck with terror all th' affembly round,

Except the queen, who ftood unmov'd alone,

By her diftreffes more prefumptuous grown.

Near the pale corfes ftood their fifters fair

In fable veftures and difhevell'd hair ;

One, while fhe draws the fatal fhaft away,   195

Faints, falls, and fickens at the light of day.

To footh her mother, lo ! another flies,

And blames the fury of inclement fkies,

And, while her words a filial pity fhow,

Struck dumb——indignant feeks the fhades

    below.   200

                    Now

Now from the fatal place another flies,
Falls in her flight, and languishes, and dies.
Another on her sister drops in death;
A fifth in trembling terrors yields her breath;
While the sixth seeks some gloomy cave in
 vain,   205
Struck with the rest, and mingl'd with the slain.

One only daughter lives, and she the least;
The queen close clasp'd the daughter to her breast:
" Ye heav'nly pow'rs, ah spare me one," she cry'd,
" Ah! spare me one," the vocal hills reply'd: 210
In vain she begs, the Fates her suit deny,
In her embrace she sees her daughter die.

* " The queen of all her family bereft,
" Without or husband, son, or daughter left,
" Grew stupid at the shock. The passing air 215
" Made no impression on her stiff'ning hair.

* This Verse to the End is the Work of another Hand. [8]

" The

" The blood forfook her face : amidſt the flood
" Pour'd from her cheeks, quite fix'd her eye-balls
    " ſtood.
" Her tongue, her palate both obdurate grew,
" Her curdled veins no longer motion knew ; 220
" The uſe of neck, and arms, and feet was gone,
" And ev'n her bowels hard'ned into ſtone:
" A marble ſtatue now the queen appears,
" But from the marble ſteal the ſilent tears."

P

To

To S. M. a young *African* Painter, on seeing his Works. [1]

TO show the lab'ring bosom's deep intent,
  And thought in living characters to paint,
When first thy pencil did those beauties give,
And breathing figures learnt from thee to live,
How did those prospects give my soul delight,   5
A new creation rushing on my sight?
Still, wond'rous youth! each noble path pursue,
On deathless glories fix thine ardent view:
Still may the painter's and the poet's fire
To aid thy pencil, and thy verse conspire!   10
And may the charms of each seraphic theme
Conduct thy footsteps to immortal fame!
High to the blissful wonders of the skies
Elate thy soul, and raise thy wishful eyes.
Thrice happy, when exalted to survey   15
That splendid city, crown'd with endless day,
Whose twice six gates on radiant hinges ring:
Celestial *Salem* blooms in endless spring.

Calm

Calm and ferene thy moments glide along,
And may the mufe infpire each future fong !   20
Still, with the fweets of contemplation blefs'd,
May peace with balmy wings your foul inveft !
But when thefe fhades of time are chas'd away,
And darknefs ends in everlafting day,
On what feraphic pinions fhall we move,   25
And view the landfcapes in the realms above ?
There fhall thy tongue in heav'nly murmurs flow,
And there my mufe with heav'nly tranfport glow :
No more to tell of *Damon's* tender fighs, [2]
Or rifing radiance of *Aurora's* eyes,   30
For nobler themes demand a nobler ftrain,
And purer language on th' ethereal plain.
Ceafe, gentle mufe ! the folemn gloom of night
Now feals the fair creation from my fight.

P 2   To

To His Honour the Lieutenant-Governor, on the
Death of his Lady. *March* 24, 1773. [1]

ALL-conquering Death! by thy resistless
    pow'r,
Hope's tow ring plumage falls to rise no more!
Of scenes terrestrial how the glories fly,
Forget their splendors, and submit to die!
Who ere escap'd thee, but the saint * of old   5
Beyond the flood in sacred annals told,
And the great sage, † whom fiery courses drew
To heav'n's bright portals from *Elisha's* view;
Wond'ring he gaz'd at the refulgent car,
Then snatch'd the mantle floating on the air. 10
From *Death* these only could exemption boast,
And without dying gain'd th' immortal coast.
Not falling millions sate the tyrant's mind,
Nor can the victor's progress be confin'd.
But cease thy strife with *Death*, fond *Nature*,
    cease:
                      15
He leads the *virtuous* to the realms of peace;

            Enoch.   † Elijah.

                                His

His to conduct to the immortal plains,
Where heav'n's Supreme in blifs and glory reigns.

There fits, illuftrious Sir, thy beauteous fpoufe,
A gem-blaz'd circle beaming on her brows. 20
Hail'd with acclaim among the heav'nly choirs,
Her foul new-kindling with feraphic fires,
To notes divine fhe tunes the vocal ftrings,
While heav'n's high concave with the mufic rings.
Virtue's rewards can mortal pencil paint ? 25
No—all defcriptive arts, and eloquence are faint ;
Nor canft thou, *Oliver*, affent refufe
To heav'nly tidings from the *Afric* mufe.

As foon may change thy laws, eternal *fate*,
As the faint mifs the glories I relate; 30
Or her *Benevolence* forgotten lie,
Which wip'd the trick'ling tear from *Mis'ry's* eye.
Whene'er the adverfe winds were known to blow,
When lofs to lofs * enfu'd, and woe to woe,

* Three amiable Daughters who died when juft arrived to
Womens Eftate.

Calm

Calm and ferene beneath her father's hand   35
She fat refign'd to the divine command.

No longer then, great Sir, her death deplore,
And let us hear the mournful figh no more,
Reftrain the forrow ftreaming from thine eye,
Be all thy future moments crown'd with joy !   40
Nor let thy wifhes be to earth confin'd,
But foaring high purfue th' unbodied mind.
Forgive the mufe, forgive th' advent'rous lays,
That fain thy foul to heav'nly fcenes would raife.

A Farewel

A Farewel to AMERICA.[1] To Mrs. S. W. [2]

I.

ADIEU, *New-England's* smiling meads,
    Adieu, the flow'ry plain:
I leave thine op'ning charms, O spring,
    And tempt the roaring main.

II.

In vain for me the flow'rets rife,   6
    And boaft their gaudy pride,
While here beneath the northern fkies
    I mourn for *health* deny'd.

III.

Celeftial maid of rofy hue,
    O let me feel thy reign!   10
I languifh till thy face I view,
    Thy vanifh'd joys regain.

IV. *Sufannah*

261

IV.

Sufannab mourns, nor can I bear
  To fee the cryftal fhow'r,
Or mark the tender falling tear   15
  At fad departure's hour;

V.

Not unregarding can I fee
  Her foul with grief oppreft:
But let no fighs, no groans for me,
  Steal from her penfive breaft.   20

VI.

In vain the feather'd warblers fing,
  In vain the garden blooms,
And on the bofom of the fpring
  Breathes out her fweet perfumes,

VII.

While for *Britannia's* diftant fhore   25
  We fweep the liquid plain,
And with aftonifh'd eyes explore
  The wide-extended main.

VIII. Lo!

VIII.

Lo! *Health* appears! celeſtial dame!
  Complacent and ſerene,
With *Hebe*'s mantle o'er her Frame,   30
  With ſoul-delighting mein.

IX.

To mark the vale where *London* lies
  With miſty vapours crown'd,
Which cloud *Aurora*'s thouſand dyes,   35
  And veil her charms around,

X.

Why, *Phœbus*, moves thy car ſo ſlow?
  So ſlow thy riſing ray?
Give us the famous town to view,
  Thou glorious king of day!

XI.

For thee, *Britannia*, I reſign
  New-England's ſmiling fields;
To view again her charms divine,
  What joy the proſpect yields!

Q

XII. But

XII.

But thou! Temptation hence away,   45
    With all thy fatal train
Nor once feduce my foul away,
    By thine enchanting ftrain.

XIII.

Thrice happy they, whofe heav'nly fhield
    Secures their fouls from harms,   50
And fell *Temptation* on the field
    Of all its pow'r difarms!

Bofton, May 7, 1773.

A REBUS,

A REBUS, by *I. B.*[1]

I.

A BIRD delicious to the taste,
   On which an army once did feast,
  Sent by an hand unseen;
A creature of the horned race,
Which *Britain's* royal standards grace;   5
  A gem of vivid green;

II.

A town of gaiety and sport,
Where beaux and beauteous nymphs resort,
  And gallantry doth reign;
A *Dardan* hero fam'd of old   10
For youth and beauty, as we're told,
  And by a monarch slain;

III.

A peer of popular applause,
Who doth our violated laws,
  And grievances proclaim.   15
Th' initials show a vanquish'd town,
That adds fresh glory and renown
  To old *Britannia's* fame.

Q 2

An

An ANSWER to the *Rebus*, by the Author of thefe
POEMS. [1]

THE poet afks, and *Phillis* can't refufe
   To fhew th'obedience of the Infant mufe,
She knows the *Quail* of moft inviting tafte
Fed *Ifrael's* army in the dreary wafte;
And what's on *Britain's* royal ftandard borne,   5
But the tall, graceful, rampant *Unicorn?*
The *Emerald* with a vivid verdure glows
Among the gems which regal crowns compofe;
Bofton's a town, polite and debonair,
To which the beaux and beauteous nymphs repair,
Each *Helen* ftrikes the mind with fweet furprife,
While living lightning flafhes from her eyes.
See young *Euphorbus* of the *Dardan* line
By *Menelaus'* hand to death refign : [2]
The well known peer of popular applaufe
Is C—n [3] zealous to fupport our laws.
   Quebec now vanquifh'd muft obey,
   She too muft annual tribute pay
   To *Britain* of immortal fame,
   And add new glory to her name.   20

F I N I S.

CONTENTS.

On

CONTENTS.

On

CONTENTS.

NOTES

Title page.

1. The facsimile of this edition is reprinted with the permission of Kraus Reprint, a division of Kraus-Thomson Organization Limited.

Dedication page.

1. Having left Boston on May 8, and reaching London on June 17, 1773, Phillis probably wrote this mistaken date en route. She had received permission to dedicate her book to the Countess of Huntingdon as early as February or March of that year.

John Wheatley's letter to Phillis Wheatley's London publisher.

1. For a briefer version of this biographical sketch, signed "Nath¹ Wheatley/ Boston New England Oct. 12th, 1772," see "Phillis Wheatley's Variant Poems and Letters."

2. Sailing from Boston on December 23, 1765, the celebrated Mohegan Indian converted minister, Samson Occom (1732–1792) and a white fellow minister, the Reverend Nathaniel Whittaker, were in London and Scotland until 1768, lecturing to raise a record-breaking total of almost £12,000 for the benefit of Occom's alma mater, Moor's Indian Charity School in Lebanon, Connecticut, before it would move and become the Dartmouth College of Hanover, New Hampshire. Phillis's letter to Occom is not extant.

3. See Phillis's translation of Virgil's story of Niobe, below.

To the PUBLICK.

1. This attestation was first printed separately in London newspapers as part of a promotional campaign staged by Archibald Bell, Phillis's London publisher, anxious to make sales of his printing of the book to London readers. (See "Phillis Wheatley's Variant Poems and Letters.") Appearing in such newspapers as the *London Chronicle* for September 9–11 and *Lloyd's Evening Post and British Chronicle* for September 10–13 and 13–15, 1773, this attestation was dated "*Boston Oct.* 28, 1772." Because he had already cited them as part of his promotion campaign in the aforementioned and other London newspapers, Archibald Bell omitted the dedication, the preface, the biographical sketch of Phillis, and the attestation from his first London, 1773 edition of Wheatley's *Poems on Various Subjects, Religious and Moral.* At least three other London, 1773 editions of this volume, and subsequent American and London reprintings, did include the dedication, the preface, the biographical sketch, and the attestation, undated.

2. Several of these eighteen wealthy merchants, statesmen, and ministers were related through marriage and blood. Marrying sisters, Governor Thomas Hutchinson (1711–1780) and Lieutenant-Governor Andrew Oliver (1706–1774) were brothers-in-law; a cousin of the Reverend Mather Byles (1706–1788), the Reverend Samuel Mather (1723–1791) married a sister of Hutchinson; James Bowdoin (1726–1790) married a daughter of John Erving (1728–1816), while James Pitts (1710–1776) married Bowdoin's sister. Nevertheless, factions of them were implacable political rivals and enemies. In less than a year after signing this document, many of them would rejoice to learn of Governor Hutchinson's political downfall and his ultimately ignominious departure from Boston in 1774 for England, where he would die, a broken man. That these men all signed, or agreed to have signed, this nonpolitical attestation is something of a tribute to Mrs. Susanna Wheatley's unrelenting persistence, and Phillis's respected reputation. John Wheatley was tailor to John Hancock (1737–1793).

Phillis wrote poems to and about Oliver, Hubbard (1702–1773), Bowdoin, Cooper (1725–1783), and Moorhead (1704–1773). When he published his sermon on the death of the Reverend George Whitefield in London in 1771, the Reverend Ebenezer Pemberton (1704–1777) kindly appended Phillis's already well-known elegy on Whitefield. See the note to the volume poem, "To the Rev. Dr. Thomas Amory . . . ," for her relationship with the Reverend Charles Chauncy (1705–1787). The Reverend Andrew Eliot, of the New North Church, had defied his own congregation's proffering of a gift slave, and was known for his anti-slavery views. Harrison Gray (1711?–1794) had introduced anti-slavery legislation to the council who tabled it. Joseph Green (1706–1780) was a popular wit and Tory merchant who boasted one of the largest libraries in Boston. In a letter dated May 25, 1772, Richard Carey (1717–1790) described Phillis favorably to the Countess of Huntingdon in London; he also wrote a kindly letter of introduction for Phillis on May 3, 1773, which she carried with her a few days later when she sailed from Boston to London.

3. In other 1773 editions, the name is spelled correctly as "Hutchinson."

4. I.e., *The Rev.* Charles Chauncy, D.D., as spelled in other 1773 printings of the volume.

5. I.e., *The Rev.* Eb[enezer] Pemberton, D.D., so spelled in other 1773 printings and subsequent English and American reprintings.

6. Last known to have been in the possession of Archibald Bell, the London publisher of Phillis's volume, the manuscripts for this attestation, and for all other original texts of the volume, are non-extant.

To Maecenas.

1. Gaius Cilinius Maecenas was known as a powerful Roman statesman and wealthy patron of poets Horace and Virgil, but he was not known for his own poetry-writing talents, and Phillis's "Maecenas" seems to refer to a much admired contemporary poet (lines 23–28).

2. The alphabetical letters running at the bottom of pages throughout this facsimile are indications for bookbinders who arranged and gathered the printed sheets into signatures, folded units of which physically make up the succession of a book's pages.

3. See "Phillis Wheatley's Variant Poems and Letters," for variants of lines 7–14.

4. *Pelides.* The son of Peleus, i.e., Achilles of *The Iliad.*

5. *Maro.* Publius Vergilius Maro, i.e., Virgil, born near Mantua, hailed by many as the greatest of Latin poets.

6. *The Nine.* The nine muses in Greek mythology, various ones of which were traditionally invoked for inspiration by poets.

7. *Helicon.* One of the mountain homes of the muses.

8. Line 42 reads "With the first glory in the realms of fame" in the 1834, 1835, and 1838 Boston reprinted editions, and in W.G. Allen's *Wheatley, Banneker and Horton* (Boston, 1849). Throughout this facsimile are noted only selections of the many such variants found in successive reprintings of the 1773 volume.

9. *Thames.* The Thames River in London.

10. *Naiads.* Water nymphs.

11. *Phoebus.* I.e., Phoebus Apollo, god of the sun, Phillis's favorite mythological god.

12. *Aurora.* Goddess of the dawn.

13. *Parnassus.* Another mountain home of the muses.

To the University of Cambridge, in New-England.

1. See "Phillis Wheatley's Variant Poems and Letters" for a variant version.

2. Line 17 is omitted from the 1834, 1835, and 1838 reprinted editions.

To the KING's Most Excellent Majesty. . . .

1. See "Phillis Wheatley's Variant Poems and Letters" for a variant version.

2. In the 1793 reprinted edition line 10 reads "Live with heav'ns choicest blessings crown'd."

On being brought from AFRICA to AMERICA.
  1. Often cited as an instance of Phillis's Negrophobic denigration of her native African homeland, this poem is rather to be read as a terse refutation of some white Christians' racist notions that, by biblical mandate, the souls of black people were everlastingly doomed. Phillis is not disparaging Africa because of its black populations but because it is pagan, i.e., not Christian.

On the Death of the Rev. Dr. SEWELL. 1769.
  1. See "Phillis Wheatley's Variant Poems and Letters" for variant versions.

On the Death of the Rev. Mr. GEORGE WHITEFIELD. 1770.
  1. See "Phillis Wheatley's Variant Poems and Letters" for variant versions.

On the Death of a young Lady of Five Years of Age.
  1. See "Phillis Wheatley's Variant Poems and Letters" for a variant version.

To a Lady on the Death of her Husband.
  1. See "Phillis Wheatley's Variant Poems and Letters" for a variant version.
  2. Line 18 reads "And her last groan shall shake the azure ský" in the 1793 reprinted edition.

Goliath of Gath.
  1. See Appendix A.
  2. Line 103 reads "The prey deliver'd and the lion kill'd" in the 1834, 1835, 1838 reprinted editions, and also in Wm. G. Allen's *Wheatley, Banneker and Horton* (Boston, 1849), p. 26.

To a Lady on the Death of Three Relations.
  1. Line 4 reads "To blacken Phoebus, and desolate the sky" in John R. Slattery's review, "Phillis Wheatley, The Negro Poetess," *The Catholic World*, XXX (April–September, 1884), 494.

To a Clergyman on the Death of his Lady.
  1. See "Phillis Wheatley's Variant Poems and Letters" for a variant version.

An HYMN to the Morning.
  1. *Feather'd race.* I.e., birds.
  2. *Calliope.* Greek muse of epic poetry.

Isaiah lxiii 1–8.
  1. See Appendix B.

On Recollection.
  1. See "Phillis Wheatley's Variant Poems and Letters" for a variant version.
  2. *Mneme.* I.e., Mnemosyne, mother of Greek muses; especially known as the goddess of memory of great events.
  3. Phillis's age at the time she composed this piece.
  4. An instance of pious hyperbole.

On Imagination.
  1. This line reads "And soft captivity invades the mind" in a fourteen-line excerpt from this poem in J.G. Steadman, *A Narrative of a five years' expedition against the/ Revolted Negroes of Surinam,/ in Guiana . . .* 2 volumes (London, 1796), II, 259–260.
  2. This line reads "The frozen deeps may burst their iron bands" in Gilbert Imlay, *Topographical Description of the Western Territory of North America . . .* (London, 1797), p. 229; in the 1834, 1835, and 1838 Boston reprinted editions; and in Benjamin Brawley, *Early Negro American Writers* (Chapel Hill, 1935), p. 43.
  3. This line reads "Cease then, my son, cease then th'unequal lay" in Brawley, ibid., p. 43.

A Funeral POEM on the Death of C.E./ an Infant of Twelve Months.

1. See "Phillis Wheatley's Variant Poems and Letters" for variant versions.

To Captain H——d, of the 65th Regiment.

1. Mindful of how increasingly demonstrative Patriot Bostonians would likely react to this poem applauding the virtues of a British officer, Captain John Hanfield, of a royal regiment which, with other royal troops garrisoning the town since late 1769, had been seen as part of an "army of occupation," Phillis quietly omitted this piece from her 1772 proposals. Bostonians rejected these 1772 proposals, however. When her volume was to be published in London, Phillis included the poem.

To the Right Honourable WILLIAM, Earl/ of Dartmouth . . .

1. See "Phillis Wheatley's Variant Poems and Letters" for variant versions.

ODE to NEPTUNE.

1. There are those who believe that this poem refers to a trip taken by Phillis's mistress, Susanna Wheatley, to London, but there is no evidence that she ever sailed there. When Captain Robert Calef, a Wheatley employee, sailed the Wheatley-owned ship, *London*, for London on November 19, 1772, Mrs. Wheatley's name was not noted among the passengers. In fact, Calef wrote to Mrs. Wheatley from London on January 5, 1773. As late as May 13, 1773, the Countess of Huntingdon wrote to Mrs. Wheatley saying, among other things, ". . . I shall probably never see one of you/ upon earth. . . ."

2. *Susannah.* A 1773 volume of Phillis's *Poems* in the American Antiquarian Society includes a handwritten note saying that this poem was dedicated to a "Mrs. Susana Wright," a celebrated artist who worked in wax.

To a Lady on her remarkable Preservation in an Hurricane . . .

1. *Nereids.* Nymphs of the ocean waters.

2. *His* [Aeolus's] "*winged sons*" were the four winds (North, South, East, and West).

To a Lady and her Children, on the Death of her Son and their Brother.

1. In her 1772 proposals for a volume Phillis had hoped to publish in Boston that year (see below), she had first used the title "To Mrs. Boylston and Children on the Death of Her Son and Their Brother."

To a Gentleman and Lady on the Death of the Lady's Brother and Sister. . . .

1. In her 1772 proposal list of poems (see below), Phillis had first used the title "To James Sullivan, Esq: and Lady on the Death of her Brother and Sister, and a Child, Avis, aged 12 Months." Such revision shows how Phillis revised from the original specificity that would have flattered Bostonians, for whom her 1772 volume was at first intended, to the generality that would make more sense to her readers in London, where her volume was finally published.

On the Death of Dr. Samuel Marshall. . . .

1. See "Phillis Wheatley's Variant Poems and Letters" for a variant version.

To a Gentleman on his Voyage to Great-Britain. . . .

1. O R——, A comma should follow the expletive "O," preceding the letter "R" (the first letter of the last name of Joseph Rotch, Jr. (1743–1773) whom she is addressing in the poem.) Ill, young Rotch sailed from Boston at the end of 1772 for a trip to London that he hoped would help him regain his failing health. He died in London shortly after landing there.

To the Rev. Dr. THOMAS AMORY. . . .

1. According to a catalogue card in the American Antiquarian Society, in a non-extant copy of Thomas Amory, *Daily Devotions Assisted and Recommended in Four Sermons*, 2ed. corr/ ected/ (London, printed: Boston: Reprinted, E. Russell, MDCCLXXII), Boston's Reverend Charles Chauncy had

inscribed "The gift of Dr. Charles Chauncy to Phl^s Wheatley, Boston, Oct. 4, 1772." On the verso of this inscription page was noted "This book the gift of Miss Phillis Wheatley—Boston—March 20, 1774," written by Thomas Wallcutt (1758–1804), a grandnephew of Phillis's mistress, a friend, admirer, and correspondent, and one of the founders of the Massachusetts Historical Society.

2. This line reads "In vain would Vice her works conceal" in the 1793 reprinted edition.

On the Death of J.C. an Infant.

1. Line 3 has been omitted from the 1834, 1835, and 1838 reprinted editions.

2. This line reads "No more shall smile, no more shall raise his head" in Armistead Wilson, *A Tribute for the Negro* (Manchester, England, 1848), p. 337.

3. This line reads "'Where flies my child?' 'tis thus I seem to hear" in Wilson, ibid., p. 337. Other variants in Wilson's version of this poem, also in 42 lines, are routine modernizations in punctuation and spelling.

To the Honourable T.H. Esq: on the Death of his Daughter.

1. See "Phillis Wheatley's Variant Poems and Letters" for a variant version.

Niobe in Distress for her Children slain by Apollo. . . .

1. Richard Wilson (1714–1782) was one of the most prominent landscape artists of his day. He painted several landscapes for Lord Dartmouth and rendered his "Niobe" three times. It is unclear which of the three Niobe paintings or their 1761 engravings Phillis refers to here.

2. *Dodonean Jove.* Dodona was especially venerated as the site of an ancient oracle of Zeus.

3. This line reads "Seven daughters, beauteous as the rising morn" in the 1834, 1835, and 1838 reprinted editions, and in Brawley, op. cit., p. 44.

4. *Manto.* Prophetess and daughter of Tiresias (line 39), himself a prophet.

5. *Coeus' offspring.* Latona. Her father, Coeus, was a Titan, whose race was overthrown by the gods, according to one version, leaving him dominionless.

6. *Delos.* The only place that would receive dominionless Latona when, pregnant by Zeus who had abandoned her to avoid the wrath of his wife, Hera, she roamed, rejected, from place to place, looking for a locale in which to deliver her children, Artemis and her brother, Phoebus Apollo.

7. This line reads "To punish and to scourge the rebel mind" in the 1834, 1835, and 1838 reprinted editions, and in Brawley, ibid., p. 47.

8. *The Work of another Hand.* This writer is unknown; it was probably the work of Mary Wheatley, Phillis's tutor in English and Latin. See Appendix C.

To S.M. a young African Painter. . . .

1. S[cipio] M[oorhead], a black servant of the Reverend John Moorhead of the Federal Street Presbyterian Church. Scipio is so identified from a pencilled note in a 1773 volume of Phillis's *Poems* housed at the American Antiquarian Society. John Moorhead's wife, Sarah (1712–1774), enjoyed a local reputation as an instructor of art to Bostonians; she also instructed Scipio "whose genius inclined him that way." At a watch-maker's shop, not far from where Phillis lived on King Street, there was, in 1773 ". . . a Negro man whose extraordinary genius has been assisted by one of the best masters in London; he takes faces at the lowest Rates. Specimens of his Performances may be seen at said Place." This notice may, or may not, refer to Scipio who may, or may not, have painted Phillis's portrait that was engraved for the celebrated frontispiece of her volume of *Poems.* Dr. Dorothy Porter Wesley, curator emerita of the Moorland-Spingarn collection at Howard University, reports that, in 1945, the antiquarian Charles Heartman offered for sale an original pen and ink portrait of Phillis, dated 1774 (which may have been the model for W.E. Braxton's pen and ink drawing of Phillis that was printed in Charles Johnson, editor, *Ebony and Topaz Col-*

lecteana (for the National Urban League in 1927). See Illustrations, above. In 1947, Dr. Porter received a letter from a dealer in early Americana, offering for sale a pencilled portrait of Phillis, which, the dealer believed, was the portrait on which the engraving in Phillis's 1773 volume was based.

2. *Damon's tender sighs.* As none of Phillis Wheatley's known poems concerns a Damon (of the Damon and Pythias story?), this name may refer to a poem or painting by Scipio.

To His Honour the Lieutenant-Governor. . . .

1. Mary Sanford (1714–1774) married Andrew Oliver (1706–1774) in 1734, as his second wife, and delivered seventeen children before he rose to become Lieutenant-Governor of the Province of Massachusetts in 1770.

A Farewel to America. To Mrs. S.W.

1. See "Phillis Wheatley's Variant Poems and Letters" for a variant version.

2. Mrs. S.W. Mrs. Susanna Wheatley, Phillis's mistress.

A Rebus, by I.B.

1. *I.B.* James Bowdoin?

An Answer to the Rebus. . . .

1. Phillis's "answer" to the Rebus is "QUEBEC," initial letters of which are found in lines 3, 6, 7, 8, 12, and 15. "I learn . . . that Phillis . . . excelled particularly in acrostics and in other equally difficult tricks of literary dexterity," from Rufus Griswold, ed., *The Female Poets of America* (Philadelphia, 1849), p. 31.

2. In Book XVII of Homer's *Iliad*, Menelaus, a Greek leader, slays Euphorbus, a Trojan who had slain Patroclus, the dearest friend of Achilles, the hero of the book. See Phillis's poem, "To Maecenas," lines 17–20.

3. *C——m.* William Pitt, 1st Earl of Chatham (1708–1778), seen by some Bostonians as sympathetic to the colonials' grievances. See Appendix G.

PHILLIS WHEATLEY'S LATER POEMS
1773–1784

An
ELEGY
To Miss. Mary Moorhead,
On the DEATH of her Father,
The Rev. Mr. John Moorhead.[1]

Involv'd in Clouds of Wo, *Maria* mourns
And various Anguish wracks her Soul by turns;
See thy lov'd Parent languishing in Death,
His Exit watch, and catch his flying Breath;
"Stay happy Shade," distress'd *Maria* cries;
"Stay happy Shade," the hapless Church replies;
"Suspend a while, suspend thy rapid flight,
"Still with thy Friendship, chear our sullen Night,
"The sullen Night of Error, Sin, and Pain;
"See Earth astonish'd at the Loss, complain;"
Thine, and the Church's Sorrows I deplore;
Moorhead is dead, and Friendship is no more;
From Earth she flies, nor mingles with our Wo,
Since cold the Breast, where once she deign'd to glow;
Here shone the heavenly Virtue, there confess'd,
Celestial Love, reign'd joyous in his Breast;
Till Death grown jealous for his drear Domain,
Sent his dread Offspring, unrelenting Pain.
With hasty Wing, the Son of Terror flies,
Lest *Moorhead* find the Portal of the Skies;
Without a Passage through the Shades below,
Like great *Elijah*, Death's triumphant Foe;
Death follows soon, nor leaves the Prophet long,
His Eyes are seal'd, and every Nerve unstrung;
Forever silent is the stiff'ning Clay,
While the rapt Soul, explores the Realms of Day,
Oft has he strove to raise the Soul from Earth,
Oft has he travail'd in the heavenly Birth;

1. The Reverend John Moorhead (1703–1773), popular Irish-born pastor of the Scotch Presbyterian Church on Long Lane (today's Federal Street) from 1730 until his death. Mary Moorhead, his daughter, born in 1732, had an older brother, Parsons, and a younger brother, John. Moorhead's wife, Sarah, instructed Bostonians in drawing, and she also instructed Scipio, the Moorhead's black servant, who had native artistic ability. Phillis included a poem, "To S.M. A Young African Painter, On Seeing His Works," in her volume of 1773. The text is from a broadside in the American Antiquarian Society.

Till Jesus took possession of the Soul,
Till the new Creature liv'd throughout the whole.
   When fierce conviction seiz'd the Sinner's Mind,
The Law-loud thundering he to Death consign'd;
JEHOVAH'S Wrath revolving, he surveys,
The Fancy's terror, and the Souls amaze.
Say, what is Death? The Gloom of endless Night,
Which from the Sinner, bars the Gates of Light:
Say, what is Hell? In Horrors passing strange;
His Vengeance views, who seals his final Change;
The winged Hours, the final Judgment brings,
Decides his Fate, and that of Gods and Kings;
Tremendous Doom! And dreadful to be told,
To dwell in Tophet 'stead of shrines of Gold.
"Gods. Ye shall die like Men," the Herald cries,
"And stil'd no more the Children of the Skies."
   Trembling he sees the horrid Gulf appear,
Creation quakes, and no Deliverer near;
With Heart relenting to his Feelings kind,
See Moorhead hasten to relieve his Mind.
See him the Gospel's healing Balm impart,
To sooth the Anguish of his tortur'd Heart.
He points the trembling Mountain, and the Tree,
Which bent beneath th'incarnate Deity,
How God descended, wonderous to relate,
To bear our Crimes, a dread enormous Weight;
Seraphic Strains too feeble to repeat,
Half the dread Punishment the GOD-HEAD meet.
Suspended there, (till Heaven was reconcil'd,)
Like *Moses'* Serpent in the Desert wild
The Mind appeas'd what new Devotion glows,
With Joy unknown, the raptur'd Soul o'erflows;
While on his GOD-like Savior's Glory bent,
His Life proves witness of his Heart's intent.

Lament ye indigent the Friendly Mind,
Which oft relented, to your Mis'ry kind.
   With humble Gratitude he render'd Praise,
To Him whose Spirit had inspir'd his Lays;
To Him whose Guidance gave his Words to flow,

Divine instruction, and the Balm of Wo:
To you his Offspring, and his Church, be given,
A triple Portion of his Thirst for Heaven;
Such was the Prophet; we the stroke deplore,
Which let's us hear his warning Voice no more.
But cease complaining, hush each murm'ring Tongue,
Pursue the Example which inspires my Song.
Let his Example in your Conduct shine;
Own the afflicting Providence, divine;
So shall bright Periods grace your joyful Days,
And heavenly Anthems swell your Songs of Praise.

Boston, Decem.   *Phillis Wheatley.*
  15   1773

Printed from the Original Manuscript, and Sold by William
M'Alpine, at his Sshop, in *Marlborough-Street*, 1773.

[TO A GENTLEMAN OF THE NAVY]
For the ROYAL AMERICAN MAGAZINE

By particular request we insert the following Poem[1] addressed, by/ Philis (a young Affrican, of surprising genius) to a gentleman of/ the navy, with his reply./[2] By this single instance may be seen, the importance of education,—/ Uncultivated nature is much the same in every part of the globe./ It is probable Europe and Affrica would be alike savage or po-/ lite in the same circumstances; though, it may be questioned, whe-/ ther men who have no artificial wants, are capable of becoming so/ ferocious as those, who, by faring sumptuously every day, are re-/ duced to a habit of thinking it necessary to their happiness, to/ plunder the whole human race./[3]

Celestial muse! for sweetness fam'd inspire
My wondrous theme with true poetic fire,
Rochfort,[4] for thee! And Greaves[5] deserve my lays

1. From *The Royal American Magazine, or Universal Repository of Instruction and Amusement*, 1 (December, 1774), 473–474.
2. For the naval gentleman's "reply" to Phillis's poem, see the verses, "The Answer," printed immediately below.
3. This headnote is anonymous. The editor of the magazine at this time was Joseph Greenleaf, a former Justice of the Peace, dismissed for his anti-Loyalist views. A printer of pamphlets, Greenleaf assumed the publication of the *Royal Magazine* after his Patriot colleague, Isaiah Thomas, failed as the periodical's publisher after six months; Greenleaf continued publishing the magazine until April, 1775, when the outbreak of war caused him to stop.
4. *Rochfort.* Presumably, a young officer of the Royal Navy who had served off the coast of Africa, admired Isaac Newton and John Milton (see "The Answer," below), and liked telling Phillis of his earlier adventures off the coasts of Gambia and Senegal. The name "Rochfort" or "Rochford" cannot be found in the rosters of Royal Naval officers serving in Boston in 1774; e.g., see ". . . a List *of the Squadron in* North/ America *under the command of* Adm. Graves—/ *Taken from* Mills *and* Hicks's *Register*." The names of the twenty-five royal officers based in Boston in 1774 are listed with the names of Admiral Graves and all of their ships, but "Rochfort" or "Rochford" does not appear.
5. There were several royal naval officers named Graves, two of them—cousins, and both named Thomas—had both served earlier off the coast of Africa. But as Phillis is clearly addressing "Cerulean youths" for whom "the thirst of glory burns each youthful breast," she is probably discussing the Lieutenant Thomas Graves who was born in 1747 and who died in 1814. He sailed to the colonies with his uncle, Admiral Samuel Graves (1713–1787) who assumed command of the North American station based at Boston as of June, 1774, relieving Admiral John Montagu, another of Phillis's several military heroes. (See the listing of poetic titles and letters in her 1779 proposals.) As the above poem by Phillis, "The Answer" by Rochford (?), and "Philis's Reply to the Answer" were all written within a single month and bespeak a familiarity between Phillis and the officers, both Rochford and Graves may have been billeted in John Wheatley's King Street mansion by virtue of the expansion of the 1765 British Quartering Act.

The sacred tribute of ingenuous praise.
For here, true merit shuns the glare of light,
She loves oblivion, and evades the sight.
At sight of her, see dawning genius rise
And stretch her pinions to her native skies.
  Paris, for Helen's bright resistless charms,
Made Illion bleed and set the world in arms.
Had you appear'd on the Achaian shore
Troy now had stood, and Helen charm'd no more.
The Phrygian hero had resign'd the dame
For purer joys in friendship's sacred flame,
The noblest gift, and of immortal kind,
That brightens, dignifies the manly mind.
  Calliope,[6] half gracious to my prayer,
Grants but the half and scatters half in air.
  Far in the space where ancient Albion[7] keeps
Amidst the roarings of the sacred deeps,
Where willing forests leave their native plain,
Descend, and instant, plough the wat'ry main.
Strange to relate! with canvas wings they speed
To distant worlds; of distant worlds the dread.
The trembling natives of the peaceful main,
Astonish'd view the heroes of the main,
Wond'ring to see two chiefs of matchless grace,
Of generous bosom, and ingenuous face,
From ocean sprung, like ocean foes to rest,
The thirst of glory burns each youthful breast.
  In virtue's cause, the muse implores for grace,
These blooming sons of Neptune's royal race;
Cerulean youths![8] your joint assent declare,
Virtue to rev'rence, more than mortal fair,
A crown of glory, which the muse will twine,
Immortal trophy! Rochfort shall be thine:
Thine too O Greaves! for virtue's offspring share,
Celestial friendship and the muse's care.
Yours is the song, and your's the honest praise,
Lo! Rochfort smiles, and Greaves approves my lays.
                BOSTON, October 30th, 1774.

6. *Calliope*. The muse of epic poetry.
7. *Albion*. England.
8. *Cerulean youths*. Probably a reference to the royal naval officers' blue uniforms.

The ANSWER[1]

Celestial muse! sublimest of the nine,
Assist my song, and dictate every line;
Inspire me once, nor with imperfect lays,
To sing this great, this lovely virgin's praise:
But yet, alas! what tribute can I bring,
WH——TL-Y but smiles, whilst I thus faintly sing,
    Behold with reverence, and with joy adore;
The lovely daughter of the Affric shore,
Where every grace, and every virtue join,
That kindles friendship and makes love divine;
In hue as diff'rent as in souls above;
The rest of mortals who in vain have strove,
Th'immortal wreathe, the muse's gift to share,
Which heav'n reserv'd for this angelic fair.

    Blest be the guilded shore,[2] the happy land,
Where spring and autumn gently hand in hand;
O'er shady forests that scarce know a bound,
In vivid blaze alternately dance round:
Where cancers[3] torrid heat the soul inspires;
With strains divine and true poetic fires;
(Far from the reach of Hudson's chilly bay)
Where cheerful phoebus makes all nature gay;
Where sweet refreshing breezes gently fan;
The flow'ry path, the ever verdant Lawn,
The artless grottos, and the soft retreats;
"At once the lover and the thea [sic] muse's seats."
Where nature taught, (tho' strange it is to tell,)
Her flowing pencil Europe to excell.
Britania's glory long hath fill'd the skies;

Whilst other nations, tho' with envious eyes,
Have view'd her growing greatness, and the rules;
That's long been taught in her untainted schools:

1. From *The Royal American Magazine, or Universal Repository of Instruction and Amusement*, 1 (December, 1774), 474–475, these flattering lines were written in anonymous reaction to Wheatley's poem, immediately above.
2. *The guilded shore*. I.e., "Guinea," or "the Gold Coast," the West African coast. In 1768, when he was a Captain, Samuel Graves and his nephew, Thomas, were despatched to patrol the coast lines of Senegal and Gambia where England had slaving interests that were coveted by other western nations, including France.
3. *Cancers*. I.e., Cancer's, the zodiacal reference to Africa.

Where great Sir Isaac![4] whose immortal name;
Still shines the brightest on the seat of fame;
By ways and methods never known before;
The sacred depth of nature did explore:
And like a God, on philosophic wings;
Rode with the planets thro' their circling rings:
Surveying nature with a curious eye,
And viewing other systems in the sky.

   Where nature's bard[5] with true poetic lays,
The pristine state of paradise displays,
And with a genius that's but very rare
Describes the first the only happy pair
That in terrestrial mansions ever reign'd,
View'd happiness now lost, and now regain'd,
Unravel'd all the battles of the Gods,
And view'd old night below the antipodes.
On his imperious throne, with awful sway,
Commanding regions yet unknown today,

   Or where these lofty bards have dwelt so long,
That ravish'd Europe with their heavenly song,

   But now this blessful clime, this happy land,
That all the neighbouring nations did command;
Whose royal navy neptunes waves did sweep,
Reign'd Prince alone, and sov'reign of the deep:
No more can boast, but of the power to kill,
By force of arms, or diabolic skill.
For softer strains we quickly must repair
To Wheatly's song, for Wheatly is the fair;
That has the art, which art could ne'er acquire:
To dress each sentence with seraphic fire.

   Her wondrous virtues I could ne'er express!
To paint her charms, would only make them less.

December 2d. 1774.

---

4. *Great Sir Isaac.* Sir Isaac Newton (1642–1727), English mathematician.
5. *Nature's bard.* I.e., John Milton (1608–1674), English poet, author of *Paradise Lost* and *Paradise Regained*, both of which works are referred to five lines lower in this poem.

PHILIS's *Reply to the Answer in our last by the Gentleman in the Navy*[1]

For one bright moment, heavenly goddess! shine,
Inspire my song and form the lays divine.
Rochford, attend. Beloved of Phoebus! hear,
A truer sentence never reach'd thine ear;
Struck with thy song, each vain conceit resign'd
A soft affection seiz'd my grateful mind,
While I each golden sentiment admire
In thee, the muse's bright celestial fire.
The generous plaudit 'tis not mine to claim,
A muse untutor'd, and unknown to fame.

The heavenly sisters pour thy notes along
And crown their bard with every grace of song.
My pen, least favour'd by the tuneful nine,
Can never rival, never equal thine;
Then fix the humble Afric muse's seat
At British Homer's and Sir Isaac's feet.[2]
Those bards whose fame in deathless strains arise
Creation's boast, and fav'rites of the skies.

In fair description are thy powers display'd
In artless grottos, and the sylvan shade;
Charm'd with thy painting, how my bosom burns!
And pleasing Gambia[3] on my soul returns,

1. From The *Royal American Magazine*, 11 (January, 1775), 34–35.
2. *British Homer's and Sir Isaac's feet.* John Milton and Sir Isaac Newton.
3. *Gambia.* In this poem, Phillis responds specifically to names mentioned in "The Answer." As Gambia is not mentioned in that poem, this may be a reference to her remembered African homeland. If she were too young to have remembered her African homeland when, at age 7 or 8, she was kidnapped, enslaved, and transported to Boston, she might have inquired of Timothy Fitch, one-time successful slave merchant living in nearby Medford, Massachusetts. Fitch could have asked such information from Captain Peter Gwin, who commanded Fitch's slave ship, the *Phillis*, which carried Phillis and other slaves to Boston in the summer of 1761. Fitch repeatedly ordered Gwin to get slaves from the coasts of Senegal and Gambia, smallest of today's independent African nations, a finger shaped peninsula country jutting out into the Atlantic ocean from the inner south-western side of Senegal. An anecdote tells of Phillis's having tea with Fitch's second wife and their daughters in the Fitch's Medford home. See Appendix H4. If Gwin could remember where, on the African coast, he had purchased Phillis, it need not have meant that she was a native of that locale. Slaves were often brought from miles distant from coastal locales where they were bought by European slavers. Whether she is being poetically extravagant or defensive or indeed autobiographical in this poem, Phillis is the first black American poet to rhapsodize about black Africa.

With native grace in spring's luxuriant reign,
Smiles the gay mead, and Eden blooms again,
The various bower, the tuneful flowing stream,
The soft retreats, the lovers golden dream,
Her soil spontaneous, yields exhaustless stores;
For phoebus revels on her verdant shores.
Whose flowery births, a fragrant train appear,
And crown the youth throughout the smiling year,
 There, as in Britain's favour'd isle, behold
The bending harvest ripen into gold!
Just are thy views of Afric's blissful plain,
On the warm limits of the land and main.
 Pleas'd with the theme, we see sportive fancy play,
In realms devoted to the God of Day!
 Europa's bard, who the great depth explor'd,
Of Nature, and thro' boundless systems soar'd,
Thro' earth, thro' heaven, and hell's profound domain,
Where night eternal holds her awful reign.
But, lo! in him Britania's prophet dies,
And whence, ah! whence, shall other *Newtons* rise?
Muse, bid thy Rochford's matchless pen display
The charms of friendship in the sprightly lay.
Queen of his song, thro' all his numbers shine,
And plausive glories, goddess! shall be thine.
With partial grace thou mak'st his verse excel,
And *his* the glory to describe so well.
Cerulean bard! to thee these strains belong,
The Muse's darling and the prince of song.

DECEMBER 5th, 1774.

Mess. DIXON & HUNTER,/ *Pray insert the enclosed letter and verses, written by the famous*/ PHILLIS WHEATLEY, *the* AFRICAN poetess, in your next/ gazette.[1]

[To His Excellency General Washington]

Celestial choir! enthron'd in realms of light,
Columbia's[2] scenes of glorious toils I write.
While freedom's cause her anxious breast alarms,
She flashes dreadful in refulgent arms.
See mother earth her offspring's fate bemoan,
And nations gaze at scenes before unknown!
See the bright beams of heaven's revolving light
Involv'd in sorrows and the veil of night!

The goddess comes, she moves divinely fair,
Olive and laurel bind her golden hair:
Wherever shines this native of the skies,
Unnumber'd charms and recent graces rise.

Muse! bow propitious, while my pen relates
How pour her armies through a thousand gates;
As when Eolus heaven's fair face deforms,
Enwrap'd in tempest, and a night of storms;
Astonish'd ocean feels the wild uproar,
The refluent surges beat the sounding shore;
Or thick as leaves in autumn's golden reign,

1. From the *Virginia Gazette* (20 March 1776), p. 1. The headnote was written by Joseph Reed, former adjutant to General George Washington. In a letter dated "Cambridge, 10 February, 1776," Washington enclosed the manuscripts of this poem and its accompanying headnote letter written by Phillis from "Providence, Oct. 26, 1775" to Colonel Reed who was then in Philadelphia. In deference to the Virginia-born Washington, Reed forwarded Phillis's manuscript letter and poem to John Dixon and William Hunter, of the *Gazette*. Phillis's letter and poem were reprinted in *The Pennsylvania Magazine, or American Monthly Museum* for April, 1776, when Tom Paine was editing that periodical. Wheatley's manuscript letter and poem are no longer extant.
2. Phillis Wheatley was not the first American poet to use "Columbia" as a poetical reference to America. See Albert H. Hoyt, "The Name Columbia," *New England Historical and Genealogical Registry for the Year 1886* (New York, 1886), pp. 310–313. Also, contrary to a long-standing notion, Wheatley was not the second American female to publish a volume of her verses, after Anne Bradstreet's *The Tenth Muse* (London, 1650); Jane Turell's posthumous *Reliquiae Turellae et Lacrymae* . . . (Boston, 1735), Maria Wadsworth Brewster's *Poems on Divers Subjects* (New London, Printed, Boston Reprinted, 1757), and Jane Dunlap's *Poems,/ Upon Several SERMONS, Preached/ By the Rev'd and Renowned/ GEORGE WHITEFIELD* (Boston, 1771) are only three volumes by American females which appeared before Wheatley's *Poems* (London, 1773).

Such, and so many, moves the warrior train.
In bright array they seek the work of war,
Where high unfurl'd the ensign waves in air.
Shall I to Washington their praise recite?
Enough thou know'st them in the fields of fight.
Thee, first in place[3] and honours,—we demand
The grace and glory of thy martial band.
Fam'd for thy valour, for thy virtues more,
Hear every tongue thy guardian aid implore!

One century scarce perform'd its destin'd round,
When Gallic powers Columbia's fury found;
And so may you, whoever dares disgrace
The land of freedom's heaven-defended race!
Fix'd are the eyes of nations on the scales,
For in their hopes Columbia's arm prevails.
Anon Britannia droops the pensive head,
While round increase the rising hills of dead.
Ah! cruel blindness to Columbia's state!
Lament thy thirst of boundless power too late.

Proceed, great chief, with virtue on thy side,
Thy every action let the goddess guide.
A crown, a mansion, and a throne that shine,
With gold unfading, WASHINGTON! be thine.

3. *Place.* "Peace" in other readings.

The following thoughts on his Excellency Major General Lee being/ betray'd into the hands of the Enemy by the treachery of a pretended/ Friend; To the Honourable James Bowdoin Esq[r] are most respectfully/ Inscrib'd By his most obedient and devoted humble servant./ Phillis Wheatley.[1]

[On The Capture of General Lee.]

The deed perfidious, and the Hero's fate
In tender strains, celestial Muse! relate.
The latent foe to friendship makes pretence,
The name assumes without the sacred sense!
He, with a rapture well dissembl'd, press'd
The hero's hand, and fraudful, thus address'd,
   "O friend belov'd! may heaven its aid afford,
"And spread yon troops beneath thy conquering sword!
"Grant to America's united prayer
"A glorious conquest on the field of war.
"But thou indulgent to my warm request
"Vouchsafe thy presence as my honour'd guest:
"From martial cares a space unbend thy soul
"In social banquet, and the sprightly bowl."
Thus spoke the foe; and warlike *Lee* reply'd,
"Ill fits it me, who such an army guide;
"To whom his conduct each brave soldier owes,
"To waste an hour in banquet or repose.
"This day important, with loud voice demands
"Our wisest Counsels, and our bravest hands."
Thus having said he heav'd a boding sigh.
The hour approach'd that damps Columbia's Joy.
Inform'd, conducted by the treach'rous friend
With winged speed the adverse train attend
Ascend the Dome, and seize with frantic air

1. Writing without knowledge of top level military personality clashes, Phillis Wheatley here wrongly romanticizes the genuine feelings of Major General Charles Lee (1731–1782). Ever annoyingly jealous of Washington as commander-in-chief of the Continental forces, Lee forced his own court-martial and eventual discharge from the service. In fact, Lee was strongly suspected of becoming an American traitor after he was captured by the British in Morristown, New Jersey, on December 13, 1776; a plan in his handwriting devising a stratagem for the British capture of Washington's army was unearthed in 1858. First printed by the Massachusetts Historical Society in their proceedings for 1863–1864, pp. 7, 165–167, the manuscript, in slightly variant form, is in the Bowdoin College Library.

The self surrender'd glorious prize of war!
On sixty coursers, swifter than the wind
They fly, and reach the British camp assign'd.
Arriv'd, what transport touch'd their leader's breast!
Who thus deriding, the brave Chief address'd.
"Say, art thou he, beneath whose vengeful hands
"Our best of heroes grasp'd in death the sands?
"One fierce regard of thine indignant eye
"Turn'd Brittain pale, and made her armies fly;
"But Oh! how chang'd! a prisoner in our arms
"Till martial honour, dreadful in her charms,
"Shall grace Brittannia at her sons' return,
"And widow'd thousands in our triumphs mourn."
While thus he spoke, the hero of renown
Survey'd the boaster with a gloomy frown
And stern reply'd. "Oh arrogance of tongue!
"And wild ambition, ever prone to wrong!
"Believ'st thou Chief, that armies such as thine
"Can stretch in dust that heaven-defended line?
"In vain allies may swarm from distant lands
"And demons aid in formidable bands.
"Great as thou art, thou shun'st the field of fame,
"Disgrace to Brittain, and the British name!
"When offer'd combat by the noble foe,
"(Foe to mis-rule,) why did thy sword forgo
"The easy conquest of the rebel-land?
"Perhaps *too* easy for thy martial hand.
"What various causes to the field invite!
"For plunder *you*, and we for freedom fight:
"Her cause divine with generous ardor fires,
"And every bosom glows as she inspires!
"Already, thousands of your troops are fled
"To the drear mansions of the silent dead:
"Columbia too, beholds with streaming eyes
"Her heroes fall—'tis freedom's sacrifice!
"So wills the Power who with convulsive storms
"Shakes impious realms, and nature's face deforms,
"Yet those brave troops innum'rous as the sands
"One soul inspires, one General Chief commands.
"Find in your train of boasted heroes, one

"To match the praise of Godlike Washington.
"Thrice happy Chief! in whom the virtues join,
"And heaven-taught prudence speaks the man divine!"
   He ceas'd. Amazement struck the warrior-train,
   And doubt of conquest, on the hostile plain.

Boston Dec.ʳ 30. 1776

[On The Death of General Wooster][1]

From this the Muse rich consolation draws
He nobly perish'd in his Country's cause
His Country's Cause that ever fir'd his mind
Where martial flames, and Christian virtues join'd.
How shall my pen his warlike deeds proclaim
Or paint them fairer on the list of Fame—
Enough, great Chief—now wrapt in Shades around
Thy grateful Country shall thy praise resound—
Tho' not with mortals' empty praise elate
That vainest vapour to th'immortal State
Inly serene the expiring hero lies
And thus (while heav'nward roll his swimming eyes)
Permit, great power while yet my fleeting breath
And Spirits wander to the verge of Death—
Permit me yet to paint fair freedom's charms
For her the Continent shines bright in arms
By thy high will, celestial prize she came—
For her we combat on the feild of fame
Without her presence vice maintains full sway
And social love and virtue wing their way
O still propitious be thy guardian care
And lead *Columbia* thro' the toils of war.
With thine hand conduct them and defend
And bring the dreadful contest to an end—
For ever grateful let them live to thee
And keep them ever Virtuous, brave, and free—
But how, presumptuous shall we hope to find
Divine acceptance with th'Almighty mind—
While yet, O deed ungenerous! they disgrace

---

1. David Wooster (1710–1777). Born in Stratford, Connecticut, and educated at Yale, Wooster married Mary Clap (sister to Temperance Clap, who married the Rev. Mr. Timothy Pitkin; see Wheatley's poem, "To the Rev. Mr. Pitkin, on the Death of His Lady," above). A New Haven merchant, Wooster rose through command ranks to become Major General of Patriot forces, dying on May 2, 1777, from mortal wounds inflicted by the British. This poem is imbedded in a letter dated "Queenstreet/ Boston July/ 15.th 1778" (see "Phillis Wheatley's Letters and Proposals," below), written by Phillis to Mary Wooster. Phillis fails to punctuate, with quotation marks, Wooster's dying apostrophe expressed in lines 13–32. The manuscript of this poem is in the Hugh Upham Clark Papers of the Library of Congress.

And hold in bondage Afric's blameless race?
Let virtue reign—And thou accord our prayers
Be victory our's, and generous freedom theirs.
The hero pray'd—the wond'ring Spirit fled
And sought the unknown regions of the dead—
Tis thine fair partner of his life, to find
The virtuous path and follow close behind—
A little moment steals him from thy sight
He waits thy coming to the realms of light
Freed from his labours in the ethereal Skies
Where in succession endless pleasures rise!

AN/ ELEGY,/ Sacred to the/ MEMORY/ Of That Great Divine,/
THE REVEREND AND LEARNED/ DR. SAMUEL COOPER,/
Who departed this Life December 29, 1783,/ AETATIS 59./ By
PHILLIS PETERS./ Boston: Printed and Sold by E. Russell,/ in
Essex-Street. near Liberty-Pole./ M,DCC,LXXXIV.

To the Church and Congregation/ assembling in Brattle-Street,
the following/ ELEGY,/ Sacred to the Memory of their late Re-/
verend and Worthy Pastor, Dr./ Samuel Cooper, is, with/ the
greatest Sympathy, most respectfully/ inscribed by their Obedient,/
Humble Servant,/ Phillis Peters./ Boston, Jan. 1784.[1]

An/ ELEGY, &c./ O Thou whose exit wraps in boundless woe,
For Thee the tears of various Nations flow:
For Thee the floods of virtuous sorrows rise
From the full heart and burst from streaming eyes,
Far from our view to Heaven's eternal height,
The Seat of bliss divine, and glory bright;
Far from the restless turbulence of life,
The war of factions, and impassion'd strife.
From every ill mortality endur'd,
Safe in celestial *Salem's* walls secur'd.

E'er yet from this terrestrial state retir'd,
The Virtuous lov'd Thee, and the wise admir'd.
The gay approv'd Thee, and the grave rever'd;
And all thy words with rapt-attention heard!
The Sons of Learning on thy lessons hung,
While soft persuasion mov'd th'illit'rate throng.
Who, drawn by rhetoric's commanding laws,
Comply'd obedient, nor conceiv'd the cause.
Thy every sentence was with grace inspir'd,
And every period with devotion fir'd;

1. The Reverend Samuel Cooper (1725–1783) from 1746 until his death was pastor
of the Brattle Street Congregational Church in Boston. A handsome, eloquent
preacher, he was even more of a pronounced Patriot, being friendly with the likes
of John Adams and Benjamin Franklin; John Hancock attended his church. His
daughter, Judith, married Gabriel Johonot, one of the "Sons of Liberty," who
rose to become Lieutenant-Colonel in the Continental Army. On August 18, 1771,
Cooper baptized Phillis into membership of the Old South Church, that church
then being temporarily without its own pastor. See "On Phillis Wheatley and Her
Boston," above. The eight-page pamphlet is in the Boston Athenaeum. For a
variant version of this poem, see "Phillis Wheatley's Variant Poems and Letters,"
below.

Bright Truth thy guide without a dark disguise,
And penetration's all-discerning eyes.
Thy Country mourns th'afflicting Hand divine
That now forbids thy radiant lamp to shine,
Which, like the sun, resplendent source of light
Diffus'd its beams, and chear'd our gloom of night.

What deep-felt sorrow in each *Kindred* breast
With keen sensation rends the heart distress'd!
Fraternal love sustains a tenderer part,
And mourns a Brother with a Brother's heart.[2]

Thy Church laments her faithful Pastor fled
To the cold mansions of the silent dead.
There hush'd forever, cease the heavenly strain,
That wak'd the soul, but here resounds in vain.
Still live thy merits, where thy name is known,
As the sweet Rose, its blooming beauty gone
Retains it's fragrance with a long perfume:
Thus COOPER! thus thy death-less name shall bloom
Unfading, in thy *Church* and *Country's* love,
While Winter frowns, or spring renews the grove.

The hapless Muse her loss in Cooper mourns,
And as she sits, she writes and weeps by turns;
A Friend sincere, whose mild indulgent grace
Encourag'd oft, and oft approv'd her lays.

With all their charms, terrestrial objects strove,
But vain their pleasures to attract his love.
Such Cooper was—at Heaven's high call he flies;
His task well finish'd, to his native skies.
Yet to his fate reluctant we resign,
Tho' our's to copy conduct such as thine:
Such was thy wish, th'observant Muse survey'd
Thy latest breath, and this advice convey'd.

---

2. *A Brother's heart.* William Cooper (1729–1809), Reverend Cooper's brother and for forty-nine years the Town Clerk of Boston. When, less than six months earlier, on July 28, 1784, Phillis's husband, John Peters, had written a petition to the Boston Selectmen for a license to retail liquor from his North End shop, his character was attested to by the Selectmen and signed by William Cooper.

LIBERTY AND PEACE,[1]
A POEM.
By *Phillis Peters.*
Boston:
Printed by WARDEN *and* RUSSELL,
At Their Office in Marlborough-Street.
M,DCC,LXXXIV.

LO! Freedom comes. Th'prescient Muse foretold,
   All Eyes th'accomplish'd Prophecy behold:
Her Port describ'd, *"She moves divinely fair,*
"Olive and Laurel bind her golden Hair."[2]
She, the bright Progeny of Heaven, descends,
And every Grace her sovreign Step attends;
For now kind Heaven, indulgent to our Prayer,
In smiling *Peace* resolves the Din of *War.*
Fix'd in *Columbia* her illustrious Line,
And bids in thee her future Councils shine.
To every Realm her Portals open'd wide,
Receives from each the full commercial Tide.
Each Art and Science now with rising Charms
Th'expanding Heart with Emulation warms.
E'en great *Britannia* sees with dread Surprize,
And from the dazz'ling Splendor turns her Eyes!
Britain, whose Navies swept th'*Atlantic* o'er,
And Thunder sent to every distant Shore:
E'en thou, in Manners cruel as thou art,
The Sword resign'd, resume the friendly Part!
For *Galia's* Power espous'd *Columbia's* Cause,[3]
And new-born *Rome* shall give *Britannia* Laws,
Nor unremember'd in the grateful Strain,
Shall princely *Louis'* friendly Deeds remain;
The generous Prince th'impending Vengeance eye's,
Sees the fierce Wrong, and to the rescue flies.
Perish that Thirst of boundless Power, that drew

---

1. The text is from a four-page pamphlet located in the American Antiquarian Society.
2. Lines 3–4 repeat her description of Columbia (i.e., America) in lines 9–10 of her 1775 poem to General Washington, q.v. above.
3. France joined the Americans as allies on June of 1778.

On *Albion's* Head the curse to Tyrants due.
But thou appeas'd submit to Heaven's decree,
That bids this Realm of Freedom rival thee!
Now sheathe the Sword that bade the Brave attone
With guiltless Blood for Madness not their own.
Sent from th' Enjoyment of their native Shore
Ill-fated—never to behold her more!
From every Kingdom on *Europa's* Coast
Throng'd various Troops, their Glory, Strength and Boast.
With heart-felt pity fair *Hibernia* saw
Columbia menac'd by the Tyrant's Law:
On hostile Fields fraternal Arms engage,
And mutual Deaths, all dealt with mutual Rage;
The Muse's Ear hears mother Earth deplore
Her ample Surface smoak with kindred Gore:
The hostile Field destroys the social Ties,
And ever-lasting Slumber seals their Eyes.
Columbia mourns, the haughty foes deride,
Her Treasures plunder'd, and her Towns destroy'd:
Witness how *Charlestown's* curling Smoaks arise,
In sable Columns to the clouded Skies!
The ample Dome, high-wrought with curious Toil,
In one sad Hour[4] the savage Troops despoil.
Descending *Peace* and Power of War confounds;
From every Tongue celestial *Peace* resounds:
As for the East th'illustrious King of Day,
With rising Radiance drives the Shades away,
So Freedom comes array'd with Charms divine,
And in her Train Commerce and Plenty shine.
Britannia owns her Independent Reign
Hibernia, Scotia, and the Realms of *Spain*;
And great *Germania's* ample Coast admires
The generous Spirit that *Columbia* fires.
Auspicious Heaven shall fill with fav'ring Gales,

4. *In one sad Hour.* From 3 until 4 p.m. on June 17, 1775, the Battle of Bunker
Hill, on Charlestown peninsula, across the bay from Boston, was fought between
outnumbered American and ultimately victorious British troops, who achieved a
costly pyrrhic victory, losing over 1000 soldiers, while the Americans lost 450 men.
Vindictively, the British burned down the town of Charlestown, of some 2000 persons, the flames burning all that afternoon and into the evening, the rising smoke
blackening the skies, or as Phillis puts it, "The ample Dome" was "high-wrought
with curious Toil."

Where e'er *Columbia* spreads her swelling Sails:
To every Realm shall *Peace* her Charms display,
And Heavenly *Freedom* spreads her golden Ray.

TO MR. AND MRS. *******, ON THE
DEATH OF THEIR INFANT SON.
By Phillis Wheatly[1]

O DEATH! whose sceptre, trem/ bling realms obey,
And weeping millions mourn thy sa/ vage sway;
Say, shall we call thee by the name of/ friend,
Who blasts our joys, and bids our glo/ ries end?
Behold, a child who rivals op'ning/ morn,
When its first beams the eastern hills/ adorn;
So sweetly blooming once that lovely/ boy,
His father's hope, his mother's only/ joy,
Nor charms nor innocence prevail to/ save,
From the grim monarch of the gloomy/ grave!
Two moons revolve when lo! among/ the dead
The beauteous infant lays his weary/ head:
For long he strove the tyrant to with/ stand,
And the dread terrors of his iron hand;
Vain was his strife, with the relentless/ power,
His efforts weak; and this his mortal/ hour;
He sinks—he dies—celestial muse, re/ late
His spirit's entrance at the sacred gate.
Methinks I hear the heav'nly courts/ resound,
The recent theme inspires the choirs around.
His guardian angel with delight un/ known,
Hails his bless'd charge on his immortal/ throne;
His heart expands at scenes unknown/ before,
Dominions praise, and prostrate/ throngs adore;
Before the Eternal's feet their crowns/ are laid,
The glowing seraph vails his sacred/ head,
Spirits redeem'd, that more than an/ gels shine,
For nobler praises tune their harps di/ vine:
These saw his entrance; his soft hands/ they press'd,
Sat on his throne, and smiling thus/ address'd,
"Hail! thou! thrice welcome to this/ happy shore,
Born to new life where changes are no more;
Glad heaven receives thee, and thy/ God bestows,
Immortal youth exempt from pain/ and woes.
Sorrow and sin, those foes to human/ rest,

---

1. The last known published poem by Phillis Wheatley Peters, this piece appeared in *The Boston Magazine* for September, 1784, p. 488, less than three months before her death on December 5.

Forever banish'd from thy happy/ breast."
Gazing they spoke, and raptur'd thus/ replies,
The beauteous stranger in th'ethereal/ skies,
"Thus safe conducted to your bless'd/ abodes,
With sweet surprize I mix among the/ Gods;
The vast profound of this amazing/ grace,
Beyond your search, immortal powers,/ I praise;
Great Sire, I sing thy boundless love/ divine,
Mine is the bliss, but all the glory/ thine."
All heaven rejoices as your ******* sings,
To heavenly airs he tunes the sound/ ing strings;
Mean time on earth the hapless parents/ mourn,
"Too quickly fled, ah! never to re/ turn."
Thee, the vain visions of the night/ restore,
Illusive fancy paints the phantom o'er;
Fain would we clasp him, but he wings/ his flight;
Deceives our arms, and mixes with/ the night;
But oh! suppress the clouds of grief/ that roll,
Invading peace, and dark'ning all the/ soul.
Should heaven restore him to your/ arms again,
Oppress'd with woes, a painful endless/ train,
How would your prayers, your ardent/ wishes, rise,
Safe to repose him in his native skies.

PHILLIS WHEATLEY'S LETTERS
AND PROPOSALS
1770–1779

Mr Eleazer Wheelock[1]   Boston Jany 2d 1770

Sir,

I recd your favr p[er] Mr Brimmer by which observe Jn Thorn-
ton[2]/ Esqr of London has given you orders to draw on him for
Forty or fifty/ Pounds Sterling for the assistance of Mr Occum if
you thought it/ necessary, and that you had inquired into Mr
Occum's Circum-/ stances and had found he stood in need of that
Gents charity

I have therefore this day paid Mr John Brimmer Forty/ Pounds
Stg on your account, which you will please to reimburse/ in a Bill
of Exchange on that Gent for that sum. This I have/ done out of
pure regard for Mr Occum for I think him a very/ just man. you
[sic] will please to acquaint Mr Occum that/ Bills of Exchange
are from 5 to 7½ PCt under par, wch/ will make a loss on this Bill
of yours 40 or 50/ Stg but/ this loss I do not value, as it is to serve
Mr Occum.

I am, with due respects to you & Mr Occum

                                                    Sir
                                            Your most hume Sert
                                            Nathl. Wheatley[3]

1. Eleazer Wheelock (1711–1779) was a one-time pastor of the Second Congregational Church of Lebanon, Connecticut, where he later superintended Moor's
Indian Charity School, which the celebrated Mohegan Indian minister, Reverend
Samson Occom, attended from 1743 to 1747. Having preached and lectured
throughout England, Scotland, and Ireland for two years, with a white fellow
minister, the Reverend Nathaniel Whitaker (1732–1795), to raise almost £12,000
for the avowed assistance of the Indian school, Occom harbored an everlasting
sense of rank betrayal when, in 1769, Wheelock used that money to found Dartmouth College in Hanover, New Hampshire, where, at first, no Indian students
were enrolled. The first Dartmouth College commencement on August 28, 1771
graduated four white students. Occom never did visit Dartmouth College where
Wheelock was president from 1769 to 1779. The manuscript is in the Bowdoin
College Library.
2. Jn (i.e., John) Thornton, the London Christian philanthropist, was treasurer
of the Board of Trustees for Moor's Indian Charity School and later for Dartmouth
College and an eventually long-time supporter of Wheelock's educational and
Christian plans for American Indians. Thornton was especially helpful to Samson
Occom, a selflessly dedicated minister among other Indians who was usually in
financial straits.
3. Although this letter bears the name of Nathaniel Wheatley, son of Phillis's
master, it was Phillis who actually wrote the letter from dictation by Nathaniel.
See also Nathaniel's dictated letter, written by Phillis, to William Channing of
Providence, Rhode Island, on November 12, 1770, below, and the earlier, briefer
biographical sketch of Phillis with Nathaniel Wheatley's name, dated October 12,
1772, below.

To the R! Hon'ble the Countess of Huntingdon[1]
Most noble Lady,

The occasion of my addressing your Ladiship/ will, I hope, apologize for this my boldness in doing it. it is/ to enclose a few lines on the decease of your worthy chap-/ lain, the Rev'd Mr. Whitefield, in the loss of whom I sincere-/ ly sympathize with your Ladiship: but your great loss/ which is his Greater gain, will, I hope, meet with infinite/ reparation, in the presence of God, the Divine Benefactor/ whose image you bear by filial imitation.

The Tongues of the learned are insufficient, much less/ the pen of an untutor'd African, to paint in lively char/ acters, the excellencies of this Citizen of Zion! I beg an/ Interest in your Ladiship's Prayers, and am

With great humility
Your Ladiship's most Obedient
Humble Servant

Phillis Wheatley

Boston   Oct.r 25th 1770

---

1. Covering a non-extant manuscript version of Wheatley's eulogy on the death of the Reverend George Whitefield, personal chaplain to the countess since 1749, this manuscript letter is among the Countess of Huntingdon Papers. This and two other Phillis Wheatley manuscript letters were first printed by Sarah Dunlap Jackson, "Letters of Phillis Wheatley and Susanna Wheatley," *The Journal of Negro History*, 57, No. 2, (April, 1972), 211–215. The Right Honourable the Countess of Huntingdon was Selina Hastings (1707–1791) who continued her interest in Phillis. She asked about Phillis in a letter to Richard Carey of Charlestown, Massachusetts, who responded in a flattering letter dated May 25, 1772. In December of that year, the countess "was greatly pleas'd" in hearing selections of Wheatley's manuscript poems read aloud to her for her approval. ". . . Is not this, or that, fine? Do read another," she ordered her reader, Archibald Bell, the London printer who would publish the volume of verses. Lady Huntingdon approved the planned dedication of the volume to herself, and insisted that an engraved likeness of Phillis be the frontispiece. In another letter to Carey, she asked about Phillis again. Carey wrote back a still more flattering introductory letter dated May 3, 1773, which Phillis carried with her when she left Boston on May 8, 1773, for London. In a letter of May 13 of that year, to Mrs. Susanna Wheatley, the countess twice asked to be remembered "to your poet, unworthy, unknown but companion & friend. . . . Your little poetess remember me to her. May the Lord keep her heart alive with the fire of that other that never goes out. . . ." See "Phillis Wheatley's Variant Poems and Letters," below, for other versions of this letter.

Mr. William Channing[1]   Boston Nov 12   1770

Sir,

Your much esteem'd favor of 8 Inst I duly rec'd & observe/ Mr. Chaloner the Sherriff has returnd the Execution against the/ Harts' for an Alias & that they had assignd over the Policy of the/ Sloop wheel of fortune to me. Since I had the pleasure of seeing/ you at Providence I have been informd by an officer that Mr./ Elizer had given Mr Manly a power to recieve the money of the/ underwriters to Settle with them at 80 PCT & Mr Manly had/ laid an attachment in their hand, that they cant, nor will/ they pay the money until [?] that attachment is dropped, now/ shall be glad to know whether the assignment of the Policy is good/ I am afraid they will cheat us at Last. Shall be glad if you wou'd/ write the Sherriff & desire him to wait on Harts & Elizer & get them/ to desire Mr Manly to write his lawyer to drop the attachment/ & at same time desire Mr. Elizer to give me orders to Settle with/ the underwriters if they will pay 80 PCT & to send Mr Manly/ to Town, for my lawyer says he is a very material Evidence/ in the case. As the post just going prevents my Enlarging/ must Conclude, with dependence on your doing all in your/ power for my Interest. Sir   Your very hble Ser.

Nath.! Wheatley

[Phillis's hand writing]

[Son of John recieved 27 (illegible)]

1. Addressed "To/ William Channing Esq;/ Attorney at Law/ In/ Providence," this manuscript letter, in the Perkins Library of Duke University, was once owned by Charles Deane, the prominent 19th-century antiquarian, who identified this letter as being in the handwriting of Phillis Wheatley. The bracketed comments, bottom of letter, are Deane's. A leading Boston merchant, Nathaniel Wheatley, the son of John, Phillis's master, dealt with many other merchants, including Newport's slave-trader, Aaron Lopez, and Boston's John Hancock. He dictated a brief biographical sketch of Phillis, q.v., below. William Channing (1751–1793) graduated Princeton in 1769 and practiced law in his native province of Rhode Island. He was District Attorney and Attorney General there, and dealt in the slave trade in the face of Rhode Island legal efforts to do away with that traffic.

MADAM,[1]

Agreeable to your proposing *Recollection* as a/ subject proper for me to write upon, I enclose these/ few thoughts upon it; and as you was the first per-/ son who mentioned it, I thought none more proper/ to dedicate it to; and, if it meets with your appro-/ bation, the poem is honoured, and the authoress/ satisfied.

I am, Madam,
Your very humble servant,
PHILLIS.[2]

---

1. From *The London Magazine: Or, Gentleman's Monthly Intelligencer*, 41 (March, 1772), 134–135. Phillis's note, above, is preceded by a headnote, and a letter by an unknown "L" which read:

To the Author of the London Magazine.
Boston, in New-England, Jan. 1, 1772.

Sir,

As your Magazine is a proper repository for/ any thing valuable or curious, I hope you/ will excuse the communicating the following by/ one of your subscribers. L.

There is in this town a young *Negro woman*, who/ left *her* country at ten years of age, and has been/ in *this* eight years. She is a compleat sempstress, an/ accomplished mistress of her pen, and discovers a/ most surprising genius. Some of her productions/ have seen the light, among which is a poem on the/ death of the Rev. Mr. George Whitefield.—The/ following was occasioned by her being in company/ with some young ladies, when one of them/ said she did not remember, among all the poetical/ pieces she had seen, ever to have met with a poem/ upon RECOLLECTION. The *African* (so let me/ call her, for so in fact she is) took the hint, went/ home to her master's, and soon sent what follows.

2. The poem, "Recollection," in 58 lines, then follows this note. This poem was reprinted in the *Massachusetts Gazette and Boston Post Boy and Advertiser* (1 March 1773), and in the *Essex Gazette* (16–23 March 1773), just prior to Phillis's departure from Boston for London. It was reprinted also in *The Annual Register, or a View of the History, Politics, and Literature for the Year 1772*, 5th edition (London: J. Dodsley, 1795), 214–215, without the headnote and letter by "L," and the above letter of dedication by Phillis. See "Phillis Wheatley's Variant Poems and Letters," below.

PROPOSALS
For Printing By Subscription[1]

A Collection of POEMS, wrote/ at several times, and upon various occasions, by PHILLIS,/ a Negro Girl, from the strength of her own Genius, it being/ but a few Years since she came to this Town an uncultivated/ Barbarian from *Africa*. The Poems having been seen and/ read by the best judges, who think them well worthy of the/ Publick View; and upon critical examination, they find/ that the declared Author was capable of writing them./ The Order in which they were penned, together with the/ Occasion, are as follows;

[1.] On the Death of the Rev. Dr. *Sewell*, when sick, 1765—;/ [2.] On virtue, 66—;/ [3.] On two Friends, who were cast away, do.—;[2]/ [4.] To the University of Cambridge, 1767—; [5.] An Address to/ the Atheist, do.—; [6.] An Address to the Deist, do.—; [7.] On/ America, 1768—; [8.] On the King, do.—; [9.] On Friend-ship,/ do.—; [10.] Thoughts on being brought from Africa to Ameri-/ ca, do.—; [11.] On the Nuptials of Mr. *Spence* to Miss *Hooper*, do.—;/ [12.] On the Hon. Commodore Hood, on his pardoning a Deserter,/ 1769—; [13.] On the Death of Reverend Dr. *Sewell*, do.—;/ [14.] On the Death of Master *Seider*, who was killed by *Ebenezer/ Richardson*, 1770.—; [15.] On the Death of the Rev. *George White-/ field*, do.—; [16.] On the Death of a young Miss, aged 5 years, do.—;/ [17.] On the Arrival of the Ships of War, and landing of the/ Troops. [No date]—; [18.] On the Affray in King-Street, on the Evening of/ the 5th of March, [no date]—; [19.] On the death of a young Gentleman [no date]—;/ [20.] To *Samuel Quincy*, Esq; a Panegyrick. [no date]—; [21.] To a Lady on her/ coming to America for her Health. [no date]—; [22.] To Mrs. *Leonard*, on/ the Death of her Husband. [no date]—; [23.]

1. These proposals were printed in the *Boston Censor* for February 29, March 14, and April 11, 1772, but were rejected, mostly for racist reasons. See William H. Robinson, "Phillis Wheatley," *Black New England Letters* (Boston, Boston Public Library, 1977), pp. 27–62. This volume of poems was not published as here presented. Titles numbered [3], [4], [8], [10], [13], [15], [16], [21], [22], [23], [25], [26], and [28] were revised as, presumably, were their respective texts and in-cluded in the 1773 volume. Manuscripts for titles numbered [4], [5], [6], [7], [8], [12], and [14] have been found and printed. See Robert C. Kuncio, "Some Unpub-lished Poems of Phillis Wheatley," *The New England Quarterly*, 43, No. 2 (June, 1970), 287–297. Not included in the original printings, the numbers have been added to facilitate cross-reference.
2. *Do.* Ditto, i.e., 1776.

To Mrs. Boylston and Chil-/ dren, on the Death of her Son and their Brother. [no date]—; [24.] To a/ Gentleman and Lady on the Death of their Son, aged 9/ Months. [no date]—; [25.] To a Lady on her remarkable Deliverance in a/ Hurricane. [no date]—; [26.] To *James Sullivan*, Esq; and Lady on the/ Death of her Brother and Sister, and a child *Avis*, aged 12/ Months. [no date]—; [27.] *Goliah* [sic for Goliath] of Gath. [no date]—; [28.] On the Death of Dr. *Sa-/ muel* Marshall. [no date].

It is supposed they will make one small Octavo Volume,/ and will contain about 200 Pages./ They will be printed on Demy Paper, and beautiful Types./ The Price to Subscribers, handsomely bound and lettered,/ will be Four Shillings.—Stitched in blue, Three Shillings./ It is hoped Encouragement will be given to this Publicati-/ on, as a reward to a very uncommon Genius, at present a/ Slave./ This Work will be put to the Press as soon as three/ Hundred Copies are subscribed for, and shall be pub-/ lished with all Speed./ Subscriptions are taken in by E. Russell, in Marlborough/ Street.

Hon'd, sir[1]

I rec'd your instructive favṛ of Feb. 29, for which, return/ you ten thousand thanks. I did not flatter myself with the tho'ts/ of your honouring me with an Answer to my letter. I thank/ you for recommending the Bible to be my chief study. I find/ and acknowledge it the best of Books, it contains an endless/ treasure of wisdom, and knowledge. O that my eyes were more/ open'd to see the real worth, and true excellence of the word/ of truth, my flinty heart soften'd with the grateful dews of/ divine grace and the stubborn will, and affections, bent on God/ alone their proper object, and the vitiated palate may be/ corrected to relish heav'nly things. It has pleas'd God to lay me/ on a bed of sickness, and I

1. John Thornton (1720–1790), of London's Clapham Sect, was a pious and wealthy English merchant and philanthropist, said to have spent annually "two to three thousand pounds sterling on charitable purposes (perhaps £150,000 in his lifetime)." He corresponded with Phillis from sometime before the date of the above letter up to March 29th, 1774, the date of the fourth extant Wheatley letter to him. A friend and generous financial supporter of the Countess of Huntingdon and of the Reverend George Whitefield, whose elegy in two versions Phillis had published in London in 1771, Thornton very likely learned personal details of Phillis from her friend, the Reverend Samson Occom, whom Thornton hosted in his Clapham home during Occom's 1766–1768 fund-raising tour of England. During these years, Phillis and Occom exchanged non-extant letters. Wheatley's letter to Thornton sometime before the April 21, 1772, date of the above letter, and his February 29 reply are non-extant, but the manuscripts of four of her letters to him are in the Scottish Records Office in Edinburgh. All four of these letters were first published by Kenneth Silverman, "Four New Letters By Phillis Wheatley," *Early American Literature*, 7, No. 3 (Winter, 1974), 257–271. Mrs. Susanna Wheatley also corresponded with John Thornton, two of her manuscript letters, dated October 26, 1771, and February 9, 1772, being extant in the Scottish Records Office. In a copyist's handwriting, Thornton's reply to Phillis's letter of December 1, 1773, (see below) is extant. In this long, sententious letter, Thornton, in typical piety, counsels Phillis, the much celebrated black poetess, against the pitfalls of succumbing to earthly vanity:

"... Many a good man is often a snare/ to another, by too openly commending his good quali-/ ties, and not aware how undesignedly he spreads a net for the feet of his friend. Your present situation, and the kindness you meet with from many good people, and the respect/ that is paid to your uncommon genius, extort this friendly hint from me. I have no reason/ to charge you with any indiscretions of this kind: I mean only to apprize you of the danger./ I feared for you when here, lest the notice many took of you, should prove a snare. For half of our religious folks kill one another with kindness: that is, they get into a religious/ gossiping, they commend each others good qualities: praise is agreeable to corrupt nature:/ and the consequence is, we begin to be of the same opinion, are off our guard, become proud of our graces, the power of grace gradually dwindles away and little more than the/ empty name and profession remains. ..."

knew not but my death bed, but he/ has been graciously pleas'd to restore me in a great measure. I beg/ your prayers, that I may be made thankful for his paternal/ corrections, and that I may make a proper use of them to the/ glory of his grace. I am still very weak & the Physicians seem/ to think there is danger of a consumpsion. And O that when my/ flesh and my heart fail me God would be my strength and/ portion for ever, that I might put my whole trust and Confidence/ in him, who has promis'd never to forsake those who seek him/ with the whole heart, you could not, I am sure have expres'd/ greater tenderness and affection for me, than by being a welwisher/ to my soul, the friends of soul bear [some][2] resemblance to the father/ of spirits and are made partakers of his divine Nature.

I am afraid I have entruded on your patient, but if I had not/ tho't it ungrateful [to omit writing in answer to your favour][3] I should not have troubl'd you, but I can't/ expect you to answer this. I am sir with greatest respect,-/ your very hum. sert./ Phillis Wheatley

[To John Thornton in London]

---

2. Bracketed word inserted by Phillis.
3. Bracketed words inserted by Phillis.

Boston May 19.th 1772

Dear Sister[1]

I rec'd your favour of February 6.th for which I give you/ my sincere thanks. I greatly rejoice with you in that realizing/ view, and I hope experience, of the saving change which you so/ emphatically described. Happy were it for us if we could arrive to/ that evangelical Repentance, and the true holiness of heart which/ you mention. Inexpressibly happy should we be could we/ have a due sense of the Beauties and excellence of the Crucified/ Saviour. In his Crucifixion may be seen marvellous displays/ of Grace and Love, sufficient to draw and invite us to the rich/ and endless treasures of his mercy, let us rejoice in and adore/ the wonders of God's infinite Love in bringing us from a land/ Semblant of darkness itself, and where the divine light of reve-/ lation (being obscur'd) is as darkness. Here the knowledge of the/ true God and eternal life are made manifest; But there,/ profound ignorance overshadows the Land. Your observation/ is true, namely, that there was nothing in us to recommend us/ to God. Many of our fellow creatures are pass'd by, when the/ bowels of divine love expanded toward us. May this goodness/ & long suffering of God lead us to unfeign'd repentance [.]

It gives me very great pleasure to hear of so many of my/ Nation, seeking with eagerness the way to true felicity. O may/ we all meet at length in that happy mansion. I hope the/ correspondence between us will continue, (my being much indispos'd/ this winter past was the reason of my not answering yours/ before now) which correspondence I hope may have the happy/ effect of improving our mutual friendship. Till we meet/ in the regions of consumate blessedness, let us endeavor/ by the assistance of divine grace, to live the life, and we/ shall die the death of the Righteous.

1. The manuscript is in The Quaker Collection of the Haverford College Library.

may this be our/ happy case and of those who are travelling to the region/ of Felicity is the earnest request of your affectionate/ Friend & hum. Ser! Phillis Wheatley

[To/ Arbour Tanner[2]/ in/ New port]

2. Arbour (sometimes spelled Obour or Abour) Tanner, a lifelong friend and soul mate to Phillis. She was a fellow servant, to the family of James Tanner in Newport, Rhode Island. Baptized by the Reverend Samuel Hopkins in his First Congregational Church on July 10, 1768, she married Barra Tanner on November 14, 1789, and died in Newport on June 21, 1835. It was Obour who saved the seven known Wheatley letters to her and gave them to the wife of the Reverend William Beecher, who in turn gave them to the Reverend Edward A. Hale, who donated them to the Massachusetts Historical Society, in whose *Proceedings* for November, 1863, they were printed. They were printed again, separately, in 1864. Although it is clear that Obour wrote Phillis as many as, if not more, letters than Phillis wrote to her, not one Tanner letter to Phillis is known. Six of these original manuscript letters remain at the Massachusetts Historical Society.

My dear friend[1]

I rec'd your kind Epistle a few days ago; much disappointed/ to hear that you had not rec'd my answer to your first letter.* I/ have been in a very poor state of health all the past winter/ and spring, and now reside in the country for the benefit of its/ more wholesome air. I came to town this morning to spend the/ Sabbath with my master and mistress. Let me be interested in yr/ Prayers that God would please to bless to me the means us'd for my/ recovery, if agreeable to his holy Will. While my outward man/ languishes under weakness and pa[in], may the inward be refresh'd/ and strengthen'd more abundantly by him who declar'd from/ heaven that his strength was made perfect in weakness! may/ he correct our vitiated taste, that the meditation of him may/ be delightful to us. No longer to be so excessively charm'd with/ fleeting vanities: But pressing forward to the fix'd mark for/ the prize. How happy that man who is prepar'd for that Night/ Wherein no man can work! Let us be mindful of our high/ calling, continually on our guard, lest our treacherous hearts/ should give the adversary an advantage over us. O! who can/ think without horror of the snares of the Devil. Let us, by frequent/ meditation on the eternal Judgment/ prepare for it. May the/ Lord bless to us these thoughts, and teach us by his Spirit to/ live to him alone, and when we leave this world may we be/ his: That this may be our happy case, is the sincere desire/ of, your affectionate friend & humble serv't/ Phillis Wheatley.

*I sent the letter/ to Mr. Whitwell's[2] who said he/ wou'd forward it.

[To Arbour Tanner,/ in Newport. Rhode Island./ To the care of/ Mr. Pease's Servant.]

---

1. The manuscript is in the Massachusetts Historical Society.
2. William Whitwell (1714–1795), thrice-married merchant of Boston was a long-time member of the Old South Church, Phillis's place of worship since 1771.

My Lord,

The joyful occasion which has given me this Confidence in ad-/ dressing your Lordship in the inclos'd Piece, will, I hope, sufficiently apologize for/ this freedom from an African, who with the (now) happy America, exults with/ equal transport in the view of one of its greatest advocates Presiding, with the/ Special tenderness of a Fatherly heart, over the American department.[1]

Nor can they, my Lord, be insensible of the Friendship so much/ exemplified in your endeavors in their behalf, during the late unhappy/ disturbances. I sincerely wish your Lordship all Possible success, in your/ undertakings for the Interest of North America.

That the united Blessings of Heaven and Earth, may attend you/ here, and the endless Felicity of the invisible State, in the presence of the/ Divine Benefactor, may be your portion here after, is the hearty desire

of, My Lord,
Your Lordship's most ob^t &
devoted Hum^e Serv!
Phillis Wheatley

Boston, N.E. Oct 10. 1772

To/ The Right Hon'ble/ The Earl of Dartmouth/ &.&.&.
p.^r favour of/ Mr Wooldridge[2]

---

1. Lord Dartmouth was appointed His Majesty's Secretary of State for North America in August of 1772, to the general satisfaction of many colonists who, appreciative of his part in the repeal of the widely hated Stamp Act, and, aware of his well-known concerns for Christian piety and the reform-minded Methodism of Lady Huntingdon, were hopeful he would become even more partisan in their behalf.

2. Thomas Wooldridge (d. 1795) an obscure, minor English functionary and one-time London politician who toured the colonies and informed Dartmouth of American sentiments on various issues. Anxious to see first-hand the much discussed black poetess of Boston, Phillis Wheatley, he visited her King Street home, was astounded to behold her writing verses before his eyes, and promised to deliver her extemporaneously composed poem on Dartmouth (see Wheatley's "Variant Poems and Letters"), and a biographical sketch of Phillis (see Wheatley's "Letters and Proposals"). The manuscript for the above letter is among Lord Dartmouth's Papers in the County Record Office, Stafford, England. For variant versions of this letter, see "Phillis Wheatley's Variant Poems and Letters" below.

PROPOSALS[1]

For Printing in *London* by Subscription,
A Volume of POEMS,
Dedicated by Permission to the Right Hon. the
Countess of Huntingdon.
Written by PHILLIS,
A Negro Servant to Mr. J. Wheatley of *Boston*
in *New England.*
Terms of Subscription

I. The Book to be neatly printed in 12 mo.[2] on a new
Type and a fine Paper, adorned with an elegant
Frontispiece, representing the Author.
II. That the Price to Subscribers shall be Two Shillings
Sewed, or Two Shillings and Six pence, neatly bound.
II [sic]. That every Subscriber deposit One Shilling at
the Time of Subscribing; and the Remainder to be paid
on Delivery of the Book.

* *

* Subscriptions are received by Cox and Berry,/ in *Boston.*

---

1. From the *Massachusetts Gazette and Boston Post Boy and the Advertiser* (19 and 22 April 1773). These same proposals were also printed in *The Massachusetts Gazette and Boston Weekly News Letter* (16 April 1773).
2. *12 mo.* An abbreviation for duodecimo, meaing a book whose pages were the size of a piece of paper cut into 12 leaves from a printers sheet. Wheatley's 1772 volume was to have made "one small ocatvo," a book with pages the size of a piece of paper cut into 8 leaves from a printer's sheet.

London
June 27th 1773

Madam[1]

It is with pleasure I acquaint your Ladyship of my safe arri/ val in London after a fine passage of 5 weeks, in the Ship London, with/ my young Master:[2] (advis'd by my Physicians for my Health) have/ Brought a letter from Rich'd Carey Esqr[3] but was disappointed by your/ absence of (the?) honour of waiting upon your Ladyship with it. I woud/ have inclos'd it, but was doubtful of the safety of the conveyance.

I should think my self very happy in seeing your Ladyship,/ and if you was so desirous of the Image of the Author as to propose it/ for a Frontispiece I flatter myself that you would accept the Reality.

I conclude with thanking your Ladyship for permitting the/ Dedication of my Poems to you; and am not insensible, that under/ the patronage of your Ladyship, not more eminent in the station/ of life than in your exemplary Piety and Virtue, my feeble/ efforts will be shielded from the severe trials of unpitying criticism/ and being encourag'd by your Ladyship's Indulgence, I the more freely/ resign to the world these Juvenile productions, and am, Madam/ with greatest humility, your Dutiful Hm! Ser.!

Phillis Wheatley

1. The manuscript is among the Countess of Huntingdon's Papers.
2. Nathaniel Wheatley, son of Phillis's master, who provided protection for Phillis during the trip to London.
3. Richard Carey (1717–1790) of Charlestown, Massachusetts, one of the eighteen "most respectable Characters in *Boston*," whose signatures attested to Phillis Wheatley's authenticity as author of the 1773 volume. Carey's letter of introduction, dated May 3, 1773, reads in part

> This will be delivered your Ladyship by/ Phillis, the Christian Poetess, Whose Behaviour in England/ I wish may be as exemplary, as it has been in Boston./ This appears remarkable for her Humility, and/ spiritual-mindedness, hope she will continue an ornament for/ the Christian name and profession, as she grows older/ and has more experience, I doubt not her writings will/ run more in Evangelical strain. I think your Ladyship/ will be pleased with her. . . .

A year earlier, in reply to a query about Phillis from the countess, Carey reported in a letter dated May 25, 1772:

> . . . The Negro girl of Mr. Wheatley's, by her virtuous Behaviour/ and Conversation in life, gives Reason to believe, she is a Subject/ of Divine Grace—remarkable for her Piety, of an extraordinary/ Genius, and in full communion with one of the Churches,/ the family & girl was affected at the kind enquiry your Ladyship/ made after her. . . .

318

[The Right Honourable/ The Countess of Huntington (sic)/ at Talgarth[4]/ South Wales]

4. Ailing, the countess had retired to her estate in Talgarth, South Wales, for recuperation at the time of Phillis's London visit.

Madam[1]

I rec'd with the mix'd sensations of pleasure & disappoint!/ ment your Ladiship's message favored by Mr. Rien acquainting us with/ your pleasure that my Master & I should wait upon you in S? Wales, de-/ lighted with your Ladiship's condescention to me so unworthy of it. Am sorry/ to acquaint your Ladiship that the Ship is certainly to sail next Thurs/ [day? on?][2] which I must return to America. I long to see my friends there,/ [I am] extremely reluctant to go without having first seen your Ladiship.[3]/ It gives me very great satisfaction to hear of an African so worthy/ to be honour'd with your Ladiship's approbation & Friendship as him/ whom you call your Brother.[4] I rejoice with your Ladiship in that Fund of/ mental felicity which you cannot but be possessed of, in the consider-/ ation of your exceeding great reward. My great opinion of your/ Ladiship's goodness, leads to believe I have an interest in your most hap-/ py hours of communion, with your most indulgent Father and our great/ and common Benefactor. With greatest humility I am,

most dutifully
your Ladiship's obed[t] Sert
Phillis Wheatley

London July 17
    1773

---

1. The manuscript is among the Countess of Huntingdon's Papers.
2. The manuscript is torn at the beginnings of lines 6 and 7. Words torn away are suggested by words in the two sets of brackets.
3. Prompted by an urgent call to Boston where her mistress was sinking rapidly, Phillis left London in late July. Reported *The Morning Chronicle and London Advertiser* (26 July 1773), p. 4: "Cleared OUTWARDS. Boston, London, Califf." (i.e., The ship, *London*, under the command of Captain Robert Calef, was cleared from London for a destination of Boston in New England.) Phillis and the countess never did meet personally.
4. The worthy African referred to here as enjoying the countess's "approbation & Friendship" was very likely James Albert Ukawsaw Gronniosaw (b. 1710?), who as a child of African royalty routinely costumed himself in gold pieces, but who later fell into several enslavements and eventual London poverty. During this time of unemployment he was reduced to watching his English wife and three children eat a single raw carrot a day for four days. Eventually he dictated his *Narrative of the Most Remarkable Particulars in the Life of James Albert Ukawsaw Gronniosaw* (Bath, England, 1770; reprinted in Newport, Rhode Island, and sold by S. Southwick, in Queen Street, 1774), which is dedicated "To The/ Right Honorable/ The/ Countess of Huntingdon/ . . . Through Her Ladyship's Permis-

My master is yet undetermind about going home, and/ sends his dutiful respects to your Ladiship.[5]

[To The Countess of Huntingdon at Talgarth, South Wales]

sion . . ." (The title of the 1774 reprinted edition claims that Ukawsaw's narrative was "Written by HIMSELF," when, as the "Preface to the Reader" plainly states, Ukawsaw's story "was taken from his own mouth/ and committed to paper by the elegant pen of a/ young Lady of the town of Leominster. . . .")

5. When Phillis departed London for Boston, Nathaniel Wheatley remained to marry Mary Enderby of Thames Street the following November. With his English wife, Nathaniel visited Boston in the fall of 1774, but returned to London that same fall, and died there in 1783.

Sir   Oct. 18, 1773

Having an opportunity by a servant of Mr. Badcock's who
lives/ near you, I am glad to hear you and your Family are well, I
take the/ Freedom to transmit to you a short sketch of my voyage
and re-/ turn from London where I went for the recovery of my
health as ad-/ vis'd by my Physicians. I was reciev'd in England
with such kindness,/ Complaisance, and so many marks of
esteem and real Friendship/ as astonishes me on the reflection,
for I was no more than 6/ weeks there—Was introduced to Lord
Dartmouth and had/ near half an hour's conversation with his
Lordship, with whom/ was Alderman Kirkman.—Then to Lord
Lincoln, who visited/ me at my own Lodgings with the Famous
D⸢r⸣ Solander, who/ accompany'd M⸢r⸣ Banks in his late expedition
round the World./ Then to Lady Cavendish, and Lady Carteret
Webb.—M⸢rs⸣ Pal-/ mer a Poetess, an accomplish'd Lady.—D⸢r⸣
Tho⸢s⸣ Gibbons, Rhe-/ toric Proffesor, to Israel Mauduit Esq⸢r⸣
Benjamin Franklin/ Esq⸢r⸣ F.R.S. Grenville [sic] Sharp Esq⸢r⸣[1] who

1. John Kirkman was an Alderman for the city of London during Phillis's visit.
Lord Lincoln (Henry Fiennes Clinton, 1720–1790), was an Eton and Oxford
educated English sportsman politician, who married his cousin, the eldest daugh-
ter of his uncle, Henry Pelham, the Prime Minister. Dr. Daniel Solander (1736–
1782), Swedish-born English botanist, had been engaged by his wealthy friend, Sir
Joseph Banks (1743–1820) as a companion researcher aboard the *Endeavor*, under
the famous Captain James Cook, for an extended trip throughout the South
Pacific, 1768–1771, visiting Tierra del Fuego, Otahite (among the Society Islands),
New Zealand, Australia, and the Dutch East Indies. Lady Cavendish and Lady
Carteret-Webb, were sisters and devoted associates of the Countess of Huntingdon's
religious work in London. Mary (Reynolds) Palmer (1716–1796), was the sister of
the celebrated London artist, Sir Joshua Reynolds, a mother of six children, and
author of two short books on the Devonshire dialect. Phillis speaks of Mrs. Palmer
as "a Poetess, an accomplish'd Lady," but neither of her posthumously published
books on the Devonshire dialect (1837, 1839) is in verse; both are in prose.
Dr. Thomas Gibbons (1720–1785), a dissenting English minister and long-time
tutor at Mile End Academy, was the author of several dozen pieces, including a
Latin poem, "Epitaphium," (London, 1771) on the death of George Whitefield.
During Reverend Samson Occom's London lecture tour, Gibbons contributed to
the solicited funds. Israel Mauduit (1708–1787), wealthy English bachelor, classical scholar, and a long-time (since 1763) agent in London for the province of
Massachusetts Bay. Phillis sent a copy of her manumission papers to Mauduit,
and planned to publish a letter to him. See letter title number 8 in her 1779
proposals, above. Her manumission papers are, reportedly, not to be found
among Mauduit's papers in either the British Library or the Public Records Office
in London. At the prompting of his nephew in Boston, Franklin, in London,
visited with Phillis during the summer of 1773 "and offered her any services I
could do her." On October 30, and throughout November and December of 1779,
Phillis published proposals for a volume of her poems and letters that was to be
*"Dedicated to the Right Honourable,/ Benjamin Franklin, Esq:/ One of the
Ambassadors of the United States, at/ the Court of France. . . ."* Granville Sharp

attended me to the Tower &/ show'd the Lions, Panthers, Tigers, &c The Horse Armoury, [small?]/ Armoury, the Crowns, Sceptres, Diadems, the Font for christening/ the Royal Family. Saw Westminster Abbey, British Museum,/ Coxe's Museum, Saddler's wells, Greenwich Hospital, Park/ and Chapel, the royal Observatory at Greenwich, &ᶜ &ᶜ too/ many things & Places to trouble you with in a letter.—The Earl of/ Dartmouth made me a Compliment of 5 guineas, and desir'd me to/ get the whole of Mʳ Pope's Works,[2] as the best he could recommend/ to my perusal, this I did. also got Hudibrass, Don Quixot,[3] & Gay's Fables/ — was presented with a Folio Edition of Milton's Paradise Lost, prin-/ ted on a silver Type, so call'd from its elegance, (I suppose) By Mʳ/ Brook Watson, Merchᵗ whose Coat of Arms is prefix'd.[4]— Since my/ return to America my Master, has at the desire of my friends in/ England given me my freedom. The Instrument is drawn, so as/ to secure me and my property from the hands of the Exectutʳˢ admin-/ istrators, &ᶜ of my master, & secure whatsoever should be given me as/ my Own. A Copy is sent to Isra. Mauduit Esqʳ F.R.S.

I expect my Books which are publish'd in London in Capt./

(1735–1813), English philanthropist, was a tirelessly dedicated abolitionist and founded the English Society for the Abolition of Slavery.

2. These works consist of four volumes of Pope's translation of Homer's *Odyssey* (London, 1771) and nine of Pope's *Works* (London, 1766), and each volume is inscribed by Phillis. They are housed in the Rare Book Room of the Atkins Library of the University of North Carolina at Charlotte. Thanks to Professor Julian D. Mason, Jr., himself a Wheatley scholar, of the University of North Carolina at Charlotte, for this information.

3. Said to have been translated by the novelist, Tobias Smollett, the London, 1770, edition of Don Quixote, inscribed "The Earl of Dartmouth/ To Phillis Wheatley/ London July-1773," is at the Schomburg Center for Research in Black Culture. Also at the Schomburg Center are volumes II and III of William Shenstone's four-volume *Complete Works in Verse and Prose*, Third edition (London, 1773), inscribed "Mary Everleigh to/ Phillis Wheatley Sept. 24/ 1774."

4. The 1770 copy of the Foulis Folio edition of John Milton's *Paradise Lost* is in Houghton Library of Harvard University. On one flyleaf is inscribed "A Gift from/ D.L. Pickman/ of Salem./ Recᵈ May 9th/ 1824"; on the following flyleaf, "Mr. Brook Watson to Phillis Wheatley/ London July—1773," and on the lower right-hand side, "This Book was given by Brook Watson/ formerly Lord Mayor of London, to Phillis Wheatley—and after her death was sold in/ payment of her Husband's debts./ It is now presented to the Library/ of Harvard University at Cambridge,/ by Dudley L. Pickman of Salem/ March 1824." However, during Phillis's summer, 1773, visit to London, Frederick Bull was Lord Mayor of London. Watson (1735–1807), who served as a commissary agent throughout the Revolutionary War, and later as the king's Commissary General, did not become Lord Mayor of London until 1796.

Hall, who will be here I believe in 8 or 10 days. I beg the favour/ that you would honour the enclos'd Proposals, & use your inte-/ rest with Gentlemen & Ladies of your acquaintance to subscribe/ also; for the more subscribers there are, the more it will be for/ my advantage as I am to have half the sale of the Books. This I/ am the more solicitous for, as I am now upon my own footing/ and whatever I get by this is entirely mine, & it is the Chief I have to/ depend upon. I must also request you would desire the Printers/ in New Haven, not to reprint that Book, as it will be a great/ hurt to me, preventing any further Benefit that I might so/ recieve from the Sale of my Copies from England. The price is/ 2/6^d Bound or 2/ Sterling sewed—[if any][5] should be so ungene-/ rous as to reprint them the genuine Copy may be known, for it/ is sign'd in my own handwriting. My dutiful respects attend your/ Lady and Children and I am/ ever respectfully your oblig'd Hm^e sert./ Phillis Wheatley/ Boston October/ 18!^{h} 1773/ I found my mistress very sick on my return./ But she is somewhat better, we wish we could depend on it./ She gives her Compliments to you & your Lady.

[To/ Col. David Worcester (sic)/ in/ New Haven./ favour'd by M!/ Badcock's Servant.]

5. Torn from the manuscript at this place are the words "if any," which are visible elsewhere in the manuscript. As the British burned most of Wooster's papers when they pillaged New Haven in 1777, this especially valuable manuscript letter from Phillis Wheatley has survived merely by chance. The manuscript is in the Hugh Upham Clark Papers in the Library of Congress.

Dear Obour

I rec'd your most kind epistle of Aug! 27th, & Oct/ 13th, by a young man of your acquaintance, for which I am/ oblig'd to you. I hear of your welfare with pleasure; but this/ acquaints you that I am at present indispos'd by a cold, &/ since my arrival have been visited by the asthma.—/ Your observations on our dependence on the Deity, &/ your hopes that my wants will/ be supply'd from his fulness/ which is in Christ Jesus, is truely worthy of your self.—/ I can't say but my voyage to England has conduced to/ the recovery (in a great measure) of my Health. The Friends/ I found there among the nobility and gentry, their bene-/ volent conduct towards me, the unexpected and unmerited/ civility and Complaisance with which I was treated by all,/ fills me with astonishment. I can scarcely Realize it.—/ This I humbly hope has the happy Effect of lessening/ me in my own Esteem. Your Reflections on the sufferings/ of the Son of God, & the inestima-ble price of our immortal/ Souls, Plainly demonstrate the sensa-tions of a soul united/ to Jesus. What you observe of Esau is true of all/ mankind, who, (left to themselves) would sell their hea-/ venly Birth Rights for a few moments of sensual pleasure,/ whose wages at last (dreadful wages!) is eternal condemna-/ tion. Dear Obour, let us not sell our Birth right/ for a thousand worlds, which indeed would be as dust upon/ the Ballance.—The God of the seas & dry land, has gracious/ ly Brought me home in safety Join with me in thanks to him/ for so great a mercy, & that it may excite me to praise him/ with cheerfulness, to Persevere in Grace & Faith, & in the know-/ ledge of our Creator and Redeemer,— that my heart may be/ fill'd with gratitude. I should have been pleas'd greatly to see/ Miss West, as I imagine she knew you. I have been very bu-/ sy ever since my arrival, or should have now wrote a more par/ ticular account of my voyage, But must submit that satisfac-/ tion to some other opportunity. I am Dear friend,/ most affectionately ever yours,

Phillis Wheatley

My mistress has been very sick above 14 weeks, & confin'd to her/ Bed the whole time, but is I hope somewhat Better, now./ The young man by whom this is handed you seems/ to me to be a very clever man knows you very well, & is/ very Complaisant and agreeable.—[1] P.W./ I enclose Proposals for my book, and beg you'd use your/ interest to get Subscriptions as it is for my Benefit.

[To/ Obour Tanner,/ in New Port]

1. Some Wheatley observers believe that the young man so warmly referred to here was John Peters, who would marry Phillis five years later in April of 1778. The manuscript is at the Massachusetts Historical Society.

Hon'd sir

It is with great satisfaction, I acquaint you with my experience of the/ goodness of God in safely conducting my passage over the mighty waters, and returning/ me in safety to my American Friends. I presume you will join with them and me/ in praise to God for so distinguishing a favour, it was amazing Mercy, alto-gether/ unmerited by me: and if possible it is augmented by the consideration of the bitter re-/ verse, which is the deserved wages of my evil doings. The Apostle Paul, tells us/ that the wages of sin is death. I don't imagine he excepted any sin whatsoever,/ being equally hateful in its nature in the sight of God, who is essential Purity.

Should we not sink hon'd sir, under this sentence of Death, pronounced/ on every sin, from the comparatively least to the greatest, were not this blessed Con-/ trast annexed to it, "But the Gift of God is eternal Life, through Jesus Christ/ our Lord?["] It is his Gift. O let us be thankful for it! What a load is taken from/ the sinner's shoulder, when he thinks, that Jesus has done that work for him/ which he could never have done, and suffer'd, that punishment of his imputed/ Rebellions, for which a long Eternity of Torments could not have made suffici-/ ent expiation. O that I could meditate continually on this work of wonder/ ous Deity itself. This, which Kings & Prophets have desir'd to see, & have not seen[.]/ This, which Angels are continually exploring, yet are not equal to the search,—/ Millions of Ages shall roll away, and they may try in vain to find out to/ perfection, the sublime mysteries of Christ's Incarnation. Nor will this desire/ to look into the deep things of God, cease, in the Breasts of glorified saints & Ang-/ els. It's duration will be coeval with Eternity. This Eternity how dreadful,/ how delightful! Delightful to those who have an interest in the Crucified/ Saviour, who has dignified our Nature, by seating it at the Right Hand of/ the divine Majesty.— They alone who are thus interested, have cause to rejoice/ even on the brink of that Bottomless Profound: and I doubt not (without the/ least Adulation) that you are one of that happy number. O pray that I may/ be one also, who shall join with you in songs of praise at the Throne of him, who/ is no respecter of Persons, being equally the great Maker of all:—Therefor disdain/ not to be called the Father of Humble Africans and Indians; though de-spis'd/ on earth on account of our colour, we have this Consolation, if he enables us to/ deserve it. "That God dwells in the humble & contrite heart." O that I were/ more & more possess'd of this inestimable blessing; to be directed by the imme/ diate influence of the divine spirit in my daily walk & Conversation.

Do you, my hon'd sir, who have abundant Reason to be thankful for/ the great share you possess of it, be always mindful in your Closet, of those/ who want it, of me in particular.

When I first arriv'd at home my mistress was so bad as not to be expec-/ ted to live above two or three days, but through the goodness of God, she is/ still alive but remains in a very weak & languishing Condition. She begs/ a continued interest in your most earnest prayers, that she may be daily/ prepar'd for that great Change which she is likely soon to undergo; She in-/ treats you, as her son is still[1] ~~now~~ in England, that you would take all opportuni-/ ties to advise & counsel him. [She says she is going to leave him & desires you'd be a spiritual Father to him.][2] She will take it very kind. *She thanks you/ heartily for the kind notice you took of me while in England.* please/ to give my best Respects to Mᴿˢ & miss Thornton, and masters Henry/ and Robert who held with me a long conversation on many subjects/ which Mᴿˢ Drinkwater knows very well.[3] I hope she is in better Health/ than when I left her. Please to remember me to your whole family & I thank/ them for their kindness to me, begging still an interest in your best hours/ I am Hon'd sir/ most respectfully your Humble servᵗ

Phillis Wheatley

Boston Dec. 1, 1773}
I have written to Mᴿˢ Wilberforce,[4] some time since please to give/ my duty to her; Since writing the above the Rev'd Mr. Moorhead has made his/ Exit from this world, in whom we lament the loss of the Zealous Pious & true christian

[To John Thornton Esqʳᵉ Merchant London]

1. The word "now" is cancelled and the word "still" inserted.
2. In the manuscript, the sentence in brackets is written above the sentence following the brackets. The last two words of the bracketed sentence, "to him," are squeezed below "Father."
3. Miss Thornton was Jane Thornton; Henry and Robert were Thornton's sons. Mrs. Drinkwater is unidentified.
4. See Phillis Wheatley's 1779 proposals, letter titled number 9. Mrs. Wilberforce was a half-sister to John Thornton, and aunt to the distinguished English statesman and abolitionist, William Wilberforce (1759–1833). The manuscript is in the Scottish Records Office.

Boston Feb. 9!ᵗh 1774—

Rev'd Sir

I take with pleasure this opportunity by the Post, to acquaint you of the arr! (i.e., arrival)/ of my books from London. I have seal'd up a package, containing 17 for you 2 for/ Mʳˢ Tanner and one for Mʳˢ Mason, and only wait for you to appoint some proper per-/ son by whom I may convey them to you. I recᵈ some time ago 20/ sterling, upon them/ by the hands of your Son in a Letter from Obour Tanner; I recᵈ at the same time/ a paper by which I understood there are two negro men who are desirous of returning/ to their native Country to preach the Gospel;[2] But

---

1. The bracketed words have been added by another hand.
2. The two were Bristol Yamma (1744?–1793) and John Quamine (1743?–1779), who, as African children, were differently transported to Newport, Rhode Island. Although Yamma was born "in the inland country, some hundreds of miles (as it is supposed) North of Annamaboe," and Quamine was "a Fantee, from Fantin adjacent to Annamaboe," the two of them spoke the same language in which they remained fluent throughout their lives. "The son of a rich man of Annamaboe," Quamine, at ten years of age, was entrusted by his naive father to a well-rewarded Rhode Island slave ship captain to be taken to Newport for an education and returned to Africa. After educating the boy for a short while, the captain betrayed his word, and sold Quamine as a "slave for life." Yamma came to Newport as a slave. Sharing $300.00 in a lottery, the two of them eventually purchased their freedom, Quamine for $180.00, and Yamma, only after some difficulty, for $200.00. Married, both with a child apiece, the two blacks were communicants at Newport's First Congregational Church, Quamine being baptized there in 1765, and Yamma in 1768. Both of them often discussed in Fanti their wish to become Christian missionaries in Africa. They caught the attention of Reverend Samuel Hopkins (1721–1803), installed as pastor of their church in 1770, who also had plans for a black Christian mission in Africa. Toward that end, Hopkins and Reverend Ezra Stiles of the Second Congregational Church of Newport prepared and signed a circular in August, 1773, which solicited funds for the missionary project from interested persons, mostly clergymen in Scotland, England, New England, New Jersey, and Philadelphia. They collected £102 ls. 4d. 3f. (one hundred pounds, one shilling, four pence, and three farthings) by the end of 1776, which was used to prepare the barely literate Quamine and Yamma for missionary work at the College of New Jersey (today's Princeton University) with the Reverend Levi Hart of Preston, Connecticut, with whom the two blacks lived for some months. Then the blacks attended the college from 1774 to 1776, when they were declared fit for work abroad. But, before additional monies could be secured for their transportation to Africa, and for the establishment of a missionary school there, the Revolutionary War broke out and donor monies found other channels. Hopkins persisted in his project, however, as late as July 29, 1793, writing Dr. Hart of his hopes of sending the ailing Bristol Yamma to Sierra Leone for both recuperation and mission work. With Hopkins's support, on January 4, 1826, thirty-two other Rhode Island blacks sailed aboard the brig, *Vine*, from Boston for Liberia and new lives as Afro-American Africans.

being much indispos'd by the return of/ my Asthmatic complaint, besides, the sickness of my mistress who has been long con-/ fin'd to her bed, & is not expected to live [~~above~~]³ a great while; all these things render it/ impracticable for me to do anything at present with regard to that paper, but what/ I can do in influencing my Christian friends and acquaintances to promote this laudable/ design shall not be wanting. Methinks Rev'd Sir, this is the beginning of that happy/ period foretold by the Prophets, when all shall know the Lord from the least to the great-/ est, and that without the assistance of human art & eloquence, my heart ex-panded,/ with sympathetic Joy, to see at distant time the thick cloud of ignorance dispersing from/ the face of my benighted Country. Europe and America have long been fed with the/ heavenly provision, and I fear they loathe it, while Africa is perishing with a spiritu-/ al Famine. O that they could partake of the crumbs, the precious crumbs which/ fall from the table, of these distinguish'd children of the Kingdom.

Their minds are unprejudiced against the truth therefore tis to be hoped they wou^d receive it with their whole heart. I hope that which the divine royal Psalmist says/ by inspiration is now on the point of being accomplish'd, namely, Ethiopia shall/ soon stretch forth her hands Unto God, of this Obour Tanner (and I trust many/ others within your knowledge are living witnesses.⁴ Please to give my love to her/ & I intend to write to her soon, my best respects attend every kind inquirer after/ your oblig'd Humble servant.

Phillis Wheatley.

[The Rev'd M.ʳ Sam.ˡ/ Hopkins/ New Port/ Rhode Island/ pʳ Post.]

3. Phillis cancelled the word "above."
4. Obour Tanner was one of almost a dozen members of Hopkins's church, all of whom were restricted to the balcony area. The manuscript is at the Historical Society of Pennsylvania. For a printed variant of this letter, see Wheatley's "Variant Poems and Letters," below.

THIS DAY IS PUBLISHED,
Adorn'd with an elegant Engraving of the Author.
[Price 3s.4d. L.M. Bound][1]
POEMS,
On various subjects-Religious and Moral.
By PHILLIS WHEATLEY,
A Negro Girl.

Sold by Messrs. Cox & Berry,
At their Store in King Street, Boston.
N. B. The Subscribers are requested to apply for
their Copies.

---

1. From The *Boston Gazette and Country Journal* (17 January 1774), p. 3; repeated in the same newspaper for 24, 31 January and 7 February; and, in The *Massachusetts Gazette and Boston Weekly News Letter* for 24 January, and 3, 10, 17 of February, 1774. Although Phillis—a free woman since October, 1773—did not write this notice of the Boston availability of her London-published volume, she very likely did inform the printers of her new status as "A Negro Girl." Previously, and in many subsequent advertisements of sales of her book, she was listed as "a Negro servant of Mr. John Wheatley of Boston."

The following is an extract of a letter from Phillis, a Negro girl of Mr. Wheatley's of this town, to the Reverend Samson Occom, which we are desired to insert as a specimen of her ingenuity. It is dated the 11th of February, 1774.

Reverend and honoured Sir,[1]
I have this Day received your obliging kind Epistle, and am greatly satisfied with your Reasons respecting the negroes, and think highly reasonable what you offer in Vindication of their natural Rights: Those that invade them cannot be insensible that the divine Light is insensibly chasing away the thick Darkness which broods over the Land of Africa; and the Chaos which has reigned so long is converting into beautiful Order, and reveals more and more clearly the glorious Dispensation of civil and religious Liberty, which are so inseparably united, that there is little or no Enjoyment of one without the other: Otherwise, perhaps the Israelites had been less solicitous for their Freedom from Egyptian slavery; I do not say they would have been contented without it, by no means, for in every human Breast, God has implanted a Principle, which we call Love of Freedom; it is impatient of oppression, and pants for Deliverance—and by the Leave of our modern Egyptians I will assert that the same principle lives in us. God grant Deliverance in his own Way and Time, and get him honour upon all those whose Avaraice impels them to countenance and help forward the Calamities of their fellow Creatures. This I desire not for their Hurt, but to convince them of the strange Absurdity of their Conduct whose Words and Actions are so diametrically opposite. How well the Cry for Liberty, and the reverse Disposition for the exercise of oppressive power over others agree I humbly think it does not require the penetration of a Philosopher to determine.

---

1. From *The Massachusetts Spy* (24 March 1774), this letter was first printed in the *Connecticut Gazette* (11 March 1774) and thereafter in almost a dozen New England newspapers. A free, black woman for some four months when she composed the biting scoring of the hypocritical absurdity of slave-holding Christian ministers, this is Phillis Wheatley's strongest indictment of American slavery in print.

Dear Obour

I rec'd your obliging Letter, enclos'd in your revd Pastor's & handed/ me by his Son. I have lately met with a great trial in the death of my/ mistress.[1] Let us imagine the loss of a Parent, Sister, or Brother the tender/ ness of all these were united in her. I was a poor little outcast &/ a stranger when she took me in, not only into her house, but I pre-/ sently became a sharer in her most tender affections. I was treated by her/ more like her child than her servant, no opportunity was left unim/ prov'd of giving me the best of advice, but in terms how tender! how/ engaging! This I hope ever to keep in remembrance. Her exampla-/ ly [i.e., exemplary] life was a greater monitor than all her precepts and Instruction/ thus we may observe of how much greater force example is than/ Instruction. To alleviate our sorrows we had the satisfaction to see/ her depart in inexpressible raptures, earnest longings, & impatient/ thirstings for the *upper* Courts of the Lord. Do, my dear friend, remem/ ber me & this family in your Closet, that this afflicting dispensation/ may be sanctify'd to us. I am very sorry to hear that you are indispos'd,/ but hope this will find you in better health. I have been unwell the/ greater Part of the winter, but am much better as the Spring approaches./ Pray excuse my not writing to you so long before, for I have been so bu-/ sy lately that I could not find leisure. I shall send the 5 books you/ wrote for, the first convenient opportunity, if you want more, they/ shall be ready for you. I am very affectionately your Friend

                                        Phillis Wheatley.

Boston March 21, 1774

[To/ Miss Obour Tanner/ New Port/ Rhode Island/ favd by Mr./ Pemberton.]

1. Mrs. Susanna Wheatley died March 3, 1774, aged sixty-five years, according to her obituaries, but, according to Christopher Wallcutt, a grandnephew of Mrs. Wheatley, in a letter to his brother, Thomas, a student at Dartmouth College, "Aunt Weatly after a lingering Deseas died a Wensday Morning the 2 of March aboute nine o'clock. . . ." The text, above, is from a manuscript at the Massachusetts Historical Society.

Much honoured sir

I should not so soon have troubled you with the 2ᵈ Letter, but/ the mournful *Occasion* will sufficiently Apologize. It is the death of Mͬ ͤˢ/ Wheatley. She has been labouring under a languishing illness for many months past/ and has at length took her flight from hence to those blissful regions, which need/ not the light of any, but the sun of Righteousness. O could you have been/ present, to see how she long'd to drop the tabernacle of Clay, and to be freed from/ the cumbrous shackles of a mortal Body, which had so many Times retarded/ her desires when soaring upward. She has often told me how your Letters had quicken'd her in her spiritual Course: when she has been in darkness of mind/ they have rais'd and enliven'd her insomuch, that she went on, with chearfulness/ and alacrity in the path of her duty. She did truely, *run with patience the/ race that was set before her*, and hath, at length obtained the celestial Goal./ She is now, sure, that the afflictions of this present time, were not worthy/ to be compared to the Glory, which is now revealed in her, Seeing they/ have wrought out for her, *a far more exceeding and eternal weight of/ Glory*. This, sure, is sufficient encouragement under the bitterest suffer-/ ings, which we can endure.— About half an hour before her Death, she/ spoke with a more audible voice, than she had for 3 months before. She/ call'd her friends & relations around her, and charg'd them not to leave/ their great work undone till *that* hour, but to fear God, and keep his Com-/ mandments. being asked if her faith fail'd her, she answer'd, no. Then [spread? word unclear]/ out her arms crying come! come quickly! come, come! O pray for an easy/ and quick Passage! She eagerly longed to depart to be with Christ. She retain'd/ her senses till the very last moment when "fare well, fare well" with a very/ low voice, were the last words she utter'd. I sat the whole time by her bed/ side, and saw with Grief and Wonder, the Effects of Sin on the human race./ Had not Christ taken away the envenom'd sting, where had been our hopes?/ what might we not have fear'd, what might we not [have] expect'd from the dreadful/ King of Terrors? But *this* is matter of endless praise, to the King eterrnal/ immortal, invisible, that, *it is finished*. I hope her son will be interested in/ your Closet duties, & that the prayers which she was continually putting up & wᶜʰ/ are recorded before God in the Book of his remembrance for her son & for me/ may be

334

answer'd. I can scarcely think that an Object of so many prayers,/ will fail of the Blessings implor'd for him ever since he was born. I intreat/ the same Interest in your best thoughts for myself, that her prayers, in/ my behalf, may be favour'd with an Answer of *Peace*. We received and for/ warded your Letter to the rev'd Mr Occom, but first took the freedom to/ peruse it, and am exceeding glad, that you have order'd him to draw immediate-/ ly for £25, for I really think he is in absolute necessity for that and as much more,/ he is so loth to run in debt for fear he shall not be able to repay, that he has/ not the least shelter for his Creatures [to defend them] from the inclemencies of the weather, and/ he has lost some already for want of it. his hay is quite as defenceless, thus the/ former are in a fair way of being lost, and the latter to be wasted; it were to be/ wished that his *dwelling house* was like the Ark, with appartments, to contain/ the beasts and their provision; He said Mrs Wheatley and the rev'd Mr Moorhead[1]/ were his best friends in Boston. But alass! they are gone. I trust [gone] to receive the/ rewards promis'd to those, who offer a Cup of cold water in the name [& for the sake] of Jesus./ They have both been very instrum[ental in meeting? the next word or two are torn from manuscript][2] the wants of that child of/ God, Mr Occom—but I fear your pa[tience has been? the next words are torn from manuscript][2] exhausted, it remains only that/ we thank you for your kind letter to my Mistress it came above a fortnight after her/ Death.—Hoping for an interest in your prayers for these santification of this be-/ reaving Providence, I am hon'd sir, with dutiful respect ever your obliged/ and devoted Humble servant   Phillis Wheatley

Boston

N England March 29th
1774

John Thornton Esqr

1. See Phillis's "Elegy To Miss. Mary Moorhead, on the DEATH of her Father, The Rev. Mr. JOHN MOORHEAD," above. The manuscript is in the Scottish Records Office.
2. Except for words in brackets marked with superscript 2, all other words in brackets were inserted by Phillis Wheatley.

Dear Obour

I rec'd last evening your kind & friendly Letter and am not a little/ animated thereby. I hope ever to follow your good advices and be resigned to/ the afflicting hand of a seemingly frowning Providence. I have rec'd the/ money you sent for the 5 books & 2/6 more for another, which I now send/ & wish safe to hand. Your tenderness for my welfare demands my gratitude./ Assist me, dear Obour! to Praise our great benefactor, for the innumerable/ Benefits continually pour'd upon me, that while he strikes one Comfort *dead*/ he raises up another. But O, that I could dwell on & delight in him alone/ above every other object! While the world hangs loose about us we shall/ not be in painful *anxiety* in giving up to God, that which he first gave to us./ Your letter came by Mr. Pemberton who brings you the book you write/ for. I shall wait upon Mr. Whitwell with your Letter and am,

Dear Sister, ever affectionately, your

Phillis Wheatley

I have rec'd by some of the last ships/ 300 more of my Poems.[1]

Boston/ May 6, 1774

[To/ Miss Obour Tanner/ New Port/ Rhode Island. favd by Mr. Pemberton.]

---

1. In lots of 300 copies each, at least four editions of Phillis's book had been printed in London in the fall of 1773; the first American edition arrived in Boston in January of 1774. With the lot of her volume referred to in this letter, at least 1800 copies of her book appeared within eight months. The manuscript is at the Massachusetts Historical Society.

Rev'd Sir

I received your kind letter last Evening by Mr Pemberton, by whom also/ this is to be handed you. I have also rec^d the Money for the 5 books I sent to Obour, & 2/6/ more for another. She has wrote me, but the date is 29 April. I am very sorry to/ hear that Philip Quaque[1] has very little or no *apparent*/ Success in his mission—/ Yet, I wish that what you hear respecting him, may be only a misrepresentation—/ Let us not be discouraged, but still hope, that God will bring about his great/ work, tho' Philip may *not* be the instrument in the Divine Hand to perform this/ work of wonder, turning the African *"from darkness to light."* Possibly, if Philip/ would introduce himself properly to them, (I don't know the reverse) he might/ be more Successful, and in setting a good example which is more powerfully win-/ ning than Instruction. I Observe your Reference to the Maps of Guinea & Salmon's/ Gazetteer, and I shall consult them. I have rec^d in some of the last ships from London/ 300 more copies of my Poems, and wish to dispose of them as soon as Possible: If you/ know of any being wanted I flatter myself you will be pleas'd to let me know it,/ which will be adding one more to the many Obligations already confer'd on/ her, who is, with a due Sense of your kindness,

Your most humble
And Obedient servant
Phillis Wheatley

Boston
  May 6, 1774
The revd S. Hopkins.

[To—/ The Rev'd Mr Saml Hopkins/ New Port/ Rhode Island fav'd by Mr./ Pemberton.]

---

1. Philip Quaque (1741–1816), African-born, English educated, had been, in 1765, the first African ordained as an Episcopalian priest in the Church of England and was working in Africa. For an account of the many problems, personal, social, financial, plaguing Quaque as he struggled in the capacities of Chaplain and Missionary School Master and Catechist to the Negroes on the Gold Coast (today's Ghana), see Phillip D. Curtin, editor, *Africa Remembered* (Madison, 1968), pp. 99–139. This letter was first printed in Carter G. Woodson, editor, *The Mind of The Negro* (Washington, D.C., 1926), pp. xvi–xvii. The manuscript is in the Chamberlain Collection of the Boston Public Library. For a printed variant of this letter from another manuscript, see "Phillis Wheatley's Variant Poems and Letters," below.

This Day is published[1]
Adorned with a beautiful Frontispiece of the Author, taken from Life (Price 2s.6d. Sterling)

POEMS

on various Subjects
Religious and Moral,
By Phillis Wheatley
A Negro Girl

Printed for the Benefit of the Author and Sold by
Cox & Berry
At their Store in King - Street, Boston.[2]

---

1. The expression "This Day is published" is misleading to modern readers. There was no edition published in Boston in 1774. Phillis refers to the 300 copies recently sent to her from London, where her book was published in September, 1773.

2. From The *Massachusetts Gazette and Boston Post Boy and Advertiser* (4–11 July 1774), p. 4. Having received "by some of the last ships/ 300 more of my Poems," as Phillis wrote to her friend, Obour, in May 6, 1774, she promoted sales of her book by dictating the information of the above advertisement to the printers. In her 1772 proposals, she had solicited Boston subscribers for a projected volume that was to have sold for "Four Shillings bound" or "Three Shillings, stitched in blue paper." When notices of the Boston availability of her book appeared in January and February of 1774, the book price became "3s. 4d. L.M. Bound" (i.e., three shillings, four pence, Legal Money). By July of 1774, the price dropped to "2s. 6d. Sterling," which would remain until 1778, when Phillis would write Mrs. Mary Wooster in New Haven to report that she could "easily dispose of them here at 12 Lm⁰ each. . . ." (that is, twelve shillings each). Before the above July advertising of her volume for sale, Phillis had been trying to sell copies with the help of friends: see *The Connecticut Gazette* (17 June 1774): "TO BE SOLD B.T. GREEN, POEMS ON VARIOUS SUBJECTS, RELIGIOUS AND MORAL. BY PHILLIS WHEATLEY. NEGRO SERVANT TO MR. JOHN WHEATLEY OF BOSTON, IN NEW ENGLAND. A few of the above are likewise to be sold by Samson Ocum (sic)."

Much hon.^d Sir

I have the honour of your Obliging favour of August 1.st By M.^r/ Wheatley who arriv'd not before the 27.th Ultimo after a tedious passage of near two/ months; the obligations I am under to the family I desire to retain a grateful sense of,/ and consequently rejoice in the bountiful dealings of providence towards him—[1]

By the great loss I have sustain'd of my best friend, I feel like One/ forsaken by her parent in a desolate wilderness, for such the world appears to/ me, wandring thus without $\frac{my^2}{a}$ friendly guide. I fear lest every step should lead me/ into error and confusion. She gave me many precepts and instructions; which/ I hope I shall never forget. Hon'd sir, pardon me if after the retrospect of such uncom-/ mon tenderness for thirteen years from my earliest youth—such unwearied deligence/ to instruct me in the principles of the true Religion, this in some degree Justifies me/ while I deplore my misery— [If] I readily join with you in wishing that you could/ in these respects supply her place, but this does not seem probable from the great/ distance of your residence. However I will endeavour to compensate it by a/ strict Observance of hers and your good advice from time [to] time, which you/ have given me encouragement to hope for—What a Blessed source of consolati/ on that our greatest friend is an immortal God whose friendship is invariable!/ from whom I

---

1. Nathaniel Wheatley and his English bride of almost a year, Mary Enderby, were reported landing in Salem, Massachusetts, as early as September 22 by the *Massachusetts Gazette and Boston Weekly Newsletter,* Boston harbor having been officially closed by the British since March, 1774. Phillis may here be expressing her gratitude to Nathaniel Wheatley for his approving his father's plan to allow her to remain in the King Street mansion, which now belonged to Nathaniel. On October 27, 1774, the Wheatley family lawyer, Samuel Quincy, signed a deposition that attested John Wheatley had sold part of the King Street home to his son in 1771 for the token sum of £100, and that, in October, 1774, for the "token sum" of £200 Nathaniel became the sole owner of the residence and other John Wheatley properties. In November, 1774, he and his wife would return to London where he would die in the spring of 1783.
2. The "a" has been crossed out and replaced with "my."

have all that is [in me] praiseworthy in $^{mental^3}_{\;\;my}$ possession. This

consideration/ humbles me much under encomiums on the gifts of God, the fear that I should/ not improve them to his glory and the good of mankind, it almost hinders a com-/ mendable self estimation (at times) but quite beats down the boldness of presump-/ tion. The world is a severe Schoolmaster, for its frowns are far less dang'rous/ than its smiles and flatteries, and it is a difficult task to keep in the path/ of Wisdom. I attended, and find exactly true your thoughts on the behaviour/ of those who seem'd to respect me while under my mistresses patronage: you said/ right, for some of those have already put on a reserve; but I submit while God/ rules; who never forsakes any till they have ungratefully forsaken him—

My old master's generous behaviour in granting me my freedom, and still so/ kind to me I delight to acknowledge my great obligations to him. this he did about/ 3 months before the death of my dear mistress & at her desire, as well as his own/ humanity, [of w.^{ch}] I hope ever to retain a grateful sense, and treat [him] with that respect/ which is ever due to a paternal friendship—If this had not been the Case, yet/ I hope I should willingly submit to Servitude to be free in Christ—But since it [is?] thus—Let me be a *Servant of Christ*, and that is the most perfect freedom.—[4]

You propose my returning to Africa with Bristol Yamma/ and John Quamine if either of them upon strict enquiry is such, as I dare/ give my heart and hand to, I believe they are either of them good enough/ if not too good for me, or they would not be fit for missionaries; but/ why do you, hon'd sir, wish those poor men so much trouble as to carry/ me so long a voyage? Upon my arrival, how like a Barbarian shou'd/ I look to the Natives; I can promise that my tongue shall be quiet [for a strong reason indeed] being/ an utter stranger to the Language of Anamoboe.[5] Now to be

3. The "my" has been crossed out and replaced with "mental." Other words in brackets throughout the letter are insertions by Phillis.

4. Actually, as she well knew, Phillis was manumitted before October 18, 1773, nearly six months before the death of her mistress. Also, as Phillis well knew, she coveted her personal freedom very much.

5. For some time, both Mrs. Susanna Wheatley and the Reverend Samson Occom had been suggesting Phillis's return to Africa as a Christian missionary. Wrote Occom in March of 1771, "P.S. Please to remember me to Phillis and the rest of your Servants./ Pray madam what harm would it be to send Phillis to her/ Native Country as a Female Preacher to her kindred,/ you know Quaker women are allow'd to preach, and why/ not others in an extraordinary case—."

serious, this/ undertaking appears too hazardous, and not sufficiently Eligible, to go—/ and leave my British & American
Friends—I am also unacquain-/ ted with those Missionaries in
Person. The reverend gentleman who under-/ takes their Education has repeatedly inform^d me by Letters of their progress/ in
Learning also an account of John Quamine's family and kingdom[.]^6

But be that as it will I resign it all to God's all wise governance;
I thank you heartily for your generous Offer—with sincerity—/ I
am hon^d sir/ most respectfully your Devoted Servt

Phillis Wheatley

Boston Oct 30!^h 1774.

[To/ John Thornton/ Merchant/ London]

6. "The reverend gentleman" was Reverend Samuel Hopkins of Newport, Rhode
Island. Through an exchange of letters with the African priest, Phillip Quaque,
missionary-teacher on the Gold Coast, Hopkins was able to put John Quamine,
who had been enslaved and brought to Newport, back in touch with his African
mother and uncle in Anamaboe (in today's Ghana). On April 10, 1776, the
Reverends Ezra Stiles and Samuel Hopkins signed a second circular soliciting
funds for the education and transportation of John Quamine and Bristol Yamma
to Africa to serve as Christian missionaries. This second circular included the
printing of the account of an exchange of letters between Hopkins and Quaque.
By 1773 Quaque could write Hopkins

> It was with inexpressible pleasure and satisfaction that I acquaint you, that
> my inquiries after the friends and relatives of that gentleman [i.e., John
> Quamine, living in Newport] have met with the desired success. . . . I have
> found his father's name to be the same which you mention, who has been
> dead many years. His mother's name is as you have written it, who is still
> alive, and whom I had the pleasure of seeing. But the bowels of maternal
> affection—in truth I do declare it—seem ready to burst. . . . The joy it
> kindled on the occasion, in expectation of seeing once more the fruit of her
> loins before she with her gray hair goes down to the grave, threw her into
> ecstacies resembling Jacob's, and in raptures she breaks forth and says *It is
> enough! My son is yet alive! I hope, by God's blessing, to see him before I
> die.* . . . A great personage of his family, whose name is *Oforee*, and now
> enjoys the father's estate, desires with great importunity, that I would
> earnestly petition you that he may be returned to them as soon as may be,
> and promises that nothing shall be wanting to make him, and all about
> him, comfortable and happy among his own kindred. . . .

See Edward A. Parks, *Memoir of the Life and Character of Samuel Hopkins, D.D.*
second edition (Boston, 1834), pp. 134–135. The manuscript is at the Scottish
Records Office.

SIR,[1]

I have taken the freedom to address your Excellency in the/ enclosed poem, and entreat your acceptance, though I am not/ insensible of its inaccuracies. Your being appointed by the/ Grand Continental Congress to be Generalissimo of the armies of/ North America, together with the fame of your virtues, excite/ sensations not easy to suppress. Your generosity, therefore, I pre-/ sume, will pardon the attempt. Wishing your Excellency all/ possible success in the great cause you are so generously engaged/ in, I am

    Your Excellency's

Most obedient humble servant,
PHILLIS WHEATLEY.

Providence, *Octo.* 26, 1775.
His Excellency General Washington.

---

1. Washington enclosed the manuscript of this letter (and the accompanying poem, "To His Excellency General Washington," q.v., above) in a letter dated "Cambridge, February 10, 1776," to his adjutant, Colonel Joseph Reed. In another letter, dated "Cambridge, February 28, 1776," Washington answered Phillis's note. Both of these Washington letters were published in Jared Sparks, editor, *The Writings of George Washington*, 12 volumes (Boston, 1834), 111, 288, 297–298. See Appendices G and H. The manuscripts of the poem and the covering letter are not extant.

Boston May 29th '78

Dear Obour,—

I am exceedingly glad to hear from you by Mrs. Tanner, and wish you/ had timely notice of her departure,[1] so as to have wrote me; next to/ that is the pleasure of hearing that you are well. The vast variety of/ scenes that have pass'd before us these 3 years past, will to a reasonable mind serve to convince us of the uncertain duration of all things/ temporal, and the proper result of such a consideration is an ardent/ desire of, & preparation for, a state and enjoyments which are more/ suitable to the immortal mind. —You will do me a great favour/ if you'll write me by every opp'y.—Direct your letters under cover/ to Mr. John Peters in Queen Street.[2] I have but half an hour's no-/ tice; and must apologize for this hasty scrawl. I am most affection-/ ately, my dear Obour your sincere friend,

Phillis Wheatley.

[To/ Miss Obour Tanner/ Worcester]

1. The Tanner family fled British-besieged Newport for Worcester, Massachusetts, where several other Tanner family members are buried in the Mechanic Street cemetery. Likely freed in 1784, Obour returned to Newport, where she would die in 1835. The manuscript is at the Massachusetts Historical Society.
2. Phillis married black, literate, ambitious John Peters in Boston in the previous month, their marriage bans having been printed and noting them both as "free Negroes."

343

Madam[1]

I rec'd your favour by Mr. Dennison inclosing a paper contain-/ ing the Character of the truely worthy General Wooster. It was with the/ most sensible regret that I heard of his fall in battle;[2] but the pain so/ afflicting a dispensation of Providence must be greatly alleviated to you and/ all his friends in the consideration that he fell a martyr in the Cause of/ Freedom————[3] You will do me a great favour by returning to me by the first opp'y/ those books that remain unsold and remitting the money for those that/ are sold—I can easily dispose of them here for 12/Lm^{O4} each—/ I am greatly obliged to you for the care you show me, and your/ condescention in taking so much pains for my Interest—I am/ extremely sorry not to have been honour'd with a personal acquaintance/ with you—if the foregoing lines meet with your acceptance/ and approbation I shall think them highly honour'd./ I hope you will pardon the length of my letter, when the rea-/ son is apparent—fondness of the subject, &c—the highest/ respect for the deceas'd—I sincerely sympathize with you in/ the great loss you and your family Sustain and am sincerely

Your friend & very humble sert.
Phillis Wheatley

Queenstreet
Boston   July—
15th 1778

[Mrs. Mary Wooster/ New Haven]

---

1. This was Mary Clap Wooster, sister of Temperance Clap Pitkin, who married the Reverend Timothy Pitkin. See Wheatley's piece, "To the Rev. Mr. *Pitkin*, On the Death of his Lady," in "Phillis Wheatley's Variant Poems and Letters," above.
2. Brigadier-General David Wooster died on May 2, 1777, from wounds inflicted April 27 by the British in an ambush during the Danbury Raid. A Connecticut Masonic order caused a monument to him to be erected in Danbury in 1854.
3. The untitled eulogy on the death of General Wooster follows. See the poem, "On The Death of General Wooster," in "Phillis Wheatley's Later Poems," above.
4. This is twelve shillings, Legal Money. The manuscript is in the Hugh Upham Clark Papers at the Library of Congress.

Dr. Obour—[1]

By this opportunity I have the pleasure to inform/ you that I am well and hope you are so; tho' I have been/ silent, I have not been unmindful of you but a variety of/ hindrances was the cause of my not writing to you./ But in time to come I hope our correspondence will/ revive—and revive in better times—pray write me/ soon—for I long to hear from you—you may depend on constant/ replies—I wish you much happiness, and am

    Dr. Obour, your friend & sister   Phillis Peters.
Boston May 10 1779

[Miss Obour Tanner, Worcester. favd by Cumberland.]

1. This is the last extant letter written by Phillis to Obour Tanner. The manuscript is at the Massachusetts Historical Society.

Prayer of Phillis's accidentally discovered in her bible[1]

Sabbath—June 13, 1779

Oh my Gracious Preserver.
hithero thou hast brot [me,]
be pleased when thou bringest
to the birth to give [me] strength
to bring forth living & perfect a
being who shall be greatly in
strumental in promoting thy [glory]
Tho conceived in Sin & brot forth
in iniquity yet thy infinite wisdom
can bring a clean thing out of an
unclean, a vesse[l] of Honor filled
for thy glory—grant me to
to live a life of gratitude to thee
for the innumerable benefits—
O Lord my God. instruct my ignorance
& enlighten my Darkness
Thou art my King, take [thou]
the entire possession of [all] my
powers & faculties & let me be
no longer under the dominion
of sin—give me a sincere &
hearty repentance for all my
[illegible] offences & strengthen
by thy grace my resolutions
on amendment & circumspection
for the time to come—Grant me
[also] the spirit of Prayer & Suppli-
[cation] according to thy own
most gracious Promises.

1. Most curiously, this headnote is written in the same handwriting as the prayer
itself. Of lifelong poor health, Phillis here, on the eve of her first pregnancy—she
was married on April 1, 1778—seems almost traumatized. The manuscript, in very
poor condition, is at the Schomburg Center for Research in Black Culture,
whose authorities supplied the bracketed information.

PROPOSALS[1]

For Printing/ By Subscription/ A Volume of Poems,/ And/ Letters/ on Various Subjects,/ Dedicated to the Right Honourable,/ Benjamin Franklin Esq:/ One of the Ambassadors of the United States, at/ the Court of France,/ By Phillis Peters.

Poems.

Thoughts on the Times./ On the Capture of General Lee, to I.B. Esq./ To His Excellency General Washington./ On the death of General Wooster./ An Address to Dr ———./ To Lieut. R——— of the Royal Navy./ To the same./ To T.M. Esq. of Granada./ To Sophia of South Carolina./ To Mr. A. M'B——— of the Navy./ To Lieut R——— D——— of the Navy./ Ocean./ The choice and advantages of a Friend; to Mr. T———./ Farewell to England., 1773./ To Mrs. W———ms on Anna Eliza./ To Mr. A. Mc-B———d./ Epithalamium to Mrs. H———./ To P.N.S. & Lady on the death of their infant son./ To Mr. El———y on the death of his Lady./ On the death of Lieut. L———ds./ To Penelope./ To Mr. & Mrs. L——— on the death of their daughter./ A Complaint./ To Mr. A.I.M. on Virtue./ To Dr. L———d and Lady on the death of their son/ aged 5 years./ To Mr. L———g on the death of his son./ To Capt. F———r on the death of his granddaughter./ To Philandra an Elegy./ Niagara./ Chloe to Calliope./ To Musidora on Florello./ To Sir E. ——— Esq./ To the Hon. John Montague Esq. Rear Admiral/ of the Blue.

1. These proposals were printed in Boston's *Evening Post and General Advertiser* (30 October; 6, 27 November; 4, 11, 18 December, 1779); like her 1772 proposals they were rejected, and this volume was never published as planned. However, various of these poems—the second, third, fourth, sixth, and seventh—and possibly letters numbered 1, 7, 12, and 13—have been published separately by various hands over the years.

LETTERS[2]

1. To the Right Hon. Wm E. of Dartmouth/ Sec. of State of N. America./ 2. To the Rev. Mr. T.P. Farmington./ 3. To Mr. T. W——— Dartmouth College./ 4. To the Hon. T.H. Esq./ 5. To Dr. B. Rush, Phila./ 6. To the Rev. Dr. Thomas, London./ 7. To the Right Hon. Countess of H———./ 8. To I. M——— Esq. London./ 9. To Mrs. W———e in the County of Surrey./ 10. To Mr. T.M. Homerton, near London./ 11. To Mrs. S.W.———./ 12. To the Rt. the Hon. the Countess of H———./ 13. To the same.

Messieurs Printers,—/ The above collection of Poems and Letters was put/ into my hands by the desire of the Ingenious author in order/ to be introduced to public View.

The subjects are various and curious, and the author a/ Female African, whose lot it was to fall into the hands of a/ *generous* master and *great* benefactor. The learned and ing-/ enuous as well as those who are pleased with novelty, are/ invited to incourage the publication by a generous subscrip/ tion—the former, that they may fan the sacred fire which,/ is self-enkindled in the breast of this *young* African—The/ ingenuous that they may by reading this collection have/ a large play for their imaginations, and be exited [sic for excited] to please/ and benefit mankind, by some brilliant production of their/ own pens.—Those who are *always* in search of some *new*/ thing, that they may obtain a sight of this *rara avis in*/ *terra*—And every one, that the ingenious author may be/ encouraged to improve her own mind, and benefit and please/ mankind.

---

2. In the November 27 printing of these proposals, "Letters" is misprinted "LETTEES." These proposals were printed in an especially careless manner. In this same printing, "France" appears as "FRANEC." A few other such examples of such sloppy printing are: The correct title of the poem, "To Mr. A.I.M. on Virtue," in the October 30 and November 6 printings, appears as "To Mr. T.I.M. on Virtue" in the other printings. The November 7 and December 4 printings misprint "Chine to Calliope" for "Chloe to Calliope," which apears in the other printings. The November 27 and December 4 issues misprint "To Mogdera on Florello" for "To Musidora on Florello" in all other printings. Among the letters, number 2, "To the Rev. Mr. T.P. Farmington," reads, "To the Rev. Mr. T.P. Framington," which is Reverend Timothy Pitkin's hometown, in the October 30 and November 6 printings. In the November 27, December 4, and December 11 printings, "To Mr. T. W——— Dartmouth College" appears as "To Mr. D——— C———."

CONDITIONS.

They will be printed and good Paper and a neat Type;/ and will Contain about 300 Pages in Octavo./ The price to Subscribers will be *Twelve Pounds*, neatly/ Bound & Lettered, and *Nine Pounds*, sew'd in blue paper,[3] one Half to be paid on Subscribing, the other Half,/ on Delivery of the Books./ The Work will be put to the Press as soon as a sufficient Number of Encouragers offer./ Those who subscribe for Six will have a Seventh Gratis./ Subscriptions are taken by White and Adams, the/ Publishers, in School-Street, *Boston.*

3. Despite the notoriously swollen inflation rate in Boston in the mid and late 1770's, these advertised prices of *"Twelve Pounds*, neatly/ Bound & Lettered, and *Nine Pounds*, sew'd in blue paper"* seem unusually high. Just fifteen months earlier, Phillis had declared that she could easily dispose of remainder copies of her 1773 volume "for 12/Lm⁰" (i.e., 12 shillings, Legal money). In 1773, bound copies of this volume in London sold for "3s. 4d." (i.e., 3 shillings and 4 pence) while in Boston in the first of 1774 and thereafter, sewn copies cost "2s. 6d. Sterling." Now she advertises a projected second volume of her writings for sale at twelve pounds bound, and nine pounds sewn. If the printed prices above are an accurate printing of the manuscript, they could reflect the inflation of the times, or they might reflect John Peters's grandiose notions of the book's worth. Perhaps, as has been suggested, the compositor for the *Evening Post and General Advertiser* misread Phillis's handwritten "12 Lm⁰" to mean "twelve pounds." However, in her manuscript letters, Phillis used the pound sign raised above the level of the written line, and immediately *preceding* the number of pounds. For instance, she wrote to John Thornton on March 29th, 1774, thanking him for making monies available for her Indian friend, the Reverend Samson Occom: ". . . am exceeding glad, that you have order'd him to draw immediately for £25, for I really think he is in absolute necessity for it. . . ." Also, Mrs. Susanna Wheatley, who surely helped Phillis in learning how to write, did the same thing. Writing to Thornton on February 9, 1773, again about money for Occom, she said ". . . tho he has a salary of £50 Sterlg, it seems he has little benefit of it. . . ." In making up the font for the printing of Phillis's proposals, the compositor made several mistakes and changes, but not in the advertised sale price of the projected book, which remained the same in all six issues of the paper. The text above is from the October 30 printing, which differs from the reprinting in the *Proceedings of the Massachusetts Historical Society*, VIII (September, 1865). See also Mukhtar Ali Isani, "'On the Death of General Wooster': An Unpublished Poem by Phillis Wheatley," *Modern Philology*, 77, no. 3 (February, 1980), 308n.

The Poem, in page 488, of/ this Number, was selected/ from a manuscript Volume of Poems,/ written by PHILLIS PETERS, formerly/ PHILLIS WHEATLEY—and is inserted/ as a Specimen of her Work; should/ this gain the Approbation of the Pub-/ lick and sufficient encouragement be/ given, a Volume will be shortly Pub-/ lished, by the Printers hereof, who/ received subscriptions for said Work.[1]

1. From *The Boston Magazine* (September, 1784), p. 488. For two different volumes that were to have been published in Boston, Phillis printed proposals three times in 1772, six times in 1779, and once in 1784. For Bostonians who wished to subscribe to her first volume, newly planned for London publication, Phillis ran proposals three times in 1773. Each of her thirteen solicitations for Boston publication of her books was rejected. The proposals above were printed in *The Boston Magazine* for September, 1784, p. 462. "The Poem, in page 488, of/ this Number . . ." refers to "To Mr. and Mrs. *******, On the Death of Their Infant Son, By Phillis Wheatly [sic]." See "Phillis Wheatley's Later Poems," above.

PHILLIS WHEATLEY'S VARIANT POEMS
AND LETTERS

With noble warmth shows man created free,
" When GOD, from chaos, gave this world to be."
What plaintive song, what melancholy tale,
Rides on the breeze and spreads upon the vale ?
'Tis BARLOW'S* strain, which solemn pours along,
For HOSMER's dead, and saddened is the song.

Here the fair volume shows the far-spread name
Of wondrous WHEATLY,† *Afric's* heir to fame.
Well is it known what glowing genius shines,
What force of numbers, in her polished lines:
With magic power the grand descriptions roll
Thick on the mind, and agitate the soul.‡

---

* Mr. Joel Barlow, of Connecticut. At the time when this was written, the author had only seen his Elegy on Judge Hosmer, which contains much sublimity.

† Phillis Wheatly, a negress, and the authoress of some ingenious poems, which seem to be entitled to a remembrance here, although not written by a native of America.

‡ We need only peruse the following lines, extracted from her poems, to be convinced of this:

" When Homer paints, lo ! circumfused in air,
Celestial gods in mortal forms appear: _
Swift as they move, hear each recess rebound,
Earth quakes, heaven thunders, and the shores resound.
Great sire of verse, before my mortal eyes
The lightnings flash along the gloomy skies:
And as the thunder shades the heavenly plains,
A deep-felt horror creeps through all my veins." ⌉

---

1. When she edited her late brother's collected papers as *The Literary Remains of Joseph Brown Ladd, M.D.* (New York: H.S. Sleight, 1832), Mrs. Elizabeth Haskins included Ladd's poem, "The Prospect of America," which praises poets Joel Barlow, Philip Freneau, and Phillis Wheatley. Several lines from this excerpt, however, are variant from lines 7–14 of the poem, "To Maecenas," as it was published in Wheatley's volume of 1773. Born and reared in Newport, Rhode Island, Ladd (1764–1786) published poems when he was quite young, as did Phillis Wheatley. He may have secured an early manuscript version of "To Maecenas" from Phillis during one of her visits with her lifelong black friend, Obour Tanner, of that town, or Mrs. Haskins may have misquoted the printed poem, "Maecenas." The date of composition of this version of Wheatley's piece is unknown; it is placed first here only because "To Maecenas" appears first in her 1773 volume, which follows a rough chronology. Line 7 would seem to misprint "shades" for "shakes."

1

1. "The University of Cambridge," i.e., Harvard College in Cambridge, Massachusetts, where, in 1766, students generated a publicized commotion over being served bad butter in their commons.

2. *The dark abode.* In lines 3–7, Phillis disparages the African lack of formalized, western, literate education, and especially Christianity, which she serendipitously found, and thereafter enjoyed, in New England and London. She does not denigrate Africa, her "native shore,/ The sable Land of error's darkest night/ . . . the dark abode," because its peoples are black-skinned. Her use of colors, black and white especially, is a traditional, symbolic use. Thus, in line 28, "the sable monster" does not refer to any real color, but to "hateful vice so baneful to the Soul," line 26.

354

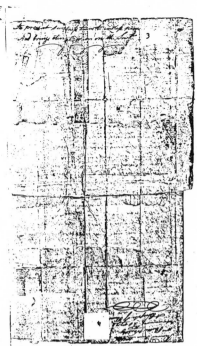

3. Written on a second sheet of paper, these two lines read,

> Its present sweetness turns to endless pain
> And brings eternal ruin on the soul

and are not included in all printings of this manuscript.

4. Reading "Received from Mrs P.W./ ("Mrs P.W." being crossed out) Mrs Phillis Wheatly/ February 2d 1773/ A Couple of Poems," this notation was written by Thomas Wallcutt (1758–1840), a grandnephew of Phillis's mistress, and an admiring friend. One of two extant letters written to Phillis was written by him from Montreal, Canada, on "Nov 17, 1774." She planned to publish one of her letters to Wallcutt. See letter title 3 of her 1779 Proposals for a volume of verses and letters that was never published. Wallcutt's mother, Elizabeth Wallcutt (1721–1811), a niece to Phillis's mistress, mailed the manuscript of the above poem, and the manuscript of Phillis's elegy on the death of the Reverend Dr. Sewall (q.v., below) on January 30, 1773, when Wallcutt was a student at Dartmouth College. On April 20, 1773, Wallcutt acknowledged receipt of the two manuscripts:

> . . . Honored & kind Mama, yours of January 30 I have received with Phillis's letters and the Poems on the Death of Dr. Sewall and his picture with an address to the scholars of Cambridge. . . .

This poem's manuscript, at the American Antiquarian Society, would be revised as "To the University of Cambridge in New-England," in 30 lines, and included in Wheatley's volume, *Poems on Various Subjects, Religious and Moral* (London, 1773). Another manuscript is said to be in the Schomburg Center for Research in Black Culture. The legibility of this manuscript has been greatly improved by the skillful work of the expert restoration team of the American Antiquarian Society.

The following Lines are said to be compos'd by a Native/ of Africa, about 15 years of age,—& who (few years ago)/ could not speak one word of English,—She belong'd to/ John Wheatley of Boston—[1]

on Atheism

Where now shall I begin this Spacious field
To Tell what Curses,—Unbelief doth Yield,
Thou that Doest, daily, feel his hand & rod,
And dar'st deny the Essence of a God,
If there's no heaven—whither wilt Thou go,
Make thy Elysium—in the shades below,
If there's no God—from whence did all things spring,
He made the Greatest, & minutest Thing
With great astonishment my soul is struck
O weakness great?—hast Thou thy sense forsook?
Hast Thou forgot thy Preterperfect days
They are recorded, in the book of praise
If 'Tis not written with the hand of God,
Why is it seal'd with dear Imanuel's blood,

Now Turn, I pray Thee, from ꝑ dang'rous road
Rise from ꝑ Dust,—& see the Mighty God;
Tis by his Mercy, we do move & live
His loving kindness doth our Sin's forgive,
Tis Satan's power, (our Adversary great)
With holds us, from the kingdom & ꝑ state,
Bliss weeping, wants us, in her arms to fly,
To the vast Regions of felicity,
Prehaps Thy Ignorance, will ask us, where?
Go to the Cornerstone, it will declare,
Thy heart in Unbelief will harder grow,
Altho' thou hidest it, for Pleasure Now,

1. Chief of Reference Services, Phil Lapsansky, of the Library Company of Philadelphia, which holds the manuscript, advises that this version of this poem is "not in Wheatley's hand," but comes from a collection of poems copied and authored by Hannah Griffitts (or Griffith), a local Philadelphia minor poet, who may well have made this copy after seeing the poem 'Atheism.'" It is included here because it varies from other manuscript versions. Lorenzo Greene, in *The Negro in Colonial New England* (New York, 1942), p. 245, prints, with variant punctuation, the first sixteen lines of this version (which make up the first of the three manuscript pages), from a photostat of a manuscript. Another copy of this version of the poem is in the Library of Congress. The first of the three pages of this manuscript is unreproducible.

Thou Takes Unusual means, the Path forbear,
Unkind to others, to thyself severe?
Methinks I see the Consequence,—thou'rt blind,
Thy Unbelief destroys thy Peace of Mind,
If Men such wise inventions then coud know,
In the high firmament, who made the Bow,
Which Covenant was made, for to insure,
Made to Establish, Lasting to endure,
Who made the Heaven's & Earth, a lasting spring
Of Admiration,—To whom doest Thou bring
Thy Thanks & Tribute,— Thy adoration pay,
To heathen God's, & own their fabled sway,
Doth Pluto Tell thee thou shall see ♀ Shades,
Of fell Perdition,—for thy learning made
Doth Cupid in thy breast that warmth inspire,
To Love thy B (sic) Brother which is God's desire,
Look thou above, & see who made ♀ sky
Nothing more Lucid, to an Atheist's eye,
Look Thou beneath & see each Purling stream,
It surely canot all Delusion seem.
Mark rising Phebus, when he spreads his ray,
And his Comission is—to Rule ♀ day,
At Night keep watch,—& see a Cynthia bright
And her Comission is,—to rule the Night.

                                        Africania

Atheism [1]

Where now shall I begin this Spacious Feild
To tell what curses unbelief doth yield
Thou that dost daily feel his hand and rod
And dare deny the essence of a god
If there's no god from whence did all things spring
He made the greatest and minutest thing
If there's no heaven whither wilt thou go
Make thy Elysium in the shades below
With great astonishment my soul is struck
O rashness great hast thou thy sense forsook
Hast thou forgot the preterperfect days
They are recorded in the Book of praise
If twas not written by the hand of God
Why was it sealed with Immanuel's blood
Tho' tis a second point thou dost deny
Unmeasur'd vengeance Scarlet sins do cry
Turn now I pray thee from the dangerous road
Rise from the dust and seek the mighty God

---

1. This is another variant of "An Address to the Atheist. By P. Wheatley at the age of/ 14 Years—1767"; see "Phillis Wheatley's Early Poems," above. The manuscript is at the Library Company of Philadelphia.

By whose great mercy we do move and live
Whose Loving kindness doth our sins forgive.
'Tis Beelzebub our adversary great
Withholds from us the kingdom and the seat
Bliss weeping waits us in her arms to fly
To the vast regions of Felicity
Perhaps thy Ignorance will ask us where
Go to the corner stone it will declare
Thy heart in unbelief will harder grow
Altho thou hidest it for pleasure now
Thou tak'st unusual means, the path forbear
Unkind to others to thyself severe
Methinks I see the consequence thou art blind
Thy unbelief disturbs the peaceful mind
The endless Scene too far for me to tread
Too great to Accomplish from so weak a head
If men such wise inventions then should know
In the high Firmament who made the bow
That covenant was made for to ensure
Made to establish lasting to endure
Who made the heavens and earth a lasting Spring
Of Admiration, to whom dost thou bring

Thy thanks, and tribute, Adoration pay,
To heathen gods, can wise Apollo say
'Tis I that saves thee from the deepest hell
Minerva teach thee all thy days to tell
Doth pluto tell thee thou shalt see the shade
Of fell perdition for thy learning made
Doth cupid in thy breast that warmth inspire
To love thy brother which is Gods desire
Look thou above and see who made the sky
Nothing more lucid to an Atheists eye
Look thou beneath, behold each purling stream
It surely cannot a Delusion seem.

Mark rising Phœbus when he spreads his ray
And his commission for to guide the day
At night keep watch, and see a Cynthia bright
And her commission for to guide the night
See how the stars when the do sing his praise
Witness his essence in celestial lays

(Deism)[1]

Must Ethiopians be imploy'd for you
Greatly rejoice if any good I do
I ask O unbeliever satans child
Has not thy saviour been too meek & mild
The auspicious rays that round his head do shine
Do still declare him to be christ divine
Doth not the Omnipotent call him son?
And is well pleas'd with his beloved One
How canst thou thus divide the trinity
What canst thou take up for to make the three
Tis satans snares a fluttering in the wind
Whereby he hath ensnar'd thy foolish mind
God the eternal Orders this to be
See thy vain arg'ments to divide the three
Canst thou not see the consequence in store
Begin the Omnipotent to adore
Arise the pinions of Persuasions here
Seek the Eternal while he is so near

1. This is a variant of "An address to the Deist—1767," one of Wheatley's "Early Poems," (q.v., above). In the Library Company of Philadelphia, the manuscript was printed by Phil Lapsansky, "Deism An Unpublished Poem by Phillis Wheatley," *New England Quarterly*, 50, No. 3 (September, 1977), 517–520.

At the last day where wilt thou hide thy face
The day approaching is no time for grace
Then wilt thou cry Myself undone and lost
Proclaiming Father, Son, and Holy Ghost
Who trod the wine press of Jehovahs wrath
Who taught us prayer and gave us grace and faith
Who but the great and the Supreme who bleſsd
Ever and ever in Immortal rest
The meanest prodigal that comes to God
Is not cast off, but brought by Jesus Blood
When to the faithleſs Jews he oft did cry
One call'd him Teacher some made him a lye
He came to you in mean apparell clad
He came to save you from your sins and had
Far more Compaſsion then I can expreſs
Paine his companions, and his Friends Distreſs

362

Immanuel God with us these pains did bear
Must the Eternal our Petitions hear?
Ah! cruel destiny his life he laid
Father Forgive them thus the saviour said
They nail'd King Jesus to the cross for us
For our Transgressions he did bear the curse.

May I O Eternal salute aurora. to begin thy
Praise, shall mortal dust do that. which Immortals scarcely
can comprehend, then O omnipotent I with humbly ask. after
imploring thy pardon for this presumpsion. when shall we ap-
=proach thy majestys presence crowned with celestial Dignities
When shall we see the resting place of the great supreme.
When shall we behold thee. O redeemer in all the resplendent
Graces of a suffering God,

yet wise men sent from the Orient clime
Now led by seraphs to the bliss'd abode

To the King's most excellent Majesty on his repealing the american Stamp act [1]
Your Subjects hope

The crown upon your head may flourish long .
And in great wars your royal arms be strong
May your Sceptre many nations sway
Resent it on them that dislike Obey
But how shall we exalt the British king
Who ralets france Rejicting every thing
The sweet remembrance of whose favours past .
The meanest peasants bless the great the last
May George beloved of all the nations round
Live and by earths and heavens blessings crown'd
May heaven protect and guard him from on high
And at his presence every evil fly
Thus every clime with equal gladness see
When kings do smile it sets their Subjects free
When wars came on the proudest rebel fled .
God thunder'd fury on their guilty head

Phillis

---

1. This is the original version of "To the King's Most Excellent Majesty. 1768," in 15 lines, which was included in Wheatley's 1773 volume of *Poems*. In her 1772 proposals (q.v., above), Phillis noted that she had composed this piece in 1768, but news of the repeal of the heartily despised Stamp Act reached Boston by the Spring of 1766. The manuscript is in the Historical Society of Pennsylvania.

The Decease of the rev'd Dr. Sewell ——

E'r yet the morning heav'd its Orient head
Behold him praising with the happy dead
Hail happy Saint, on the Immortal Shore.
We hear thy warnings and advice no more
Then let each one. behold with wishful eyes
The Saint ascending to his native Skies
From hence the Prophet wing'd his rapturous way
To mansions pure, to fair celestial day ——
Then begging for the Spirit of his God
And panting eager for the blest abode
Let every one with the same vigour soar
To bliss and happiness unseen before
Then be christs image on our minds impress'd
And plant a saviour in each glowing Breast
Thrice happy thou, arriv'd to joy at last
What compensation for the evil past ——
Thou Lord incomprehensible unknown
By sense — we bow at thy exalted throne

1. This is one of two manuscript versions of this poem among the Countess of Huntingdon's Papers at Cheshunt Foundation, Cambridge University, England. Showing slight punctuational differences, this version, above, includes two lines more—lines 36-37—than the other version.

While thus we beg thy excellence to feel
Thy Sacred Spirit in our hearts reveal
To make each one of us thy grace partake
Which thus we beg for the Redeemers Sake
Sewell is dead, swift pinion'd fame there cry'd
Is Sewell dead, my trembling heart reply'd
Behold to us a benefit deny'd
But when our Jesus had ascended high
With captive bands he led captivity
And gifts receiv'd for such as knew not God
Lord, send a Pastor for thy Churches good;
O ruin'd world, my mournful thots reply'd
And ruin'd continent the ecco cry'd
How oft for us the holy Prophet pray'd
But now behold him in his clay cold bed.
By duty urg'd my weeping verse to close.
I'll on his Tomb, an Epitaph compose.
Here lies a man bought with Christs precious blood
Once a poor Sinner, now a saint with God

Behold ye rich and poor and fools and wise
Nor let this monitor your hearts Surprize
I'll tell you all, what this great Saint has done
That makes him brighter than the glorious Sun
Listen ye happy, from the Seats above
I speak sincerely and with truth and Love
He sought the paths of virtue and of truth
'Twas this that made him happy in his Youth
In blooming years he found that grace divine
That gives admittance to the Sacred Shrine

Mourn him ye indigent, whom he has fed
Seek yet more earnest for the living bread
Even Christ, your bread that cometh from above
Implore his pity and his grace and Love
Mourn him ye youth, whom he hath often told
Gods bounteous mercies from the times of old
I too have cause this heavy loss to mourn
For this my monitor will not return
Now this faint semblance of his life complete
He is thro' Jesus made divinely great
And Set a Glorious pattern to repeat —
But when shall we to this bless'd State Arrive
When the same graces in our hearts do thrive

                              Phillis Wheatley

*On the Death of the Rev. D. Sewall 176_*

Ere yet the morning heav'd its Orient head
Behold him praising with the happy dead.
Hail! happy Saint, on the immortal shore,
We hear thy warnings and advice no more:
Then let each one behold with wishful eyes
The Saint ascending to his native Skies,
From hence the Prophet wing'd his rapturous way
To mansions pure, to fair celestial day —
Then begging for the Spirit of his God
And panting eager for the bless'd abode,
Let every one, with the same vigour, strive
To bliss, and happiness, unseen before
Then be Christ's image on our minds impress'd
And plant a Saviour in each glowing Breast —
Thrice happy thou, arriv'd to joy at last,
What compensation for the evil past!
Thou Lord, incomprehensible, unknown;
To Sense, we bow, at thy creative Throne!
While thus we beg thy excellence to feel,
Thy Sacred Spirit, in our hearts reveal
And make each one of us, that grace partake
Which thus we ask for the Redeemer's Sake
"Sewall is dead" swift pinion'd fame thus cry'd
"Is Sewall dead?" my trembling heart reply'd
O what a blessing in thy flight deny'd!
But when our Jesus had ascended high,
With captive bands he led captivity;
And gifts receiv'd for such as knew not God
Lord, send a Pastor, for thy Churches
O round wor'd bereft of thee, we cry'd,
The rocks responsive to the voice, reply'd.

---

1. This is the earliest version of this poem which would be revised, with the same title, in 51 lines, and included in Wheatley's 1773 volume of *Poems*. The Reverend Joseph Sewall (1688–1769) was the pastor for fifty-six years of the Old South Congregational Church and Meeting House, which Phillis would join on August 18, 1771, when she became 18 years old (perhaps using the date of her being sold as a slave to Mrs. Susanna Wheatley in August, 1761, as an indication of the eighth year of her age). Like many of Phillis's acquaintants, Sewall was concerned with Christian reform work, especially among the Indians of New England. As a corresponding member of the Society in Scotland for Propagating Christian Knowledge, and as a commissioner for the Society for the Propagation of the Gospel in New England and parts adjacent in America, he maintained a continuing interest in Moor's Charity School in Lebanon, Connecticut, to which the

How oft for us this holy Prophet pray'd.
But ah! behold him in his Clay-cold bed
By date wrg'd my weeping verse to close
I'll on his Tomb an Epitaph compose
    Lo! here, a man bought with Christs precious blood
Once a poor sinner, now a Saint with God
Behold ye rich and poor, and fools and wise;
Nor let this monitor your hearts surprize
I'll tell you all, what thing great Saint has done
Which makes him brighter than the glorious Sun.
Listen ye happy from your seats above
I speak sincerely and with truth and love:
He sought the Paths of virtue and of Truth
'Twas this which made him happy in his Youth
In Blooming years he found that grace Divine
Which gives admittance to the sacred throne
Mourn him, ye Indigent, whom he hath fed.
Seek yet more earnest for the living Bread
Een Christ your Bread, who cometh from above
Implore his pity and his grace and Love.
Mourn him ye Youth, whom he hath often told
Gods bounteous Mercy from the times of Old.
I too, have cause this mighty loss to mourn
For this my monitor will not return
    Now this faint semblance of his life complete
He is, thro' Jesus, made Divinely great
And left a glorious pattern to repeat
    But when shall we, to this blessd State arrive?
When the same graces in our hearts do thrive.

Countess of Huntingdon made financial contributions. Phillis had a long-time fondness for Sewall, as can be gathered from the fact that she wrote a poem for him, ambiguously titled, "On the Death of the Rev. Dr. *Sewell* when Sick, 1765," the earliest poem she could remember ever having written. She listed that title in her 1772 proposals, as being the first of twenty-eight titles of poems she had hoped, in vain, to publish in Boston in that year. There are four variant versions of this poem (three in manuscript, and one printed in her 1773 volume). One of two manuscript versions among the Countess of Huntingdon's Papers is 58 lines long; the other version also entitled "The Decease of the rev'd Dr. Sewell," is 60 lines long (q.v., above). A third manuscript version, also 60 lines long and printed above is in the American Antiquarian Society.

An ELEGIAC

P O E M,

On the DEATH of that celebrated Divine, and eminent Servant of JESUS CHRIST, the late Reverend, and pious

GEORGE WHITEFIELD,

Chaplain to the Right Honourable the Countess of Huntingdon, &c. &c.

Who made his Exit from this transitory State, to dwell in the celestial Realms of Bliss, on LORD's-Day, 30th of September, 1770, when he was seiz'd with a Fit of the Asthma, at Newbury-Port, near Boston, in New-England. In which is a Condolatory Address to His truly noble Benefactress the worthy and pious Lady Huntingdon,—and the Orphan-Children in Georgia; who, with many Thousands, are left, by the Death of this great Man, to lament the Loss of a Father, Friend, and Benefactor.

By Phillis, a Servant Girl of 17 Years of Age, belonging to Mr. J. Wheatley, of Boston:—And has been but 9 Years in this Country from Africa.

HAIL happy Saint on thy immortal throne!
　To thee complaints of grievance are unknown;
We hear no more the music of thy tongue,
Thy wonted auditories cease to throng.
Thy lessons in unequal'd accents flow'd!
While emulation in each bosom glow'd;
Thou didst, in strains of eloquence refin'd,
Inflame the soul, and captivate the mind.
Unhappy we, the setting Sun deplore!
Which once was splendid, but it shines no more;
He leaves this earth for Heaven's unmeasur'd height,
And worlds unknown, receive him from our sight;
There WHITEFIELD wings, with rapid course his way,
And sails to Zion, through vast seas of day.

　When his AMERICANS were burden'd sore,
When streets were crimson'd with their guiltless gore:
Unrival'd friendship in his breast now strove:
The fruit thereof was charity and love
Towards America——couldst thou do more
Than leave thy native home, the British shore,
To cross the great Atlantic's wat'ry road,
To see America's distress'd abode?
Thy prayers, great Saint, and thy incessant cries,
Have pierc'd the bosom of thy native skies!
Thou moon hast seen, and ye bright stars of light
Have witness been of his requests by night!
He pray'd that grace in every heart might dwell:
He long'd to see America excell;
He charg'd its youth to let the grace divine
Arise, and in their future actions shine;
He offer'd THAT he did himself receive,

A greater gift not GOD himself can give:
He urg'd the need of men to every one;
It was no less than GOD's co-equal SON!
Take HIM ye wretched for your only good,
Take HIM ye starving souls to be your food;
Ye thirsty, come to this life giving stream:
Ye Preachers, take him for your joyful theme:
Take HIM, "my dear AMERICANS," he said,
Be your complaints in his kind bosom laid:
Take HIM ye Africans, he longs for you;
Impartial SAVIOUR, is his title due;
If you will chuse to walk in grace's road,
You shall be sons, and kings, and priests to GOD.

　Great COUNTESS! we Americans revere
Thy name, and thus condole thy grief sincere:
We mourn with thee, that TOMB obscurely plac'd,
In which thy Chaplain undisturb'd doth rest.
New-England sure, doth feel the ORPHAN's smart;
Reveals the true sensations of his heart;
Since this fair Sun, withdraws his golden rays,
No more to brighten these distressful days!
His lonely Tabernacle, sees no more
A WHITEFIELD landing on the British shore:
Then let us view him in yon azure skies:
Let every mind with this lov'd object rise.
No more can he exert his lab'ring breath,
Seiz'd by the cruel messenger of death.
What can his dear AMERICA return?
But drop a tear upon his happy urn,
Thou tomb, shalt safe retain thy sacred trust,
Till life divine re-animate his dust.

Sold by Ezekiel Russell, in Queen-Street, and John Boyles, in Marlboro'-Street.

1. This is the original text of a Wheatley poem that was widely advertised in Boston newspaper for October, 1770, as selling for "7 coppers,/ (Embellished with a plate representing the position in/ which the Rev. Mr. Whitefield lay before and after/ his interment.)" In broadside and pamphlet form, it was reprinted almost a dozen times in New England, New York, and Philadelphia. As a pamphlet, it was also appended to *Heaven the Residence of Saints,* a sermon preached by Boston's Reverend Ebenezer Pemberton on the occasion of Whitefield's death, and printed in London in 1771 by "E. and C. Dilly in the Poultry;/ And sold in the Chapel in Tottenham Court Road,/ And at the Tabernacle near Moorfields./ (Price Sixpence)." Phillis mailed a non-extant manuscript version of the poem to the Countess of Huntingdon in London on October 25, 1770. The poem established Phillis's international reputation. With differing headnotes and differing punctuation supplied by its various printers, the poem exists in three variant texts. The broadside version, below, "An Ode of Verses," is in 64 lines; Phillis would revise the piece to 47 lines and include it in her 1773 volume, *Poems,* q.v. above.
2. Bethesda, Whitefield's orphanage 12 miles outside of Savannah, Georgia, burned to the ground in June of 1773.
3. *Great Countess!* The Countess of Huntingdon was supportive of Whitefield's plans for his orphanage. Whitefield bequeathed the orphanage and its fifty or sixty black slaves to the Countess.

AN ODE OF VERSES[1]

On the much-lamented Death of the

Rev. Mr. GEORGE WHITEFIELD,

Late Chaplain to the Countefs of *Huntingdon*;

Who departed this Life, at *Newberry* near *Boſton* in *New England*, on the Thirtieth of *September*, 1770, in the Fifty-feventh Year of his Age.

Compos'd in *America* by a Negro Girl Seventeen Years of Age, and ſent over to a Gentleman of Character in *London*.

HAIL Happy Saint, on thy Immortal Throne!
To thee Complaints of Grievance are unknown,
We hear no more the Muſic of thy Tongue,
Thy wonted Auditories ceaſe to throng.
Thy Leſſons in unequal'd Accents flow'd,
While Emulation in each Boſom glow'd.
Thou didſt, in Strains of Eloquence refin'd,
Inflame the Soul, and captivate the Mind.
Unhappy we thy ſetting Sun deplore,
Which once was ſplendid, but it ſhines no more.
He leaves the Earth for Heaven's unmeaſur'd Height,
And Worlds unknown receive him out of Sight.
There *Whitefield* wings with rapid Courſe his Way,
And ſails to *Zion* thro' vaſt Seas of Day.
When his *Americans* were burthen'd ſore,
When Streets were crimſon'd with their guiltleſs Gore,
Wond'rous Compaſſion in his Breaſt now ſtrove,
The Fruit thereof was Charity and Love.
Towards *America* what could he more!
Than leave his native Home, the *Britiſh* Shore,
To croſs the Great *Atlantick* wat'ry Road,
To ſee *New England's* much-diſtreſs'd Abode.
Thy Prayers, great Saint, and thy inceſſant Cries,
Have often pierc'd the Boſom of the Skies.
Thou, Moon, haſt ſeen, and thou, bright Star of Light,
Haſt Witneſs been of his Requeſts by Night.

He pray'd for Grace in ev'ry Heart to dwell,
He long'd to ſee *America* excel.
He charg'd its Youth to let the Grace Divine
Ariſe, and in their future Actions ſhine.
He offer'd that he did himſelf receive:
A greater Gift not God himſelf could give.
He urg'd the Need of Him to ev'ry one,
It was no leſs than God's co-equal Son.
Take him, ye Wretched, for your only Good;
Take him, ye hungry Souls, to be your Food;
Take him, ye Thirſty, for your cooling Stream;
Ye Preachers, take him for your joyful Theme;
Take him, my dear *Americans*, he ſaid,
Be your Complaints in his kind Boſom laid;
Take him, ye *Africans*, he longs for you;
Impartial Saviour is his Title due.
If you will walk in Grace's heavenly Road,
He'll make you free, and Kings, and Prieſts to God.
No more can he exert his lab'ring Breath,
Seiz'd by the cruel Meſſenger of Death.
What can his dear *America* return,
But drop a Tear upon his happy Urn.
Thou, Tomb, ſhalt ſafe retain thy ſacred Truſt,
Till Life Divine reanimate his Duſt.

Our *Whitefield* the Haven has gain'd,
Outflying the Tempeſt and Wind;
His Reſt he has ſooner obtain'd,
And left his Companions behind.

With Songs let us follow his Flight,
And mount with his Spirit above;
Eſcap'd to the Manſions of Light,
And lodg'd in the *Eden* of Love.

The CONCLUSION.

May *Whitefield's* Virtues flouriſh with his Fame,
And Ages yet unborn record his Name.
All Praiſe and Glory be to God on High,
Whoſe dread Command is, That we all muſt die.
To live to Life eternal, may we emulate
The worthy Man that's gone, e'er tis too late.

Printed and ſold for the Benefit of a poor Family burnt out a few Weeks ſince near *Shoreditch Church*, that loſt all they poſſeſſed, having nothing inſur'd.

Price a Penny apiece, or 5 s. a Hundred to thoſe that ſell them again.

1. This is a variant of Wheatley's elegy on the death of the Reverend George Whitefield. Although the headnote points out that this poem was "sent over to a Gentleman of Character in *London*," there is no other evidence to document that Phillis ever mailed any other version of this poem than the non-extant manuscript version she mailed to the Countess of Huntingdon under a covering letter dated "Boston Oct.ʳ 25th 1770." The "Gentleman of Character in London" was probably John Thornton, a close friend and supporter of the countess for whom Whitefield was personal chaplain since 1749. The last fourteen lines may have been added by another hand; lines 51–58, with their anapestic meters, are most unusual for Phillis, who uses them nowhere else. The broadside, #41245, is located at the Henry E. Huntington Library and Art Gallery, San Marino, California.
2. *He'll make you free.* In no other version of this poem does this reference to black freedom occur.

To Mrs. LEONARD, on the Death of her HUSBAND.

Grim Monarch ! see depriv'd of vital breath,
A young Physician in the dust of death !
Dost thou go on incessant to destroy :
The grief to double, and impair the joy ?
Enough thou never yet wast known to say,
Tho' millions die thy mandate to obey.
Nor youth, nor science nor the charms of love,
Nor aught on earth thy rocky heart can move.
The friend, the spouse, from his dark realm to save,
In vain we ask the tyrant of the grave.

Fair mourner, there see thy own LEONARD spread,
Lies undistinguish'd from the vulgar dead ;
Clos'd are his eyes, eternal slumbers keep,
His senses bound in never-waking sleep,
Till time shall cease ; till many a shining world,
Shall fall from Heav'n, in dire confusion hurl'd :
Till dying Nature in wild torture lies ;
Till her last groans shall rend the brazen skies !
And not till then, his active Soul shall claim,
In body, now, of more than mortal frame.
But ah ! methinks the rolling tears space,
Pursue each other down the alter'd face.
Ah ! cease ye sighs, nor rend the mourner's heart :
Cease thy complaints, no more thy griefs impart.
From the cold shell of his great soul arise !
And look above, thou native of the skies !
There fix thy view, where fleeter than the wind
Thy LEONARD flies, and leaves the earth behind.

Thyself prepare to pass the gloomy night,
To join forever in the fields of light ;
To thy embrace, his joyful spirit moves,
To thee the partner of his earthly loves ;
He welcomes thee to pleasures more refin'd
And better suited to the deathless mind.

Phillis Wheatley.

---

1. This was Thankfull (Hubbard) Leonard (1745–1772) of whom Phillis was especially fond. Besides this piece, Phillis wrote three other poems and variants to and about her. She revised this broadside as "To A Lady on the Death of Her Husband" (in 30 lines) and it was included in the 1773 volume. See also "To the Hon'ble Thomas Hubbard, Esq;/ On the Death of/ Mrs. Thankfull Leonard," below.
2. Dr. Thomas Leonard (1744–1771). He married Thankfull Hubbard on October 4, 1770, and died less than a year afterward on June 21, 1771. The broadside is at the Historical Society of Pennsylvania.

On the Death of Doctor SAMUEL MARSHALL.[1]

Thro' thickest glooms, look back, immortal Shade!
On that confusion which thy flight has made.
Or from Olympus' height look down, and see
A Town involv'd in grief for thee:
His *Lucy* sees him mix among the dead.
And rends the graceful tresses from her head:
Frantic with woe, with griefs unknown, oppres'd,
Sigh follows sigh, and heaves the downy breast.

Too quickly fled, ah! whither art thou gone:
Ah! lost for ever to thy Wife and Son!
The hapless child, thy only hope and heir,
Clings round her neck, and weeps his sorrows there.
The loss of thee on *Tyler's* soul returns,
And *Boston* too, for her Physician mourns.

When sickness call'd for *Marshall's* kindly hand,
Lo! how with pity would his heart expand!
The sire, the friend, in him we oft have found,
With gen'rous friendship did his soul abound.

Could Esculapius[2] then no longer stay?
To bring his ling'ring infant into day!
The babe unborn, in dark confines is toss'd.
And seems in anguish for its father lost.

Gone, is Apollo![3] from his house of earth,
And leaves the sweet memorials of his worth.
From yonder world unseen, he comes no more,
The common parent, whom we thus deplore:

---

1. Dr. Samuel Marshall (1735–1771) graduated from Harvard College in 1754, and studied medicine in London hospitals, qualifying as an M.D. by 1761. He returned to Boston and on October 14, 1765, married Lucy Tyler, sold his Cornhill Street home for a newer place on Congress Street, but died on September 29, 1771. His obituary, in *The Boston Evening Post* (30 September 1771), p. 3, describes him as "highly esteemed . . . a very skillful Physician, Surgeon and Man Midwife; his death is therefore to be lamented as a public loss to the community as well as to his more intimate Friends & Acquaintances, to whom his many social Virtues, and agreeable, obliging Disposition rendered him peculiarly endearing." Dr. Marshall was also a relative of Phillis's mistress.
2. *Esculapius* (Aesculapius, Asclepius). In Greek mythology he was called "the father of physicians."
3. *Apollo*. Apollo was the father of Esculapius.

Yet, in our hopes, immortal joys attend
The Sire, the Spouse, the universal Friend.[4]

4. This poem appeared anonymously in *The Boston Evening Post* (7 October 1771), p. 3, and does not reproduce well. Phillis revised this piece, with the same title (in 28 lines) and included it in her 1773 volume.

Verses by a young African Negro Woman, at Boston in New-England; who did not quit her own country till she was ten years old, and has not been above eight in Boston.

RECOLLECTION. 1

To Miss A—— M——, humbly inscribed by the Authoress.

MNEME, begin; infpire, ye facred Nine!
   Your vent'rous *Afric* in the deep defign.
Do ye rekindle the cœleftial fire,
Ye god-like powers! the glowing thoughts infpire,
Immortal Pow'r! I trace thy facred fpring,
Affift my ftrains, while I *thy* glories fing.
By *thee*, paft afts of many thoufand years,
Rang'd in due order, to the mind appears;
The *long fergot* thy gentle hand conveys,
Returns, and foft upon the fancy plays. 2
Calm, in the vifions of the night he pours
'Th' exhauftlefs treafures of his fecret ftores.
Swift from above he wings his downy flight
"Thro' *Phœbe's* realm, fair regent of the night,
Thence to the raptur'd poet gives his aid,
Dwells in his heart, or hovers round his head;
To give inftruction to the lab'ring mind,
Diffufing light cœleftial and refin'd.

Still he purfues, unweary'd in the race,
And wraps his fenfes in the pleafing maze.
The Heav'nly Phantom *points* the aftions done
In the paft worlds, and tribes beneath the fun.
He, from his throne in ev'ry human breaft,
Has *vice* condemn'd, and ev'ry *virtue* blefs'd.
Sweet are the founds in which thy words we hear,
Cœleftial mufic to the ravifh'd ear.

---

1. From *The Annual Register, or a View of the History, Politics, and Literature for the Year 1772*, 5th edition. (London: Dodsley, 1795). The poem is printed here without the headnote and introductory letter written by an unknown "L," and without the headnote letter written by Phillis, all three pieces being included in the first printing of this poem in *The London Magazine: Or, Gentleman's Monthly Intelligencer* for March, 1772, vol. 41, pp. 134–135. See "Phillis Wheatley's Letters and Proposals," above. This poem would be revised as "On Recollection" (in 50 lines) and included in the 1773 volume of *Poems*.

2. *He pours*. Phillis nods here, and in lines 12, 13, 15, 19, 20, and 23, where she ascribes masculine references to Mnemosyne, the Greek mythological goddess of memory and great events. When she revised the poem for inclusion in her 1773 volume, she correctly ascribed female references to the goddess.

We hear thy voice, refounding o'er the plains,
Excelling Maro's fweet Mencllian ftrains.
But awful *Thou!* to that perfidious race,
Who fcorn thy warnings, nor the good embrace;
By *Thee* unveil'd, the horrid crime appears,
Thy mighty hand redoubled fury bears;
The time mif-fpent augments their hell of woes,
While through each breaft the dire contagion flows,
Now turn and leave the rude ungraceful fcene,
And paint fair Virtue in immortal green.
For ever flourifh in the glowing veins,
For ever flourifh in poetic ftrains.
Be *Thy* employ to guide my early days,
And *Thine* the tribute of my youthful lays.

   Now * *eighteen years* their deftin'd courfe have run,
In due fucceffion, round the central fun;
How did each folly unregarded pafs!
But fure 'tis graven on eternal brafs!
To *recalled*, inglorious I return;
'Tis mine paft follies and paft crimes to mourn.
The *virtue*, ah! unequal to the *vice*,
Will fcarce afford fmall reafon to rejoice.

   Such, RECOLLECTION! is thy pow'r, high thron'd,
In ev'ry breaft of mortals, ever own'd.
The wretch, who dar'd the vengeance of the fkies,
At laft awakes with horror and furprize.
By *Thee* alarm'd, he fees impending fate,
He howls in anguifh, and repents too late.
But oft *thy* kindnefs moves with timely fear
The furious rebel in his mad career.
Thrice blefs'd the man, who in *thy* facred fhrine
Improves the REFUGE from the wrath divine.

To the Rev. Mr. *Pitkin*, on the
DEATH of his LADY.[1]

WHERE Contemplation finds her sacred Spring;
  Where heav'nly Music makes the Centre ring;
  Where Virtue reigns unsulled (sic), and divine;
  Where Wisdom thron'd, and all the Graces shine;
There sits thy Spouse, amid the glitt'ring Throng;
There central Beauty feasts the ravish'd Tongue;
With recent Powers, with recent glories crown'd,
The Choirs angelic shout her Welcome round.

  The virtuous Dead, demand a grateful Tear—
But cease thy Grief a-while, thy Tears forbear,
Nor thine alone, the Sorrow I relate,
Thy blooming Off-spring[2] feel the mighty Weight;
Thus, from the Bosom of the tender Vine,
The Branches torn, fall, wither, sink supine.

  Now flies the Soul, thro' Aether unconfin'd.
Thrice happy State of the immortal Mind!
Still in thy Breast tumultuous Passions rise,
And urge the lucent Torrent from thine Eyes.
Amidst the Seats of Heaven, a Place is free
Among those bright angelic Ranks for thee.
For thee, they wait—and with expectant Eye,
Thy Spouse leans forward from th'ethereal Sky,
Thus in my Hearing, "Come away," she cries,
"Partake the sacred Raptures of the Skies!
"Our Bliss divine, to Mortals is unknown,
"And endless Scenes of Happiness our own;
"May the dear Off-spring of our earthly Love,
"Receive Admittance to the Joys above!
"Attune the Harp to more than mortal Lays,

1. The Reverend Timothy Pitkin (1727–1811) was the second son of Governor William Pitkin of Connecticut. A graduate of Yale (1747), where he was a tutor (1750–1751), Trustee member (1769–1773), and Fellow (1777–1804), he was also a Trustee of Dartmouth College (1769–1773) and worked with Christian Indian ministers. Wealthy, patrician, a patriot and a classical scholar, he was a Congregationalist minister in Farmington, Connecticut, from 1752 to 1785. In 1752, he married Temperance Clap (daughter of the president of Yale), who died on May 19, 1772, giving birth to her eighth child, also named Temperance.
2. *Thy blooming Off-spring.* Fitch's children were Samuel (b. 1754), Catherine (b. 1757), Charles (b. 1759), Elizabeth (b. 1761), Timothy (b. 1766), Mary (b. 1769), and Temperance (b. 1772).

"And pay with us, the Tribute of their Praise
"To Him, who died, dread Justice to appease,
"Which reconcil'd, holds Mercy in Embrace;
"Creation too, her MAKER'S Death bemoan'd,
"Retir'd the Sun, and deep the Centre groan'd.
"He in his Death slew ours, and as he rose,
"He crush'd the Empire of our hated Foes.
"How vain their Hopes to put the God to flight,
"And render Vengeance to the Sons of Light!"
　　Thus having spoke she turn'd away her Eyes,
Which beam'd celestial Radiance o'er the skies.
Let Grief no longer damp the sacred Fire,
But rise sublime, to equal Bliss aspire;[3]
Thy sighs no more be wafted by the Wind,
Complain no more, but be to Heav'n resign'd.
'Twas thine to shew those Treasures all divine,
To sooth our Woes, the Task was also thine.
Now Sorrow is recumbent on thy Heart,
Permit the Muse that healing to impart,
Nor can the World, a pitying tear refuse,
They weep, and with them, ev'ry heavenly Muse.

Phillis Wheatley.

Boston, June 16th, 1772.

The above *Phillis Wheatley*, is a Negro Girl, about 18 Years/ old, who has been in this Country 11 years.

3. Pitkin outlived a second wife, Eunice, who died in 1778, but his grave is between those of both wives in Farmington, Connecticut. A photocopy of this broadside, which would be revised as "To A Clergyman on the Death of His Wife," (in 43 lines) and included in the 1773 volume, is in C.F. Heartman, *Phillis Wheatley (Phillis Peters) A Critical Attempt And a Bibliography of Her Writings* (New York, 1915).

A Poem on the Death of Charles Eliot, aged 12. Months [1]

Thro' airy realms he wings his infant flight;
To purer regions of celestial light;
Unmov'd he sees unnumber'd systems roll
Beneath his feet, the universal whole
In just succession run their destin'd round,
And circling wonders spread the dread profound:
Th'etherial now, and now the starry skies,
With glowing splendors, strike his wond'ring eyes.
The heav'nly legions, view with joy unknown,
Press his soft hand, and seat him on the throne, —
And smiling, thus: "To this divine abode.
"The seat of Saints, of Angels, and of GOD:
"Thrice welcome thou.—— The raptur'd babe replies,
"Thanks to my God, who snatch'd me to the skies,
"Ere vice triumphant had possess'd my heart;
"Ere yet the tempter claim'd my better part: —
"Ere yet on sin's most deadly actions bent;
"Ere yet I knew temptation's dread intent; —
"Ere yet the rod for horrid crimes I knew,
"Nor rais'd with vanity, or press'd with wo; —
"But soon arriv'd to heav'n's bright port assign'd.
"New glories rush on my expanding mind;
"A noble ardor now, my bosom fires,
"To utter what the heav'nly muse inspires!"

1. Charles Eliot was the son of Samuel Eliot, who married the sister of Ruth (Barrell) Andrews, wife of John Andrews, well-known Boston merchant and Patriot, and extensive letter writer to William Barrell, his brother-in-law, and fellow merchant in Philadelphia. John Andrews was very familiar with Phillis and her poems, mailing a manuscript version of this poem to Barrell in a letter dated September 22, 1772, which said in part "The 3d Instant I wrote you by the/ post, acquainting you with/ the death of little Charles./ Ruthy has inclos'd you by this opp^y a Poem by P. Wheatly (sic)/ addressed to the father on this melancholy occasion,/ wch I/ think is a masterly performance." Several letters written by Andrews to Barrell between 1772 and 1774 concern Phillis's progress with her poetry, two of these letters describing Boston racist difficulties Phillis encountered as she tried to publish a volume of poems in Boston in 1772, and failed for lack of Boston subscribers to her proposals. Phillis's closeness to the Andrews-Eliot family can be deduced from her note on the outside of this manuscript: "Poem/ On the Death of Charles/ Eliot/ My Dear Polly/ I take this opport-/ unity to write to/ you—," "Polly" being an 18th-century term of familiar endearment. This poem would be revised as "A Funeral Poem on the Death of C.E. an Infant of Twelve Months" (in 46 lines) and was included in the 1773 volume of *Poems*. The manuscript is in the Massachusetts Historical Society.

Joyful he spoke—exulting cherubs round
Clasp loud their pinions, and the plains resound.—
Say, parents! why this unavailing moan?
Why heave your bosoms with the rising groan?—
To Charles, the happy subject of my song,
A happier world, and nobler strains belong.
Say, would you tear him from the realms above?
Or make less happy, frantic in your love?—
Doth his beatitude increase your pain,
Or could you welcome to this earth again,
The son of bliss?—— No, with superior air,
Methinks he answers with a smile severe,
"Thrones and dominions cannot tempt me there!"

But still you cry, "O Charles! thy manly mind,
"Enwrapt our souls, and all thy actions bind;
"Our only hope, more dear than vital breath,
"Twelve moons revolv'd, and sunk in shades of death!
"Engaging infant! Nightly visions give,
"Thee to our arms, and we with joy reciev:
"We fain would clasp the phantom to our breast,
"The phantom flies, and leaves the soul unblest!"
Prepare to meet your dearest infant friend,
Where joys are pure, and glory's without end.

Boston. Septr 1st 1772.   Phillis Wheatley.

A Poem on the death of Charles Eliot aged 12 m°. To Mr S Eliot

Thro' airy realms, he wings his instant flight
To purer regions of celestial light.
Unmov'd he sees unnumber'd Systems roll,
Beneath his feet, the Universal whole
In just succession run their destin'd round
And circling wonders spread the dread profound,
Th'ethereal now, and now the starry Skies;
With glowing Splendors, strike his wond'ring eyes.
The heav'nly legions, view, with joy unknown,
Press his soft hand, and seat him on the throne;
And smiling, thus. To this divine abode;
The seat of saints, of angels and of God:
Thrice welcome thou. — The raptur'd babe replies,
Thanks to my God, who snatch'd me to the Skies!
" E'er yet triumphant had possess'd my heart;
" E'er yet the tempter claim'd my better part:__
" E'er yet on sin's most deadly actions bent;
" E'er yet I knew temptation's dread intent:
" E'er yet the rod for horrid crimes I knew,
" Not rais'd with vanity or press'd with woe;
" But soon arriv'd to heaven's bright port assign'd
" New glories rush on my expanding mind!
" A noble ardor now, my bosom fires,
" To utter what the heav'nly muse inspires!"
Joyful he spoke — exulting cherubs round.
Clap loud their pinions, and the plains resound.

1. A better punctuated, slightly variant manuscript copy of the manuscript above.
This manuscript is in the Houghton Library of Harvard University.

Say, parents: why this unavailing moan,?
Why heave your bosoms with the rising groan ?,
To Charles the happy subject of my Song:
A happier world, and nobler strains belong.
Say, would you tear him from the realms above)?
Or make less happy, frantic in your Love).
Doth his beatitude increase your pain.
Or could you welcome to this earth again.
The son of bliss. — no with superior air,
Methinks he answers with a smile severe,
"Thrones and Dominions cannot tempt me there !"
    But still you cry. "O Charles! thy manly mind,
"Enwrap our souls, and all thy actions bind,
" Our only hopes, more dear than vital breath.
" Twelve moons revolv'd, and sank in shades of death.
" Engaging Infant! Nightly visions give
" Thee to our arms, and we with joy receive.
" We fain would clasp; the Phantom to our breast.
" The Phantom flies, and leaves the soul unblest !"
    Prepare to meet your dearest Infant friend,
    Where Joys are pure, and Glory without end.

                                        Phil: Wheatley

Boston Sept: 1st 1772.

384

Hail! happy day! when smiling like the Morn,
Fair Freedom rose. New England to adorn:
The northern clime, beneath her genial ray,
Beholds exulting, thy Paternal sway,
For big with hope, her race no longer mourns
Each soul expands, each ardent bosom burns,
While in thy hand, with pleasure, we behold
The silken reins and Freedom's charms unfold.
Long lost to Realms beneath the northern skies,
She shines supreme, while hated Faction dies,
Soon as he saw the triumph long desir'd
Sick of the view, he languish'd and expir'd.
Thus, from the splendors of the rising Sun
The sickning Owl explores the dark unknown.
    No more of grievance unredress'd complain;
Or injur'd Rights, or groan beneath the chain,

---

1. This is the original manuscript version of "To the Right Honourable William,
Earl of Dartmouth, His Majesty's Principal Secretary of State for North America,
&c" (in 43 lines), which was included in Wheatley's 1773 volume. The manuscript is among the Earl of Dartmouth's papers in the County Records Office,
Stafford, England.

Which Wanton Tyranny with lawless hand
Made to enslave, O Liberty! thy Land.

My Soul rekindles at thy glorious name
Thy beams essential to the vital flame.

The Patriots' breast, what Heav'nly virtue warms!
And adds new lustre to his mental charms:
While in thy speech, the Graces all combine;
Apollos too, with Sons of Thunder join,
Then shall the Race of injur'd Freedom bless
The Sire, the Friend, and messenger of Peace.

While you, my Lord, read o'er th' adventrous Song
And wonder whence such daring boldness sprung;
Hence flow my wishes for the common good
By feeling hearts alone, best understood.

From Native clime, when seeming cruel fate
Me snatch'd from Afric's fancy'd happy seat
Impetuous.————Ah! what bitter pangs molest
What sorrows labour'd in the Parent breast!
That more than Stone, ne'er soft compassion mov'd
Who from its Father seiz'd his much belov'd.

Each once my case. —— Thus I deplore the day
When Britons weep beneath Tyrannic sway.
To thee, our thanks for favours past are due,
To thee, we still solicit for the new;
Since in thy pow'r as in thy Will before,
To sooth the griefs which thou didst then deplore
May heav'nly grace the sacred sanction give
To all thy works, and thou for ever live,
Not only on the wing of fleeting Fame,
(Immortal Honours grace the Patriot's name!)
Thee to conduct to Heav'ns refulgent fane,
May fiery coursers sweep th'ethereal plain!
Thou, like the Prophet, find the bright abode
Where dwells thy Sire, the Everlasting God.

[We have had several Specimens of the poetical Genius of an African Negro Girl, belonging to Mr. Wheatley of Boston, in New England, who was Authoress of the following Epistle[1] and Verses, addressed to Lord Dartmouth—They were written, we are told on the following Occasion, viz/:/ A Gentleman[2] who had seen several of the Pieces ascribed to her, thought them so much superior to her Situation, and Opportunities of Knowledge, that he doubted their being genuine—And in order to be satisfied, went to her Master's House, told his Doubts, and to remove them, desired that she should write something before him. She told him she was then busy and engaged for the Day, but if he would propose a Subject, and call in the Morning, she would endeavour to satisfy him. Accordingly he gave for a Subject, The Earl of Dartmouth, and calling the next Morning, she wrote in his presence, as follows.][3]

To the Right Honourable William Legge, Earl of Dart-/ mouth, his Majesty's Secretary of State for America, &.&[4]

HAIL, happy Day! when smiling like the Morn,
Fair *Freedom* rose, New England to adorn:
The Northern Clime beneath her genial Ray
Beholds, exulting, thy paternal Sway;
For, big with Hopes, her Race no longer mourns;   5
Each Soul expands, and every Bosom burns:
While in thy Hand, with Pleasure we behold,
The silken Reins, and *Freedom's* Charms unfold!
Long lost to Realms beneath the Northern skies,
She shines supreme; while hated *Faction* dies: 10
Soon as appear'd the Triumph long desir'd
Sick at the View, he languish'd and expir'd.
   No more, of Grievance unredress'd complain,

---

1. *The following Epistle.* The letter covering this poem is in "Phillis Wheatley's Letters and Proposals," above.
2. Thomas Wooldridge (d. 1795), a minor English functionary travelling through the American colonies in the service of Dartmouth.
3. This headnote is unsigned. The editor of the *New York Journal,* which printed this poem on June 3, 1773, was Virginia-born John Holt (1720–1784).
4. The *New York Journal* copyist of Wheatley's manuscript has omitted two entire lines from this poem and changed several words and punctuation from the original; see the manuscript poem, above. The text for this *New York Journal* printing is from Mukhtar Ali Isani, "Early Versions of Some Works of Phillis Wheatley," *Early American Literature,* 14, No. 2 (Fall, 1979), pp. 150–151.

Or injur'd Rights, or groan beneath the Chain,
Which wanton Tyranny, with lawless Hand,   15
Made to enslave, O *Liberty*! thy Land.—
My Soul rekindles, at thy glorious Name
Thy Beams, essential to the vital Flame—
The Patriot's Breast, what Heavenly Virtue warms,
And adds new Lustre to his mental Charms!   20
While in thy Speech, the Graces all combine,
Apollo's too, with Sons of Thunder join.
Then shall the Race of injur'd Freedom bless,
The Sire, the Friend, and Messenger of Peace.
   While you, my Lord, read o'er the advent'rous Song   25
And wonder, whence such daring Boldness sprung;
Whence flow my Wishes for the common Good,
By feeling Hearts alone best understood?
From native Clime, when seeming cruel Fate
Me snatch'd from Afric's fancy'd happy Seat,   30
Impetuous—Ah! what bitter Pangs molest,
What Sorrows labour'd in the Parent Breast?
That, more than Stone, ne'er soft Compassion mov'd,
Who from its Father seiz'd his much belov'd.
Such once my Case—Thus I deplore the Day,   35
When Britons weep beneath Tyrannick Sway.
To thee our Thanks for Favours past are due;
To thee we still solicit for the new:
Since in thy Pow'r, as in thy will before,
To sooth the Griefs which thou di[d]st then, deplore;   40
May Heav'nly Grace the sacred Sanction give,
To all thy Works, and thou for ever live;
Not only on the Wings of fleeting Fame,
(Immortal Honours Grace the Patriot's Name,)
Thee to conduct to Heaven's refulgent Fane;[5]   45
May fiery Courses sweep the ethereal Plain,
There, like the Prophet, find the bright Abode,
Where dwells thy Sire, the Everlasting GOD.

5. *Refulgent Fane*. I.e., "shining realm." Both this printing of this poem and the facsimile, above, are variant from the version (in 43 lines) published in Wheatley's volume of 1773. Having gotten the original manuscript for this poem directly from the hand of Phillis Wheatley, whom he visited in October, 1772, the touring Englishman, Thomas Wooldridge, was in New York by November of 1772 (see his letter to the Earl of Dartmouth, dated "New York Nov. 24th 1772, in Appendix G); it is not clear why the *New York Journal* printed the poem as late as June, 1773.

To the Hon'ble THOMAS HUBBARD, Esq; On the Death of Mrs. THANKFULL LEONARD. [1]

WHILE thus you mourn beneath the Cyprefs fhade
That hand of Death, a kind conductor made
To her whofe flight commands your tears to flow
And wracks your bofom with a fcene of wo :
Let Recollection bear a tender part
To footh and calm the tortures of your heart ;
To ftill the tempeft of tumultous grief ;
To give the heav'nly Nectar of relief :
Ah ! ceafe, no more her unknown blifs bemoan !
Sufpend the figh, and check the rifing groan.
Her virtues fhone with rays divinely bright,
But ah ! foon clouded with the fhades of night.
How free from tow'ring pride, that gentle mind !
Which ne'er the haplefs indigent declin'd,
Expanding free, it fought the means to prove
Unfailing Charity, unbounded Love !

She unreluctant flies, to fee no more
Her much lov'd Parents on Earth's dufky fhore,
'Till dark mortality fhall be withdrawn,
And your blefs'd eyes falute the op'ning morn. • { *Meaning the Refurrection.
Impatient heav'n's refplendent goal to gain

---

1. At the Historical Society of Pennsylvania, this broadside is the earlier variant of "To the Honourable T.H. Esq; on the Death of his Daughter," (in 40 lines) in the 1773 volume of *Poems*. Phillis's fondness for Thankfull (Hubbard) Leonard developed from the late 1760's when the Hubbards were her King Street neighbors. She was thus familiar with the untimely death of Thankfull in 1772, and of her sister, Mary, who died in 1768, after 14 months of marriage. Thomas Hubbard was a long-time Deacon of the Old South Church, treasurer of Harvard College, successful merchant (and one time slave trader); he left over £200 to the Old South's poor. He died in July of 1773, while Phillis was abroad. Hubbard's wife, Mary, died in 1774.

She with fwift progrefs fcours the azure plain,
Where grief fubfides, where paffion is no more
And life's tumultous billows ceafe to roar,
She leaves her earthly manfions for the fkies
Where new creations feaft her won'dring eyes.
To heav'n's high mandate chearfully refign'd
She mounts, fhe flies, and leaves the rolling Globe behind.
She who late figh'd for LEONARD to return
Has ceas'd to languifh, and forgot to mourn.
Since to the fame divine dominions come
She joins her Spoufe, and fmiles upon the Tomb :
And thus addreffes ;—— (let Idea rove)——
Lo ! this the Kingdom of celeftial Love !
Cou!d our fond Parents view our endlefs Joy,
Soon would the fountain of their forrows dry ;
Then would delightful retrofpect infpire, —·
Their kindling bofoms with the facred fire !
Amidft unutter'd pleafures, whilft I play,
In the fair funfhine of celeftial day :
As far as grief affects a deathlefs Soul,
So far doth grief my better mind controul :
To fee on Earth, my aged Parents mourn,
And fecret, wifh for THANKFULL to return !
Let not fuch thought their lateft hours employ
But as advancing faft, prepare for equal Joy.

Bofton, January 2,
1773.   *Phillis Wheatley.*

BOSTON, May 10. 1773.

Saturday laft Capt. Calef failed for London, in whom went Paffengers Mr. Nathaniel Wheatley, Merchant; alfo, Phillis, the extraordinary Negro Poet, Servant to Mr. John Wheatley. 1

FAREWELL to AMERICA.

To Mrs. S—— W——. By Phillis Wheatley.

ADIEU New England's fmiling Meads;
    Adieu the flow'ry Plain,
I leave thy opening Charms, O Spring !
    To try the Azure Reign.

In vain for me the Flow'rets rife
    And fhow their gawdy Pride,
While here beneath the Northern Skies
    I mourn for Health deny'd.

Thee, charming Maid ! while I purfue
    In thy luxuriant Reign;
And figh and languifh, thee to view
    Thy Pleafures to regain.

Sufanna mourns, nor can I bear
    To fee the Chriftal Show'r
Faft falling—the indulgent Tear
    In fad Departure's Hour.

Not unregarding lo ! I fee
    Thy Soul with Grief opprefs'd ;
Ah ! curb the rifing Groan for me,
    Nor Sighs difturb thy Breaft.

In vain the feather'd Songfters fing,
    In vain the Garden Blooms,
And on the Bofom of the Spring,
    Breaths out her fweet Perfumes.

While for Britannia's diftant Shore,
    We fweep the liquid Plain,
Till Aura to the Arms reftore
    Of this belov'd Domain.

Lo ! Health appears ! Celeftial Dame,

---

1. From *The Massachusetts Gazette and Boston Weekly News Letter* (13 May 1773), p. 4. In this 60-line version, the poem was printed in more than a half-dozen New England newspapers throughout May (and in *The London Chronicle* of 1–3 July) of 1773. It would be revised and shortened to 52 lines, dated May 7, 1773, and included in the 1773 volume of *Poems.*

Complacent and serene,
With Hebe's Mantle o'er her Frame,
  With Soul-delighting Mein.
Deep in a Vale where London lies,
  With misty Vapours crown'd,
Which cloud Aurora's thousand Dyes,
  And Veil her Charms around.
Why Phœbus ! moves thy Car so slow,
  So slow thy rising Ray;
Nor gives the mantled Town to View
  Thee glorious King of Day !
But late from Orient Skies, behold !
  He Shines benignly bright,
He decks his native Plains with Gold,
  With chearing Rays of Light.
For thee Britannia ! I resign
  New-England's smiling Face,
To view again her Charms divine,
  One short reluctant Space.
But thou Temptation ! hençe, away,
  With all thy hated Train
Of Ills—nor tempt my Mind astray
  From Virtue's sacred Strain.
Most happy ! who with Sword and Shield
  Is screen'd from dire Alarms,
And fell Temptation, on the Field,
  Of fatal Power disarms.
But ceafe thy Lays, my Lute forbear
  Nor frown my gentle Muse,
To see the secret falling Tear,
  Nor pitying look refufe.

It was mentioned in our last that Phillis the Negro
Poet, had taken her Paffage for England, in confequence
of an Invitation from the Countefs of Huntington,
which was a miftake.

An Elegy Sacred to the Memory of the Rev'd Samuel Cooper D.D. By Phillis Wheatley [1]

O Thou whose exit wraps in boundless woe;
For thee the tears of various nations flow.
In thee the floods of virtuous sorrows rise—
From the full heart and burst from streaming eyes.
Far from our view to heaven's eternal height   5
The seat of bliss divine and glory bright.
Far from the restless turbulence of life,
The war of factions and impassion'd strife,
From every ill mortality endured
Safe in Celestial Salem's walls secured.   10
    E'er yet from this terrestrial state retir'd
The Virtuous lov'd thee and the wise admir'd.
The gay approv'd thee and the grave rever'd,
And all thy words with rapt attention heard.
The Sons of learning on thy lessons hung.   15
While soft persuasion mov'd the illiterate throng
Who drawn by rhetoric's commanding laws,
Comply'd obedient nor conceived the cause;
Thy every sentence was with grace inspir'd,
And every period with devotion fir'd,   20
Bright Truth thy guide without disguise,
And penetration's all discerning eyes.
    Thy Country mourns th' afflicting hand divine
That now forbid thy radiant lamp to shine,
Which like the sun resplendent source of light   25
Diffus'd the beams and cheard our gloom of night.

1. This is the original version of the broadside, "AN/ ELEGY,/ SACRED TO THE/ MEMORY/ OF THAT GREAT DIVINE,/ THE REVEREND AND LEARNED/ DR. SAMUEL COOPER,/ Who departed this Life December 29, 1783,/ AETATIS 59./ BY PHILLIS PETERS." (See "Phillis Wheatley's Later Poems," above.) This manuscript is at the Massachusetts Historical Society.

What deep felt sorrow in each kindred breast
With keen sensations rends the heart oppress'd!
Fraternal love sustains a tenderer part
And mourns a Brother with a Brother's heart.   30

Thy Church laments her faithfull Pastor fled
To the cold mansions of the silent dead.
There hush'd forever cease the heavenly strains
That wak'd the soul but here resound in vain
Still live thy merits, where thy name is known   35
As the sweet Rose, its blooming beauty gone
Retains its fragrance with a long perfume:
Thus Cooper! True thy deathless name shall bloom
Unfading, in thy Church and Country's Eve,
While Winter frowns or Spring renews the grove   40
The hapless Muse, her loss in Cooper mourns
And as she sits, she writes, and weeps by turns:
A Friend sincere, whose mild indulgent rays
Encouraged oft, and oft approv'd her lays.

With all their charms terrestrial objects strove,   45
But vain their pleasures to attract his love;
Such Cooper was —— at Heaven's high call he flies,
His task well finished, to his native skies
Yet to his fate reluctant just design —————
Tho' mine to copy conduct such as thine: 50
Such was thy wish, th' observant Muse survey'd
Thy latest breath, and this advice convey'd.

On the Death of J.C. an Infant.[1]

No more the flow'ry scenes of pleasure rise,
No charming prospects greet the mental eyes,
No more with joy we view that lovely face,
Smiling, disportive, flush'd with ev'ry grace.

The tear of sorrow flows from ev'ry eye,   5
Groans answer groans, and sighs respond to sigh;
What sudden pangs shot through each aching heart,
When ruthless death dispatch'd his mortal dart?

"Where flies my James?" ('tis thus I seem to hear
The parent ask) " some angel tell me where   10
He wings his passage through the yielding air?"

Methinks a cherub, bending from the skies,
Observes the question, and serene replies,
"Before his Saviour's face, your babe appears:
Prepare to meet him, and dismiss your tears.   15

"There, there behold him, like a seraph glow:
While sounds celestial in his numbers flow:
Melodious, while the soul-enchanting strain
Dwells on his tongue, and fills th'ethereal plain."

Enough—for ever cease your murmuring breath;   20
Not as a foe, but friend, converse with death,
Since to the parts of happiness unknown
Is gone the treasure which you call your own.

---

1. Found in the Philadelphia *Methodist Magazine* for September of 1797,
pp. 431–432, this poem is a variant of a poem with the same title (in 42 lines)
in Wheatley's 1773 volume. With notes, this piece was first reprinted by Mukhtar
Ali Isani, "Early Versions of Some Works by Phillis Wheatley," *Early American
Literature*, 14, No. 2 (Fall, 1979), 149–155. The text is from Isani's article.

ON THE DEATH OF A YOUNG GIRL.

From dark abodes to fair ethereal light,
The enraptured innocent has winged her flight;
On the kind bosom of eternal love
She finds unknown beatitudes above.
This know, ye parents, nor her loss deplore —
She feels the iron hand of pain no more;
The dispensations of unerring grace
Should turn your sorrows into grateful praise;
Let, then, no tears for her henceforward flow
Nor suffer grief in this dark vale below.

Her morning sun, which rose divinely bright,
Was quickly mantled with the gloom of night;
But hear, in heaven's best bowers, your child so fair,
And learn to imitate her language there.
Thou, Lord, whom I behold with glory crowned,
By what sweet name, and in what tuneful sound,
Wilt thou be praised? Seraphic powers are faint
Infinite love and majesty to paint.
To thee let all their grateful voices raise,
And saints and angels join their songs of praise

Perfect in bliss, now from her heavenly home
She looks, and, smiling, beckons you to come;
Why then, fond parents, why these fruitless groans?
Restrain your tears, and cease your plaintive moans.
Freed from a world of sin, and snares, and pain,
Why would ye wish your fair one back again?

1. From William Wells Brown, *The Black Man, His Antecedents, His Genius, And His Achievements.* Fourth edition (Boston: Robert F. Wallcutt, 1865), pp. 141–142. This is a variant of "On The Death of A Young Lady Of Five Years of Age," (in 36 lines) in Wheatley's 1773 volume, *Poems.* As Brown gave to Harvard College an 1834 Boston reprinting of Wheatley's volume (inscribed "Harvard College Library./ From Wm. Wells Brown./ March 28, 1863") in which this poem is printed as it was in the 1773 original volume, he may here possibly have been copying an otherwise unknown manuscript. More probably, Brown seems to be further "correcting" a version of this poem already "corrected" in Wilson Armistead's *A Tribute for the Negro . . .* (Manchester, England, 1848), p. 339. Brown's *Black Man* was widely criticized for its careless writing and mistakes. See William E. Farrison, *Wiliam Wells Brown, Author and Reformer* (Chicago and London: The University of Chicago Press, 1969), passim.

Nay, bow resigned ; let hope your grief control,
And check the rising tumult of the soul.
Calm in the prosperous and the adverse day,
Adore the God who gives and takes away ;
See him in all, his holy name revere,
Upright your actions, and your hearts sincere,
Till, having sailed through life's tempestuous sea,
And from its rocks and boisterous billows free,
Yourselves, safe landed on the blissful shore,
Shall join your happy child to part no more.

Most Noble Lady:[1]

The occasion of my addressing your Ladiship will, I hope, apologize for this my boldness in doing it. it is to inclose a few lines on the decease of your worthy Chaplain the Reverend Mr. Whitefield, in the loss of whom, I sincerely Sympathize with your Ladiship; but your great loss, which is his greater gain, will I hope, meet with infinite reparation in the presence of God the divine Benefactor, whose image you are by filial imitation. The tongues of the learned are insufficient, much less the pen of an untutor'd African, to paint in lively Characters, the excellencies of this citizen of Zion —

I am with great humility, your Ladiship's

Most Obedient humble Servant, Phillis Wheatley

I beg an interest in your Ladiship's Prayers
Boston Octr 25.th 1770

---

1. Among the papers of the Countess of Huntingdon, this manuscript letter, covering an enclosed but now non-extant elegy on the death of the Reverend George Whitefield, is a variant of another manuscript version; see "Phillis Wheatley's Letters and Proposals," above.

My Lord [1]

The Joyful occacion which has given me this Confidence in Addressing your Lordship with inclosed peice will, I hope sufficiently apologize for this freedom in an African who with the now happy America exults with equal transport in the view of one of its greatest advocates presiding with the Special tenderness of a Fatherly Heart over that Department.

Nor can they my Lord be insensible of the Friendship so much exemplified in your Endeavours in their behalf during the late unhappy Disturbances

---

1. Found in the Massachusetts Historical Society, this manuscript is a slight variant of the same letter, above. Accompanying this manuscript is another manuscript note, undated but signed. "C.D." (Charles Deane, 19th-century antiquarian and member of this Society) who attests to the authenticity of this letter. "This letter is probably an original," wrote Deane to an inquiring woman from Philadelphia. "Phillis learned to write a better hand later. . . ." Yet the handwriting here is unlike Phillis's penmanship before or after this date. Still another variant version of Wheatley's letter to Dartmouth was printed, along with the poem to him, in the *New York Journal* for June 13, 1773, which see immediately following.

I sincerely wish your Lordship all possible success in your Undertaking for the Interest of north America

That the united blessings of Heaven & Earth may attend you here and the endless Felicity of the invisible State in the presence of the divine Benefactor may be your portion hereafter is the hearty Desire of

My Lord
Your Lordships
Most Obedient
H'ble Servant
Phillis Wheatley

Boston N. E. Octo. 10th 1772

MY LORD,[1]

The joyful Occasion which has given me this Confidence in addressing/ your Lordship in the inclos'd piece, will, I hope sufficiently apologize/ for this Freedom in an African, who, with the now happy America, ex-/ ults with equal Transport, in the View of one of its greatest Advocates,/ presiding with the special Tenderness of a fatherly Heart over that/ Department.

Nor can they, my Lord, be insensible of the Friendship so much ex-/ emplified in your Endeavours in their Behalf, during the late unhappy/ Disturbances,—I sincerely wish your Lordship all possible Success in/ your Undertakings, for the Interest of North America.—That the united/ Blessings of Heaven and Earth may attend you here; and that the/ endless Felicity of the invisible State, in the Presence of the divine/ Benefactor, may be your Portion hereafter, is the hearty Desire of,

My LORD,
Your Lordship's
Most obedient humble Servant,
PHILLIS WHEATLEY.

Boston, N.E. October 10th, 1772.

1. From *The New York Journal* (3 June 1773), as reprinted in Mukhtar Ali Isani, "Early Versions of Some Works of Phillis Wheatley," *Early American Literature,* 14, No. 2 (Fall, 1979), p. 149. This version was "corrected" by a copyist for the *New York Journal.* Although he was working from the original manuscript loaned to him by Thomas Wooldridge, the format and punctuation of this printing are variant from the original. Touring the American colonies and reporting to Lord Dartmouth in London, the Englishman, Wooldridge, visited Boston in October of 1772, when, after promising to deliver them personally to Dartmouth, he secured from Phillis's own hand the manuscripts for this letter, her poem to Dartmouth, and the Nathaniel Wheatley dictated biographical sketch of Phillis. Wooldridge reached New York in November, 1772, when he permitted the *New York Journal* to copy Phillis's manuscript letter and poem. For a copy of the manuscript letter, above, see "Phillis Wheatley's Letters and Proposals," above.

Phillis was brought from Africa to America in 1761, between 7 & 8 years old. Without any assistance from School education, she in 16 months time from her first arrival, ... not only attain'd the English language, (to which she was an utter Stranger before) but also to read, any, the most difficult part of the Sacred Writings, to the great astonishment of those who heard her. As to her writing, her own Curiosity led her to it; and in 1765, she wrote a Letter to the rev'd mr. Occom [1] while in England. This account is given by Her Mistress who bought her, and with whom she now Lives. ——

Boston New England Oct. 12th 1772.   Nath: Wheatley [2]

---

1. Leaving Boston in late December, 1765, Occom was abroad from 1766 to 1768. Phillis's letter to him is non-extant, as is a letter she reportedly wrote him in Boston in the summer of 1773 when she was in London. The manuscript is among the Earl of Dartmouth's Papers.

2. In the handwriting of Phillis Wheatley, this biographical sketch was dictated by Mrs. Susanna Wheatley and signed for Nathaniel Wheatley—as the male head of the household (John Wheatley had retired the previous year), and was delivered by Thomas Wooldridge to Lord Dartmouth, along with Phillis's poem, and a covering letter. Phillis would revise this sketch, sign John Wheatley's name to it, date it November 14, 1772, and have this version added to the prefatory materials for the volume of poems published in London in September of 1773 and to subsequent reprinted editions.

Dedicated, by permiffion, to the Right Hon. the
Countefs of Huntingdon.

This Day was publifhed,

Price 2s. fewed, or 2s. 6d. neatly bound, adorned
with an elegant engraved likenefs of the Author,

A Volume of POEMS, on various Subjects,
Religious and Moral.
By PHILLIS WHEATLEY,
Negro Servant to Mr. John Wheatley, of Bofton.
London, printed for A. Bell, Bookfeller, Aldgate;
and at Bofton, for Meff. Cox and Berry, in King-
ftreet.

To the PUBLIC.[1]

THE Book here propofed for publication difplays
perhaps one of the greateft inftances of pure, unaf-
fifted genius, that the world ever produced. The
Author is a native of Africa, and left not that dark
part of the habitable fyftem, till fhe was eight years
old. She is now no more than nineteen, and many
of the Poems were penned before fhe arrived at near
that age.

They are wrote upon a variety of interefting fub-
jects, and in a ftile rather to have been expected from
thofe who, to a native genius, have had the happi-
nefs of a liberal education, than from one born in the
wilds of Africa.

The Writer, while in England a few weeks fince,
was converfed with by many of the principal Nobility
and Gentry of this country, who have been fignally
diftinguifhed for their learning and abilities, among
whom was the Earl of Dartmouth, the late Lord
Lyttelton, and others, who unanimoufly expreffed   2
their approbation of her genius, and their amazement at the gifts with which Infinite Wifdom had
furnifhed her.

---

1. From *Lloyd's Evening Post and British Chronicle* (10–13 September 1773), p. 3.
This is one of at least two slightly variant announcements of the London publication of Wheatley's volume, printed also in several other London newspapers at the
behest of Archibald Bell, London bookseller, promoter, and publisher of Wheatley's book, *Poems*. Because Bell printed the biographical information in these
variant announcements, the very first London edition of Wheatley's *Poems* did
not include a Dedication to the Countess of Huntingdon; or a Preface; or a
biographical sketch of Phillis signed by her master, John Wheatley; or an attestation page. Subsequent London editions, and American reprinted editions did
include these four prefatory pieces, although the attestation page in all printed
editions is not dated "Boston, Oct. 28, 1772," as in this newspaper announcement.
2. Lord Lyttelton (1709–1773), English poet, man of letters, and statesman, was
fond of cultivating poetry from unlikely sources, such as Stephen Duck (1705–
1756), a humble English farmer who wrote verses.

But the Publisher means not, in this advertisement, to deliver any peculiar eulogiums on the present publication; he rather desires to submit the striking beauties of its contents to the unbiassed candour of the impartial Public.

As it has indeed been repeatedly suggested to him, by persons, who have seen the manuscript, that numbers would be ready to suspect they were not really the writings of PHILLIS, he has procured the following attestation, from the most respectable characters in Boston, that none might have the least ground for disputing their original.

 3

THE ATTESTATION.

WE whose names are underwritten, do assure the world, that the POEMS specified in the following page * were (as we verily believe) written by Phillis, a young Negro Girl, who was, but a few years since, brought an uncultivated barbarian from Africa, and has ever since been; and now is, under the disadvantage of serving as a slave in a family in this town. She has been examined by some of the best judges, and is thought qualified to write them.

Boston, Oct. 28, 1772.

His Excellency Thomas Hutchinson, Governor,
The Hon. Andrew Oliver, Lieutenant Governor.

Hon. Thomas Hubbard,	Rev. Ch. Chauncy, D.D. **4**
Hon. John Erving,	Rev. Mather Bayles, D.D.
Hon. James Pitts,	Rev. E. Pemberton, D.D.
Hon. Harrison Gray,	Rev. And. Elliott, D.D.
Hon. James Bowdoin,	Rev. Sam. Cooper, D.D.
John Hancock, Esq;	Rev. Samuel Mather,
Joseph Green, Esq;	Rev. John Moorhead,
Richard Carey, Esq;	J. Wheatley, her master.

N. B. The original attestation, signed by the above **5** gentlemen, may be seen, by applying to Archibald Bell, Bookseller, No. 8, Aldgate-street.

* The words " following page," alludes to the contents of the manuscript copy, which are wrote on the back of the above attestation.

---

3. This headnote and the immediately following attestation paragraph are slightly variant from the same paragraphs included in Wheatley's volume.
4. *Bayles.* I.e., Byles.
5. The manuscript for this "original attestation" is no longer extant.

LETTER FROM JOSHUA COFFIN.

3*Albany, April 29, 1839.*

Dear Whittier,—Having had the pleasure, during the past week of examining the rich and valuable collection of pamphlets, manuscripts, and autographs, in the possession of the Rev. W. B. Sprague, D. D. of this city, I was gratified with the perusal of a letter in the hand-writing of the celebrated Phillis Wheatley. It is beautifully written, and with the consent of the good Doctor, I herewith send you a copy, verbatim et literatim, from the original. It is addressed to the Rev. Mr. Samuel Hopkins of New Port, Rhode Island, and commences thus:

Boston, February 9, 1774.

"Rev'd Sir,—I take with pleasure the opportunity by the Post to acquaint you of the arrival of my books from London. I have sealed up a package containing 17 for you and 2 for Mr. Tanner and one for Mrs. Mason and only wait for you to appoint some proper person, by whom I may convey them to you. I rec'd some time ago 20s. sterling upon them by the hands of your son in a letter from About Tanner. I rec'd at the same time a paper, by which I understand there are two negro men, who are desirous of returning to their native Country to preach the Gospel, But being much indisposed by the return of my asthmatic complaint, besides the sickness of my mistress, who has been long confined to her bed and is not expected to live a great while; all these things render it impracticable for me to do any thing at present with regard to that paper, but what I can do in influencing my Christian friends and acquaintance to promote this laudable design, shall not be wanting. Methinks, Rev'd Sir, this is the beginning of that happy period foretold by the Prophets, when all shall know the Lord from the least to the greatest, and that without the assistance of human Art or Eloquence. My heart expands with sympathetic joy to see at distant time

---

1. From *The Pennsylvania Freeman* (9 May 1839). It was reprinted in Benjamin Quarles, "A Phillis Wheatley Letter," *The Journal of Negro History*, 34 (1949), 462–464. Although it is stated in the headnote that this printing is based on a "verbatim et literatim" copy of a manuscript among the Albany, New York, papers of the Reverend W.B. Sprague, it is variant from the manuscript version in the Historical Society of Pennsylvania; see "Phillis Wheatley's Letters and Proposals," above. Other Wheatley to Hopkins manuscripts were lost when Hopkins's home in Newport was destroyed by fire shortly after his death in 1803.
2. Joshua Coffin was a 19th-century abolitionist and reformist writer.
3. John Greenleaf Whittier (1807–1892), Quaker, abolitionist, poet, and tireless worker for social reform. he edited *The Pennsylvania Freeman* from 1838 to 1840.

the thick cloud of ignorance dispersing from the face of my benighted country. Europe and America have long been fed with the heavenly provision, and I fear they loathe it, while Africa is perishing with a spiritual Famine. O that they could partake of the crumbs, the precious crumbs, which fall from the table of these distinguished children of the kingdom.

Their minds are unprejudiced against the truth, therefore tis to be hoped they would receive it with their whole heart. I hope that which the divine royal Psalmist says by inspiration is now on the point of being accomplished, namely, Ethiopia shall soon stretch forth her hands unto God. Of this, Abour Tanner and I trust many others within your knowledge are living witnesses. Please to give my love to her, and I intend to write to her soon. My best respects attend every kind enquirer after your obliged Humble servant,

PHILLIS WHEATLEY."

The correspondence of our philanthropist, on his favorite project of evangelizing Africa, was more extensive than has been supposed. He wrote to Britons and Americans, to men and women, to blacks and whites. Among others whom he addressed on the subject, was that interesting negress, Phillis Wheatley. One would scarcely expect that a logical divine, at the age of fifty-three, would devote himself to the business of selling copies of a poetical volume, which was written by a female slave at the age of twenty. But there was nothing, honest and proper, which this enterprising man was unwilling to do for the welfare of the African race. He was not so versatile as he was strong, yet he had a richer variety of gifts than has been commonly ascribed to him. The nature of his correspondence with Phillis Wheatley is disclosed in the following letter, which she wrote to him, a few months after her book of poetry was published in London. She was about twenty-one years old at the date of her epistle. The chirography of it is remarkably beautiful. It is here copied *verbatim et literatim.*

"Reverend Sir: I received your kind letter last evening by Mr. Pemberton, by whom also this is to be handed you. I have also received the money for the five books I sent Obour, and 2s. 6d. more for another. She has wrote me, but the date is 29 April. I am very sorry to hear, that Philip Quaque has very little or no *apparent* success in his mission. Yet I wish that what you hear respecting him may be only a misrepresentation. Let us not be discouraged, but still hope that God will bring about his great work. though Philip may *not* be the instrument in the divine hand to perform this work of wonder, turning the Africans '*from darkness to light.*' Possibly, if Philip would introduce himself properly to them, (I don't know the reverse,) he might be more successful; and in setting a good example, which is more powerfully winning than instruction. I observe your reference to the maps of Guinea and Salmon's Gazetteer, and shall consult them. I have received, in some of the last ships from London, three hundred more copies of my poems, and wish to dispose of them as soon as possible. If you know of any being wanted, I flatter myself you will be pleased to let me know it, which will be adding one more to the many obligations already conferred on her, who is, with a due sense of your kindness, your most humble and obedient servant, PHILLIS WHEATLEY.
"Boston, May 6, 1774. — The Reverend S. Hopkins."

1. From Edward A. Parks, *Memoir of the Life and Character of Samuel Hopkins, D.D.* Second edition (Boston, 1854), pp. 137–138. Although Parks explains that he "copied *verbatim et literatim*" the manuscript for this letter, he is working with a manuscript that is slightly variant of the manuscript of the same letter, copied above in "Phillis Wheatley's Letters and Proposals."

SELECTIVE BIBLIOGRAPHY

Manuscripts

Andrews-Barrell Letters, at the Massachusetts Historical Society.
Countess of Huntingdon Papers, at Cambridge University.
Cushing Letters, at the Massachusetts Historical Society.
Earl of Dartmouth Papers, County Record Office, Stafford, England.
Fitch Papers, at the Medford Historical Society.
Hugh Upham Clark Papers, at the Library of Congress.
Moses Brown Papers, at the Rhode Island Historical Society.
Phillis Wheatley Letters, at the Massachusetts Historical Society.
Quaker Collection, at Haverford College.
Scottish Record Office, Edinburgh.

Newspapers

Boston Censor, 1771–1772.
Boston Evening Post, 1761, 1770–1771.
Boston Gazette and Country Journal, 1761, 1773–1778.
Boston Post Boy and Advertiser, 1773–1774.
Boston Weekly News Letter, 1769, 1770–1775.
Connecticut Courant, 1774, 1784.
Connecticut Gazette, 1774.
Connecticut Journal, 1774.
Essex Journal and Merrimack Packet, 1774.
Independent Chronicle and Advertiser (Boston), 1784–1785.
Lloyd's Evening Post and British Chronicle, 1773–1774.
London Chronicle, 1773.
London Morning Post and Advertiser, 1773.
London Public Advertiser, 1773–1774.
Massachusetts Gazette, 1769.
Massachusetts Spy and Thomas's Boston Journal, 1772–1775.
Massachusetts Spy, 1770–1772.

Massachusetts Spy; or, American Oracle of Liberty, 1775.
Massachusetts Spy; or, Worcester Gazette, 1788.
New Hampshire Gazette and Historical Chronicle, 1772–1773.
Newport Mercury (Rhode Island), 1767, 1773–1774.
New York Journal, 1773.
Pennsylvania Chronicle, 1770.
Providence Gazette and Country Journal, 1773–1774.
St. James Chronicle, or British Evening Post, 1773.
Virginia Gazette, 1776.

Magazines and Periodicals

Akers, Charles W., "Our Modern Egyptians. Phillis Wheatley and the Whig Campaign Against Slavery in Revolutionary Boston," *Journal of Negro History*, 60, No. 3 (July, 1975), 397–410.

Bridenbaugh, Carl, "The Earliest Published Poem by Phillis Wheatley," *New England Quarterly*, 42, No. 4 (December, 1969), 583–584.

Deane, Charles, [on Phillis Wheatley's life and correspondence] in *Massachusetts Historical Society Proceedings*, Vol. 7, pp. 165–167, 267–278, 269, 269n, 270.

"F.," "Phillis Wheatley," *The Anti-Slavery Record*, 2, No. 5 (May, 1836), 7–8.

Gentleman's Magazine and Historical Chronicle, 43 (September, 1773), 456.

Jackson, Sarah Dunlap, "Letters of Phillis Wheatley and Susanna Wheatley," *Journal of Negro History*, 57, No. 2 (April, 1972), 211–215.

Kuncio, Robert C., "Some Unpublished Poems by Phillis Wheatley," *New England Quarterly*, 43, No. 2 (June, 1970), 287–297.

Lapsansky, Phil, "'Deism,' an Unpublished Poem by Phillis Wheatley," *New England Quarterly*, 50, No. 3 (September, 1977), 517–520.

Parks, Carol, "Phillis Wheatley Comes Home," *Black World*, 23 (February, 1974), 92–97.

Quarles, Benjamin, "A Phillis Wheatley Letter," *Journal of Negro History*, 34, No. 4 (October, 1949), 462–464.

Records Relating to the Early History of Boston, Containing Boston Marriages 1752 to 1789. Boston, 1903.

Report of the Record Commissioners of the City of Boston, Containing the Selectmen's Minutes from 1754 through 1769. Boston, 1889.

——, *Containing the Selectmen's Minutes from 1776 through 1786.* Boston, 1894.

——, *Containing the Selectmen's Minutes from 1782 through 1798.* Boston, 1896.

The Scots Magazine, 26 (September, 1773), 93.

Shipton, Clifford K., *Sibley's Harvard Graduates*, Vols. 5–15. Boston, 1937–1970.

Silverman, Kenneth, "Four New Letters by Phillis Wheatley," *Early American Literature*, 7, No. 3 (Winter, 1974), 257–271.

"T., J.H.," [Letter from Susanna Wheatley to Samson Occom] in *The Historical Magazine and Notes and Queries*, 2 (June, 1858), 178–179.

Books

Bailyn, Bernard, *The Ordeal of Thomas Hutchinson.* Cambridge, Mass., 1974.

Bergh, Albert E., ed., *The Writings of Thomas Jefferson.* 20 vols. Washington, D.C., 1903.

Blodgett, Harold, *Samson Occom.* Hanover, N.H., 1935.

Bluett, Thomas, *Some Memoirs of Job, the Son of Solomon . . . the High Priest of Boonda in Africa. . . .* London, 1734.

Brawley, Benjamin, *The Negro in Literature and Art.* New York, 1930.

Bridgman, Thomas, *Memorials of the Dead in Boston.* Boston, 1853.

Butterfield, L.H., ed., *Letters of Benjamin Rush.* 2 vols. Princeton, 1951.

Cleveland, Charles, *A Compendium of American Literature.* Philadelphia, 1859.

Cunningham, Anne Rowe, ed., *Letters and Diaries of John Rowe, Boston Merchant 1759–1763; 1764–1779.* Boston, 1903.

Donnan, Elizabeth, ed., *Documents Illustrative of the History of the Slave Trade to America.* 4 vols. New York, 1919.

Douglass, William, *Annals of the First African Church in the United States of America.* Philadelphia, 1862.

Drake, Francis, *A Dictionary of American Biography.* Boston, 1812.

Drake, Samuel, *History and Antiquities of Boston*. Boston, 1856.

———, *Old Boston Taverns and Tavern Clubs*. Boston, 1917.

Earle, Alice M., *Customs and Fashions of Old New England*. Fourth printing. Putney, Vt., 1980.

Forbes, Esther, *Paul Revere and the World He Lived In*. Boston, 1942.

Gillies, John, *Memoir of the Reverend George Whitefield, Revised and corrected with large Additions and Improvements*. London, 1872.

Greene, Lorenzo J., *The Negro in Colonial New England*. New York, 1942.

Grégoire, Henri, *De La Littérature Des Negrès* . . . . Paris, 1808.

Griswold, Rufus, *The Female Poets of America*. Philadelphia, 1849.

Gronniosaw, James, *A Narrative of the Most Remarkable Particulars in the Life of James Albert Gronniosaw, an African Prince, as Related by Himself*. Bath, England, 1770.

Heartman, Charles F., *Phillis Wheatley (Phillis Peters) Poems and Letters, First Collected Edition*. New York, 1915.

———, *Phillis Wheatley (Phillis Peters) A Critical Attempt and A Bibliography*. New York, 1915.

Higginbotham, A. Leon, *In the Matter of Color, Race and the American Legal Process: The Colonial Period*. New York, 1978.

Hill, Hamilton, *A History of the Old South Church*. 2 vols. Boston, 1890.

Hurlburt, Mabel, *Farmington Town and Church*. Stonington, Conn., 1967.

Jea, John, *The/ Life,/ History,/ And/ Unparalleled Suffering/ of/ John Jea,/ The African Preacher/ Composed and Written by Himself*. Portsea, England, [1800].

Kaplan, Sidney, *The Black Presence in the Era of the American Revolution 1770-1800*. Greenwich, Conn., 1973.

Larabee, Benjamin, *The Boston Tea Party*. London, 1966.

Loggins, Vernon, *The Negro Author*. New York, 1931.

McCorison, Marcus, ed., *Isaiah Thomas, The History of Printing in America*. New York, 1970.

Morrison, Samuel E., *John Paul Jones: A Sailor's Biography*. Boston, 1959.

New, Reverend Alfred E., *Memoirs of Selina, Countess of Huntingdon, Revised Edition*. New York, 1858.

Park, Edward, *Memoir of the Life and Character of Samuel Hopkins, D.D.* Second edition. 2 vols. Boston, 1854.

Quarles, Benjamin, *The Negro in the American Revolution.* Chapel Hill, N.C., 1961.

Richmond, Merele A., *Bid the Vassals Soar. Interpretive Essays on the Life and Poetry of Phillis Wheatley and George Moses Horton.* Washington, D.C., 1974.

Robertson, William S., *The Life of Miranda.* 2 vols. Chapel Hill, 1929.

Robinson, William H., ed., *The Proceedings of the Free African Union Society . . . 1780–1824.* Providence, 1975.

Schlesinger, Arthur M., *The Birth of the Nation.* Boston, 1968.

Smith, Venture, *A Narrative of the Life and Adventures of Venture, A Native of Africa.* Middletown, Conn., 1897.

Smyth, Albert H., ed., *The Writings of Benjamin Franklin.* 10 vols. New York, 1906.

Sparks, Jared, ed., *The Writings of George Washington.* 12 vols. Boston, 1833.

Stiles, Ezra, *The Literary Diary of.* New York, 1901.

Thwing, Anne H., *Crooked and Narrow Streets of Boston.* Boston, 1920.

Vassa, Gustavus, *The/ Interesting Narrative/ of the/ LIFE/ of/ Olaudah Equiano,/ or/ Gustavus Vassa,/ The African./ Written by Himself.* A New Edition, corrected. Leeds, England, 1814.

Watts, Emily S., *The Poetry of American Women from 1632 to 1945.* Austin, Tex., 1977.

Winslow, Anna Green, *The Diary of.* New York, 1894.

Winsor, Justin, ed., *Memorial History of Boston.* 4 vols. Boston, 1880–1881.

Zobel, Hiller B., *The Boston Massacre.* New York, 1970.

APPENDICES

1 SAMUEL. Chapter XVII

NOW the Phĭ-lĭs′tĭneṣ gathered together their armies to battle, and were gathered together at ᵃShō′choh, which *belongeth* to Jū′dah, and pitched between Shō′choh and Ă-zē′kah, in Ĕ′phes–dăm′mim.

2 And Ṣaul and the men of Ĭṣ′ra-el were gathered together, and pitched by the valley of Ĕ′lah, and ²set the battle in array against the Phĭ-lĭs′tĭneṣ.

3 And the Phĭ-lĭs′tĭneṣ stood on a mountain on the one side, and Ĭṣ′ra-el stood on a mountain on the other side: and *there was a* valley between them.

4 ¶ And there went out ³a champion out of the camp of the Phĭ-lĭs′tĭneṣ, named ᵇGȯ-lī′ath, of ᶜGăth, whose height *was* ⁴six cubits and a span.

5 And *he had* an helmet of brass upon his head, and he *was* ⁵armed with a coat of mail; and the weight of the coat *was* five thousand shekels of brass.

6 And *he had* greaves of brass upon his legs, and a ⁶target of brass between his shoulders.

7 And the ⁴staff of his spear *was* like a weaver's beam; and his spear's head *weighed* six hundred shekels of iron: and one bearing a shield went before him.

8 And he stood and cried unto the armies of Ĭṣ′ra-el, and said unto them, Why are ye come out to set *your* battle in array? *am* not I a Phĭ-lĭs′tĭne, and ye ᵉservants to Ṣaul? choose you a man for you, and let him come down to me.

9 If he be able to fight with me, and to kill me, then will we be your servants: but if I prevail against him, and kill him, then shall ye be our servants, and ᶠserve us.

10 And the Phĭ-lĭs′tĭne said, I ᵍdefy the armies of Ĭṣ′ra-el this day; give me a man, that we may fight together.

11 When Ṣaul and all Ĭṣ′ra-el heard those words of the Phĭ-lĭs′tĭne, they were dismayed, and greatly afraid.

12 ¶ Now Dā′vid *was* ʰthe son of that ᶦĔph′rath-ite of Bĕth′–lĕ-hĕm–jū′dah, whose name *was* Jĕs′se; and he had ʲeight sons: and the man went among men *for* an old man in the days of Ṣaul.

13 And the three eldest sons of Jĕs′se went *and* followed Ṣaul to the battle: and the ᵏnames of his three sons that went to the battle *were* Ĕ-lī′ab the firstborn, and next unto him Ă-bĭn′a-dăb, and the third Shăm′mah.

See "Goliath of Gath,/ 1 Sam. Chap. XVII," in Phillis's volume, *Poems on Various Subjects*, above.

14 And Dā'vid *was* the youngest: and the three eldest followed
Saul.
15 But Dā'vid went and returned from Saul to feed his
father's sheep at Běth'-lě-hěm.
16 And the Phĭ-lĭs'tĭne drew
near morning and evening, and
presented himself forty days.
17 And Jěs'se said unto Dā'vid
his son, Take now for thy brethren an ephah of this parched *corn,*
and these ten loaves, and run to
the camp to thy brethren;
18 And carry these ten [7]cheeses
unto the [8]captain of *their* thousand, and [l]look how thy brethren
fare, and take their pledge.
19 Now Saul, and they, and all
the men of Ĭs'ra-el, *were* in the
valley of Ē'lah, fighting with the
Phĭ-lĭs'tĭnes.
20 ¶ And Dā'vid rose up early
in the morning, and left the sheep
with a keeper, and took, and
went, as Jěs'se had commanded
him; and he came to the [9]trench,
as the host was going forth to the
[10]fight, and shouted for the battle.
21 For Ĭs'ra-el and the Phĭ-lĭs'-
tĭnes had put the battle in array
army against army.
22 And Dā'vid left [11]his carriage in the hand of the keeper of
the carriage, and ran into the
army, and came and [12]saluted his
brethren.
23 And as he talked with them,
behold, there came up the champion, the Phĭ-lĭs'tĭne of Găth,
Go-lī'ath by name, out of the
armies of the Phĭ-lĭs'tĭnes, and
spake according to the same
words: and Dā'vid heard *them.*
24 And all the men of Ĭs'ra-el,
when they saw the man, fled
[13]from him, and were sore afraid.
25 And the men of Ĭs'ra-el said,
Have ye seen this man that is
come up? surely to defy Ĭs'ra-el
is he come up: and it shall be,
that the man who killeth him,
the king will enrich him with
great riches, and [m]will give him
his daughter, and make his
father's house free in Ĭs'ra-el.
26 And Dā'vid spake to the men
that stood by him, saying, What
shall be done to the man that
killeth this Phĭ-lĭs'tĭne, and
taketh away [n]the reproach from
Ĭs'ra-el? for who *is* this [o]un-
circumcised Phĭ-lĭs'tĭne, that he
should defy the armies of [p]the
living God?
27 And the people answered
him after this manner, saying,
So shall it be done to the man
that killeth him.
28 ¶ And Ē-lī'ab his eldest
brother heard when he spake unto the men; and Ē-lī'ab's [q]anger
was kindled against Dā'vid, and
he said, Why camest thou down
hither? and with whom hast
thou left those few sheep in the
wilderness? I know thy pride,
and the naughtiness of thine
heart; for thou art come down
that thou mightest see the
battle.
29 And Dā'vid said, What have
I now done? [r]*Is there* not a
cause?
30 ¶ And he turned from him
toward another, and spake after
the same [14]manner: and the
people answered him again after
the former manner.
31 And when the words were
heard which Dā'vid spake, they
rehearsed *them* before Saul: and
he [15]sent for him.
32 ¶ And Dā'vid said to Saul,
[s]Let no man's heart fail because
of him; [t]thy servant will go and
fight with this Phĭ-lĭs'tĭne.
33 And Saul said to Dā'vid,
[u]Thou art not able to go against
this Phĭ-lĭs'tĭne to fight with him:
for thou *art but* a youth, and he a
man of war from his youth.
34 And Dā'vid said unto Saul,
Thy servant kept his father's
sheep, and there came a lion, and
a bear, and took a [16]lamb out of

the flock:

35 And I went out after him, and smote him, and delivered it out of his mouth: and when he arose against me, I caught him by his beard, and smote him, and slew him.

36 Thy servant slew both the lion and the bear: and this uncircumcised Phĭ-lĭs′tĭne shall be as one of them, seeing he hath defied the armies of the living God.

37 Dā′vid said moreover, ʼThe LORD that delivered me out of the paw of the lion, and out of the paw of the bear, he will deliver me out of the hand of this Phĭ-lĭs′tĭne. And Sạul said unto Dā′vid, Go, and ʷthe LORD be with thee.

38 ¶ And Sạul ¹⁷armed Dā′vid with his armour, and he put an helmet of brass upon his head; also he armed him with a coat of mail.

39 And Dā′vid girded his sword upon his armour, and he assayed to go; for he had not proved it. And Dā′vid said unto Sạul, I cannot go with these; for I have not proved them. And Dā′vid put them off him.

40 And he took his staff in his hand, and chose him five smooth stones out of the ¹⁸brook, and put them in a shepherd's ¹⁹bag which he had, even in a scrĭp; and his sling was in his hand: and he drew near to the Phĭ-lĭs′tĭne.

41 And the Phĭ-lĭs′tĭne came on and drew near unto Dā′vid; and the man that bare the shield went before him.

42 And when the Phĭ-lĭs′tĭne looked about, and saw Dā′vid, he ʷdisdained him: for he was but a youth, and ʷruddy, and of a fair countenance.

43 And the Phĭ-lĭs′tĭne said unto Dā′vid, ʼAm I a dog, that thou comest to me with staves? And the Phĭ-lĭs′tĭne cursed Dā′-

vid by his gods.

44 And the Phĭ-lĭs′tĭne ªsaid to Dā′vid, Come to me, and I will give thy flesh unto the fowls of the air, and to the beasts of the field.

45 Then said Dā′vid to the Phĭ-lĭs′tĭne, Thou comest to me with a sword, and with a spear, and with a shield: ᵇbut I come to thee in the name of the LORD of hosts, the God of the armies of Ĭṣ′ra-el, whom thou hast defied.

46 This day will the LORD ²⁰deliver thee into mine hand; and I will smite thee, and take thine head from thee; and I will give ᶜthe carcases of the host of the Phĭ-lĭs′tĭneṣ this day unto the fowls of the air, and to the wild beasts of the earth; ᵈthat all the earth may know that there is a God in Ĭṣ′ra-el.

47 And all this assembly shall know that the LORD ᵉsaveth not with sword and spear: for ᶠthe battle is the LORD'S, and he will give you into our hands.

48 And it came to pass, when the Phĭ-lĭs′tĭne arose, and came and drew nigh to meet Dā′vid, that Dā′vid hasted, and ran toward the army to meet the Phĭ-lĭs′tĭne.

49 And Dā′vid put his hand in his bag, and took thence a stone, and slang it, and smote the Phĭ-lĭs′tĭne in his forehead, that the stone ²¹sunk into his forehead; and he fell upon his face to the earth.

50 So ᵍDā′vid prevailed over the Phĭ-lĭs′tĭne with a sling and with a stone, and smote the Phĭ-lĭs′tĭne, and slew him; but there was no sword in the hand of Dā′vid.

51 Therefore Dā′vid ran, and stood upon the Phĭ-lĭs′tĭne, and took his sword, and drew it out of the sheath thereof, and slew him, and cut off his head therewith. And when the Phĭ-lĭs′-

tines saw their champion was dead, ᴬthey fled.

52 And the men of Ĭṣ'ra-el and of Jū'dah arose, and shouted, and pursued the Phĭ-lĭs'tĭneṣ, until thou come to the valley, and to the gates of Ĕk'rŏn. And the wounded of the Phĭ-lĭs'tĭneṣ fell down by the way to ᶦShā-a-rā'im, even unto Găth, and unto Ĕk'rŏn.

53 And the children of Ĭṣ'ra-el returned from chasing after the Phĭ-lĭs'tĭneṣ, and they spoiled their tents.

54 And Dā'vid took the head of the Phĭ-lĭs'tĭne, and brought it to Jĕ-rụ'sǎ-lĕm; but he put his armour in his tent.

55 ¶ And when Ṣaul saw Dā'-vid go forth against the Phĭ-lĭs'-tĭne, he said unto Ăb'nēr, the cap-tain of the host, Ăb'nēr, ᶦwhose son *is* this youth? And Ăb'nēr said, *As* thy soul liveth, O king, I cannot tell.

56 And the king said, Enquire thou whose son the stripling *is*.

57 And as Dā'vid returned from the slaughter of the Phĭ-lĭs'tĭne, Ăb'nēr took him, and brought him before Ṣaul with the head of the Phĭ-lĭs'tĭne iⁿ his hand.

58 And Ṣaul said to him, Whose son *art* thou, *thou* young man? And Dă'vid answered, *I am* the son of thy servant ᵏJĕs'se the Bĕth'-lĕ-hĕm-īte.

From the Book of Isaiah

CHAPTER 63   742

1 Christ shews his power for salvation. 7 God's mercy to the church. 15 The church's profession of faith.

WHO *is* this that cometh from Ê'dom, with dyed garments from Bŏz'rah? this *that is* ¹glorious in his apparel, travelling in the greatness of his strength? I that speak in right-eousness, mighty to save.

2 Wherefore ᵃ*art thou* red in thine apparel, and thy garments like him that treadeth in the winefat?

3 I have ᵇtrodden the winepress alone; and of the people *there was* none with me: for I will tread them in mine anger, and trample them in my fury; and their blood shall be sprinkled upon my garments, and I will stain all my raiment.

4 For the day of vengeance *is* in mine heart, and the year of my redeemed is come.

5 And I looked, and ᶜ*there was* none to help; and I wondered that *there was* none to uphold: therefore mine own ᵈarm brought salvation unto me; and my fury, it upheld me.

6 And I will tread down the people in mine anger, and ᵉmake them drunk in my fury, and I will bring down their strength to the earth.

7 ¶ I will mention the loving-kindnesses of the LORD, *and* the

See "ISAIAH LXIII. 1-8." in Phillis's volume, *Poems*, above.

praises of the LORD, according
to all that the LORD hath bestowed on us, and the great goodness toward the house of Ĭs′ra-el,
which he hath bestowed on them
according to his mercies, and
according to the multitude of his
lovingkindnesses.

8 For he said, Surely they *are*
my people, children *that* will not
lie: ²so he was their Saviour.

NIOBE

Lydia tota fremit, Phrygiaeque per oppida facti
Rumor it et magnum sermonibus occupat orbem.
Ante suos Niobe thalamos cognoverat illam,
Tum cum Maeoniam virgo Sipylumque colebat:
Nec tamen admonita est poena popularis Arachnes

Cedere caelitibus, verbisque minoribus uti.
Multa dabant animos. sed enim nec coniugis artes
Nec genus amborum magnique potentia regni
Sic placuere illi, quamvis ea cuncta placerent,
Ut sua progenies. et felicissima matrum
Dicta foret Niobe, si non sibi visa fuisset.
Nam sata Tiresia venturi praescia Manto
Per medias fuerat, divino concita motu,
Vaticinata vias, 'Ismenides, ite frequentes
Et date Latonae Latonigenisque duobus
Cum prece tura pia, lauroque innectite crinem:
Ore meo Latona iubet.' paretur, et omnes
Thebaïdes iussis sua tempora frondibus ornant,
Turaque dant sanctis et verba precantia flammis.
Ecce venit comitum Niobe celeberrima turba,
Vestibus intexto Phrygiis spectabilis auro
Et, quantum ira sinit, formosa movensque decoro
Cum capite inmissos umerum per utrumque capillos.
Constitit: utque oculos circumtulit alta superbos,
'Quis furor, auditos' inquit 'praeponere visis
Caelestes? aut cur colitur Latona per aras,
Numen adhuc sine ture meum est? mihi Tantalus
auctor,

From R. Ehwald, editor, P. OVIDIUS NASO (Lipsiae/ In Aedibus B.G. Teubneri/ MDCCCXCI), pp. 110–114. For Phillis Wheatley's translation, see "Niobe in Distress For Her Children Slain By Apollo, from Ovid's Metamorphoses, Book VI, and from a View of The Painting of Mr. Richard Wilson," in her volume of *Poems*, above.

Cui licuit soli superorum tangere mensas.
Pleiadum soror est genetrix mea . maximus Atlas
Est avus , aetherium qui fert cervicibus axem :
Iuppiter alter avus . socero quoque glorior illo .
Me gentes metuunt Phrygiae , me regia Cadmi
Sub domina est , fidibusque mei commissa mariti
Moenia cum populis a meque viroque reguntur .
In quamcumque domus adverti lumina partem ,
Inmensa spectantur opes . accedit eodem
Digna dea facies . huc natas adice septem
Et totidem iuvenes , et mox generosque nurusque .
Quaerite nunc , habeat quam nostra superbia causam ,
Nescio quoque audete satam Titanida Coeo
Latonam praeferre mihi , cui maxima quondam
Exiguam sedem pariturae terra negavit .
Nec caelo nec humo nec aquis dea vestra recepta est
Exsul erat mundi , donec miserata vagantem
"Hospita tu terris erras , ego' dixit 'in undis ,"
Instabilemque locum Delos dedit . illa duorum
Facta parens : uteri pars haec est septima nostri .
Sum felix : quis enim neget hoc ? felixque manebo
Hoc quoque quis dubitet ? tutam me copia fecit .
Maior sum , quam cui possit Fortuna nocere ;
Multaque ut eripiat , multo mihi plura relinquet .
Excessere metum mea iam bona . fingite demi
Huic aliquid populo natorum posse meorum ,
Non tamen ad numerum redigar spoliata duorum ,
Latonae turbam : qua quantum distat ab orba ?
Ite , satis pro prole sacri est ; laurumque capillis
Ponite .' deponunt , infectaque sacra relinquunt ,
Quodque licet , tacito venerantur murmure numen
Indignata dea est , summoque in vertice Cynthi
Talibus est dictis gemina cum prole locuta :
'En ego vestra parens , vobis animosa creatis ,
Et , nisi Iunoni , nulli cessura dearum ,
An dea sim , dubitor . perque omnia saecula cultis
Arceor , o nati , nisi vos succurritis , aris .
Nec dolor hic solus : diro convicia facto
Tantalis adiecit , vosque est postponere natis
Ausa suis , et me , quod in ipsam reccidat , orbam
Dixit , et exhibuit linguam scelerata paternam .'
Adiectura preces erat his Latona relatis :
'Desine !' Phoebus ait 'poenae mora longa querella est .
Dixit idem Phoebe . celerique per aëra lapsu
Contigerant tecti Cadmeida nubibus arcem .

Planus erat lateque patens prope moenia campus,
Assiduis pulsatus equis, ubi turba rotarum
Duraque mollierat subiectas ungula glaebas.
Pars ibi de septem genitis Amphione fortes
Conscendunt in equos, Tyrioque rubentia suco
Terga premunt, auroque graves moderantur habenas.
E quibus Ismenos, qui matri sarcina quondam
Prima suae fuerat, dum certum flectit in orbem
Quadrupedis cursus, spumantiaque ora coërcet,
'Ei mihi!' conclamat, medioque in pectore fixa
Tela gerit, frenisque manu moriente remissis
In latus a dextro paulatim defluit armo.
Proximus, audito sonitu per inane pharetrae,
Frena dabat Sipylus : veluti cum praescius imbris
Nube fugit visa, pendentiaque undique rector
Carbasa deducit, ne qua levis effluat aura.
Frena dabat : dantem non evitabile telum
Consequitur, summaque tremens cervice sagitta
Haesit, et extabat nudum de gutture ferrum.
Ille, ut erat, pronus per crura adnisa iubasque
Volvitur, et calido tellurem sanguine foedat.
Phaedimus infelix et aviti nominis heres
Tantalus, ut solito finem inposuere labori,
Transierant ad opus nitidae iuvenale palaestrae:
Et iam contulerant arto luctantia nexu
Pectora pectoribus, cum tento concita nervo,
Sicut erant iuncti, traiecit utrumque sagitta.
Ingemuere simul, simul incurvata dolore
Membra solo posuere ; simul suprema iacentes
Lumina versarunt, animam simul exhalarunt.
Aspicit Alphenor, laniataque pectora plangens
Advolat, ut gelidos conplexibus allevet artus,
Inque pio cadit officio ; nam Delius illi
Intima fatifero rupit praecordia ferro.
Quod simul eductum, pars est pulmonis in hamis
Eruta, cumque anima cruor est effusus in auras.
At non intonsum simplex Damasichthona vulnus
Afflicit. ictus erat, qua crus esse incipit, et qua
Mollia nervosus facit internodia poples.
Dumque manu temptat trahere exitiabile telum,
Altera per iugulum pennis tenus acta sagitta est.
Expulit hanc sanguis, seque eiaculatus in altum
Emicat, et longe terebrata prosilit aura.

427

Ultimus Ilioneus non profectura precando
Bracchia sustulerat, 'di' que 'o communiter omnes,'
Dixerat, ignarus non omnes esse rogandos,
'Parcite!' motus erat, cum iam revocabile telum
Non fuit, arcitenens. minimo tamen occidit ille
Vulnere, non alte percusso corde sagitta.
Fama mali populique dolor lacrimaeque suorum
Tam subitae matrem certam fecere ruinae
Mirantem potuisse, irascentemque, quod ausi
Hoc essent, superi quod tantum iuris haberent.
Nam pater Amphion ferro per pectus adacto
Finierat moriens pariter cum luce dolorem.
Heu quantum haec Niobe Niobe distabat ab illa,
Quae modo Latois populum summoverat aris
Et mediam tulerat gressus resupina per urbem,
Invidiosa suis; at nunc miseranda vel hosti.
Corporibus gelidis incumbit, et ordine nullo
Oscula dispensat natos suprema per omnes.
A quibus ad caelum liventia bracchia tollens
'Pascere, crudelis, nostro, Latona, dolore,
[Pascere' ait, 'satiaque meo tua pectora luctu:]
Corque ferum satia!' dixit 'per funera septem
Efferor. exulta, victrixque inimica triumpha.
Cur autem victrix? miserae mihi plura supersunt,
Quam tibi felici. post tot quoque funera vinco.'
Dixerat, et sonuit contento nervus ab arcu:
Qui praeter Nioben unam conterruit omnes.
Illa malo est audax. stabant cum vestibus atris
Ante toros fratrum demisso crine sorores:
E quibus una trahens haerentia viscere tela
Inposito fratri moribunda relanguit ore:
Altera solari miseram conata parentem
Conticuit subito, duplicataque vulnere caeco est:
[Oraque compressit, nisi postquam spiritus ibat.]
Haec frustra fugiens collabitur: illa sorori
Inmoritur: latet haec: illam trepidare videres.
Sexque datis leto diversaque vulnera passis

Ultima restabat; quam toto corpore mater,
Tota veste tegens 'unam minimamque relinque!
De multis minimam posco' clamavit 'et unam.'
Dumque rogat, pro qua rogat, occidit. orba resedit
Exanimes inter natos natasque virumque,
Deriguitque malis. nullos movet aura capillos, т. хо.
In vultu color est sine sanguine, lumina maestis

Stant inmota genis : nihil est in imagine vivum.
Ipsa quoque interius cum duro lingua palato
Congelat , et venae desistunt posse moveri;
Nec flecti cervix nec bracchia reddere motus
Nec pes ire potest : intra quoque viscera saxum est.
Flet tamen , et validi circumdata turbine venti
In patriam rapta est . ibi fixa cacumine montis
Liquitur , et lacrimas etiam nunc marmora manant.

MEMOIR[1]

PHILLIS WHEATLEY was a native of Africa; and was brought to this country in the year 1761, and sold as a slave.

She was purchased by Mr. John Wheatley, a respectable citizen of Boston. This gentleman, at the time of the purchase, was already the owner of several slaves; but the females in his possession were getting something beyond the active periods of life, and Mrs. Wheatley wished to obtain a young negress, with the view of training her up under her own eye, that she might, by gentle usage, secure to herself a faithful domestic in her old age. She visited the slave-market, that she might make a personal selection from the group of unfortunates offered for sale. There she found several robust, healthy females, exhibited at the same time with Phillis, who was of a slender frame, and evidently suffering from change of climate. She was, however, the choice of the lady, who acknowledged herself influenced to this decision by the humble and modest demeanor and the interesting features of the little stranger.

The poor, naked child, (for she had no other covering than a quantity of dirty carpet about her like a fillibeg) was taken home in the chaise of her mistress, and comfortably attired. She is supposed to have been about

1. Appended to the 1834 Boston reprinting of Phillis's 1773 volume of *Poems*, this anonymous memoir appeared also as a separate, 36-page pamphlet. *The Liberator* of July 16, 1836, advertised it as a pamphlet costing $.25. (In 1837 the complete volume of poems, this memoir included, was advertised as costing 37½¢.) The memoir was written by Margaretta Matilda Oddell of Jamaica Plains, outside of Boston; she was a great grandniece of Phillis's mistress. The memoir has long been valued as the most authoritative of several early sketches of Phillis's life. Later scholarship has corrected its errors.

seven years old, at this time, from the circumstance of shedding her front teeth. She soon gave indications of uncommon intelligence, and was frequently seen endeavoring to make letters upon the wall with a piece of chalk or charcoal.

A daughter* of Mrs. Wheatley, not long after the child's first introduction to the family, undertook to learn her to read and write; and, while she astonished her instructress by her rapid progress, she won the good will of her kind mistress, by her amiable disposition and the propriety of her behaviour. She was not devoted to menial occupations, as was at first intended; nor was she allowed to associate with the other domestics of the family, who were of her own color and condition, but was kept constantly about the person of her mistress.

She does not seem to have preserved any remembrance of the place of her nativity, or of her parents, excepting the simple circumstance that her mother *poured out water before the sun at his rising*—in reference, no doubt, to an ancient African custom. The memories of most children reach back to a much earlier period than their seventh year; but there are some circumstances (which will shortly appear) which would induce us to suppose, that in the case of Phillis, this faculty did not equal the other powers of her mind. Should we be mistaken in this inference, the faithlessness of memory, concerning the scenes of her childhood, may be otherwise accounted for.

We cannot know at how early a period she was beguiled from the hut of her mother; or how long a time elapsed between her abduction from her first home and

* This lady was better known subsequently as Mrs. Lothrop. 2

2. Mrs. Lothrop, i.e., Mary Wheatley, was the daughter of Phillis's mistress and tutor to the slave girl; she married Reverend John Lathrop in 1771, to whom she bore six children.

her being transferred to the abode of her benevolent
mistress, where she must have felt like one awaking
from a fearful dream. This interval was, no doubt, a
long one ; and filled, as it must have been, with various
degrees and kinds of suffering, might naturally enough
obliterate the recollection of earlier and happier days.
The solitary exception which held its place so tena-
ciously in her mind, was probably renewed from day to
day through this long season of affliction; for, every
morning, when the bereaved child saw the sun emerg-
ing from the wide waters, she must have thought of her
mother, prostrating herself before the first golden beam
that glanced across her native plains.

As Phillis increased in years, the developement of
her mind realized the promise of her childhood ; and
she soon attracted the attention of the literati of the day,
many of whom furnished her with books. These ena-
bled her to make considerable progress in belles-lettres;
but such gratification seems only to have increased her
thirst after knowledge, as is the case with most gifted
minds, not misled by vanity ; and we soon find her endeavoring to master the Latin tongue.

She was now frequently visited by clergymen,[3] and
other individuals of high standing in society; but notwithstanding the attention she received, and the distinction with which she was treated, she never for a moment
lost sight of that modest, unassuming demeanor, which
first won the heart of her mistress in the slave-market.
Indeed, we consider the strongest proof of her worth to
have been the earnest affection of this excellent woman,
who admitted her to her own board. Phillis ate of her
bread, and drank of her cup, and was to her as a daugh-

3. See "To The Publick," above, for a listing of seven such divines.

ter; for she returned her affection with unbounded gratitude, and was so devoted to her interests as to have no will in opposition to that of her benefactress.

We cannot ascertain that she ever received any formal manumission[4]; but the chains which bound her to her master and mistress were the golden links of love, and the silken bands of gratitude. She had a child's place in their house and in their hearts. Nor did she, notwithstanding their magnanimity in setting aside the prejudices against color and condition, when they found these adventitious circumstances dignified by talents and worth, ever presume on their indulgence either at home or abroad. Whenever she was invited to the houses of individuals of wealth and distinction, (which frequently happened,) she always declined the seat offered her at their board, and, requesting that a side-table might be laid for her, dined modestly apart from the rest of the company[5]

We consider this conduct both dignified and judicious. A woman of so much mind as Phillis possessed, could not but be aware of the emptiness of many of the artificial distinctions of life. She could not, indeed, have felt so utterly unworthy to sit down among the guests, with those by whom she had been bidden to the banquet. But she must have been painfully conscious of the feelings with which her unfortunate race were regarded; and must have reflected that, in a mixed company, there might be many individuals who would, perhaps, think they honored her too far by dining with her at the same table. Therefore, by respecting even the prejudices of those who courteously waived them in her favor, she very delicately expressed her gratitude; and,

4. Phillis was manumitted between September 16 and October 18, 1773; see her letter to Colonel David Wooster of October 18, 1773, above.
5. For at least one exception to this notion, see the account of Phillis's visit with Mrs. Timothy Fitch, "Phillis Wheatley and Her Boston," above.

following the counsels of those Scriptures to which she was not a stranger, and taking the lowest seat at the feast, she placed herself where she could certainly expect neither to give or receive offence.

It is related that, upon the occasion of one of these visits, the weather changed during the absence of Phillis; and her anxious mistress, fearful of the effects of cold and damp upon her already delicate health, ordered Prince (also an African and a slave) to take the chaise, and bring home her *protegee*. When the chaise returned, the good lady drew near the window, as it approached the house, and exclaimed—' Do but look at the saucy varlet—if he has n't the impudence to sit upon the same seat with *my Phillis!* ' And poor Prince received a severe reprimand for forgetting the dignity thus kindly, though perhaps to him unaccountably, attached to the sable person of ' my Phillis.'

In 1770, at the age of sixteen, Phillis was received as a member of the church worshipping in the Old South Meeting house, then under the pastoral charge of the Rev. Dr. Sewall.[6] She became an ornament to her profession; for she possessed that meekness of spirit, which, in the language of inspiration, is said to be above all price. She was very gentle-tempered, extremely affectionate, and altogether free from that most despicable foible, which might naturally have been her besetting sin—literary vanity.

The little poem commencing,

' 'T was mercy brought me from my heathen land,'[7]

will be found to be a beautiful expression of her religious sentiments, and a noble vindication of the claims

---

6. Phillis was received into the Old South Congregational Church on August 8, 1771, by the Reverend Samuel Cooper, of the Brattle Street Congregational Church, temporarily filling in until a new pastor could be found for the Old South.

7. From "On Being Brought from Africa to America." See Wheatley's volume, *Poems*, above.

of her race. We can hardly suppose any one, reflecting by whom it was written—an African and a slave—to read it without emotions both of regret and admiration. Phillis never indulged her muse in any fits of sullenness or caprice. She was at all times accessible. If any one requested her to write upon any particular subject or event, she immediately set herself to the task, and produced something upon the given theme. This is probably the reason why so many of her pieces are funeral poems, many of them, no doubt, being written at the request of friends. Still, the variety of her compositions affords sufficient proof of the versatility of her genius. We find her at one time occupied in the contemplation of an event affecting the condition of a whole people, and pouring forth her thoughts in a lofty strain. Then the song sinks to the soft tones of sympathy in the affliction occasioned by domestic bereavement. Again, we observe her seeking inspiration from the sacred volume, or from the tomes of heathen lore; now excited by the beauties of art, and now, hymning the praises of nature to 'Nature's God.' On one occasion, we notice her—a girl of but fourteen years—recognizing a political event, and endeavoring to express the grateful loyalty of subjects to their rightful king—not as one, indeed, who had been trained to note the events of nations, by a course of historical studies, but one whose habits, taste and opinions, were peculiarly her own; for in Phillis we have an example of originality of no ordinary character. She was allowed, and even encouraged, to follow the leading of her own genius; but nothing was forced upon her, nothing suggested, or placed before her as a lure ; her literary efforts were altogether the natural workings of her own mind.

There is another circumstance respecting her habits of composition, which peculiarly claims our attention. She did not seem to have the power of retaining the creations of her own fancy, for a long time, in her own mind. If, during the vigil of a wakeful night, she amused herself by weaving a tale, she knew nothing of it in the morning—it had vanished in the land of dreams. Her kind mistress indulged her with a light, and in the cold season with a fire, in her apartment, during the night. The light was placed upon a table at her bedside, with writing materials, that if any thing occurred to her after she had retired, she might, without rising or taking cold, secure the swift-winged fancy, ere it fled.

We have before remarked, that Mrs. Wheatley did not require or permit her services as a domestic ; but she would sometimes allow her to polish a table or dust an apartment, (occupations which were not thought derogatory to the dignity of a lady in those days of primitive simplicity,) or engage in some other trifling occupation that would break in upon her sedentary habits ; but not unfrequently, in these cases, the brush and the duster were soon dropped for the pen, that her meditated verse might not escape her.

It has been suggested that memory was in fault in this instance ; but we have hesitated to account for this singular habit of mind in this manner ; for, upon duly considering the point, we cannot suppose that Phillis could have made such rapid progress in various branches of knowledge, if she had not possessed a retentive memory— and still less, that she could have succeeded in the at-

tainment of one of the dead languages. We are rather
inclined to refer the fact in question to some peculiar
structure of mind—possibly to its activity—perhaps occasioned by lack of early discipline—one fancy thrusting
forth another, and occupying its place.

But the difficulty still remains, that she could not recall those fancies. Most persons are aware that, by a
mental effort, (and there is no operation of the mind
more wonderful) they can recall scenes and events long
since forgotten ; but Phillis does not seem to have possessed this power, as it respects her own productions,—
for we believe this singularity to have affected her own
thoughts only, and not the impressions made upon her
mind by the thoughts of others, communicated by books
or conversation.

We consider this statement of the case corroborated
by the poem on ' Recollection.' In this little effusion,
referring so directly to the point in question, we find no
intimation or acknowledgment of any deficiency, but
rather the contrary ; and when we remember Phillis's
simplicity of character, we cannot suppose that an im-
perfection of the kind would have been thus passed unnoticed, had any such existed. But, however this singularity may be accounted for, we state the fact as we
believe it to have existed, and leave our readers to draw
their own inferences. Perhaps there may be many
gifted minds conscious of the same peculiarity.

By comparing the accounts we have of Phillis's progress, with the dates of her earliest poems, we find that
she must have commenced her career as an authoress,
as soon as she could write a legible hand, and without
being acquainted with the rules of composition. Indeed,

we very much doubt if she ever had any grammatical instruction, or any knowledge of the structure or idiom of the English language, except what she imbibed from a perusal of the best English writers, and from mingling in polite circles, where, fortunately, she was encouraged to converse freely with the wise and the learned.

We gather from her writings, that she was acquainted with astronomy, ancient and modern geography, and ancient history; and that she was well versed in the scriptures of the Old and New Testament. She discovered a decided taste for the stories of Heathen Mythology, and Pope's Homer seems to have been a great favorite with her.

Her time, when she was at home, was chiefly occupied with her books, her pen, and her needle; and when we consider the innocence of her life, the purity of her heart, and the modest pride which must have followed her successful industry, joined to the ease and contentment of her domestic lot, we cannot but suppose these early years to have been years of great happiness.

The reader is already aware of the delicate constitution and frail health of Phillis. During the winter of 1773, the indications of disease had so much increased, that her physician advised a sea voyage. This was earnestly seconded by her friends; and a son of Mr. and Mrs. Wheatley being about to make a voyage to England to arrange a mercantile correspondence, it was settled that Phillis should accompany him, and she accordingly embarked in the summer of the same year.

She was at this time but nineteen years old, and was at the highest point of her short and brilliant career. It is with emotions of sorrow that we approach the strange

8. Nathaniel Wheatley, a twin brother to Mary. An able merchant, he escorted Phillis to London on May 8, 1773, aboard the schooner, *London Packet*, owned by Phillis's master, John. In November of 1773, he married Mary Enderby of the wealthy London mercantile family. He and his wife visited Boston briefly in the fall of 1774, but returned to London where he died in the spring of 1783, the father of three daughters.

and splendid scenes which were now about to open upon her—to be succeeded by grief and desolation.

Phillis was well received in England, and was presented to Lady Huntingdon, Lord Dartmouth, Mr. Thornton,* and many other individuals of distinction; but, says our informant, 'not all the attention she received, nor all the honors that were heaped upon her, had the slightest influence upon her temper or deportment. She was still the same single-hearted, unsophisticated being.' During her stay in England, her poems were given to the world, dedicated to the Countess of Huntingdon, and embellished with an engraving which is said to have been a striking representation of the original. It is supposed that one of these impressions was forwarded to her mistress, as soon as they were struck off; for a grand niece of Mrs. Wheatley's informs us that, during the absence of Phillis, she one day called upon her relative, who immediately directed her attention to a picture over the fire-place, exclaiming—'See! look at my Phillis! does she not seem as though she would speak to me!'

Phillis arrived in London so late in the season, that the great mart of fashion was deserted. She was therefore urgently pressed by her distinguished friends to remain until the Court returned to St. James's, that she might be presented to the young monarch, George III. She would probably have consented to this arrangement, had not letters from America informed her of the declining health of her mistress, who intreated her to return, that she might once more behold her beloved protegee.

* Another of the benefactors of Dartmouth College.

9. Phillis never did see the countess who, aging and ill, was confined to her South Wales residence throughout Phillis's London visit. See Phillis's letter to the countess, dated October 25, 1770, above.

439

Phillis waited not a second bidding, but immediately re-embarked, and arrived in safety at that once happy home, which was so soon to be desolate. It will probably occur to the reader as singular, that Phillis has not borne a more decided testimony to the kindness of those excellent friends who so tenderly cherished her. Her farewell to America was inscribed to her mistress, indicated by the initials, S. W., but here she merely alludes to the pain of parting. If any other pieces were ever devoted to her, they were doubtless destroyed; for upon mentioning the singularity of her omitting to record a testimony of her gratitude to her benefactors, we were told, by one of the very few individuals who have any recollection of Mrs. Wheatley or Phillis, that the former was a woman distinguished for good sense and discretion; and that her christian humility induced her to shrink from the thought of those good deeds being blazoned forth to the world, which were performed in the privacy of her own happy home. It appears, also, that on her death-bed she requested that nothing might be written upon her decease. Indeed, Phillis was forbidden this indulgence of her grief, and it was shortly after her mournful duty to close the eyes of her indulgent mistress and unwearied friend.

The decease of this excellent lady occurred in the year 1774.[10] Her husband soon followed her to the house appointed for all living;[11] and their daughter joined them in the chambers of death.[12] The son had married and settled in England; and Phillis was now, therefore, left utterly desolate. She spent a short time with a friend of her departed mistress, and then took an apartment, and lived by herself. This was a strange change to one

10. Several Boston newspapers report the death of Mrs. Wheatley on March 3, 1774.
11. John Wheatley died March 12, 1778.
12. Mary Wheatley Lathrop died September 24, 1778.

who had enjoyed the comforts and even luxuries of life, and the happiness of a fire-side where a well regulated family were accustomed to gather. Poverty, too, was drawing near with its countless afflictions. She could hope for little extraneous aid; the troubles with the mother country were thickening around; every home was darkened, and every heart was sad.

At this period of destitution, Phillis received an offer of marriage from a respectable colored man of Boston. The name of this individual was Peters. He kept a grocery in Court-Street, and was a man of very handsome person and manners ; wore a wig, carried a cane, and quite acted out ' *the gentleman.*' In an evil hour he was accepted ; and he proved utterly unworthy of the 13 distinguished woman who honored him by her alliance. He was unsuccessful in business, and failed soon after their marriage ; and he is said to have been both too proud and too indolent to apply himself to any occupation below his fancied dignity. Hence his unfortunate wife suffered much from this ill-omened union.

'The difficulties between the colonies and the mother country had by this time increased to open hostilities. Universal distress prevailed. The provincial army was scantily provided with clothing and food ; and the families of those who were fighting for their country, most of whom had been cherished in the lap of plenty, were glad to obtain their daily bread. The inhabitants of Boston were fleeing in all directions ; and Phillis accompanied her husband to Wilmington, in this state. In an obscure country village, the necessaries of life are always obtained with more difficulty than in a populous town, and in this season of scarcity, Phillis suffered much

13. Both listed as "free Negroes," Phillis Wheatley and John Peters posted their marriage bans on April 1, 1778.

from privation—from absolute want—and from painful exertions to which she was unaccustomed, and for which her frail constitution unfitted her. We cannot be surprised that, under these distressing circumstances, her health, which had been much improved by her voyage to England, should have again declined. We rather wonder, that one who had been so tenderly reared, and so fondly nurtured, should have borne up, for so long a season, against such an increasing burthen of misfortune and affliction.

In the course of these years of suffering, she became the mother of three infants, who inherited the frail health of their parent ; and thus to her other cares was added the anxiety of a mother, watching the flickering flame glowing in the bosom of her offspring, and trembling every moment lest the breath of adversity should extinguish a life so dear to her. We know little of Phillis in her relations of wife and mother ; but we cannot suppose, that one who had been so faithful to her earliest friend, who was so meek and unassuming, and possessed of such an affectionate constitutional disposition, could have been unmindful, in any case, of her conjugal or matronly duties. Nor can we learn that a breath of complaint or reproach ever escaped her respecting her husband. There are some, however, not so tender of a name she was not allowed to bear, who speak of him as that man deserves to be spoken of, who beguiles a woman to confide in his protection, and betrays her trust and his own.

We have alluded above to the circumstance that we never heard Phillis named, or alluded to, by any other appellation than that of ' Phillis Wheatley'—a name

---

14. Phillis used her married name on each of her last three published poems and in her proposals for a projected volume of her writings, printed in the *Evening Post and General Advertiser* from October 30 through December 18, 1779. See Wheatley's "Later Poems," and her "Letters and Proposals," both above.

which she sustained with dignity and honor, not only in the vicinity of her own residence, but upon far distant shores. After the evacuation of Boston by the British troops, Phillis returned thither.[15] A niece of Mrs. Wheatley's, whose son had been slain in battle, received her beneath her own roof.[16] This lady was a widow, and not wealthy. She kept a small day school to increase her narrow income. Her mansion had been much injured by the enemy, but it afforded a shelter to herself and daughter, and they ministered to Phillis, and her three suffering children, for six weeks. At the end of that period, Peters came for his wife, and, having provided an apartment, took her thither with her little *family*.

It must be remembered that this was a season of general poverty. Phillis's friends of former days were scattered far and wide. Many of them, attached to the royal interest, had left the country. The successful patriots, during the seven years' contention, had not only lost the profits which would have arisen from their industry, but were obliged to strain every nerve to meet the exigencies of the war. The depreciation of the currency added greatly to the general distress. Mr. Thacher, for example, in his History of Plymouth, tells us of a man who sold a cow for forty dollars, and gave the same sum for a goose! We have ourselves heard an elderly lady* relate, that her husband, serving in the army, forwarded her in a letter fifty dollars, which was of so little value when she received it, that she paid the whole for a quarter of mutton, so poor and so tough, that it required great skill and patience, in the culinary

* The grandmother of the writer of this Memoir.

15. There is some confusion here. The British evacuated Boston in March of 1776, two years before Phillis was married.
16. Mrs. Elizabeth Wallcutt (1721–1811), whose daughter was named Lucy. Christopher Wallcutt (1758–1777) was killed at Bennington, Vermont, by the British. He was one of two older brothers to Thomas Wallcutt, Phillis's friend and correspondent.

department, to render it fit for the table. 'In this condition of things,' observes the lady, whom we have more than once referred to, and to whom we expressed our surprise at the neglect and poverty into which Phillis was suffered to decline, ' people had other things to attend to than prose and poetry, and had little to bestow in charity, when their own children were clamorous for bread.' Poor Phillis was left to the care of her negligent husband.

We now learn nothing of her for a long interval. At length a relative of her lamented mistress heard of her illness, and sought her out. She was also visited by several other members of that family. They found her in a situation of extreme misery. Two of her children were dead, and the third was sick unto death. She was herself suffering for want of attention, for many comforts, and that greatest of all comforts in sickness—cleanliness. She was reduced to a condition too loathsome to describe. If a charitable individual, moved at the sight of so much distress, sent a load of wood, to render her more comfortable during the cold season, her husband *was too much of a gentleman* to prepare it for her use.—It is painful to dwell upon the closing scene. In a filthy apartment, in an obscure part of the metropolis, lay the dying mother, and the wasting child. The woman who had stood honored and respected in the presence of the wise and good of that country which was hers by adoption, or rather compulsion, who had graced the ancient halls of Old England, and rolled about in the splendid equipages of the proud nobles of Britain, was now numbering the last hours of life in a state of the most abject misery, surrounded by all the emblems of squalid poverty!

Little more remains to be told. It is probable, (as frequently happens when the constitution has long borne up against disease) that the thread of life, attenuated by suffering, at last snapped suddenly ; for the friends of Phillis, who had visited her in her sickness, knew not of her death. Peters did not see fit to acquaint them with the event, or to notify them of her interment.[17] A grand niece of Phillis's benefactress, passing up Court-Street, met the funeral of an adult and a child : a bystander informed her they were bearing Phillis Wheatley to that silent mansion ' where the wicked cease from troubling, and the weary are at rest.'

They laid her away in her solitary grave, without a stone to tell that one so good and so gifted sleeps beneath ; and the waters of oblivion are rapidly erasing her name from the sands of time.—We would that her memory were engraven upon the heart of the young, and the gifted, who are striving for a niche in the temple of fame. We think, gentle reader, she is as worthy of a place in your thoughts, as the heroines of the thousand tales dressed out to beguile your fancy. Remember, that though the children of men regard feature and complexion, there is One who looketh upon the heart.

Here and there we find a solitary pilgrim, belonging to the days of the years that are gone, treasuring Phillis's poems as a precious relic. But when *they* shall have passed away, who will remember her ? May not this little record, though offered with diffidence be allowed to perpetuate her name ?

The poems now republished, are as they came from the hands of the author, without the alteration of a

---

17. But there were several notices of Phillis's funeral in Boston newspapers, including *The Massachusetts Centinel* (8 December 1784), and the *Boston Independent Chronicle and Universal Advertiser* (9 December 1784).

word or letter. Surely they lift an eloquent voice in behalf of her race.

Is it urged that Phillis is but a solitary instance of African genius? Even though this were the case (which we by no means grant) we reply—that had Phillis fallen into less generous and affectionate hands, she would speedily have perished under the privations and exertions of common servitude. Or had she dragged out a few years of suffering, she would have been of much less value to her master, than the sturdy negress of more obscure faculties, but whose stronger limbs could have borne heavier burthens. How then can it be known, among this unfortunate people, how often the light of genius is quenched in suffering and death?

The great difference between the colored man and his oppressors seems to us to be, that the great Ruler of the universe has appointed power unto the white man for a season; and verily they have bowed down their brethren with a rod of iron. From the luxuriant savannahs of America and the barren sands of Africa, the blood of their victims cries unto God from the ground.

Friends of liberty! friends of humanity! when will ye appoint a jubilee for the African, and let the oppressed go free?

We have named, in the course of the preceding Memoir, some of the remarkable privileges which fell to the lot of Phillis. We should allude also more distinctly to the general disadvantages of her condition. It must not be forgotten, that the opportunities of education allowed females, at this early period, were few and meagre. Those who coveted superior advantages for their children, sent them home (as the mother country was fondly termed) for their education. Of course, this expensive method could be adopted only by a privileged few, chiefly belonging to old English families of rank and wealth. The great mass of American females could boast of few accomplishments save housewifery. They had few books beside their Bibles. They were not expected to read—far less to write. It was their province to guide the spindle and distaff, and work willingly with their hands. *Now*, woman is allowed to establish her humble stool somewhat nearer the elbow-chair of her lord and master ; to pore over the huge tome of science, hitherto considered as his exclusive property ; to con the musty volumes of classic lore, written even in strange tongues ; to form her own opinions, and give them forth to the world. But, in the days of Phillis, these things were not so. She was not stimulated to exertion by the successful cultivation of female talent. She had no brilliant exhibition of feminine genius before her, to excite her emulation ; and we are at a loss to conjecture, how the first strivings of her mind after knowledge—her delight in literature, her success even in a dead language, the first bursting forth of her thoughts in song—can be accounted for, unless these efforts are allowed to have been the inspirations of that genius which is the gift of God. And who will dare to say, that the benevolent Sovereign of the universe has appointed her unfortunate race to be hewers of wood and drawers of water, and given them no portion with their brethren ?

The distinguished women of France were trained, as it were, in the very temple of science, to minister at its altars. Those of England stood, too, in the broad light of its wide-spreading beams; but at the time when Phillis lived, our own land was darkly overshadowed. We had no philosophers, no historians, no poets; and our statesmen—those wonderful men, who stood forth in the day of a nation's peril, the wonder and glory of the world—had not then breathed forth those mighty energies which girded the warrior for the battle, and nerved the hearts of a whole people as the heart of one man. All here was calm and passionless as the natural world upon the morning of creation, ere the Spirit of God had moved upon the face of the waters. It passed, and the day-spring knew its place. Even thus with the spirit of Liberty. It breathed upon our sleeping nation, awakening the genius of the people to appear from time to time in a thousand new and multiplying forms of ever-varying beauty.

Since that day, our philosophers have stood in the courts of monarchs, more honored than he who held the sceptre; and the recesses of the leafy forest, and the banks of the solitary stream and lonely lake, have been hallowed by the legends of the children of song. Nor has skill been wanting to embody the deeds of our fathers, or shadow forth the gentle and the brave, in tales that have stirred many hearts, even beyond the waters. But Phillis lived not amid these happy influences. True, she heard the alarum of Liberty, but it was in suffering and sorrow; and when the shout of triumph was raised, it fell upon a chilled heart and a closing ear. The pride of victory could scarce move the sympathies of one who had known the emptiness of glory, and proved the mockery of fame.

The evidences she has left us of her genius, were the productions of early and happy days, before her mind was matured by experience, the depths of her soul fathomed by suffering, or her fine powers chastened by affliction. The blight was upon her in her spring-time, and she passed away.

The reader may claim to be satisfied as to the authenticity of the facts stated in the preceding Memoir.

They were derived from grand-nieces of Phillis's benefactress, who are still living, and have a distinct and vivid remembrance both of their excellent relative and her admired protegee.

Their statements are corroborated by a grand-daughter of that lady, now residing in Boston ; who, though much younger than the individuals alluded to, recollects the circumstance of Phillis's visiting at the house of her father.] 8Other company was probably present; for the lady in question relates, that the domestics observed, ' it was the first time they ever carried tea to a colored woman.'

This lady communicates some particulars which we state with great pleasure, as they remove from Phillis the supposition of her having formed a matrimonial connection from unworthy or mercenary motives. She assures us that Peters was not only a very remarkable looking man, but a man of talents and information ; and that he wrote with fluency and propriety, and at one period read law. It is admitted, however, that he was disagreeable in his manners, and that on account of his

18. Jane Tyler Lathrop (1777–1846), one of several daughters born to Mary Wheatley Lathrop and her husband, John.

improper conduct, Phillis became entirely estranged from the immediate family of her mistress : they were not seasonably informed of her suffering condition, or of her death.

Lastly, the author of this Memoir is a collateral descendant of Mrs. Wheatley, and has been familiar with the name and fame of Phillis from her childhood. [19]

NOTE.

Previous to Phillis's departure for Wilmington, she entrusted her papers to a daughter of the lady who received her on her return from that place. After her death, these papers were demanded by Peters, as the property of his deceased wife, and were, of course, yielded to his importunity. Some years after, he went to the South, and we have not been able to ascertain what eventually became of the manuscripts. [20]

19. Margaretta Matilda Odell, whose mother was a daughter of Christopher Marshall, a nephew of Mrs. Susanna Wheatley, Phillis's mistress.
20. In the *Independent Chronicle and Universal Advertiser* (10 February 1785), John Peters ran the following:

> The person who borrowed a volume of manuscript
> poems & & of Phillis Peters, formerly Phillis
> Wheatley, deceased, would very much oblige her
> husband, John Peters, by returning it immediately,
> as the whole of her works are intended to be published.

No such collection was ever published, and most of the poems and letters advertised in 1779 are lost. The "daughter" with whom Phillis had entrusted her papers before going to Wilmington was Lucy Wallcutt (born 1762), sister to Thomas Wallcutt, Phillis's correspondent and friend.

Appendix E

[General Washington to Joseph Reed][1]

". . . I recollect nothing else worth giving you the trouble of, unless you can be amused by reading a letter and poem addressed to me by Miss Phillis Wheatley. In searching over a parcel of papers the other day, in order to destroy such as were useless, I brought it to light again. At first, with a view of doing justice to her poetical genius, I had a great mind to publish the poem; but not knowing whether it might not be considered rather as a mark of my own vanity, than as a compliment to her, I laid it aside, till I came across it again in the manner just mentioned. . . ."

1. From a letter dated Cambridge, 10 February 1776, written by George Washington to his former secretary, Colonel Joseph Reed, then in Philadelphia, as published in Jared Sparks, editor, *The Writings of George Washington* (Boston, 1833) 111, 288. Enclosed in the above letter were Phillis's letter from Providence on "*Octo.* 26, 1775," and her poem, "To His Excellency General Washington," which see in "Phillis Wheatley's Early Poems," above.

Appendix F

[General Washington to Phillis Wheatley][1]

Cambridge

Miss Phillis,

Your favor of the 26th of October did not reach my hands, till the middle of December. Time enough, you will say, to have given an answer ere this. Granted. But a variety of important occurrences, continually interposing to distract the mind and withdraw the attention, I hope will apologize delay, and plead my excuse for the seeming but not real neglect. I thank you most sincerely for your polite notice of me, in the elegant lines you enclosed; and however undeserving I may be of such encomium and panegyric, the style and manner exhibit a striking proof of your poetical talents; in honor of which, and as a tribute justly due to you, I would have published the poem, had I not been apprehensive, that, while I only meant to give the world this new instance of your genius, I might have incurred the imputation of vanity. This, and nothing else, determined me not to give it place in the public prints.

If you should ever come to Cambridge, or near headquarters, I shall be happy to see a person so favored by the Muses, and to whom nature has been so liberal and beneficent in her dispensations.[2] I am, with great respect, your obedient humble servant.

1. From Jared Sparks, editor, *The Writings of George Washington* (Boston, 1833), 111, 297–298.
2. "Washington invited her to visit him at Cambridge, which she did a few days before the British evacuated Boston. . . . She passed half an hour with the commander-in-chief, from whom and his officers she received marked attention," from Benson J. Lossing, *The Pictorial Field Book of the Revolution*. Two volumes (New York, 1855), 1, 556. Phillis's visit with Washington is nowhere else cited. Lossing should be used with caution.

Appendix G

My Lord

If I never had experienced the Honour/ of your Lordship's Friendship, I should rejoice on your being called by/ His Majesty to preside over the American department;[1] when I reflect how much the general voice in this Country Exults in the/ appointment: Yes, my Lord, I cannot but rejoice on the Important occasion/ and such is the weakness of the human heart, that I seem be/ sensibly interested in it myself, As I still retain the warmest/ gratitude for your many kind offices towards me, (which promoted/ my happiness in the wilds of Florida),[2] even at a time, when your/ Lordship did not choose to be concerned with administration./ Though my congratulation on your Lordship's appointment is late,/ be assured it is not less sincere. I flatter myself that you will/ receive this poor mark of my attachment as the real effusions/ of a heart deeply impresse'd with gratitude. Indeed, my dear Lord,/ nothing could have given me more pleasure that your Lordship's/ appointment. The beneficient Parent of all good has now in/ his own time, chose his faithful servant to preside over the/ scattered Tribes of his Children in America.[3] I have lately travelled/ through all the New England Provinces, where they rejoiced with/ me on the Happy occasion. Their Fears are removed, and they seem to/ anticipate the full enjoyment of Civil & Religious Liberty. Permit me,/ my Lord, to mention that I shall soon visit all the West India Islands/ where I shall be happy to be honoured with your commands. My business/ there I hope to finish by the Spring, and then, with your Lordship's permission,/ embark for my native country.

1. The Earl of Dartmouth was appointed Secretary of State for North America in August, 1772, by King George III.
2. At one time, Dartmouth was considering purchasing thousands of Florida acreage.
3. Dartmouth and Lady Huntingdon and fellow Christian evangelists were much concerned with converting American Indians in both the East (hence their support of Moor's Indian Charity School—Dartmouth College) and in the American West.

While in Boston, I heard of a very extra-/ ordinary female slave, who had made some verses on our mutually dear/ deceased Friend;[4] I visited her mistress, and found by conversing with the/ African, that she was no Impostor; I asked if she could write on any Subject;/ she said Yes; we had just heard of your Lordship's appointment; I gave her/ your name, which she was acquainted with. She immediately wrote/ a rough Copy of the inclosed Adress & Letter, which I promised to convey or deliver. I was astonish'd, and could hardly believe my own Eyes. I was present/ while she wrote and can attest that it is her own production; she shew'd/ me her Letter to Lady Huntingdon,[5] which I daresay, Your Lordship has/ seen; I send you an account signed by her master of her Importation, Education/ &c. they are all wrote in her own hand.[6] Pardon the account I have given/ you of this poor untutor'd slave, when, possibly, your precious time may/ be very ill bestowed in reading my scrawls. . . .

          . . . suffer me to subscribe myself with the great Truth and Esteem
                My Lord,
                Your Lordship's
                    most Obliged and most
                      Humble Servant,
                        Tho.ˢ Wooldridge

New York   Nov. 24ᵗʰ 1772

The Earl of Dartmouth

---

4. The Reverend George Whitefield (1714–1770) who died in Newburyport, Massachusetts, during one of his many evangelizing tours of America.
5. Phillis's letter of October 25, 1770, covering a non-extant manuscript elegy on the death of the Reverend George Whitefield (see "Phillis Wheatley's Letters and Proposals," above).
6. Phillis Wheatley prepared and asked Wooldridge to deliver the manuscripts for a biographical sketch of herself, signed by Nathaniel Wheatley; a congratulatory poem to Dartmouth; and a covering letter (see "Phillis Wheatley's Variant Poems and Leters," above). All three manuscripts were delivered and are today among the papers of Lord Dartmouth in the County Record Office, Stafford, England.

ACADEMIC AFFAIRS OFFICE

TO:

FROM:

MESSAGE

Pam'la

TIME: _____ a.m./ p.m.

DATE: _____

Unsigned Poems [by Phillis Wheatley?]

1

[From "On The Affray in King Street, on the
Evening of the 5th of March"?][1]

With Fire enwrapt, surcharg'd with sudden Death,
Lo, the pois'd Tube convolves its fatal breath!
The flying Ball with heaven-directed Force,
Rids the Spirit of its fallen corse.
   Well sated Shades! let no unwomanly Tear
From Pity's Eye, disdain in your honour'd Bier;
Lost to their View, surviving Friends may mourn,
Yet on thy Pile shall Flames celestial burn;
Long as in *Freedom's* Cause the wise contend,
Dear to your unity shall Fame extend;
While to the World, the letter'd *Stone* shall tell,
How *Caldwell, Attucks, Gray,* and *Mav'rick* fell . . .

1. In the Boston *Evening Post* for March 12, 1770, these anonymous lines were printed, and are included here because the style, sentiment, and vocabulary are very much like Phillis's, and may be part of her poem whose title, above, is listed in her 1772 proposals.

2

[On William Pitt, Earl of Chatham][1]

Hail first of Patriots! whose extensive mind,
Revolves the vast concernments of mankind:
Contending realms accept controul from thee;
And Briton's glory hangs on thy decree;
War deals destruction, *Peace* her olive brings.
As thy supreme direction, governs Kings.
Where'er thou bidst, the wreaths of conquest fall,
The guide, the friend, the guardian of us all.

---

1. A 1772 *Isaac Bickerstaff Boston ALMANAC./ for the Year of our LORD/ 1772./ Being LEAP YEAR.* printed a likeness of Pitt, beneath which these eight lines of verse appear. Although not listed among her 1772 proposals, and not included among her London-published volume of poems, the verses very much resemble Phillis's kind of writing. For a Wheatley poem about Pitt, see the last poem in her 1773 volume.

On The Birthday of Pompey Stockbridge[1]

While hireling scribblers prostitute their pen,
Creating virtues for abandoned men,
Ascribing merit to the vicious great,
And basely flatter whom they ought to hate—
Be mine the just, the grateful task to scan
Th'effulgent virtues of a *sable* man;
Trace the good action to its source sublime
And mark its progress to the death of time.
Alternate seasons quickly pass away,
And the *sixth* lustre crowns this natal day
Since first my Pompey, humble, modest, wise,
Shot the bright dawn of reason from his eyes:
Nor was his morn o'ercast by folly's cloud;
Ne'er pressed his footsteps 'mong the giddy crowd:
Even the gay season of luxuriant youth
Was wisely spent to ascertain the truth.
Religious precepts formed his darling plan,
And virtue's dictates stamped him *real* man,—
Long may Pompey live, long live to prove
The sweets of virtue, and the joys of love;
And when these happy annual feasts are past,
That day be happiest which will be his last;
Then may his soul triumphantly ascend,
Where *perfect bliss* shall never know an end.

1. Unsigned and undated, this broadside is found in the Moorland Collection at Howard University in the probability that it was written by Phillis, who in fact expressed similar concern for another black, Scipio Moorhead, the black servant of the Reverend Moorhead, whose artist wife instructed Scipio. See Phillis's poem, "to S.M. A Young African Painter, On Seeing His Works," in her volume, above.

For the A.S. Record[1]

Phillis Wheatley

Many of our young readers have heard of Phillis Wheatley, the African slave, who wrote poems, and published a book. She was only seven or eight years old, when the men-stealers took her from her friends and playmates, and confined her in a slave ship. The vessel which brought her to America was owned by Colonel Fitch, a rich man, who traded in slaves, and lived in the city of Boston. Phillis had not been long here before she was sold to Mr. John Wheatley, and from him she took her surname. She soon learned to read, for in those days slaves were taught to read, and were instructed in the Bible. She also learned to write, and after a while began to write verses. Some of these were seen by the family, who showed them to several of the ministers and schoolmasters in Boston, and they were greatly surprised and pleased in finding a poor slave able to write so well. At length she wrote a number of poems, and some of them were printed. It was thought to be a great wonder that a colored person, and one born in Africa, should be able to write poetry in the English language. Some of the friends of Phillis thought she had better go to England, where she would receive many presents, which would assist her to acquire further knowledge, and enable her to print her poems in a book.

Accordingly, she sailed for England, and when she arrived there, she was treated with much kindness. The people were much pleased to see her, for they had heard about her being a poet before her arrival. The Countess of Huntingdon, a good and kind lady, was her friend, and invited Phillis to stay with her some time, and took her to her chapel, where Mr. Whitefield had so often preached. She had her poems published in London in 1773.

After she returned to Boston, she went to see her old master's family, for they had treated her kindly. Col. Fitch had a large house, and lived in much splendor. He had white servants and colored servants. He had a large family of daughters, and they

---

1. From *The Anti-Slavery Record*, 11, No. 5 (May, 1836), whole No. 17, pp. 7–8.

thought much of their father's wealth and station. Mrs. Fitch[2] was a very kind woman, and invited Phillis to spend the afternoon with her. The daughters, though they were glad to see her, could not imagine how she would be disposed of at *tea time*; for, like many persons at the present day, they could not bear the idea of sitting down at table with a colored person, even though she had sat at table with a countess. They were therefore very anxious to learn of their mother, *what she should do with Phillis at tea time.* Mrs. Fitch told them at once that she was to be seated with them. They pouted a little, but submitted to their mother's directions.

When tea was brought in, Phillis took her seat with the fair daughters of Col. Fitch. She soon began to give an account of her visits at various places in England, and describe the persons and things she had seen. She had seen King George III and his queen, and told them how Queen Charlotte was dressed. She told them of St. Paul's Cathedral, one of the largest churches in the world; of Westminster Abby, and of London Bridge, with its numerous arches. She told them much about the Countess of Huntingdon, and of her charity to the poor—that she was kind alike to all, and that she had often been to her chapel, and been seated by her side in her pew.[3] In short, as she went on with her pleasant and entertaining stories, the young ladies became delighted with Phillis; they became more and more inquisitive to learn what she had seen, and found that with all their wealth and advantages she knew more than they did. As she went on with her stories, they forgot she had been a slave; they felt no prejudice against her because she was black, and they felt ashamed they had ever made any objections to her having a seat at the tea-table.

F.

2. Eunice (Brown) Fitch (1731-1799) became in 1760 the second wife of Timothy Fitch, and birthed four daughters, to add to the six daughters Fitch had by his first wife, Abigail.
3. Phillis and the Countess never did meet personally. See "Phillis Wheatley's Letters and Proposals," above.

INDEX